OXFORD REFERENCE

# A Dictionary of Finance

**Editors**
Brian Butler (Lloyds Bank plc)
Alan Isaacs (Market House Books Ltd)

**Market House Books Ltd Editorial Staff**
Elizabeth Martin
Anne Stibbs
Fran Alexander
Edmund Wright

**Contributors**
Brian Butler
Brian Johnson
Graham Sidwell
Andrew Wood
Brian Clutterbuck
Alan Isaacs
Barry Brindley
R. M. Walters
Matthew Wright

# A Dictionary of Finance

Oxford   New York

OXFORD UNIVERSITY PRESS

1993

*Oxford University Press, Walton Street, Oxford* OX2 6DP

*Oxford New York Toronto*
*Delhi Bombay Calcutta Madras Karachi*
*Kuala Lumpur Singapore Hong Kong Tokyo*
*Nairobi Dar es Salaam Cape Town*
*Melbourne Auckland Madrid*

*and associated companies in*
*Berlin Ibadan*

*Oxford is a trade mark of Oxford University Press*

*British Library Cataloguing in Publication Data*
*Data available*

*Library of Congress Cataloging in Publication Data*
*A dictionary of finance.*
*p. cm. — (Oxford reference)*
*1. Finance—Dictionaries. I. Series.*
*332'.03—dc20 HG151.D54 1993 92–42735*
*ISBN 0–19–215363–3*
*ISBN 0–19–285279–5 (Pbk.)*

10 9 8 7 6 5 4 3 2 1

*Text prepared by*
*Market House Books Ltd,*
*Aylesbury*

*Printed in Great Britain by*
*Biddles Ltd.*
*Guildford and King's Lynn*

# Preface

*A Dictionary of Finance* is a companion volume to *A Concise Dictionary of Business* (also in Oxford Reference). It is intended for students and professionals in the field of finance as well as private investors and the readers of the financial pages of newspapers.

The 3,300 entries in this book cover the vocabulary used in banking, money markets, foreign exchanges, financial futures and options, commodity markets, and takeovers and mergers, as well as business loans and debt-collecting.

Public finance is also included, with a substantial coverage of the terms used in government finance, the money supply, public-sector borrowing, local finance, central banking, and European finance.

The private investor and borrower will find full coverage of terms relating to savings, stock-exchange dealing, mortgages, pensions, life assurance, and taxation.

The contributors and editors of this book have been at great pains to make the entries as clear and as easy to understand as possible. Although jargon is not used in definitions, many of the jargon words and phrases are themselves entries.

The coverage is wide and international, with entries for the world's standard currency units and many of the financial institutions in London, New York, Tokyo, Hong Kong, Frankfurt, and Paris.

AI
BB
(1993)

Note: An asterisk (*) placed before a term in a definition indicates that this term can be found as an entry in the dictionary and will provide further information. Synonyms and abbreviations are usually found within brackets immediately following a headword.

**A1** A description of property or a person that is in the best condition. In marine insurance, before a vessel can be insured, it has to be inspected to check its condition. If it is 'maintained in good and efficient condition' it will be shown in *Lloyd's Register of Shipping as 'A' and if the anchor moorings are in the same condition the number '1' is added. This description is also used in life assurance, in which premiums are largely based on the person's health. After a medical examination a person in perfect health is described as 'an A1 life'.

**ABI** Abbreviation for *Association of British Insurers.

**above-the-line 1.** Denoting entries above the horizontal line on a company's *profit and loss account that separates the entries that establish the profit (or loss) from the entries that show how the profit is distributed. **2.** Denoting advertising expenditure on mass media advertising, including press, television, radio, and posters. It is traditionally regarded as all advertising expenditure on which a commission is payable to an advertising agency. **3.** Denoting transactions concerned with revenue, as opposed to capital, in national accounts. *Compare* below-the-line.

**absorption costing** The process of costing products or activities by taking into account the total costs incurred in producing the product or service, however remote. This method of costing ensures that full costs are recovered provided that goods or services can always be sold at the price implied by full-cost pricing. However, if sales are lost due to the high sales price opportunities may be lost of making some contribution to overheads. *Compare* marginal costing.

**ACA** Abbreviation for Associate of the *Institute of Chartered Accountants.

**ACC** Abbreviation for *Agricultural Credit Corporation Ltd.

**ACCA** Abbreviation for Associate of the Chartered Association of Certified Accountants. *See* certified accountant; chartered accountant.

**acceptance 1.** The signature on a *bill of exchange indicating that the person on whom it is drawn accepts the conditions of the bill. Acceptance is usually written: 'Accepted, payable at … (name and address of bank): (*Signature*)'. *See also* non-acceptance. **2.** A bill of exchange that has been so accepted. **3.** Agreement to accept the terms of an offer; for example, the agreement of an insurance company to provide a specified insurance cover or of a trader to accept a specified parcel of goods at the offer price.

**acceptance credit** A means of financing the sale of goods, particularly in international trade. It involves a commercial bank or merchant bank extending credit to a foreign importer whom it deems creditworthy. An acceptance credit is opened against which the exporter can draw a *bill of exchange. Once accepted by the bank, the bill can be discounted on the *money market or allowed to run to maturity.

**acceptance supra protest (acceptance for honour)** The acceptance or payment of a *bill of exchange, after it has been dishonoured, by a person wishing to save the honour of the drawer or an endorser of the bill.

**accepting house** An institution specializing in accepting or guaranteeing *bills of exchange. A service fee is charged for guaranteeing payment, enabling the bill to be discounted at preferential rates on the *money market. The decline in the use of bills of exchange has forced the accepting houses to widen their financial activities; many of them have returned to their original function of merchant banking (*see* merchant bank).

**Accepting Houses Committee** A committee representing the 16 *accepting houses in the City of London. Members of the committee are eligible for finer discounts on bills bought by the Bank of England, although this privilege has been extended to other banks.

**acceptor** The drawee of a *bill of exchange accepting the bill, i.e. after the drawee has accepted liability by signing the face of the bill.

**accommodation bill** A *bill of exchange signed by a person (the accommodation party) who acts as a guarantor. The accommodation party is liable for the bill should the *acceptor fail to pay at maturity. Accommodation bills are sometimes known as **windbills** or **windmills**. *See also* kite.

**accomodation endorser** A person or a bank that endorses a loan to another party; for example, a parent company may endorse a bank loan to a subsidiary. The endorser becomes a guarantor and is secondarily liable in case of default. Banks may endorse other banks' acceptance notes, which can then be traded on the secondary market.

**account** **1.** A statement of indebtedness from one person to another; an invoice. A provider of professional services or of goods may render an account to a client or customer; a solicitor selling a house on a person's behalf will render an account of the sale, which may show that the solicitor owes the seller the proceeds of the sale, less expenses. **2.** A named segment of a ledger recording transactions relevant to the person or the matter named. Accounts consist of two sides; increases are recorded on one side and decreases on the other. Accounts may be kept in a written form in a ledger, they may be on loose cards, or they may be on a magnetic medium in a computer. **3.** A record maintained by a *bank or a *building society of the amount of money a customer has deposited or been lent. *See* cheque account; current account; deposit account. **4.** A period during which dealings on the London Stock Exchange are made without immediate cash settlement. There are 24 accounts in the year, most of two weeks duration, but a few last for three weeks to accommodate public holidays. Up to the end of each account transactions are recorded but no money changes hands, which enables speculators to operate with the minimum capital outlay (for shares bought and sold within an account only differences have to be settled). Settlement of all transactions made within an account is made ten days after the account ends (*see* account day). Most other world stock markets use rolling accounts in which deals are settled a fixed number of days after the transaction is agreed. **5.** *See* annual accounts.

**accountant**  A person trained to keep books of account, which record all the financial transactions of a business or other organization, and to prepare periodic accounts. The accounts normally consist of a *balance sheet; a *profit and loss account or, in the case of a non-trading organization, an *income and expenditure account; and sometimes a statement of sources and application of funds. Other roles of accountants are to *audit the accounts of organizations and to give advice on taxation and other financial matters. Qualified accountants are normally members of one of several professional bodies to which they gain admission through a period of work experience and examinations (*see* chartered accountant; certified accountant). *See also* cost accountant; financial accountant.

**account day (settlement day)**  The day on which all transactions made during the previous *account on the London Stock Exchange must be settled. It falls on a Monday, ten days after the account ends.

**accounting concepts**  The basic theoretical ideas devised to support the activity of accounting. As accounting developed largely from a practical base, it has been argued that it lacks a theoretical framework. Accountants have therefore tried to develop such a framework; although various concepts have been suggested, few have found universal agreement. However, four are deemed to be important (*see* statements of standard accounting practice): the first, the **on-going concern concept**, assumes that the business is a going concern until there is evidence to the contrary, so that assets are not stated at their break-up value; the second, the **accruals concept**, involves recording income and expenses as they accrue, as distinct from when they are received or paid; the third, the **consistency concept**, demands that accounts be prepared on a consistent basis from one period to another; and the fourth, the **prudence concept**, calls for accounts to be prepared on a conservative basis, not taking credit for profits or income before they are realized but making provision for losses when they are foreseen. *Depreciation and *deferred taxation are concepts relating to accounting, but are not often considered when reference is made to accounting concepts.

**accounting period**  **1.** The period for which an organization makes up its accounts, usually an annual period. *Profit and loss accounts (or *income and expenditure accounts) are drawn up to cover that period and *balance sheets are prepared for the closing date. It is often a legal requirement that these accounts should be published. However, an organization might make use of shorter accounting periods for internal management purposes, e.g. monthly, quarterly, or six-monthly periods.  **2.** An accounting period for tax purposes, as defined by the taxation Acts. For unincorporated businesses it is the period for which the businesses prepare their accounts. For companies it is broadly the same except that if an accounting period exceeds twelve months it is divided into two or more accounting periods of twelve months, each excluding the last.

**accounting rate of return (ARR)**  The net profit to be expected from an investment, calculated as a percentage of the book value of the assets invested. *Compare* net present value (NPV).

**Accounting Standards Board (ASB)**  A UK company limited by guarantee, set up in 1989 as a subsidiary of the *Financial Reporting Council according to the provisions of the Companies Act 1989. Its purpose is to promote better standards in financial reporting by UK companies, some of which are enforceable in law. If a court is satisfied that a company's accounts do not provide a true and fair record of its activities, the court can compel the company to revise the accounts and circulate them at the company's expense, to all members entitled to receive them. Large companies are obliged to show that they have complied with the legally enforceable accounting standards laid down. The ten-member board, which is autonomous, oversees, revises, and issues accounting standards.

**account payee** The words added to a crossed cheque ensuring that the funds will only be paid to the individual to whom the cheque was made payable. The *Cheques Act 1992 strengthened the law relating to account payee status.

**accounts** **1.** The *profit and loss account and the *balance sheet of a company. **2.** *See* account.

**accounts payable** The amounts due to suppliers of goods and services to an organization. Originally a US term, it is gaining popularity in the UK.

**accounts receivable** The amounts owed to an organization for goods and services that it has supplied. Originally a US term, it is gaining popularity in the UK.

**accrual (accrued charge)** An amount incurred as a charge in a given accounting period but not paid by the end of that period, e.g. the last quarter's electricity charge. *See* accruals concept.

**accruals concept** One of the four principal *accounting concepts. Merely to record cash received or paid would not give a fair view of an organization's profit or loss, since it would not take account of goods sold but not yet paid for nor of expenses incurred but not yet paid. Accordingly, it is considered good accounting practice to prepare accounts taking note of such accruals. This is also akin to the **matching concept**, which suggests that costs should, as far as possible, be matched with the income to which they give rise.

**accrued benefits** The benefits that have accrued to a person in respect of a pension, for the service given up to a specified date, whether or not that person continues in office.

**accrued income scheme** An arrangement that applies in the UK when the owner of interest-bearing securities disposes of them. The interest accrued between the date of the last interest payment and the date of disposal is regarded, for tax purposes, as the income of the transferor. The transferee is able to deduct this sum from taxable income. The scheme does not apply to non-residents or if the transfer is part of a trade. Exemption also applies to individuals (husband and wife being regarded as one) if the total nominal value of the securities held does not exceed £5000.

**accumulated depreciation** The total amount written off the value of an asset. It is the sum of the yearly instalments of depreciation since the asset was acquired.

**accumulated dividend** A dividend that has not been paid to a company's preference shareholders. It is, therefore, shown as a liability in its accounts.

**accumulated profits** The amount showing in the *appropriation of profits account that can be carried forward to the next year's accounts, i.e. after paying dividends, taxes, and putting some to reserve.

**accumulating shares** Ordinary shares issued to holders of ordinary shares in a company, instead of a dividend. Accumulating shares are a way of replacing annual income with capital growth; they avoid income tax but not capital-gains tax. Usually tax is deducted by the company from the declared dividend, in the usual way, and the net dividend is then used to buy additional ordinary shares for the shareholder.

**accumulation trust** *See* discretionary trust.

**accumulation unit** A unit in an *investment trust in which dividends are ploughed back into the trust, after deducting income tax, enabling the value of the unit to increase. It is usually linked to a life-assurance policy.

**acid-test ratio** *See* liquid ratio.

**ACII** Abbreviation for Associate of the *Chartered Insurance Institute.

**acquisition accounting** The accounting procedures adopted when one company is taken over by another. This often involves controversial issues as to the way in which goodwill is to be treated.

**ACT** Abbreviation for *advance corporation tax.

**active stocks** The stocks and shares that have been actively traded, as recorded in the Official List of the London Stock Exchange.

**actuals (physicals)** Commodities that can be purchased and used, rather than goods traded on a *futures contract, which are represented by documents (although the documents give a right to physical possession of the goods, futures contracts are often cancelled out by offsetting a purchase against a sale). *See also* spot goods.

**actuary** A person trained in the mathematics of statistics and probability theory. Some are employed by insurance companies to calculate probable lengths of life and advise insurers on the amounts that should be put aside to pay claims and the amount of premium to be charged for each type of risk. Actuaries also advise on the administration of pension funds; the *government actuary is responsible for advising the government on National Insurance and other state pension schemes. *See also* Institute of Actuaries.

**additional personal allowance** An income-tax allowance available, in addition to the personal allowance, to a single person who has a qualifying child living with him or her, or to a married man with such a child and a totally incapacitated wife. A qualifying child is either under the age of 16 at the beginning of the income-tax year, or if over that age is undergoing full-time education. The allowance ceases in the income-tax year following the child's 18th birthday. *See also* personal allowances.

**additional rate tax** A tax payable by the trustees of *discretionary trusts in the UK on income arising in any *tax year which is either accumulated by them or payable at their discretion.

**adjudication 1.** The judgment or decision of a court, especially in bankruptcy proceedings. **2.** An assessment by the Commissioners of Inland Revenue of the amount of stamp duty due on a document. A document sent for adjudication will either be stamped as having no duty to pay or the taxpayer will be advised how much is due. An appeal may be made to the High Court if the taxpayer disagrees with the adjudication.

**adjustable-rate mortgage (ARM)** A *mortgage in which the interest rate is adjusted at periodic intervals, usually to reflect the prevailing rate of interest in the *money markets. Borrowers are often protected by a *cap, or ceiling, above which the interest rate is not allowed to rise. Such a cap may be reviewed annually or may cover the whole term of the mortgage. Such variable-rate mortgages usually start with a lower rate than a *fixed-rate mortgage in order to attract borrowers. In the USA this low initial rate is often known as a **teaser rate**.

**adjustable-rate preferred stock (ARP)** Stock or cumulative preference shares in the USA whose dividends are linked to Treasury Bill interest rates. Minimum and maximum rates are specified by the application of a *collar. **Convertible adjusted-rate preferred stock** can be converted to common stock at a fixed price at specified dates.

**adjustment credit** An advance made by a US Federal Bank to smaller banks to satisfy short-term lending needs. The loans may be made for as short a term as 15 days. Adjustment credits are most often used when interest rates are high and money supply is short.

**administration order 1.** An order made in a county court for the administration of the estate of a judgment debtor (*see* judgment creditor). The order normally requires the debtor to pay the debts by instalments; so long as this is done, the creditors referred to in the order cannot enforce their individual claims by other methods without the leave of the court. Administration orders are issued when the debtor has multiple debts but it is thought that *bankruptcy can be avoided. **2.** An order of the court under the Insolvency Act 1986 made in relation to a company in financial difficulties with a view to securing its survival as a going concern or, failing that, to achieving a more favourable realization of its assets than would be possible on a *liquidation. While the order is in force, the affairs of the company are managed by an **administrator**.

**administrative receiver** *See* receiver.

**administrator 1.** Any person appointed by the courts, or by private arrangement, to manage the property of another. **2.** Any person appointed by the courts to take charge of the affairs of a deceased person, who died without making a will. This includes collection of assets, payment of debts, and distribution of the surplus to those persons entitled to inherit, according to the laws of *intestacy. The administrator must be in possession of *letters of administration as proof of the authority vested by the courts.

**ADR** Abbreviation for *American Depository Receipt.

**ad valorem** (Latin: according to value) Denoting a tax or commission that is calculated as a percentage of the total invoice value of goods rather than the number of items. For example, *VAT is an ad valorem tax, calculated by adding a fixed percentage to an invoice value.

**advance corporation tax (ACT)** A feature of the *imputation system of taxation that has applied in the UK since 1972. When dividends (or other distributions) are made by UK companies to their shareholders, the companies must account to the Inland Revenue for advance corporation tax at a rate that would equal the basic rate of income tax on a figure consisting of the distribution plus the ACT. Thus, if the basic rate of income tax is 25%, the rate of ACT would be 1/3, so that a dividend of £750 with its ACT of 1/3 × £750 = £250 would total £1000, on which the tax at 25% would be £250 (the amount of the

ACT). The ACT thus paid serves two purposes: (1) it is a payment on account of the individual shareholder's personal income tax on the dividend, and (2) for the paying company it constitutes a payment on account of that company's corporation tax for the period in which the dividend is paid. There are limits to the amount of ACT that may be set against corporation tax liabilities for any given period. Unrelieved ACT may also be carried backwards or forwards or surrendered to other subsidiary companies.

**adventure** A commercial undertaking of a speculative nature, often associated with overseas trading.

**advise fate** A request by a collecting bank wishing to know, as soon as possible, whether a cheque will be paid on its receipt by the paying bank. The cheque is sent direct and not through a clearing house, asking that its fate should be advised immediately.

**AFBD** Abbreviation for *Association of Futures Brokers and Dealers Ltd.

**affinity card** A *credit card issued to an affinity group (such as the members of a club, college, etc.) in the USA. In the UK, an affinity card is linked to a particular charity; the credit-card company pledges to make a donation to a specified charity for each card issued and may also donate a small proportion of the money spent by card users. In the UK, affinity cards are sometimes called **charity cards**.

**afghani** (AF) The standard monetary unit of Afghanistan, divided into 100 puls.

**after date** The words used in a *bill of exchange to indicate that the period of the bill should commence from the date inserted on the bill, e.g. '… 30 days after date, we promise to pay …'. *Compare* after sight; at sight.

**after-hours deals** Transactions made on the London Stock Exchange after its official close at the end of its mandatory quote period. These deals are recorded as part of the next day's trading and referred to as early bargains. The mandatory quote period on the London Stock Exchange for the *Stock Exchange Automated Quotations System (SEAQ) is 8.30 am to 4.30 pm, and on SEAQ International, 9.30 am to 4.00 pm.

**after sight** The words used in a *bill of exchange to indicate that the period of the bill should commence from the date on which the drawee is presented with it for acceptance, i.e. has sight of it. *Compare* after date; at sight.

**AG** Abbreviation for *Aktiengesellschaft*. It appears after the name of a German, Austrian, or Swiss company, being equivalent to the British abbreviation plc (i.e. denoting a public limited company). *Compare* GmbH.

**agency 1.** A relationship between two parties; one, the principal, on whose behalf some action with a third party is being taken by the other, the agent. An agency agreement might exist, for example, when one person gives a power of attorney to another to negotiate a contract on his or her behalf, or when a bank purchases securities for a customer. **2.** An organization or individual that provides such an agency service. **3.** Securities issued in the USA by non-Treasury Department sources, such as the National Mortgage Association. **4.** One bank that acts as the organizer for a group of banks lending money to a corporation.

**agency bill** *See* inland bill.

**agency loan** A loan available for local-government authorities, public organizations, etc., from the *European Investment Bank.

*agent de change* A stockbroker on the Paris Bourse (*see* bourse).

**age relief** An additional *personal allowance set against income for income-tax purposes in the UK for both single people and married couples over 65. At the age of 75 both the personal allowance and the married couple's allowance are increased.

**agio** **1.** The fee charged by a bank or other financial institution for changing one form of money into another, e.g. coins to notes, or one currency to another. **2.** The difference between a bank's interest rate for borrowing money and the rate at which it is prepared to lend it, also known as the **turn** or **spread**.

**agora** An Israeli monetary unit, worth one hundredth of a *sheqel.

**agreed-value policy** An insurance policy in which the sum to be paid out under any claim is set out in the policy agreement.

**Agricultural Bank (Land Bank)** A credit bank specifically established to assist agricultural development, particularly by granting loans for longer periods than is usual with commercial banks.

**Agricultural Credit Corporation Ltd (ACC)** A corporation established in 1964 to extend the availability of medium-term bank credit for buildings, equipment, livestock, and working capital to farmers, growers, and cooperatives. The ACC offers a guarantee to the farmer's bank for such loans and promises to repay the bank should the farmer fail to do so. In return for this service the farmer pays a percentage charge to the ACC.

**Agricultural Mortgage Corporation Ltd (AMC)** A corporation established to grant loans to farmers against first mortgages on their land by the Agricultural Credits Act 1928. The AMC offers loans for periods of 5 to 40 years, and typically for up to two thirds the value of the mortgaged property. The capital of the AMC is supplied by the Bank of England, the High-Street banks, and by state-guaranteed debentures. Its loans are irrevocable, except in cases of default, and are usually made through the local branches of the High-Street banks.

**aid trade provision (ATP)** A major component of the British aid programme, which seeks to combine aid to developing countries with creating business for UK companies. Subsidized loans and credits are offered to developing countries on condition that goods and services are purchased from UK-based enterprises.

**Aktb** Abbreviation for *Aktiebolaget*. It appears after the name of a Swedish joint-stock company.

*Aktiengesellschaft* A German, Austrian, or Swiss public limited company. *See* AG.

**allonge** An attachment to a *bill of exchange to provide space for further endorsements when the back of the bill itself has been fully used. With the decline in the use of bills of exchange it is now rarely needed.

**All-Ordinaries share index** The most widely quoted index of Australian shares; it is a capitalization-weighted arithmetic average of 245 ordinary shares quoted on the *Australian Stock Exchange. The index encompasses two others, which are sometimes quoted independently: the All-Mining index (accounting for 17.6% of the All-Ordinaries) and the All-Resources (34.1%).

**allotment** A method of distributing previously unissued shares in a limited company in exchange for a contribution of capital. An application for such shares will often be made after the issue of a *prospectus on the *flotation of a public company or on the privatization of a state-owned industry. The company accepts the application by dispatching a **letter of allotment** to the applicant stating how many shares have been allotted; the applicant then has an unconditional right to be entered in the *register of members in respect of those shares. If the number of shares applied for exceeds the number available (oversubscription), allotment is made by a random draw or by a proportional allocation. Applicants that have been allotted fewer shares than they applied for receive a cheque for the unallotted balance (an application must be accompanied by a cheque for the full value of the shares applied for). *See also* multiple application.

**alpha coefficient** A measure of the expected return on a share compared to the expected return on shares with a similar volatility or *beta coefficient. The term is used in *portfolio theory. *See also* capital asset pricing model.

**alpha stocks** The most actively traded securities in the *Stock Exchange Automated Quotations System (SEAQ); it was a measure of market liquidity used by the *London Stock Exchange from October 1986 until January 1991, when the system was replaced by the *Normal Market Size (NMS) measure of dealings in a company's shares. The system divided the approximately 4000 securities quoted into four categories, alpha, beta, gamma, and delta, according to the frequency with which they were traded. The classification defined the degree of commitment to trading that had to be provided by market makers. For alpha stocks, normally the 100 or so largest quoted companies on SEAQ, at least 10 market makers had continuously to display firm buying and selling prices on the TOPIC screens installed throughout dealing rooms and offices in the City and the regions. In addition, all transactions had immediately to be published on TOPIC. Other criteria for alpha stocks related to the quarterly turnover and the market capitalization of the companies concerned. Beta stocks formed the second rank of quoted companies, of which there were approximately 500; these were less actively traded but continuous prices had also to be displayed, although immediate publication of transactions was not required. For gamma stocks and delta stocks, the relatively small companies in which trade was much more infrequent, prices displayed on the screens were treated as indicative, but market makers were not necessarily required to buy and sell at those prices. The prices of delta stocks did not have to be displayed at all. The classification was replaced when it became apparent that company directors regarded the system as an indication of status and even of corporate virility.

**amalgamation** The joining together of two or more businesses. *See* merger.

**American Depository Receipt (ADR)** A certificate issued by a US bank containing a statement that a specific number of shares in a foreign company has been deposited with them. The certificates are denominated in US dollars and can be traded as a security in US markets.

**American option** *See* option.

**American Stock Exchange (AMEX)** A stock exchange in New York, on which second-tier securities are traded. It originated as an open-air market in which brokers carried out kerbstone dealings in Wall Street. The market moved indoors in 1921, when it became the market for stocks and bonds of companies whose small size did not qualify them for membership of the main *New York Stock Exchange. Listing requirements on AMEX are less stringent than on the NYSE. AMEX pioneered touch-screen technology and, in linking with the Toronto Stock Exchange in 1985, established the first international link between primary equity markets. AMEX has developed a market in options and futures.

**AMEX** Abbreviation for *American Stock Exchange.

**amortization** The process of treating as an expense the annual amount deemed to waste away from a fixed asset. The concept is particularly applied to leases, which are acquired for a given sum for a specified term at the end of which the lease will have no value. It is customary to divide the cost of the lease by the number of years of its term and treat the result as an annual charge against profit. While this method does not necessarily reflect the value of the lease at any given time, it is an equitable way of allocating the original cost between periods. *Compare* depreciation.

Goodwill may also be amortized. The *statements of standard accounting practice recommend as its preferred method the writing-off in the year of purchase of all purchased goodwill. The charge should be to the reserves and not to the *profit and loss account. However the standard also permits the writing-off of goodwill to the profit and loss account in regular instalments over the period of its economic life. Home-grown goodwill, if it is in the balance sheet at all, should be similarly dealt with by one of the two methods above.

**amortizing mortgage** A *mortgage in which all the principal and all the interest has been repaid by the end of the mortgage agreement period. Although equal payments may be made during the term of the mortgage, the sums are divided, on a sliding scale, between interest payments and repayments of the principal. In the early years most of the payments go towards the interest charges, while in later years more repays the sum borrowed, until this sum is reduced to zero with the last payment. *Compare* balloon mortgage.

**amounts differ** The words stamped or written on a cheque or bill of exchange by a banker who returns it unpaid because the amount in words differs from that in figures. Banks usually make a charge for returning unpaid cheques.

**Amsterdam International Market (AIM)** A market set up by the banks, commission houses, and institutions in 1986 on the *Amsterdam Stock Exchange to transact large business at negotiated commissions without the use of brokers.

**Amsterdam Stock Exchange** Amsterdam first established a stock exchange in 1602 to trade in shares of the Dutch East India Company; it thus claims to be the world's oldest stock exchange. On the Amsterdam Stock Exchange only members (*hoekmen*) can deal. *See also* Amsterdam International Market; European Options Exchange.

**ancillary credit business** A business involved in credit brokerage, debt adjusting, debt counselling, debt collecting, or the operation of a credit-reference agency (*see* credit rating). **Credit brokerage** includes the effecting of introductions of individuals wishing to obtain credit to persons

carrying on a consumer-credit business. **Debt adjusting** is the process by
which a third party negotiates terms for the discharge of a debt due under
consumer-credit agreements or consumer-hire agreements with the creditor or
owner on behalf of the debtor or hirer. The latter may also pay a third party to
take over an obligation to discharge a debt or to undertake any similar acitivity
concerned with its liquidation. **Debt counselling** is the giving of advice (other
than by the original creditor and certain others) to debtors or hirers about the
liquidation of debts due under consumer-credit agreements or consumer-hire
agreements. A **credit-reference agency** collects information concerning the
financial standing of individuals and supplies this information to those seeking
it. The Consumer Credit Act 1974 provides for the licensing of ancillary credit
businesses and regulates their activities.

**annual accounts** An organization's financial statements published annually,
usually to comply with a statutory obligation to do so. They include a *balance
sheet, *profit and loss account (or *income and expenditure account), and
possibly a statement of sources and application of funds. *See also* modified
accounts. The most common are those produced by companies and filed at
Companies House, in accordance with the provisions of the Companies Acts.
However, other bodies are regulated by different statutes, for example Friendly
Societies report to the Registrar of Friendly Societies. Sole traders and
partnerships have no statutory obligation to produce annual accounts,
although accounts are required of them in order to agree assessments raised by
the Inland Revenue for taxation purposes.

**annual depreciation allowance** The reduction in the book value of an asset
at a specified percentage rate per annum.

**annual percentage rate (APR)** The annual equivalent *rate of return on a
loan or investment in which the rate of interest specified is chargeable or
payable more frequently than annually. Most investment institutions are now
required by law to specify the APR when the interest intervals are more frequent
than annual. Similarly those charge cards that advertise monthly rates of
interest (say, 2%) must state the equivalent APR. In this case it would be
$[(1.02)^{12} - 1] = 26.8\%$.

**annual report** The *annual accounts and directors' report of a company,
issued to shareholders and filed at Companies House in accordance with the
provisions of the Companies Acts.

**annual return** A return made annually to the Registrar of Companies in
accordance with the Companies Acts. It records details of the share capital and
assets (subject to charges) of directors, the company secretary, and
shareholders. The return is made up to the date 14 days after the date of the
company's annual general meeting.

**annuitant** A person who receives an *annuity.

**annuity 1.** A contract in which a person pays a premium to an insurance
company, usually in one lump sum, and in return receives periodic payments
for an agreed period or for the rest of his or her life (*see* life annuity). An annuity
has been described as the opposite of a life assurance as the policyholder pays
the lump sum and the insurer makes the regular payments. Annuities are often
purchased at a time of prosperity to convert capital into an income during old

age. *See also* annuity certain; deferred annuity.   **2.** A payment made on such a contract.

**annuity certain**   An *annuity in which payments continue for a specified period irrespective of the life or death of the person covered. In general, annuities cease on the death of the policyholder (*see* life annuity) unless they are annuities certain.

**ante-date**   To date a document before the date on which it is drawn up. This is not necessarily illegal or improper. For instance, an ante-dated cheque is not in law invalid. *Compare* post-date.

**APACS**   Abbreviation for *Association for Payment Clearing Services.

**APCIMS**   Abbreviation for *Association of Private Client Investment Managers and Stockbrokers.

**application form**   A form, issued by a newly floated company with its *prospectus, on which members of the public apply for shares in the company. *See also* allotment; multiple application; pink form.

**application for quotation**   An application by a *public limited company for a quotation on the *London Stock Exchange. The company is scrutinized by the Quotations Committee to see if it complies with the regulations and if its directors have a high reputation. If the application is accepted the company is given a quotation on one of the Stock Exchange's markets.

**appraisal-surplus account**   *See* revaluation of assets.

**appreciation**   **1.** An increase in the value of an asset, through inflation, a rise in market price, or interest earned. This usually occurs with land and buildings; the directors of a company have an obligation to adjust the nominal value of land and buildings and other assets in balance sheets to take account of appreciation. *See* asset stripping.   **2.** An increase in the value of a currency with a *floating exchange rate relative to another currency. *Compare* depreciation; devaluation.

**appropriation**   **1.** An allocation of the net profit of an organization in its accounts. Some payments may be treated as expenses and deducted before arriving at net profit; other payments are deemed to be appropriations of profit, once that profit has been ascertained. Examples of the former are such normal trade expenses as wages and salaries of employees, motor running expenses, light and heat, and most interest payments on external finance. Appropriations of the net profit include payments of income tax or corporation tax, dividends to shareholders, transfers to reserves, and, in the case of partnerships, salaries and interest on capital paid to the partners. *See also* accumulated profits. **2.** The allocation of payments to a particular debt out of several owed by a debtor to one creditor. The right to make the appropriation belongs first to the debtor but if the debtor fails to make the appropriation the creditor has the right to do so.

**approved deferred share trust (ADST)**   A trust fund set up by a British company, and approved by the Inland Revenue, that purchases shares in that company for the benefit of its employees. Tax on dividends is deferred until the shares are sold and is then paid at a reduced rate.

**APR**   Abbreviation for *annual percentage rate.

**arbitrage**  The non-speculative transfer of funds from one market to another to take advantage of differences in interest rates, exchange rates, or commodity prices between the two markets. It is non-speculative because an arbitrageur will only switch from one market to another if the rates or prices in both markets are known and if the profit to be gained outweighs the costs of the operation. Thus, a large stock of a commodity in a user country may force its price below that in a producing country; if the difference is greater than the cost of shipping the goods back to the producing country, this could provide a profitable opportunity for arbitrage. Similar opportunities arise with *bills of exchange and foreign currencies.

**ARBs**  Abbreviation for arbitrageurs, i.e. dealers specializing in *arbitrage.

**arithmetic mean**  An average obtained by adding together the individual numbers concerned and dividing the total by their number. For example, the arithmetic mean of 7, 20, 107, and 350 is 484/4 = 121. This value, however, gives no idea of the spread of numbers. *Compare* geometric mean.

**ARM**  Abbreviation for *adjustable-rate mortgage.

**arm's length**  Denoting a transaction in which the parties to the transaction are financially unconnected. For example, a transaction between two subsidiaries of the same parent organization could only be said to be at arm's length if it could be shown that the deal had been carried out at current market prices with no preference of any kind being shown in the trading terms.

**ARP**  Abbreviation for *adjustable-rate preferred stock.

**ARR**  Abbreviation for *accounting rate of return.

**arrangement**  **1.** A method of enabling debtors to enter into agreements with their creditors (either privately or through the courts) to discharge their debts by partial payment, as an alternative to bankruptcy. This is generally achieved by a **scheme of arrangement**, which involves applying the assets and income of the debtor in proportionate payments to the creditors. For instance, a scheme of arrangement may stipulate that the creditors will receive 20 pence for every pound that is owed to them. This is sometimes also known as **composition**. Once a scheme of arrangement has been agreed a **deed of arrangement** is drawn up, which must be registered with the Department of Trade and Industry within seven days. **2.** *See* voluntary arrangement.

**ASB**  Abbreviation for *Accounting Standards Board.

**A shares**  Ordinary shares in a company that usually do not carry voting rights. **Non-voting shares** are issued by a company when it wishes to raise additional capital without committing itself to a fixed dividend and without diluting control of the company. They are, however, unpopular with institutional investors (who like to have a measure of control with their investments) and are therefore now rarely issued.

**as per advice**  Words written on a *bill of exchange to indicate that the drawee has been informed that the bill is being drawn on him or her.

**assented stock**  A security, usually an ordinary share, the owner of which has agreed to the terms of a *takeover bid. During the takeover negotiations, different prices may be quoted for assented and **non-assented stock**.

**assessment** The method by which a tax authority raises a bill for a particular tax and sends it to the taxpayer or the taxpayer's agent. The assessment may be based on figures already agreed between the authority and the taxpayer or it may be an estimate by the tax authorities. The taxpayer normally has a right of appeal against an assessment within a specified time limit. A **Notice of Assessment** is, under UK income tax legislation, essential before a legal liability to income tax can arise. The assessment must also be served on (or delivered to) the person being assessed.

**asset** Any object, tangible or intangible, that is of value to its possessor. In most cases it either is cash or can be turned into cash; exceptions include prepayments, which may represent payments made for rent, rates, or motor licences, in cases in which the time paid for has not yet expired. Tangible assets include land and buildings, plant and machinery, fixtures and fittings, trading stock, investments, debtors, and cash; intangible assets include goodwill, patents, copyrights, and trademarks. *See also* deferred asset.

For *capital-gains tax purposes, an asset consists of all forms of property, whether situated in the UK or abroad, including options, debts, incorporeal property, currency (other than sterling), and any form of property either created by the person disposing of it or owned without being acquired. It must, however, consist of some form of property for which a value can be ascertained. Some assets are exempt from *capital-gains tax.

**asset-backed fund** A fund in which the money is invested in tangible or corporate assets, such as property or shares, rather than being treated as savings loaned to a bank or other institution. Asset-backed funds can be expected to grow with inflation in a way that bank savings cannot. *See also* equity-linked policy; unit-linked policy.

**Asset card** *See* debit card.

**asset management** **1.** The management of the financial assets of a company in order to maximize the return on the investments. **2.** An investment service offered by banks and some other financial institutions. In the UK some private banks offer an asset management service for wealthy customers. *See also* portfolio.

**asset specificity** Tangible or intangible assets that only have value in the context of a particular relationship.

**asset stripping** The acquisition or takeover of a company whose shares are valued below their *asset value, and the subsequent sale of the company's most valuable assets. Asset stripping was a practice that occurred primarily in the decade after World War II, during which property values were rising sharply. Having identified a suitable company, an entrepreneur would acquire a controlling interest in it by buying its shares on the stock exchange; after revaluing the properties held some or all of them could be sold for cash, which would be distributed to shareholders (which now included the entrepreneur). Subsequently, the entrepreneur could either revitalize the management of the company and later sell off the acquired shareholding at a profit or, in some cases, close the business down. Because the asset stripper is totally heedless of the welfare of the other shareholders, the employees, the suppliers, or creditors of the stripped company, the practice is now highly deprecated.

**asset value (per share)** The total value of the assets of a company less its liabilities, divided by the number of ordinary shares in issue. This represents in theory, although probably not in practice, the amount attributable to each share if the company was wound up. The asset value may not necessarily be the total of the values shown by a company's balance sheet, since it is not the function of balance sheets to value assets. It may, therefore, be necessary to substitute the best estimate that can be made of the market values of the assets (including goodwill) for the values shown in the balance sheet. If there is more than one class of share, it may be necessary to deduct amounts due to shareholders with a priority on winding up before arriving at the amounts attributable to shareholders with a lower priority.

**assignment** The act of transferring, or a document (a **deed of assignment**) transferring, property to some other person. Examples of assignment include the transfer of rights under a contract or benefits under a trust to another person.

**assignment of insurable interest** Assigning to another party the rights and obligations of the *insurable interest in an item of property, life, or a legal liability to be insured. This enables the person to whom the interest is assigned to arrange insurance cover, which would not otherwise be legally permitted.

**assignment of life policies** Transfer of the legal right under a life-assurance policy to collect the proceeds. Assignment is only valid if the life insurer is advised and agrees; life assurance is the only form of insurance in which the assignee need not possess an *insurable interest. In recent years policy auctions have become a popular alternative to surrendering *endowment assurances. In these auctions, a policy is sold to the highest bidder and then assigned to him or her by the original policyholder.

**associate company** A company that is partly owned by another.

**Association for Payment Clearing Services (APACS)** An association set up by the UK banks in 1985 to manage payment clearing and overseas money transmission in the UK. The three operating companies under its aegis are: BACS Ltd, which provides an automated service for interbank clearing in the UK; Cheque and Credit Clearing Co. Ltd, which operates a bulk clearing system for interbank cheques and paper credits; and CHAPS and Town Clearing, which provides same-day clearing for high-value cheques and electronic funds transfer. In addition EftPos UK Ltd is a company set up to develop electronic funds transfer at the point of sale. APACS also oversees London Dollar Clearing, the London Currency Settlement Scheme, and the cheque card and *eurocheque schemes in the UK.

**Association of British Insurers (ABI)** A trade association representing over 440 insurance companies offering any class of insurance business, whose members transact over 90% of the business of the British insurance market. It was formed in 1985 by a merger the British Insurance Association, the Accident Offices Association, the Fire Offices Committee, the Life Offices Association, and the Industrial Life Offices Association.

**Association of Futures Brokers and Dealers Ltd (AFBD)** A former Self-Regulating Organization (SRO) set up under the Finance Act 1986 to regulate the activities of brokers and dealers on the London International

Financial Futures and Options Exchange. It merged with The *Securities Association Ltd in 1991 to form the *Securities and Futures Authority Ltd (SFA).

**Association of Private Client Investment Managers and Stockbrokers (APCIMS)**  A representative body for private-client investment managers and stockbrokers, formed in June 1990. It aims to improve the environment and expand the market in which private-investors' business is transacted. The association represents 95% of eligible firms with a network of over 250 offices throughout the UK. It publishes a directory of private-client stockbrokers, with details of members and the services they provide. It is run by an elected committee with a small permanent secretariat based in London, assisted by specialist practitioner committees.

**assurance**  *Insurance against an eventuality (especially death) that must occur. *See* life assurance.

**assured**  The person named in a life-assurance policy to receive the proceeds in the event of maturity or the death of the *life assured. As a result of the policy, the person's financial future is 'assured'.

**AST**  Abbreviation for *automated screen trading.

**at**  A monetary unit of Laos, worth one hundredth of a kip.

**at best**  An instruction to a broker to buy or sell shares, stocks, commodities, currencies, etc., as specified, at the best possible price. It must be executed immediately irrespective of market movements. *Compare* at limit.

**at call**  Denoting secured money that has been lent on a short-term basis and must be repaid immediately on demand. Discount houses in the City of London are the main borrowers of money at call, accounting for 4–6% of the banks' eligible liabilities.

**Athens Stock Exchange**  The only stock exchange in Greece. It was established in 1876 and privatized in 1990, with a new supervisory board and central depository.

**at limit**  An instruction to a broker to buy or sell shares, stocks, commodities, currencies, etc., as specified, at a stated limiting price (i.e. not above a stated price if buying or not below a stated price if selling). When issuing such an instruction the principal should also state for how long the instruction stands, e.g. for a day, a week, etc. *Compare* at best.

**ATM**  Abbreviation for *automated teller machine.

**at par**  *See* par value.

**at sight**  The words used on a *bill of exchange to indicate that payment is due on presentation. *Compare* after date; after sight.

**attachment**  The procedure enabling a creditor, who has obtained judgment in the courts (the judgment creditor), to secure payment of the amount due from the debtor. The judgment creditor obtains a further court order (the garnishee order) to the effect that money or property due from a third party (the garnishee) to the debtor must be frozen and paid instead to the judgment creditor to satisfy the amount due. For instance, a judgment creditor may, through a garnishee order, attach the salary due to the debtor from the debtor's employer (the garnishee).

**at-the-money option** A call or put *option in which the exercise price is approximately the same as the current market price of the underlying security.

**ATX** Abbreviation for Austrian Traded Index. *See* OTOB.

**audit** The inspection of an organization's *annual accounts. An **external audit** is carried out by a qualified *accountant, in order to obtain an opinion as to the veracity of the accounts. Under the Companies Acts, companies are required to appoint an *auditor to express an opinion as to whether the annual accounts give a true and fair view of the company's affairs and whether they comply with the provisions of the Companies Acts. To give such an opinion, the auditor needs to examine the company's internal accounting systems, inspect its assets, make tests of accounting transactions, etc. Some bodies have different requirements for audit; for example, accountants report to the Law Society on solicitors' accounts under the Accountants' Report Rules. Many companies and organizations now appoint internal auditors to carry out an **internal audit**, with the object of reporting to management on the efficacy and security of internal systems. In some cases these systems may not even be financial; they may include, for example, an audit of health and safety in the workplace or an audit of compliance with equal opportunities legislation. *See also* auditors' report.

**auditor** A person who carries out an *audit. **External auditors** are normally members of a body of *accountants authorized by the Companies Acts, such as the *Institute of Chartered Accountants or the Chartered Association of Certified Accountants. The principal requirement for an external audit is that the auditor should be independent of the organization audited and professionally qualified. The same is not true of **internal auditors,** who may be members of such professional bodies as the Institute of Internal Auditors or any of the accountancy bodies, but who may also be appropriately trained employees of the organizations being audited. Every company must have properly qualified auditors. If none have been appointed, the Secretary of State for Trade and Industry must be informed within one week. Failure to do so may result in the company and its officers being liable to a fine. Auditors are usually appointed at the annual general meeting of the company; the appointment of a new auditor or the removal of an auditor requires special notice. An auditor's notice of resignation must contain a statement of any matters that should be brought to the notice of the shareholders or creditors or a statement that there are no such matters. An auditor's duties must be carried out with due care and skill; an auditor may be liable to negligence to the company, the members, and third parties relying on the audited accounts. The **auditors' remuneration** has to be approved at a general meeting of the company and should be distinguished in the accounts from the cost of other accounting work. *See also* auditors' report.

**auditors' report** A report by the auditors appointed to *audit the accounts of a company or other organization. Auditors' reports may take many forms depending on who has appointed the auditors and for what purposes. Some auditors are engaged in an internal audit while others are appointed for various statutory purposes. The auditors of a limited company are required to form an opinion as to whether the annual accounts of the company give a true and fair view of its profit or loss for the period under review and of its state of affairs at the end of the period; they are also required to certify that the accounts are prepared in accordance with the requirements of the Companies Act 1985. The auditors' report is technically a report to the members of the company and it must be filed together with the accounts with the Registrar of Companies under the Companies Act 1985. Under this Act, the auditors' report must also include an audit of the directors' report. *See also* qualified report.

**audit trail**  The ability to trace the details of past transactions through accounts. It is usually applied to computer files and is important in securities dealing to enable supervisory bodies to follow transactions and ensure that fair prices have been paid. It is sometimes called a **paper trail**.

**Australian Stock Exchange (ASX)**  The stock exchange based in Sydney, which in 1987 superseded the exchanges in Brisbane, Adelaide, Hobart, Melbourne, and Perth. It abolished fixed-rate commissions in 1984 and adopted fully automated trading in October 1990. ASX issues the *All-Ordinaries share index as well as the subsidiary indices, the All-Industrials share index and All-Resources share index.

**authorized share capital**  *See* share capital.

**automated screen trading (AST)**  Electronic dealing in securities using visual-display units to display prices and the associated computer equipment to enter, match, and execute deals. The system does away with the need for face-to-face trading on a formal stock-exchange floor, and even dispenses with telephone dealing. It potentially reduces or eliminates paperwork. The removal of the need for human contact between dealers has caused some uneasiness.

**automated teller machine (ATM)**  A computerized machine usually attached to the outside wall of a High-Street bank or building society that enables customers to withdraw cash from their *current accounts, especially outside normal banking hours. The machines may also be used to pay in cash or cheques, effect transfers, and obtain statements. They are operated by *cash cards or *multifunctional cards in conjunction with a *PIN. ATMs are often known colloquially as **cash dispensers**.

**automatic debit transfer**  *See* giro.

**available earnings**  *See* earnings per share.

**aval**  **1.** A third-party guarantee of payment on a *bill of exchange or promissory note; it is often given by a bank.  **2.** A signature on a bill of exchange that endorses or guarantees the bill.

**average**  **1.** A single number used to represent a set of numbers; mean. *See* arithmetic mean; geometric mean; median.  **2.** A method of sharing losses in property insurance to combat underinsurance. This is usually applied in an **average clause** in a fire insurance policy, in which it is stated that the sum payable in the event of a claim shall be not more than the proportion that the insured value of an item bears to its actual value.  **3.** A partial loss in marine insurance.

**average stock**  A method of accounting for stock movements that assumes goods are taken out of stock at the average cost of the goods in stock. *See* base stock method; FIFO; LIFO; stock.

**averaging**  Adding to a holding of particular securities or commodities when the price falls, in order to reduce the average cost of the whole holding. **Averaging in** consists of buying at various price levels in order to build up a substantial holding of securities or commodities over a period. **Averaging out**

is the opposite process, of selling a large holding at various price levels over a long period.

**avo**  A monetary unit of Macao, worth one hundredth of a \*pataca.

**baby bonds**  Bonds offered by tax-exempt friendly societies, which produce maturing funds for an infant over a period, usually 10 years. The maximum investment allowed by the UK government is currently £18 a month or £200 a year.

**backdate   1.**  To put an earlier date on a document than that on which it was compiled, in order to make it effective from that earlier date.   **2.**  To agree that salary increases, especially those settled in a pay award, should apply from a specified date in the recent past.

**back door**  One of the methods by which the *Bank of England injects cash into the *money market. The bank purchases Treasury bills at the market rate rather than by lending money directly to the discount houses (the **front-door method**) when it acts as *lender of last resort.

**back-end load**  The final charge made by an *investment trust when an investor sells shares in the fund.

**back-to-back credit (countervailing credit)**  A method used to conceal the identity of the seller from the buyer in a credit arrangement. When the credit is arranged by a British finance house, the foreign seller provides the relevant documentation. The finance house, acting as an intermediary, issues its own documents to the buyer, omitting the seller's name and so concealing the seller's identity. The reason for not revealing the seller's identity is to prevent buyer and seller dealing direct in future transactions and thus cutting out the middle man.

**back-to-back loan**  A loan from one company to another in a different country, often in a different currency, using a bank or other financial institution as a middle man to provide the loan but not the funding, which comes from a third party. Usually the loan is between a parent company and overseas subsidiaries; a pledge is usually given to honour loans on which there may be a default.

**back-up credit**  An alternative source of funds arranged if an issue of *commercial paper is not fully taken up by the market. Back-up credit is provided by a bank for a fee or by the deposit of credit balances at the bank of the issuer. The back-up is often a stand-by facility provided by the bank, which may be drawn upon if the paper is not placed.

**backwardation   1.**  The difference between the spot price of a commodity, including rent, insurance, and interest accrued, and the forward price, when the spot price is the higher.   **2.**  A situation that occasionally occurs on the London Stock Exchange when a market maker quotes a buying price for a share that is lower than the selling price quoted by another market maker. However, with prices now displayed on screens, this situation does not now last long. Backwardation also occurs in commodity markets, especially on the London Metal Exchange. *Compare* forwardation.

**bad debt** An amount owing from a *debtor that is very unlikely to be paid. Such an amount can be treated as a loss and written off in the *profit and loss account. Doubtful debts may appear in the balance sheet of an organization as a *provision for bad debts.

**badges of trade** The criteria that distinguish trading from investment for taxation purposes. They were set out by the Royal Commission on the Taxation of Profits and Income in 1954. Dealing on the *commodity markets is normally regarded as trading and profits are subject to income tax or corporation tax; dealing on security markets is often (but not always) treated as investment and profits are subject to lower taxation by the capital-gains tax.

**baht** (B) The standard monetary unit of Thailand, divided into 100 satang.

**baiza** A monetary unit of Oman, worth one hundredth of a rial.

**balboa** (B) The standard monetary unit of Panama, divided into 100 centésimos.

**balanced-budget multiplier** The effect on the gross national product caused by a change in government expenditure that has been offset by an equal change in taxation. For example, an increase in government spending will inject more demand into the economy than the equal increase in taxation takes out, since some of the income absorbed by the tax would have been used for savings and therefore did not contribute to the aggregate demand. In effect, individuals have reduced savings, they feel worse off, and therefore work harder to build up their savings again. The balanced-budget multiplier is not usually pursued explicitly as an instrument of fiscal policy as taxation is generally unpopular.

**balance of payments** The accounts setting out a country's transactions with the outside world. They are divided into various sub-accounts, notably the **current account** and the **capital account**. The former includes the trade account, which records the balance of imports and exports (*see* balance of trade). Overall, the accounts must always be in balance. A deficit or surplus on the balance of payments refers to an imbalance on a sub-account, usually the amount by which the foreign-exchange reserves of the government have been depleted or increased. The conventions used for presenting balance-of-payments statistics are those recommended by the *International Monetary Fund.

**balance of trade** The accounts setting out the results of a country's trading position. It is a component of the *balance of payments, forming part of the *current account. It includes both the *visibles (i.e. imports and exports in physical merchandise) and the *invisible balance (receipts and expenditure on such services as insurance, finance, freight, and tourism).

**balance sheet** One of the principal statements comprising a set of *accounts, showing the financial state of affairs of an organization on a given date, usually the last day of an *accounting period. A balance sheet has three main headings: assets, liabilities, and capital. The assets must always equal the sum of the liabilities and the capital, as the statement can be looked at in either of two ways: (1) as a statement of the organization's wealth, in which case the assets less the liabilities equal the capital (the amount of wealth attributable to the proprietors); or (2) as a statement of how the assets have been funded, i.e. partly by borrowing (the liabilities) and partly by the proprietors (the capital). Although a balance sheet balances, i.e. its two sides are equal, it is actually so named since it comprises balances from the accounts in the ledgers.

**balloon** A large sum repaid as an irregular instalment of a loan repayment. **Balloon loans** are those in which repayments are not made in a regular manner, but are made, as funds become available, in balloons.

**balloon mortgage** A *mortgage in which some of the original principal and some interest is still outstanding at the end of the mortgage agreement period; it is also called a **non-amortizing mortgage**. With a balloon mortgage a lump sum has to be repaid at the end of the term to cover the remaining debt.

**ballot** A random selection of applications for an oversubscribed *new issue of shares (*see also* flotation). The successful applicants may be granted the full number of shares for which they have applied or a specified proportion of their applications. Applicants not selected in the ballot have their applications and cheques returned.

**Baltic Exchange** A former commodity and freight-chartering exchange in the City of London. It took its name from the trade in grain with Baltic ports, which was the mainstay of the business in the 18th century. Most of its trade, including the Baltic International Freight Futures Exchange (BIFFEX), has been taken over by *London FOX. The building was badly damaged by an IRA bomb in 1992.

**Baltic International Freight Futures Market (BIFFEX)** *See* London FOX.

**band 1.** A trading range, set by upper and lower limits, of a commodity or currency. For example, the ERM (*see* European Monetary System) sets a narrow band against a central rate of conversion to the Deutschmark of ± 2·5% or a broad band of ± 6%. **2.** Four ranges of maturities set by the Bank of England to influence short-term interest rates in the money market. They are set on *Treasury bills, *local authority bills, and eligible bank bills (*see* eligible paper); band 1 is from 1 to 14 days, band 2 from 15 to 33 days, band 3 from 34 to 63 days, and band 4 from 64 to 91 days.

**bani** A monetary unit of Romania, worth one hundredth of a leu.

**bank** A commercial institution licensed as a taker of deposits. Banks are concerned mainly with making and receiving payments on behalf of their customers, accepting deposits, and making short-term loans to private individuals, companies, and other organizations. In the UK, the banking system comprises the *Bank of England (the central bank), the *commercial banks, *merchant banks, branches of foreign and Commonwealth banks, the TSB Group, the *National Savings Bank, and the National Girobank (*see* giro). The first (1990) *building society to become a bank in the UK was the Abbey National, after its public *flotation. In other countries banks are also usually supervised by a government-controlled central bank.

**bank account** *See* account; cheque account; current account; deposit account; savings account.

**bank bill** A bill of exchange issued or guaranteed (accepted) by a bank. It is more acceptable than a trade bill as there is less risk of non-payment and hence it can be discounted at a more favourable rate, although this does, to some extent, depend on the credit rating of the bank.

**bank certificate** A certificate, signed by a bank manager, stating the balance held to a company's credit on a specified date. It may be asked for during the course of an audit.

**bank charge** The amount charged to a customer by a bank, usually for a specific transaction, such as paying in a sum of money by means of a cheque or withdrawing a sum by means of an automated teller machine. However, modern practice is to provide periods of commission-free banking by waiving most charges on personal current accounts. The commercial banks have largely been forced to take this step as a result of the free banking services offered by *building societies. However, business customers invariably pay tariffs in one form or another.

**bank deposit** A sum of money placed by a customer with a bank. The deposit may or may not attract interest and may be instantly accessible or accessible at a time agreed by the two parties. Banks may use a percentage of their customers' deposits to lend on to other customers; thus most deposits may only exist on paper in the bank's books. Money on deposit at a bank is usually held in either a *deposit account or a *current account, although some banks now offer special high-interest accounts.

**bank draft (banker's cheque; banker's draft)** A cheque drawn by a bank on itself or its agent. A person who owes money to another buys the draft from a bank for cash and hands it to the creditor, who will thereby have considerably less fear that it might be dishonoured. A bank draft is used if the creditor is unwilling to accept an ordinary cheque.

**banker's acceptance** A *time draft that promises to pay a certain sum and has been accepted by a bank. It is a form of promissory note, widely used in international trade; once signed and dated it can be traded before its maturity. *See also* third-country acceptance.

**banker's cheque** *See* bank draft.

**banker's reference (status enquiry)** A report on the creditworthiness of an individual supplied by a bank to a third party, such as another financial institution or a bank customer. References and status enquiries are often supplied by specialist credit-reference agencies, who keep lists of defaulters, bad payers, and people who have infringed credit agreements. References must be very general and recent legislation has given new rights to the subjects of such reports, which restrict their value even further.

**Bank for International Settlements (BIS)** An international bank originally established in 1930 as a financial institution to coordinate the payment of war reparations between European central banks. It was hoped that the BIS, with headquarters in Basle, would develop into a European central bank but many of its functions were taken over by the *International Monetary Fund (IMF) after World War II. Since then the BIS has fulfilled several roles including acting as a trustee and agent for various international groups, such as the OECD, European Monetary Agreement, etc. The frequent meetings of the BIS directors have been a useful means of cooperation between central banks, especially in combating short-term speculative monetary movements. Since 1986 the BIS has acted as a clearing house for interbank transactions in the form of *European Currency

Units. The BIS also sets *capital adequacy ratios for banks in European countries.

The original members were France, Belgium, West Germany, Italy, and the UK but now most European central banks are represented as well as the USA, Canada, and Japan. The London agent is the Bank of England, whose governor is a member of the board of directors of the BIS.

**Bank Giro** *See* giro.

**bank guarantee** An undertaking given by a bank to settle a debt should the debtor fail to do so. A bank guarantee can be used as a security for a loan but the banks themselves will require good cover in cash or counter-indemnity before they issue a guarantee. A guarantee has to be in writing to be legally binding. Such guarantees often contain indemnity clauses, which place a direct onus on the guarantor. This onus leaves the guarantor liable in law in all eventualities.

**Bank Holidays** Public holidays in the UK, when the banks are closed. They are New Year's Day, Easter Monday, May Day (the first Monday in May), Spring Bank Holiday (the last Monday in May), August Bank Holiday (last Monday in August), and Boxing Day. In Scotland, Easter Monday is replaced by 2 January and the August Bank Holiday is on the first Monday in August. In Northern Ireland St Patrick's Day (17 March) is added. In the Channel Islands Liberation Day (9 May) is included. Bank Holidays have a similar status to Sundays in that *bills of exchange falling due on a Bank Holiday are postponed until the following day and also they do not count in working out *days of grace. Good Friday and Christmas Day are also public holidays, but payments falling due (including bills of exchange) on these days are payable on the preceding day. When Bank Holidays fall on a Sunday, the following day becomes the Bank Holiday.

**banking** The activities undertaken by banks; this includes personal banking (non-business customers), commercial banking (small and medium-sized business customers), and corporate banking (large international and multinational corporations). In the USA there are many restrictions on banks opening branches across the nation, notably the Glass-Steagal Act 1933. Consequently unit banking is mainly undertaken through separate enterprises, although the restrictions have been breached on several occasions and there are now many super-regional banks in the USA, operating in a similar way to UK branches. In the UK most banking for both business and personal customers is undertaken through the High-Street banks, which is also known as **branch banking** (*see also* commercial bank).

**Banking Acts 1979 and 1987** UK Acts of Parliament defining a bank as a taker of deposits and investing supervision of banks in the *Bank of England. The Acts created safeguards to ensure that only fit and proper persons should be allowed to be managers, directors, or controllers of banks. The Acts also stipulate that the paid-up capital reserves of such an institution should be not less than £1 million. The only exceptions to this limit are authorized *building societies, municipal and school banks, and some central or international development banks. The UK legislation was made necessary by the European Community's First Banking Directive.

**Banking Ombudsman** *See* Financial Ombudsman.

**bank loan (bank advance)**  A specified sum of money lent by a bank to a customer, usually for a specified time, at a specified rate of interest. In most cases banks require some form of security for loans, especially if the loan is to a commercial enterprise, although if a bank regards a company as a good credit risk, loans may not be secured. *See also* loan account; overdraft; personal loan.

**banknote**  An item of paper currency issued by a central bank. Banknotes developed in England from the receipts issued by London goldsmiths in the 17th century for gold deposited with them for safekeeping. These receipts came to be used as money and their popularity as a *medium of exchange encouraged the goldsmiths to issue their own banknotes, largely to increase their involvement in banking and, particularly, moneylending. Now only the Bank of England and the Scottish and Irish banks in the UK have the right to issue notes. Originally all banknotes were fully backed by gold and could be exchanged on demand for gold; however, since 1931 the promise on a note to 'pay the bearer on demand' simply indicates that the note is legal tender. *See also* promissory note.

**Bank of England**  The central bank of the UK. It was established in 1694 as a private bank by London merchants in order to lend money to the state and to deal with the national debt. It came under public ownership in 1946 with the passing of the Bank of England Act. The Bank of England acts as the government's bank, providing loans through ways and means advances and arranging borrowing through the issue of gilt-edged securities. The bank helps to implement the government's financial and monetary policy as directed by the Treasury. It also has wide statutory powers to supervise the banking system, including the commercial banks to which, through the discount market, it acts as *lender of last resort.

The Bank Charter Act 1844 divided the bank into an issue department and a banking department. The issue department is responsible for the issue of banknotes and coins as supplied by the *Royal Mint. The banking department provides banking services (including accounts) to commercial banks, foreign banks, other central banks, and government departments. The bank manages the national debt, acting as registrar of government stocks. It also administers *exchange control, when in force, and manages the *exchange equalization account. The bank is controlled by a governor, deputy-governor, and a court (board) of 16 directors, appointed by the Crown for periods of 4–5 years. *See also* Banking Acts 1979 and 1987.

**Bank of England Stock Register**  The register of holders of government stocks (*see* gilt-edged security) maintained by the *Bank of England. Purchases and sales of government stocks made by stockbrokers and banks are recorded on this register. Income tax on interest paid on these stocks is deducted at source, unlike stocks on the *National Savings Stock Register.

**Bank of Japan (BOJ)**  The Japanese central bank, which controls monetary policy but does not regulate Japanese banks.

**bank rate**  The rate at which the central bank, in the UK the *Bank of England, is prepared to lend to the other banks in the banking system. From 1972 to 1981 this was known as the *minimum lending rate. It is now more commonly known as the *base rate.

**bankruptcy**  The state of an individual who is unable to pay his or her debts and against whom a **bankruptcy order** has been made by a court. Such orders deprive bankrupts of their property, which is then used to pay their debts. Bankruptcy proceedings are started by a petition, which may be presented to the court by (1) a creditor or creditors; (2) a person affected by a voluntary arrangement to pay debts set up by the debtor under the Insolvency Act 1986; (3) the Director of Public Prosecutions; or (4) the debtor. The grounds for a creditors' petition are that the debtor appears to be unable to pay his or her debts or to have reasonable prospects of doing so, i.e. that the debtor has failed to make arrangements to pay a debt for which a statutory demand has been made or that a judgment debt has not been satisifed. The debts must amount to at least £750. The grounds for a petition by a person bound by a voluntary arrangement are that the debtor has not complied with the terms of the arrangement or has withheld material information. The Director of Public Prosecutions may present a petition in the public interest under the Powers of Criminal Courts Act 1973. The debtor may also present a petition on the grounds of being unable to pay his or her debts.

Once a petition has been presented, the debtor may not dispose of any property. The court may halt any other legal proceedings against the debtor. An interim receiver may be appointed. This will usually be the *official receiver, who will take any necessary action to protect the debtor's estate. A *special manager may be appointed if the nature of the debtor's business requires it.

The court may make a bankruptcy order at its discretion. Once this has happened, the debtor is an undischarged bankrupt, who is deprived of the ownership of all property and must assist the official receiver in listing it, recovering it, protecting it, etc. The official receiver becomes manager and receiver of the estate until the appointment of a **trustee in bankruptcy**. The bankrupt must prepare a statement of affairs for the official receiver within 21 days of the bankruptcy order. A **public examination** of the bankrupt may be ordered on the application of the official receiver or the creditors, in which the bankrupt will be required to answer questions about his or her affairs in court.

Within 12 weeks the official receiver must decide whether to call a **meeting of creditors** to appoint a trustee in bankruptcy. The trustee's duties are to collect, realize, and distribute the bankrupt's estate. The trustee may be appointed by the creditors, the court, or the Secretary of State and must be a qualified insolvency practitioner or the official receiver. All the property of the bankrupt is available to pay the creditors, except for the following: equipment necessary for him or her to continue in employment or business, necessary domestic equipment; and income required for the reasonable domestic needs of the bankrupt and his or her family. The court has discretion whether to order sale of a house in which a spouse or children are living. All creditors must prove their claims to the trustees. Only unsecured claims can be proved in bankruptcy. When all expenses have been paid, the trustee will divide the estate. The Insolvency Act 1986 sets out the order in which creditors will be paid (*see* preferential creditor). The bankruptcy may end automatically after two or three years, but in some cases a court order is required. The bankrupt is discharged and receives a certificate of discharge from the court.

**Bankruptcy Reform Act 1978** A US law that brought about major changes to bankruptcy law after 40 years of the previous legislation. The reforms made it easier to file petitions, amended the previous absolute rule giving priority to secured creditors in all cases, and gave federal bankruptcy judges more powers to hear cases. The reforms also added a clause covering tests for ability to pay under Chapter 13 of the Bankruptcy Act. Under *Chapter 11 a firm can apply to the court for protection from its creditors while it undergoes a reorganization in an attempt to pay its debts.

**banque d'affaires** The French term for a *merchant bank or an *issuing house as well as an *investment bank.

**Banque de France** The central bank of France, which has approximately the same status as the Bank of England. Established in 1800 and nationalized in January 1946, it has some 214 branches.

**bargain** A transaction on the London Stock Exchange. The bargains made during the day are included in the Daily Official List.

**barometer stock** A security whose price is regarded as an indicator of the state of the market. It will be a widely held *blue chip with a stable price record.

**base rate 1.** The rate of interest used as a basis by banks for the rates they charge their customers. In practice most customers will pay a premium over base rate to take account of the bank's risk involved in lending, competitive market pressures, and to regulate the supply of credit. **2.** An informal name for the rate at which the Bank of England lends to the *discount houses, which effectively controls the lending rate throughout the banking system. The abolition of the *minimum lending rate in 1981 heralded a loosening of government control over the banking system, but the need to increase interest rates in the late 1980s (to control inflation and the *balance of payments deficit) led to the use of this term in this sense.

**base stock method** A method of accounting for stock movements that assumes a given amount of the stock never moves and therefore retains its original cost (*see* average stock; first in, first out; last in, first out).

**base-weighted index** Any index in which the values are compared with those of a *base year or base point.

**base year (base date)** The first of a series of years in an index. It is often denoted by the number 100, enabling percentage rises (or falls) to be seen at a glance. For example, if a price index indicates that the current value is 120, this will only be meaningful if it is compared to an earlier figure. This may be written: 120 (base year 1985 = 100), making it clear that there has been a 20% increase in prices since 1985.

**basic rate** The income-tax rate applied between the lower-rate band and higher-rate band (*see* income tax; higher rates). For 1992–93, it is 25%. If legislation requires the payer of covenants, royalties, annuities, etc., to deduct tax at source it will be deducted at the basic rate.

**basket of currencies** A group of selected currencies used to establish a value for some other unit of currency. The *European Currency Unit's value is determined by taking a weighted average of a basket of European currencies.

**Basle Concordat** The basis for cooperation between European banks. The concordat was agreed in 1975 and revised in 1983. It provides a moral rather than practical obligation for banks to be supervised and to help one another. It was formulated by the Cooke Committee on Banking and Regulation.

**Bay Street 1.** The street in Toronto in which the Toronto Stock Exchange is situated. **2.** The Toronto Stock Exchange itself. **3.** The financial institutions of Toronto collectively.

**BCG matrix** A scheme for categorizing businesses devised by the Boston Consulting Group, a leading firm of strategic business consultants. The scheme puts businesses into categories according to their market share and the expected growth of their markets.

**bear** A dealer on a stock exchange, currency market, or commodity market who expects prices to fall. A **bear market** is one in which prices are falling or expected to fall, i.e. a market in which a dealer is more likely to sell securities, currency, or goods than to buy them. A bear may even sell securities, currency, or goods without having them. This is known as selling short or establishing a **bear position**. The bear hopes to close (or cover) a short position by buying in at a lower price the securities, currency, or goods previously sold. The difference between the purchase price and the original sale price represents the successful bear's profit. A concerted attempt to force prices down by one or more bears by sustained selling is called a **bear raid**. A successful bear raid will produce a sharply falling market, known as a **bear slide**. In a **bear squeeze**, sellers force prices up against someone known to have a bear position to cover. *Compare* bull.

**bear closing** The purchase of securities, currency, or commodities to close an open *bear position. Bear closing can have the effect of firming up a weak market.

**bearer** A person who presents for payment a cheque or *bill of exchange marked 'pay bearer'. As a bearer cheque or bill does not require endorsement it is considered a high-risk form of transfer.

**bearer security (bearer bond)** A security for which proof of ownership is possession of the security certificate; this enables such bonds to be transferred from one person to another without registration. No register of ownership is kept by the company in whose name it is issued. This is unusual as most securities are registered, so that proof of ownership is the presence of the owner's name on the security register. *Eurobonds are bearer securities, enabling their owners to preserve their anonymity, which can have taxation advantages. Bearer bonds are usually kept under lock and key, often deposited in a bank. Dividends are usually claimed by submitting coupons attached to the certificate.

**bear hug** An approach to the board of a company by another company indicating that an offer is about to be made for their shares. If the target company indicates that it is not against the merger, but wants a higher price, this is known as a **teddy bear hug**.

**bear market** *See* bear.

**bear note** *See* bull note.

**bear position** *See* bear.

**bear raid** *See* bear.

**bear slide** *See* bear.

**bear squeeze** *See* bear.

**bed and breakfast** An operation on the London Stock Exchange in which a shareholder sells a holding one evening and makes an agreement with the broker to buy the same holding back again when the market opens the next morning. The object is to establish a loss, which can be set against other profits for calculating capital-gains tax. In the event of an unexpected change in the market, the deal is scrapped.

**Belfox** Abbreviation for the Belgian Futures and Options Exchange. Based in Brussels, it opened April 1991 and trades in Belgian government bond futures and stock index options.

**below par** *See* par value.

**below-the-line** **1.** Denoting entries below the horizontal line on a company's *profit and loss account that separates the entries that establish the profit (or loss) from the entries that show how the profit is distributed or where the funds to finance the loss have come from. **2.** Denoting advertising expenditure in which no commission is payable to an advertising agency. For example, direct mail, exhibitions, point-of-sale material, and free samples are regarded as below-the-line advertising. **3.** Denoting transactions concerned with capital, as opposed to revenue, in national accounts. *Compare* above-the-line.

**beneficiary** **1.** A person for whose benefit a *trust exists. **2.** A person who benefits under a will. **3.** A person who receives money from the proceeds of a *letter of credit. **4.** A person who receives payment at the conclusion of a transaction, e.g. a retailer who has been paid by a customer by means of a *credit card.

**benefits in kind** Benefits provided to individuals or members of their families by their employers in the UK that are regarded by the tax authorities as taxable. For directors and other employees with earnings in excess of £8500, these benefits include the use of a company car, a loan provided at a low or nil rate of interest, expenses reimbursed (unless the expenditure qualifies for relief from income tax), and the provision of accommodation. For all employees cash vouchers, medical benefits, etc., are also taxable as a benefit.

**Benelux** An association of countries in western Europe, consisting of Belgium, the Netherlands, and Luxembourg. Apart from geographical proximity these countries have particularly close economic interests, recognized in their 1947 *customs union. In 1958 the Benelux countries joined the *European Economic Community.

**Berne Union** The informal name for the International Union of Credit and Investment Insurers, an association of credit insurers from the main industrial countries, except Japan. Its main function is to facilitate an exchange of information, especially over credit terms. The *Export Credits Guarantee Department of the UK government is a member.

**BES** Abbreviation for *Business Expansion Scheme.

**best advice** *See* independent financial adviser.

**best efforts** A term used in US agreements for underwriting a stock issue in which the securities house undertakes to use its best efforts to sell an issue for the issuer, but makes no guarantee that it will sell all of the issue at the offer price.

**best price** An order to buy or sell a security, commodity, etc., at the best price available when the order is given.

**beta coefficient** The price movement of a security measured against the overall stock market. The bigger the beta coefficient of a security, the greater its volatility. The term is used in portfolio theory. *See also* alpha coefficient; capital asset pricing model.

**beta stocks** The second rank of liquidity of shares quoted on the London Stock Exchange, under the former classification system now replaced by *Normal Market Size. *See also* alpha stocks.

**bid 1.** The price (often called the **bid price**) at which a *market maker will buy shares: the lower of the two figures quoted on the *TOPIC screens of the *SEAQ system, the higher being the *offer price; the difference between the two prices is known as the **bid–offer spread**. Some dealers prefer to rely on the figure quoted, others prefer to haggle over the price. *Compare* offer price. **2.** An approach by one company to buy the share capital of another; an attempted takeover. **3.** The price at which a buyer is willing to close a deal. If the seller has made an *offer that the buyer considers too high, the buyer may make a bid at a lower price (or on more advantageous terms). Having received a bid, the seller may accept it, withdraw, or make a counteroffer. Once the buyer has made a bid the original offer no longer stands.

**bid–offer spread** *See* bid.

**bid price** *See* bid.

**bid rate** Short for *London Inter Bank Bid Rate (LIBID).

**BIFFEX** Abbreviation for Baltic International Freight Futures Market. *See* London FOX.

**Big Bang** The upheaval on the *London Stock Exchange (LSE) when major changes in operation were introduced on 27 October 1986. The major changes enacted on that date were: (a) the abolition of LSE rules enforcing a single-capacity system; (b) the abolition of fixed commission rates charged by *stockbrokers to their clients. The measures were introduced by the LSE in return for an undertaking by the government (given in 1983) that they would not prosecute the LSE under the Restrictive Practices Act. Since 1986 the Big Bang has also been associated with the *globalization and modernization of the London securities market.

**Big Blue** Colloquial name for the US information-systems group, IBM (International Business Machines Inc.).

**Big Board** Colloquial name for the *New York Stock Exchange, on which the stocks of the largest corporations in the USA are traded. *Compare* Little Board.

**Big Eight** The eight largest firms of accountants in the world, i.e. Arthur Andersen, Coopers and Lybrand, Deloitte Haskins and Sells, Ernst and Whinney, Peat Marwick Mitchell, Price Waterhouse, Touche Ross, and Arthur Young.

**Big Four 1.** The major High-Street or *commercial banks in the UK: Barclays, Lloyds, Midland, and NatWest. In terms of market capitalization the four were joined in 1990 by Abbey National, which changed its status from a *building society to a bank. **2.** In Japan, the four largest securities houses: Daiwa, Nikko, Nomura, and Yamaichi.

**bill 1.** Short for *bill of exchange. **2.** Colloquial name for an invoice.

**bill broker (discount broker)** A broker who buys *bills of exchange from traders and sells them to banks and *discount houses or holds them to maturity. Many now deal exclusively in *Treasury bills.

**billion** Formerly, one thousand million ($10^9$) in the USA and one million million ($10^{12}$) in the UK; now it is universally taken to be one thousand million.

**bill leak** A device used by UK banks to circumvent the restrictions by the Bank of England on lending and on interest-bearing eligible liabilities (*see* corset) by lending outside the banking sector to non-banking organizations by means of the acceptance of bills.

**bill mountain** Bills that have been discounted and are held at the Bank of England.

**bill of exchange** An unconditional order in writing, addressed by one person (the drawer) to another (the drawee) and signed by the person giving it, requiring the drawee to pay on demand or at a fixed or determinable future time a specified sum of money to or to the order of a specified person (the payee) or to the bearer. If the bill is payable at a future time the drawee signifies *acceptance, which makes the drawee the party primarily liable upon the bill; the drawer and endorsers may also be liable upon a bill. The use of bills of exchange enables one person to transfer to another an enforceable right to a sum of money. A bill of exchange is not only transferable but also negotiable, since, if a person without an enforceable right to the money transfers a bill to a *holder in due course, the latter obtains a good title to it. Much of the law on bills of exchange is codified by the Bills of Exchange Act 1882. *See* accommodation bill; bills in a set; dishonour.

**bill of sight** A document that an importer, who is unable fully to describe an imported cargo, gives to the Customs and Excise authorities to authorize them to inspect the goods on landing. After the goods have been landed and the importer supplies the missing information the entry is completed and the importer is said to have **perfected the sight**.

**bill rate (discount rate)** The rate on the *discount market at which *bills of exchange are discounted (i.e. purchased for less than they are worth when they mature). The rate will depend on the quality of the bill and the risk the purchaser takes. First-class bills, i.e. those backed by banks or well-respected finance houses, will be discounted at a lower rate than bills involving greater risk.

**bills in a set** One of two, or more usually three, copies of a foreign bill of exchange. Payment is made on any one of the three, the others becoming invalid on the payment of any one of them. All are made out in the same way, except that each refers to the others. The first copy is called the **first of exchange**, the next is the **second of exchange**, and so on. The duplication or triplication is to reduce the risk of loss in transit.

**bills payable** An item that may appear in a firm's accounts under current liabilities, summarizing the *bills of exchange being held, which will have to be paid when they mature.

**bills receivable** An item that may appear in a firm's accounts under current assets, summarizing the *bills of exchange being held until the funds become available when they mature.

**birr** (Br) The standard monetary unit of Ethiopia, divided into 100 cents.

**BIS** Abbreviation for *Bank for International Settlements.

**black knight** A person or firm that makes an unwelcome *takeover bid for a company. *Compare* grey knight; white knight.

**Black Monday** Either of the two Mondays on which the two largest stock market crashes occurred in this century. The original Wall Street crash occurred on Monday, 28 October 1929, when the *Dow Jones Industrial Average fell by 13%. On Monday, 19 October 1987, the Dow Jones Average lost 23%. In both cases Black Monday in the USA triggered heavy stock market falls around the world.

**Black Wednesday** Wednesday 16 September 1992, when sterling left the Exchange Rate Mechanism (*see* European Monetary System), which led to a 15% fall in its value against the Deutschmark. The Chancellor of the Exchequer and the prime minister, having previously described this measure as 'a betrayal of our future', were called upon to resign, but did not do so.

**blank bill** A *bill of exchange in which the name of the payee is left blank.

**blank cheque** *See* cheque.

**blank endorsed** *See* endorsement.

**blanket policy** An insurance policy that covers a number of items but has only one total sum insured and no insured sums for individual items. The policy can be of any type, e.g. covering a fleet of vehicles or a group of buildings.

**blank transfer** A share transfer form in which the name of the transferee and the transfer date are left blank. The form is signed by the registered holder of the shares so that the holder of the blank transfer has only to fill in the missing details to become the registered owner of the shares. Blank transfers can be deposited with a bank, when shares are being used as a security for a loan. A blank transfer can also be used when shares are held by *nominees, the beneficial owner holding the blank transfer.

**blocked account** **1.** A bank account from which money cannot be withdrawn, for any of a number of reasons, of which the most likely is that the affairs of the holder of the account are in the hands of a receiver owing to *bankruptcy (or *liquidation in the case of a company). **2.** A bank account held by an exporter of goods in another country into which the proceeds of the sale of the goods have been paid but from which they cannot be transferred to the exporter's own country. This is usually a result of a government order, when that government is so short of foreign currency that it has to block all accounts that require the use of a foreign currency.

**blocked currency** A currency that cannot be removed from a country as a result of *exchange controls. Trading usually takes place in such currencies at a discount through brokers specializing in blocked-currency trading, who convert it to other funds for importers and exporters with blocked currency accounts.

**block order exposure system (BLOX)** A system for buying or selling large blocks of securities on *TOPIC.

**block trade** The sale or purchase of large quantities of a security in the USA, normally in excess of 10 000 securities.

**block volume**  A total volume of trades in stocks in the USA exceeding 10 000 securities.

**blue chip**  Colloquial name for any of the ordinary shares in the most highly regarded companies traded on a stock market. Originating in the USA, the name comes from the colour of the highest value chip used in poker. Blue-chip companies have a well-known name, a good growth record, and large assets. The main part of an institution's equity portfolio will consist of blue chips.

**blue-sky laws**  The colloquial name for the legislation in certain US states that insist on stocks being registered in that state before they can be traded there.

**Board of Customs and Excise**  The government department responsible for collecting and administering customs and excise duties and *VAT. The Commissioners of Customs were first appointed in 1671 by Charles II; the Excise department, formerly part of the Inland Revenue Department, was merged with the Customs in 1909. The Customs and Excise have an investigation division responsible for preventing and detecting evasions of revenue laws and for enforcing restrictions on the importation of certain goods (e.g. arms, drugs, etc.). Their statistical office compiles overseas trade statistics from customs import and export documents.

**Board of Inland Revenue**  A small number of higher civil servants, known individually as Commissioners of Inland Revenue, responsible to the Treasury for the administration and collection of the principal direct taxes in the UK, but not the indirect VAT and excise duties. They are responsible for income tax, capital-gains tax, corporation tax, inheritance tax, petroleum revenue tax, and stamp duties. Under the Taxes Management Act 1970, they are under a duty to appoint inspectors and collectors of taxes who, in turn, act under the direction of the board. They also advise on new legislation and prepare statistical information.

**boiler room**  A colloquial name for a *bucket shop that specializes in selling securities over the telephone.

**bolívar**  (B) The standard monetary unit of Venezuela, divided into 100 céntimos.

**boliviano**  ($b) The standard monetary unit of Bolivia, divided into 100 centavos.

**Bombay Stock Exchange**  India's leading stock exchange, listing more than 2000 companies. British influence brought share trading to India, where trading began in the 1830s on an informal basis in Bombay, the commercial gateway from the West; exchanges now exist in seven other cities. The Indian government has created a Securities and Exchange Board of India (SEBI) to regulate the market. SEBI operates in much the same way as the *Securities and Exchange Commission in the USA and the *Securities and Investment Board in the UK.

**bond**  An IOU issued by a borrower to a lender. Bonds usually take the form of *fixed-interest securities issued by governments, local authorities, or companies. However, bonds come in many forms: with fixed or variable rates of interest, redeemable or irredeemable, short- or long-term, secured or unsecured, and marketable or unmarketable. Fixed-interest payments are usually made twice a year but may alternatively be credited at the end of the agreement (typically 5 to 10 years). The borrower repays a specific sum of money plus the face value (PAR) of the bond. Most bonds are unsecured and do not grant shares in an organization (*see* debenture). Bonds are usually sold against loans, mortgages, credit-card income, etc., as marketable securities. A discount bond is one sold below its face value; a premium bond is one sold above par. *See also* debenture; deposit bonds; income bond; premium bonds.

**bond washing**  *See* dividend stripping.

**Bonn Index FAZ**  *See* Commerzbank Index.

**bonus  1.** An extra payment made to employees by management, usually as a reward for good work, to compensate for something (e.g. dangerous work) or to share out the profits of a good year's trading.  **2.** An extra amount of money additional to the proceeds, which is distributed to a policyholder by an insurer who has made a profit on the investment of a life-assurance fund. Only holders of *with-profits policies are entitled to a share in these profits and the payment of this bonus is conditional on the life assurer having surplus funds after claims, costs, and expenses have been paid in a particular year.  **3.** Any extra or unexpected payment. *See also* no-claim bonus; reversionary bonus; terminal bonus.

**bonus issue**  *See* scrip issue.

**book value**  The value of an asset as recorded in the books of account of an organization. This is normally the historical cost of the asset reduced by amounts written off for *depreciation. If the asset has ever been revalued, the book value will be the amount of the revaluation less amounts subsequently written off for depreciation. Except at the time of purchase of the asset, the book value will rarely be the same as the market value of the asset.

**bootstrap  1.** A cash offer for a controlling interest in a company. This is followed by an offer to acquire the rest of the company's shares at a lower price. The purpose is twofold: to establish control of the company and to reduce the cost of the purchase.  **2.** A technique enabling a computer to load a program of instructions. Before computer hardware can function, a program must be loaded into it. However, as a program is needed in the computer to enable it to load a program, preliminary instructions are stored permanently in the computer making it possible for longer programs to be accepted.

**borrowed reserves**  Loans made to US banks from the Federal Reserve, which allow reserves in individual banks to remain at acceptable levels. This is usually only necessary when excessive lending is being undertaken, because otherwise reserves are kept to a workable minimum as they do not attract interest for the banks.

***borsa***  An Italian stock exchange.

***börse***  A *German stock exchange.

**bought deal**  A method of raising capital for acquisitions or other purposes, used by quoted companies as an alternative to a *rights issue or *placing. The company invites *market makers or banks to bid for new shares, selling them to the highest bidder, who then sells them to the rest of the market in the expectation of making a profit. Bought deals originated in the USA and are becoming increasingly popular in the UK, although they remain controversial as they violate the principle of *pre-emption rights. *See also* vendor placing.

**bourse** **1.** A French *stock exchange (from the French *bourse*, purse). 'The Bourse' usually refers to the stock exchange in Paris (*see* Paris Bourse), but other continental stock markets are also known by this name. Members of the Paris Bourse, who have to buy their membership for a large sum, are known as *agents de change*. **2.** In Belgium, foreign exchange dealing.

**boutique** **1.** An office, usually with a shop front and located in a shopping parade, that offers financial advice to investors, often on a walk-in basis. **2.** Specialist investment bankers, who cover a particular sector of the market, e.g. management buy-outs, acquisitions, etc.

**box spread** A combination of call and put *options held at the same exercise price.

**bracket indexation** A change in the upper and lower limits of any particular *taxation bracket in line with an index of inflation. This is needed in times of inflation to avoid fiscal drag (the tax system collecting unduly large amounts of tax).

**break-forward** A contract on the money market that combines the features of a *forward-exchange contract and a currency option. The forward contract can be undone at a previously agreed rate of exchange, enabling the consumer to be free if the market moves favourably. There is no premium on the option; the cost is built into the fixed rate of exchange.

**breaking a leg** *See* straddle.

**break-up value** **1.** The value of an asset on the assumption that an organization will not continue in business. On this assumption the assets are likely to be sold piecemeal and probably in haste. **2.** The *asset value per share of a company.

**bridging loan** A loan taken on a short-term basis to bridge the gap between the purchase of one asset and the sale of another. It is particularly common in the property and housing market.

**Britannia coins** A range of four British *gold coins (£100, £50, £25, and £10 denominations). They were introduced in October 1987 for investment purposes, in competition with the *Krugerrand. Although all sales of gold coins attract VAT, Britannia coins are widely dealt in as bullion coins.

**British Bankers Association** A London-based organization that represents the views of all the banks recognized in the UK. Founded in 1919, it is regarded as the banks' trade association. It is the British representative of the European Banking Federation.

**British Insurance and Investment Brokers Association** A trade association for insurance brokers registered with the *Insurance Brokers Registration Council and investment brokers registered under the Financial Services Act 1986. Formed in 1977 as the British Insurance Brokers Association by the amalgamation of a number of insurance broking associations, it changed to its current name in 1988 to widen its membership to include investment advisors. It provides public relations, free advice, representation in parliament, and a conciliation service for consumers.

**broad money** An informal name for M3 (*see* money supply). *Compare* narrow money.

**broker** An agent who brings two parties together, enabling them to enter into a contract to which the broker is not a principal. A broker's remuneration consists of a **brokerage**, which is usually calculated as a percentage of the sum involved in the contract but may be fixed according to a tariff. Brokers are used because they have specialized knowledge of certain markets or to conceal the identity of a principal, in addition to introducing buyers to sellers. *See* bill broker; commodity broker; insurance broker; stockbroker.

**brokerage** The commission earned by a *broker.

**broker/dealer** A member of the *London Stock Exchange who, since the *Big Bang, has functioned both as a stockbroker and a jobber, but only in a single capacity in one particular transaction.

**bucket shop** A derogatory colloquial name for a firm of brokers, dealers, agents, etc., of questionable standing and frail resources, that is unlikely to be a member of an established trade organization.

**budget 1.** A financial plan setting targets for the revenues, expenditures, etc., of an organization for a specified period. **2. (the Budget)** The UK financial plan for the coming year, presented to Parliament, usually in March or April, by the Chancellor of the Exchequer. It reveals the Chancellor's predictions for the economy and any taxation changes for the coming year.

**budget deficit** The excess of government expenditure over government income, which must be financed either by borrowing or by printing money. Keynesians have advocated that governments should run budget deficits during *recessions in order to stimulate aggregate demand (*see* pump priming). Monetarists and neo-classical macroeconomists, however, argue that budget deficits simply stimulate *inflation and crowd out private investment. Most economists now argue that, at least on average, governments should seek a balanced budget and that persistent deficits should be eliminated, either by reducing expenditure or increasing taxation. In some cases a **budget surplus** can be used during a boom to collect more revenue than is being spent.

**buffer stock** A stock of a commodity owned by a government or trade organization and used to stabilize the price of the commodity. Usually the manager of the buffer stock is authorized to buy the commodity in question if its price falls below a certain level, which is itself reviewed periodically, to enable producers to find a ready market for their goods at a profitable level. If the price rises above another fixed level, the buffer stock manager is authorized to sell the commodity on the open market. Thus, producers are encouraged to keep up a steady supply of the commodity and users are reassured that its price has a ceiling. This arrangement is often effective, but may collapse during a boom or slump. *See also* United Nations Common Fund for Commodities.

**Building Societies Act 1986** A UK Act of Parliament regulating the activities of *building societies. It widened their powers to include making unsecured loans and offering a range of financial services, such as providing foreign exchange, buying and selling shares, managing unit-trust schemes and personal-equity plans, arranging and giving advice on insurance, etc. The Act subjected building societies to a new regulatory agency, the Building Societies Commission, and additionally allowed societies to issue shares and become public limited companies, subject to the agreement of their members.

**Building Societies Ombudsman** *See* Financial Ombudsman.

**building society** A financial institution traditionally offering a variety of saving accounts to attract deposits, which are used to fund long-term *mortgages for house buyers or for house improvement. They developed from the *Friendly Society movement in the late 17th century and are non-profitmaking. They are regulated by the *Building Societies Act 1986. The societies accept deposits into a variety of accounts, which offer different interest rates and different withdrawal terms, or into 'shares', which often require longer notice of withdrawal. Interest on building-society accounts is usually paid net of income tax, the society paying the tax direct to the Inland Revenue, unless the investor is not a taxpayer. The societies attract both large and small savers, with average holdings being about £5000.

Loans made to persons wishing to purchase property are usually repaid by regular monthly instalments of capital and interest over a number of years. Another method, which is growing in popularity, is an endowment mortgage, in which the capital remains unpaid until the maturity of an assurance policy taken out on the borrower's life; in these arrangements only the interest and the premiums on the assurance policy are paid during the period of the loan.

Since the Building Societies Act 1986 societies have been able to widen the range of services they offer; this has enabled them to compete with the High-Street banks in many areas. They offer cheque accounts, which pay interest on all credit balances, cash cards, credit cards, debit cards, loans, money transmission, foreign exchange, personal financial planning services (shares, insurance, pensions, etc.), estate agency, and valuation and conveyancing services. The distinction between banks and building societies is fast disappearing; indeed some building societies have obtained the sanction of their members to become *public limited companies to enable them actually to become banks. These changes have led to the merger of many building societies to provide a national network that can compete with the *Big Four banks. Competition is well illustrated in the close relationship of interest rates between banks and building societies as they both compete for the market's funds. Moreover, the competition provided by the building societies has forced the banks into offering free banking services, paying interest on current accounts, and Saturday opening.

**bull** A dealer on a stock exchange, currency market, or commodity market who expects prices to rise. A **bull market** is one in which prices are rising or expected to rise, i.e. one in which a dealer is more likely to be a buyer than a seller, even to the extent of buying without having made a corresponding sale, thus establishing a **bull position** or a **long position**. A bull with a long position hopes to sell these purchases at a higher price after the market has risen. *Compare* bear.

**bulldog bond** A fixed-interest sterling *bond issued in the UK by a foreign borrower.

**bullet** **1.** A security offering a fixed interest and maturing on a fixed date. **2.** The final repayment of a loan, which consists of the whole of sum borrowed. In a **bullet loan**, interim repayments are interest-only repayments, the principal sum being repaid in the final bullet.

**bulletin board** *See* Company Bulletin Board Service.

**bullion** Gold, silver, or some other precious metal used in bulk, i.e. in the form of bars or ingots rather than in coin. Central banks use gold bullion in the settlement of international debts.

**bull market** *See* bull.

**bull note** A bond whose redemption value is linked to a price index (e.g. FT-SE 100 Index; *see* Financial Times Share Indexes) or a commodity price (e.g. the price of gold). Thus, a holder of a bull note will receive on redemption an amount greater than the principal of the bond if the relevant index or price has risen (but less if it has fallen). With a **bear note** the reverse happens. Bull and bear notes are therefore akin to an ordinary bond plus an *option, providing opportunities for hedging and speculating.

**bull position** *See* bull.

**Bundesbank** The German central bank (literally, federal bank). It controlled the 11 regional banks in the former West Germany and now oversees all German banks.

**burn-out turnaround** The process of restructuring a company that is in trouble by producing new finance to save it from liquidation, at the cost of diluting the shareholding of existing investors.

**burn rate** The rate at which a new company uses up its venture capital to fund fixed overheads before cash begins to come in from its trading activities.

**Business Expansion Scheme (BES)** A UK government scheme to provide tax relief to encourage investment in unlisted companies that wish to expand. The relief was available to UK residents only who subscribed for shares on their own behalf and had no connection with the company concerned. The investment had to represent new risk capital and any relief given was withdrawn if the shares were sold within 5 years or if the investor received any benefit from the company. The maximum relief available was £40,000 per individual and apart from certain ship-chartering-and-operating companies and companies for letting houses on assured tenancies, where the maximum was £5M, the maximum capital that could be raised by a company was £500,000. The scheme ended in 1993.

**business-interruption policy (consequential-loss policy; loss-of-profits policy)** An insurance policy that pays claims for financial losses occurring if a business has to stop or reduce its activities as a result of a fire or any other insurable risk. Claims can be made for lost profit, rent, rates, and other unavoidable overhead costs that continue even when trading has temporarily ceased.

**business plan** A detailed plan setting out the objectives of a business over a stated period, often three, five, or ten years. A business plan is drawn up by many businesses, especially if the business has passed through a bad period or if it has had a major change of policy. For new businesses it is an essential document for raising capital or loans. The plan should quantify as many of the objectives as possible, providing monthly *cash flows and production figures for at least the first two years, with diminishing detail in subsequent years; it must also outline its strategy and the tactics it intends to use in achieving its objectives. Anticipated *profit and loss accounts should form part of the business plan on a quarterly basis for at least two years, and an annual basis thereafter. It should also include balance-sheet projections. For a group of companies the business plan is often called a **corporate plan**.

**business strategy**  The choice of markets that a business decides to enter, or more particularly the relationship that a company decides to have with its customers, distributors, suppliers, and competitors in these markets.

**busted bond (old bond)**  A bond issued by a government or corporation that has already defaulted on the loan on which the bonds are based. Busted bonds are now collectors' items, especially those from prerevolutionary Russia and those issued by US railroad companies. Occasionally promises are made to honour Russian or Chinese bonds.

**butterfly**  A strategy used by dealers in traded *options. It involves simultaneously purchasing and selling call options (the right to buy) at different *exercise prices or different *expiry dates. A butterfly is most profitable when the price of the underlying security fluctuates within narrow limits. *Compare* straddle.

**butut**  A monetary unit of the Gambia worth one hundredth of a dalasi.

**buy-back  1.**  The buying back by a company of its shares from an investor, who put venture capital up for the formation of the company. The shares are bought back at a price that satisfies the investor, which has to be the price the company is willing to pay for its independence. The buy-back may occur if the company is publicly floated or is taken over.  **2.**  The buying back by a corporation, especially in the USA, of its shares to reduce the number on the market, either to increase the return on those shares still available or to remove threatening shareholders.  **3.**  Action by a developing country's government to reduce some or all of its debt to overseas banks by buying back that debt at the market price or at a substantial discount. The attraction for the banks is the removal of a damaging and negative debt, which may already have been provided for in its balance sheet. The advantage to the country in debt is a return to creditworthiness and the possibility of acquiring new loans.

**buy earnings**  To invest in a company that has a low *yield but whose earnings are increasing, so that a substantial capital gain can be expected.

**buyers over**  A market in securities, commodities, etc., in which the sellers have sold all they wish to sell but there are still buyers. This is clearly a strong market, with an inclination for prices to rise. *Compare* sellers over.

**buying forward**  Buying commodities, securities, foreign exchange, etc., for delivery at a date in the future in order to establish a *bull position or to cover a forward *bear sale. In the case of foreign exchange, a forward purchase may be made to cover a payment that has to be made at a later date in a foreign currency. *See also* futures contract.

**buying in**  The buying of securities, commodities, etc., by a broker because the original seller has failed to deliver. This invariably happens after a rise in a market price (the seller would be able to buy in if the market had fallen). The broker buys at the best price available and the original seller is responsible for any difference between the buying-in price and the original buying price, plus the cost of buying in. *Compare* selling out.

**buyout  1.**  An option, open to a member of an *occupational pension scheme on leaving, of transferring the benefits already purchased to an insurance company of his or her own choice.   **2.** The acquisition of its own shares by a company with a listing on a stock exchange, either by purchasing them on the open market or by means of an offer to purchase. The aim is to revert to private-company status.   **3.** *See* leveraged buyout.   **4.** *See* management buyout; employee buyout.

**BV**  Abbreviation for *Besloten Vennootschap*. It appears after the name of a Dutch company, being equivalent to the British abbreviation Ltd (denoting a private limited company). *Compare* NV.

**CA** **1.** Abbreviation for *chartered accountant. **2.** Abbreviation for *Consumers' Association.

**CAC** Abbreviation for Cotation Assistée en Continue. *See* Paris Bourse.

**CAC General Index** *See* Paris Bourse.

**CAD** Abbreviation for *cash against documents.

**call** **1.** A demand for a payment due on nil or partly paid stocks; this procedure has been common with the privatization programme of the UK government since 1979. It consists of a demand to pay a specified amount of money by a specified day; if payment is not made by the due date the shares can be forfeit. **2.** A notification that redeemable shares or bonds should be presented for repayment. **3.** A demand made on a client by a securities house, stockbroker, etc., for a partial payment of the client's debt because the value of the collateral so far provided has fallen.

**called-up capital** *See* share capital.

**call money** **1.** Money put into the money market that can be called at short notice (*see also* money at call and short notice). **2.** *See* option money.

**call-of-more option** *See* option to double.

**call option** *See* option.

**callover** A meeting of commodity brokers and dealers at fixed times during the day in order to form a market in that commodity. The callover is usually used for trading in futures, in fixed quantities on a standard contract, payments usually being settled by differences through a *clearing house. Because traders usually form a ring around the person calling out the prices, this form of market is often called **ring trading**. This method of trading is also called **open outcry**, as bids and offers are shouted out during the course of the callover. *See also* double auction.

**callover price** The price agreed for a transaction at a *callover; it may be used subsequently by the general market dealers. Callover prices, though verbal at the outset, may later be formally printed.

**cancellation price** The lowest price at which the manager of a unit trust may offer to redeem units on a particular day. The cancellation price is calculated on the basis of a formula laid down by the *Securities and Investment Board.

**cap** A ceiling on a charge; for example, an interest-rate cap would set a maximum interest rate to be charged on a loan, regardless of prevailing general interest-rate levels. A lender would charge a fee for including a cap at the outset to offset this risk. Caps may also limit annual increases to a certain level.

**CAP** Abbreviation for *Common Agricultural Policy.

**cap and collar mortgage** A *mortgage in which the variable interest rate paid by the borrower cannot rise above or fall below specified levels; such a mortgage may be granted for the first few years of a loan.

**capital** 1. The total value of the assets of a person less liabilities. 2. The amount of the proprietors' interests in the assets of an organization, less its liabilities. 3. The money contributed by the proprietors to an organization to enable it to function; thus **share capital** is the amount provided by way of shares and the **loan capital** is the amount provided by way of loans. However, the capital of the proprietors of companies not only consists of the share and loan capital, it also includes retained profit, which accrues to the holders of the ordinary shares. *See also* reserve capital. 4. In economic theory, a factor of production, usually either machinery and plant (**physical capital**) or money (**financial capital**). However, the concept can be applied to a variety of other assets (e.g. **human capital**). In general, the rate of return on capital is called *profit.

**capital account** 1. An *account recording capital expenditure on such items as land and buildings, plant and machinery, etc. 2. A budgeted amount that can only be spent on major items, especially in public-sector budgeting. *Compare* revenue account. 3. An *account showing the interest of a sole trader in the net assets of the business he or she runs. 4. A series of *accounts recording the interests of the partners in the net assets of a partnership. Capital accounts can embrace both the amounts originally contributed and the *current accounts; it may also refer, more narrowly, to the amounts originally contributed, adjusted where necessary by agreement between the partners.

**capital adequacy** The ability of a bank to meet the needs of their depositors and other creditors in terms of available funds. Many US, European, and Japanese banks are already signatories to an agreement with the *Bank for International Settlements, which requires them to maintain 8% of their risk-adjusted assets as capital.

**capital allowances** Income-tax reliefs given against business and some other profits to reflect the depreciation of certain types of asset owned by the business. Because the Inland Revenue cannot control the amount of depreciation of fixed assets that traders charge in their accounts against profits, it is customary for the trader's own depreciation charge to be disallowed for tax purposes and the Revenue's own charges (the capital allowances) substituted. These may be targeted to some types of asset (e.g. plant and machinery) and not others (office buildings); where the authorities want to create incentives for traders to invest, the allowances may be accelerated (i.e. allowed at a higher rate than would be expected if normal depreciation rates were applied), even to the extent of allowing 100% capital allowances in the year of purchase.

**capital asset (fixed asset)** An asset that is expected to be used for a considerable time in a trade or business (*compare* current assets). Examples of capital assets in most businesses are land and buildings, plant and machinery, investments in subsidiary companies, goodwill, and motor vehicles, although in the hands of dealers these assets would become current assets. The costs of these assets are normally written off against profits over their expected useful life spans by deducting an item for *depreciation from their book value each year.

**capital asset pricing model (CAPM)** A mathematical model used in *portfolio theory, in which the expected rate of return ($E$) on an investment is expressed in terms of the expected rate of return ($r_m$) on the market portfolio (*see* Markowitz model) and the *beta coefficient ($\beta$), i.e. $E = R + \beta(r_m - R)$, where $R$ is the risk-free rate of return.

**capital bond** National Savings Capital Bond, a type of UK bond, introduced by the Department of *National Savings in 1989, that offers a guaranteed rate of return over a five-year period. Tax is not deducted at source from the interest. The bonds may be bought in units of £100; the maximum holding of all series of capital bonds, excluding any holding of Series A, is £100,000.

**capital budget** The sums allocated by an organization for future *capital expenditure. The capital budget may well encompass a longer period than the next accounting period.

**capital commitments** Firm plans, usually approved by the board of directors in the case of companies, to spend sums of money on *capital assets. Capital commitments must by law be shown by way of a note, or otherwise, on company balance sheets.

**capital consumption** The total depreciation in the value of the capital goods in an economy during a specified period. It is difficult to calculate this figure, but it is needed as it has to be deducted from the *gross national product (GNP) and the *gross domestic product (GDP) to obtain the net figures.

**capital-conversion plan** An *annuity that converts capital into income. Capital-conversion policies are often used to provide an income later in life for persons who might be liable to capital-gains tax if their capital had not been reinvested in some way.

**capital expenditure** Expenditure on *capital assets. Capital expenditure is not deducted from profits, as an asset is acquired rather than a loss being made. However, as a capital asset loses value by *depreciation, the amount of the depreciation is charged against profit.

**capital gain** An increase in the capital value of an asset between the time of its acquisition by its owner and its sale by that owner. Capital gains, unless made by a business in the course of trade and subject to certain other exceptions, are taxed in many countries by means of a *capital-gains tax. In the UK, private individuals pay capital-gains tax on chargeable gains, whereas companies are assessed for *corporation tax on chargeable gains.

**capital-gains tax (CGT)** A tax on *capital gains. Most countries have a form of income tax under which they tax the profits from trading and a different tax to tax substantial disposals of assets either by traders for whom the assets are not trading stock (e.g. a trader's factory) or by individuals who do not trade (e.g. sales of shares by an investor). The latter type of tax is a capital-gains tax. Short-term gains taxes are taxes sometimes applied to an asset that has only been held for a limited time. In these cases the rates tend to be higher than for the normal capital-gains tax. In the UK, capital-gains tax applies to the net gains (after deducting losses) accruing to an individual in any tax year, with an exemption to liability if the individual's gains do not exceed a specified figure (£5800 for 1992–93); this exemption has applied separately to husbands and wives since April 1990. Other exemptions include gains on private cars, government securities and savings certificates, loan stocks, options, gambling, life-assurance and deferred-annuity contracts, main dwelling house, and works of art. The rate of tax is the taxpayer's *marginal tax rate. An indexation allowance is available when calculating a chargeable gain or allowable loss based on the *Retail Price Index between March 1982 (or, if later, the month of purchase) and the date of sale.

**capital gearing**  The ratio of the amount of fixed interest loan stock and preference shares in a company to its ordinary share capital. Because the ordinary shares of a company are known as its equity, capital gearing is also known as **equity gearing**. A company with a preponderance of ordinary share capital is **low-geared** while one in which fixed-interest capital dominates is **high-geared**. With high gearing, when profits are rising, the amounts available to ordinary shareholders rise, in percentage terms, faster than the percentage rise in profits. However, when profits are falling shareholders in high-geared companies suffer a larger percentage drop in their dividends than the percentage fall in profits. In simple terms capital gearing is the ratio of a company's debt to its total trading assets or the cost of their replacement. In the USA capital gearing is known as **leverage**. See also degearing.

**capital growth**  An increase in the value of invested capital. Investment in *fixed-interest securities or bonds provides income but limited capital growth (which may be improved in index-linked gilts; see gilt-edged security). To have a chance of making substantial capital growth it is necessary to invest in equities (see ordinary share), the value of which should increase with *inflation as well as with the improved performance of the companies invested in. Investing in equities is thus said to be a hedge against inflation. See growth stocks.

**capital investment**  See investment.

**capitalization**  **1.** The act of providing *capital for a company or other organization.  **2.** The structure of the capital of a company or other organization, i.e. the extent to which its capital is divided into share or loan capital and the extent to which share capital is divided into ordinary and preference shares. See also thin capitalization.  **3.** The conversion of the reserves of a company into capital by means of a *scrip issue.

**capitalization issue**  See scrip issue.

**capitalized value**  **1.** The value at which an asset has been recorded in the balance sheet of a company or other organization, usually before the deduction of *depreciation.  **2.** The capital equivalent of an asset that yields a regular income, calculated at the prevailing rate of interest. For example, a piece of land bringing in an annual income of £1000, when the prevailing interest rate is 10%, would have a notional capitalized value of £10,000 (i.e. £1000/0.1). This may not reflect its true value.

**capital loss**  A loss arising from the disposal, loss, or destruction of a *capital asset or from a long-term liability. For tax purposes a capital loss can be set off against a capital profit. See capital-gains tax.

**capital maintenance**  Maintaining the value of the share capital of an organization or of its share capital and reserves. More vaguely, it could refer to maintaining the operating capacity of an organization, regardless of the composition of its assets.

**capital market** A market in which long-term *capital is raised by industry and commerce, the government, and local authorities. The money comes from private investors, insurance companies, pension funds, and banks and is usually arranged by *issuing houses and *merchant banks. *Stock exchanges are also part of the capital market in that they provide a market for the shares and loan stocks that represent the capital once it has been raised. It is the presence and sophistication of their capital markets that distinguishes the industrial countries from the developing countries, in that this facility for raising industrial and commercial capital is either absent or rudimentary in the latter.

**capital market line** *See* Markowitz model.

**capital movement** The transfer of capital between countries, either by companies or individuals. Restrictions on *exchange controls and capital transfers between countries have been greatly reduced in recent years. Capital movements seeking long-term gains are usually those made by companies investing abroad, for example to set up a factory. Capital movements seeking short-term gains are often more speculative, such as those taking advantage of temporarily high interest rates in another country or an expected change in the exchange rate.

**capital profit** A profit (*see also* capital gain) arising from the disposal of a *capital asset. Capital profits, if taxable at all, are subject to *capital-gains tax, which applies to individuals, although companies pay *corporation tax on chargeable gains. The Companies Act 1980 allows capital profits made by limited companies to be distributed as revenue profits, provided that they are real, realized, have not been previously capitalized, and take into account any accumulated realized capital losses.

**capital reserves** Undistributed profits of a company that for various reasons are not regarded as distributable to shareholders as dividends. These include certain profits on the revaluation of capital assets and any sums received from share issues in excess of the nominal value of the shares, which are shown in a *share premium account. Capital reserves are now known as **undistributable reserves** under the Companies Act 1985. *See also* reserve.

**capital shares** *See* investment trust.

**capital structure** The elements, such as shares, loan stock, debt, etc., of which the *capital of a company or other organization consists.

**capital-transfer tax** A tax levied when capital is transferred from one person's estate usually into that of another, as by lifetime gifts or inheritances. There was such a tax in the UK from 1974 to 1986, when it was replaced by *inheritance tax.

**capital turnover** The ratio of sales of a company or other organization to its capital employed (i.e. its assets less liabilities). It is presumed that the higher this ratio, the better the use that is being made of the assets in generating sales.

**CAPM** Abbreviation for *capital asset pricing model.

**capped floating rate note** A floating rate note (*see* eurobond) that will mature at no more than a specified figure.

**capped mortgage** A *mortgage in which the variable interest rate paid by the borrower cannot rise above a specified level, usually for the first few years of the loan. The interest rate can, however, be reduced if interest rates fall generally.

**captive insurance company** An insurance company that is totally owned by another organization and insures only, or mostly, the parent company's risks. In this way the parent organization is able to obtain insurance cover (particularly those classes that are compulsory by law) without having to pay premiums to an organization outside its trading group.

**CAR** Abbreviation for *compound annual return.

**carrying market** A *commodity market in which goods for delivery, storage, and resale can be carried over from month to month because the particular commodity does not perish.

**carry-over** **1.** The quantity of a *commodity that is carried over from one crop to the following one. The price of some commodities, such as grain, coffee, cocoa, and jute, which grow in annual or biannual crops, is determined by the supply and the demand. The supply consists of the quantity produced by the current crop added to the quantity in the hands of producers and traders that is carried over from the previous crop. Thus, in some circumstances the carry-over can strongly influence the market price. **2.** The postponement of payment for securities from one settlement day to the next. *See also* contango.

**case of need** An endorsement written on a *bill of exchange giving the name of someone to whom the holder may apply if the bill is not honoured at maturity.

**cash against documents (CAD)** Payment terms for exported goods in which the shipping documents are sent to a bank, agent, etc., in the country to which the goods are being shipped, and the buyer then obtains the documents by paying the invoice amount in cash to the bank, agent, etc. Having the shipping documents enables the buyer to take possession of the goods when they arrive at their port of destination; this is known as **documents against presentation**. *Compare* documents against acceptance.

**cash and carry** **1.** A wholesaler, especially of groceries, who sells to retailers and others with businesses at discounted prices. **2.** An operation that is sometimes possible on the futures market (*see* futures contract), especially the *London Metal Exchange. In some circumstances the spot price of a metal, including the cost of insurance, warehousing, and interest for three months, is less than the futures-market price for delivery in three months (*see* forwardation). Under these conditions it is possible to buy the spot metal, simultaneously sell the forward goods, and make a profit in excess of the yield the capital would have earned on the money market.

**cash and new** An arrangement enabling speculators on the London Stock Exchange to carry forward a transaction from one *account day to a subsequent account day. It replaces the former *contango arrangements but is now discouraged. It involves selling the stock at the end of one account and buying it back at the start of the next. Commissions have to be paid but settlement of the transaction can be delayed.

**cash card** A plastic card enabling customers of UK banks and building societies to obtain cash from *automated teller machines, in conjunction with a *personal identification number.

**cash deal** A transaction (either buying or selling) on the *London Stock Exchange in which settlement is made immediately, i.e. usually on the following day.

**cash dispenser** *See* automated teller machine.

**cash flow** The amount of cash being received and expended by a business, which is often analysed into its various components. A **cash-flow projection** (or **cash budget**) sets out all the expected payments and receipts in a given period. This is different from the projected profit and loss account and, in times of cash shortage, may be more important. It is on the basis of the cash-flow projection that managers arrange for employees and creditors to be paid at appropriate times. *See also* discounted cash flow.

**cash ratio (liquidity ratio)** The ratio of the cash reserve that a bank keeps in coin, banknotes, etc., to its total liabilities to its customers, i.e. the amount deposited with it in current accounts and deposit accounts. Because cash reserves earn no interest, bankers try to keep them to a minimum, consistent with being able to meet customers' demands. The usual figure for the cash ratio is 8%. The *Bank of England may from time to time set specific levels of cash, which the banks must deposit with it. In the USA there have always been strict cash ratios set by the *Federal Reserve Bank. *See also* capital adequacy.

**cash settlements (cash deals)** Deals on the London Stock Exchange in which gilt-edged securities or new issues are bought by investors. These have to be paid for immediately (normally by the next business day) rather than on the next *account day.

**cash unit trust** *See* money-market unit trust.

**catching bargain (unconscionable bargain)** An unfair contract, often one in which one party has been taken advantage of by the other. Such a contract may be set aside or modified by a court.

**CBOE** Abbreviation for *Chicago Board Options Exchange.

**CCA** Abbreviation for *current-cost accounting.

**CD** Abbreviation for *certificate of deposit.

**CEC** Abbreviation for Commodities Exchange Center Inc.

**CEDEL** Abbreviation for *Centrale de Livraison de Valeurs Mobilières.

**cedi** (₵) The standard monetary unit of Ghana, divided into 100 pesewas.

**cent** **1.** A monetary unit of: Antigua and Barbuda, Australia, the Bahamas, Barbados, Belize, Bermuda, the British Virgin Islands, Brunei, the Cayman Islands, Dominica, Fiji, Grenada, Guam, Guyana, Hong Kong, Jamaica, Kiribati, Liberia, Micronesia, New Zealand, Puerto Rico, Saint Kitts and Nevis, Singapore, the Solomon Islands, Taiwan, Tuvalu, Trinidad and Tobago, the USA, the Virgin Islands, and Zimbabwe, worth one hundredth of a *dollar. **2.** A monetary unit of Ethiopia, worth one hundredth of a *birr. **3.** A monetary unit of Kenya, Tanzania, Uganda, and Somalia, worth one hundredth of a *shilling. **4.** A monetary unit of South Africa and Namibia, worth one hundredth of a *rand.

**5.** A monetary unit of the Seychelles, Sri Lanka, and Mauritius, worth one hundredth of a *rupee. **6.** A monetary unit of Swaziland, worth one hundredth of a *lilangeni. **7.** A monetary unit of the Netherlands, the Antilles, and Surinam, worth one hundredth of a *guilder. **8.** A monetary unit of Sierra Leone, worth one hundredth of a *leone. **9.** A monetary unit of Cyprus, worth one hundredth of a *pound. **10.** A monetary unit of Malta, worth one hundredth of a *lira. **11.** A monetary unit of Aruba, worth one hundredth of a *florin.

**centavo** **1.** A monetary unit of Bolivia, worth one hundredth of a *boliviano. **2.** A monetary unit of Brazil, worth one hundredth of a *cruzeiro. **3.** A monetary unit of Argentina, Chile, Colombia, Cuba, the Dominican Republic, Guinea-Bissau, Mexico, and the Philippines, worth one hundredth of a *peso. **4.** A monetary unit of Ecuador, worth one hundredth of a *sucre. **5.** A monetary unit of El Salvador, worth one hundredth of a *colón. **6.** A monetary unit of Guatemala, worth one hundredth of a *quetzal. **7.** A monetary unit of Honduras, worth one hundredth of a *lempira. **8.** A monetary unit of Nicaragua, worth one hundredth of a *córdoba. **9.** A monetary unit of Peru, worth one hundredth of a *sol. **10.** A monetary unit of Cape Verde, Portugal, and Madeira, worth one hundredth of an *escudo. **11.** A monetary unit of Mozambique, worth one hundredth of a *metical. **12.** A monetary unit of São Tomé e Principe, worth one hundredth of a *dobra.

**centésimo** **1.** A monetary unit of Italy, worth one hundredth of a *lira. **2.** A monetary unit of Panama, worth one hundredth of a *balboa. **3.** A monetary unit of Uruguay, worth one hundredth of a *peso.

**centime** **1.** A monetary unit of: Andorra, Belgium, Benin, Burkina-Faso, Burundi, Cameroon, the Central African Republic, Chad, Comoros, the Congo, Côte d'Ivoire, Djibouti, Equatorial Guinea, France, Gabon, Guinea, Liechtenstein, Luxembourg, Madagascar, Mali, Monaco, Niger, Rwanda, Senegal, Switzerland, Tahiti, and Togo, worth one hundredth of a *franc. **2.** A monetary unit of Algeria, worth one hundredth of a *dinar. **3.** A monetary unit of Haiti, worth one hundredth of a *gourde. **4.** A monetary unit of Morocco, worth one hundredth of a *dirham.

**céntimo** **1.** A monetary unit of Costa Rica, worth one hundredth of a *colón. **2.** A monetary unit of Paraguay, worth one hundredth of a *guaraní. **3.** A monetary unit of Spain and Andorra, worth one hundredth of a *peseta. **4.** A monetary unit of Venezuela, worth one hundredth of a *bolívar.

**central bank** A bank that provides financial and banking services for the government of a country and its commercial banking system as well as implementing the government's monetary policy. The main functions of a central bank are: to manage the government's accounts; to accept deposits and grant loans to the commercial banks; to control the issue of banknotes; to manage the public debt; to help manage the exchange rate when necessary; to influence the interest rate structure and control the money supply; to hold the country's reserves of gold and foreign currency; to manage dealings with other central banks; and to act as lender of last resort to the banking system. Examples of major central banks include the *Bank of England in the UK, the *Federal Reserve Bank of the USA (*see* Federal Reserve System), the *Bundesbank in Germany, the *Banque de France, and the *Bank of Japan.

**central bank discount rate** The rate of interest charged by a *central bank for discounting *eligible paper.

**Centrale de Livraison de Valeurs Mobilières (CEDEL)** A settlement service for *eurobonds in Luxembourg. It is owned by a consortium of international banks. *See also* Euroclear.

**Central Government Borrowing Requirement (CGBR)** In the UK, the *Public Sector Borrowing Requirement (PSBR) less any borrowings by local authorities and public corporations from the private sector. Since local authorities and public corporations both have a measure of freedom in deciding how much they borrow, the government does not have the complete control over the PSBR as it does over the CGBR.

**central parity** The maintenance of parity between the currencies of members of the European Community in relation to the *European Currency Unit, with a very narrow margin, up or down, for fluctuation. This parity of currency values is a major feature of the move towards a common monetary system.

**Central Registration Depository (CRD)** The computerized directory set up in the USA by the *National Association of Securities Dealers Inc. (NASD), listing the employment, qualifications, and curricula vitae of more than 40 000 professional members of the investment industry, who deal with the public.

**certain annuity (terminable annuity)** A form of investment contract that pays fixed sums at scheduled intervals to an individual after he or she attains a specified age; it runs for a specified number of years.

**certificate of deposit (CD)** A negotiable certificate issued by a bank in return for a term deposit of up to five years. CDs originated in the USA in the 1960s. From 1968, a sterling CD was issued by UK banks. They were intended to enable the *merchant banks to attract funds away from the *clearing banks with the offer of competitive interest rates. However, in 1971 the clearing banks also began to issue CDs as their negotiability and higher average yield had made them increasingly popular with the larger investors.

A secondary market in CDs has developed, made up of the *discount houses and the banks in the interbank market. They are issued in various amounts between £10,000 and £50,000, although they may be subdivided into units of the lower figure to facilitate negotiation of part holdings. *See also* roll-over CD.

**certificate of quality** A certificate to provide proof that goods to be traded in a *commodity market comply with an agreed standard.

**certified accountant** A member of the Chartered Association of Certified Accountants. Its members are trained in industry, in the public service, and in the offices of practising accountants. They often attend sandwich courses in technical colleges while still working and take the Association's exams. Members are recognized by the UK Department of Trade and Industry as qualified to audit the accounts of companies. They may be associates (ACCA) or fellows (FCCA) of the Association and although they are not *chartered accountants, they fulfil much the same role.

In the USA the equivalent is a **certified public accountant** (**CPA**), who is a member of the **Institute of Certified Public Accountants**.

**CET** Abbreviation for *Common External Tariff.

**CFC** Abbreviation for the *United Nations Common Fund for Commodities.

**CFTC** Abbreviation for *Commodity Futures Trading Commission.

**CGBR** Abbreviation for *Central Government Borrowing Requirement.

**CGT** Abbreviation for *capital-gains tax.

**chamber of commerce** In the UK, a voluntary organization, existing in most towns, of commercial, industrial, and trading businessmen who represent their joint interests to local and central government. The London Chamber of Commerce is the largest such organization in the UK; it also fulfils an educational role, running several commercial courses, for which it also sets examinations. Most UK chambers of commerce are affiliated to the Association of British Chambers of Commerce. *Compare* chamber of trade.

**chamber of trade** An organization of local retailers set up to protect their interests in local matters. They are much narrower organizations than *chambers of commerce and most in the UK are affiliated to the *National Chamber of Trade (NTC).

**Chambre Agent General Index** An arithmetically weighted index of 430 shares on the Paris Bourse.

**CHAPS** Abbreviation for Clearing House Automatic Payments System. *See* Association for Payment Clearing Services.

**Chapter 11** A section of the US Bankruptcy Reform Act 1978 that enables a business in financial difficulties to reorganize (*see* reorganization) and to be protected from its creditors while it does so. Those in charge of the business continue to run it but are under an obligation to produce a schedule of repayments for its creditors. Further loans can be made to a debtor who has filed for Chapter 11, while the restructuring takes place. Chapter 11 is the nearest US equivalent to UK *administration orders.

**charge** **1.** A legal or equitable interest in land, securing the payment of money. It gives the creditor in whose favour the charge is created (the **chargee**) the right to payment from the income or proceeds of sale of the land charged, in priority to claims against the debtor by unsecured creditors. **2.** An interest in company property created in favour of a creditor (e.g. as a *debenture holder) to secure the amount owing. Most charges must be registered by the *Registrar of Companies (*see also* register of charges). A *fixed charge (or specific charge) is attached to a specific item of property (e.g. land); a *floating charge is created in respect of circulating assets (e.g. cash, stock in trade), to which it will not attach until **crystallization**, i.e. until some event (e.g. winding-up) causes it to become fixed. Before crystallization, unsecured debts can be paid out of the assets charged. After, the charge is treated as a fixed charge and therefore unsecured debts (except those given preference under the Companies Acts) rank after those secured by the charge (*see also* fraudulent preference). A charge can also be created upon shares. For example, the articles of association usually give the company a *lien in respect of unpaid *calls, and company members may, in order to secure a debt owed to a third party, charge their shares, either by a full transfer of shares coupled with an agreement to retransfer upon repayment of the debt or by a deposit of the share certificate.

**charge card** *See* credit card.

**charitable trust** A trust set up in the UK for a charitable purpose that is registered with the **Charity Commissioners**, a body responsible to parliament.

Charitable trusts do not have to pay income tax and may have other indirect taxes reduced or exempted if they comply with the regulations of the Charity Commissioners.

**charity card**  *See* affinity card.

**chartered accountant**  A qualified member of the *Institute of Chartered Accountants in England and Wales, the Institute of Chartered Accountants of Scotland, or the Institute of Chartered Accountants in Ireland. These were the original bodies to be granted royal charters. Other bodies of accountants now have charters (the Chartered Association of Certified Accountants, the Chartered Institute of Management Accountants, and the Chartered Institute of Public Finance and Accountancy) but their members are not known as chartered accountants. Most firms of chartered accountants are engaged in public practice concerned with auditing, taxation, and other financial advice; however, many trained chartered accountants fulfil management roles in industry.

**Chartered Association of Certified Accountants**  *See* certified accountant; chartered accountant.

**chartered bank**  A bank in the USA that is authorized to operate as a bank by a charter granted either by its home state (**state-chartered bank**) or by the federal government (**nationally chartered bank**). In Canada, a similar charter is granted to banks by the Comptroller of Currency. The use of charters dates back to the use of Royal Charters, which predated Acts of Parliament.

**Chartered Institute of Management Accountants**  *See* chartered accountant.

**Chartered Institute of Public Finance and Accountancy**  *See* chartered accountant.

**Chartered Insurance Institute (CII)**  An association of insurers and brokers in the insurance industry. Its origins date back to 1873; its first Royal Charter was granted in 1912. It provides training by post and at its own college, examinations leading to its associateship diploma (ACII) and fellowship diploma (FCII), and sets high standards of ethical behaviour in the industry.

**chartist**  An *investment analyst who uses charts and graphs to record past movements of the share prices, P/E ratios, turnover, etc., of individual companies to anticipate the future share movements of these companies. Claiming that history repeats itself and that the movements of share prices conform to a small number of repetitive patterns, chartists have been popular, especially in the USA, in the past. It is now more usual for analysts to use broader techniques in addition to those used by chartists.

**cheap money (easy money)**  A monetary policy of keeping *interest rates at a low level. This is normally done to encourage an expansion in the level of economic activity by reducing the costs of borrowing and investment. It was used in the 1930s to help recovery after the depression and during World War II to reduce the cost of government borrowing. *Compare* dear money.

**check**  US spelling of *cheque.

**checkable**  Denoting a bank account in the USA upon which a check can be drawn. *See also* checking account.

**checking account** US name for a *current account, i.e. a bank account upon which checks can be drawn.

**cheque** A preprinted form on which instructions are given to an account holder (a bank or building society) to pay a stated sum to a named recipient. It is the most common form of payment of debts of all kinds (*see also* cheque account; current account).

In a **crossed cheque** two parallel lines across the face of the cheque indicate that it must be paid into a bank account and not cashed over the counter (a **general crossing**). A **special crossing** may be used in order to further restrict the negotiability of the cheque, for example by adding the name of the payee's bank. An **open cheque** is an uncrossed cheque that can be cashed at the bank of origin. An **order cheque** is one made payable to a named recipient 'or order', enabling the payee to either deposit it in an account or endorse it to a third party, i.e. transfer the rights to the cheque by signing it on the reverse. In a **blank cheque** the amount is not stated; it is often used if the exact debt is not known and the payee is left to complete it. However, the drawer may impose a maximum by writing 'under £…' on the cheque. A **rubber cheque** is one that is 'bounced' back to the drawer because of insufficient funds in the writer's account; a **stale cheque** is one in which more than three months have elapsed between the cheque's date and its presentation. In the USA the word is spelled **check**. *See also* bank draft; Cheques Act 1992; marked cheque; returned cheque; traveller's cheque.

**cheque account** An account with a *bank or *building society on which cheques can be drawn. In general, building societies pay interest on the daily credit balances in a cheque account but banks traditionally did not; they are now often doing so to meet competition from building societies. *See also* current account.

**cheque card** A plastic card issued by a UK *bank or *building society to its customers to guarantee cheques drawn on the customer's current account up to a specified limit (usually £50 or £100). The card carries the account number, the name of the customer, and has to be signed by the customer. The card number must be written on the reverse of the cheque which it is guaranteeing. Some cheque cards have now been replaced by *multifunctional cards, which also function as *cash cards and *debit cards.

**Cheques Act 1992** A UK Act of Parliament that gives legal force to the words *account payee on cheques, making them non-transferable and thus stopping fraudulent conversion of cheques intercepted by a third party. Banks require the express permission of a customer to cash an endorsed cheque. Within weeks of the legislation most High-Street banks introduced new cheque books with the words 'account payee' printed on each cheque.

**chetrum** A monetary unit of Bhutan, worth one hundredth of a *ngultrum.

**Chicago Board Options Exchange (CBOE)** A major US financial institution trading in *options. It was set up in 1973.

**Chicago Mercantile Exchange (CME)** The prime US futures and options market. It trades in currencies and livestock. It was started in 1919 as a commodity futures market, currencies trading being introduced in 1972.

**Chinese wall** A notional information barrier between the parts of a business, especially between the market-making part of a stockbroking firm and the broking part. It would clearly not be in investors' interests for brokers to persuade their clients to buy investments from them for no other reason than that the market makers in the firm, expecting a fall in price, were anxious to sell them.

**chip card** A type of *debit card that incorporates a microchip in order to store information regarding the transactions for which it is used. *See also* smart card.

**CHIPS** Abbreviation for *Clearing House Inter-Bank Payments System.

**chon** A monetary unit of North Korea and South Korea, worth one hundredth of a *won.

**churning 1.** The practice by a broker of encouraging an investor to change investments frequently in order to enable the broker to earn excessive commissions. **2.** The practice by a bank, building society, insurance broker, etc., of encouraging a householder with an endowment *mortgage to surrender the policy and to take out a new one when seeking to increase a mortgage or to raise extra funds, instead of topping up the existing mortgage. The purpose is to increase charges and commissions at the expense of the policyholder. **3.** A government policy of paying a benefit to a wide category of persons and taxing it so that those paying little or no taxes receive it while the well off return it through the tax system. There have been suggestions that a higher child benefit is suitable for churning.

**CII** Abbreviation for *Chartered Insurance Institute.

**circuity of action** The return of a *bill of exchange, prior to maturity, to the person who first signed it. Under these circumstances it may be renegotiated, but the person forfeits any right of action against those who put their names to it in the intervening period.

**circular letter of credit** *See* letter of credit.

**CISCO** Abbreviation for *City Group for Smaller Companies.

**Citibank** A major US *commercial bank with a worldwide network of branches.

**City** The financial district of London in which are situated the head offices of the banks, the money markets, the foreign exchange markets, the commodity and metal exchanges, the insurance market (including *Lloyd's), the *London Stock Exchange, and the offices of the representatives of foreign financial institutions. Occupying the square mile on the north side of the River Thames between Waterloo Bridge and Tower Bridge, it has been an international merchanting centre since medieval times.

**City Bank** One of the major 13 Japanese banks, which operates through a national network.

**City Call** A financial information service provided by British Telecom over the telephone in the UK. It gives nine bulletins of updated information each day.

**City Code on Takeovers and Mergers** A code first laid down in 1968, and subsequently modified, giving the practices to be observed in company takeovers (*see* takeover bid) and *mergers. Encouraged by the Bank of England, the code was compiled by a panel including representatives from the London Stock Exchange Association, the Issuing Houses Association, the London Clearing Bankers, and others. The code does not have the force of law but the panel can admonish offenders and refer them to their own professional bodies for disciplinary action.

The code attempts to ensure that all shareholders, including minority shareholders, are treated equally, are kept advised of the terms of all bids and counterbids, and are advised fairly by the directors of the company receiving the bid on the likely outcome if the bid succeeds. Its many other recommendations are aimed at preventing directors from acting in their own interests rather than those of their shareholders, ensuring that the negotiations are conducted openly and honestly, and preventing a spurious market arising in the shares of either side.

**City Group for Smaller Companies (CISCO)** A pressure group formed in December 1992 by 17 firms, ranging from venture capitalists to brokers, to represent the interests of smaller companies on the London Stock Exchange in anticipation of the closure of the *unlisted-securities market. Its aims are to advocate the need for a market for smaller company shares; to examine alternatives to the London Stock Exchange market; to chart investment trends of smaller companies; and to influence regulatory bodies in decisions which might affect smaller companies.

**claim** **1.** A right to assets held by another individual or organization. *See* lien. **2.** A right to all or part of the estate of a deceased person. **3.** An application by a policyholder for reimbursement for loss or damage, within the terms of an *insurance policy.

**classical system of corporation tax** A system of taxing companies in which the company is treated as a taxable entity separate from its own shareholders. The profits of companies under this system are therefore taxed twice, first when made by the company and again when distributed to the shareholders as dividends. *Compare* imputation system of taxation.

**clawback** Money that a government takes back from members of the public by taxation, especially at *higher rates, having given the money away in benefits, such as increased retirement pensions. Thus the money is clawed back from those who have no need of the extra benefit (because they are paying higher-rate taxes).

**clean floating** A government policy allowing a country's currency to fluctuate without direct intervention in the foreign-exchange markets. In practice, clean floating is rare as governments are frequently tempted to manage exchange rates by direct intervention by means of the official reserves, a policy sometimes called **managed floating** (*see also* managed currency). However, clean floating does not necessarily mean that there is no control of exchange rates, as they can still be influenced by the government's monetary policy. *See also* dirty float.

**clean price** The price of a *gilt-edged security excluding the accrued interest since the previous dividend payment. Interest on gilt-edged stocks accrues continuously although dividends are paid at fixed intervals (usually six months). Prices quoted in newspapers are usually clean prices, although a buyer will normally pay for and receive the accrued income as well as the stock itself.

**clearing bank** A bank which, in the UK, is a member of the bankers' *clearing house, to enable passage and clearance of cheques. It is often used as an alternative description for the major High-Street or joint-stock banks.

**clearing fee**  The sum charged by the agency affiliated to a *commodity exchange for settling the exchange's transactions.

**clearing house**  A centralized and computerized system for settling indebtedness between members. The best known in the UK is the *Association for Payment Clearing Services (APACS), which enables the member banks to offset claims against one another for cheques and orders paid into banks other than those upon which they were drawn. Similar arrangements exist in some commodity exchanges, in which sales and purchases are registered with the clearing house for settlement at the end of the accounting period. *See* London Clearing House.

**Clearing House Inter-Bank Payments System (CHIPS)**  A US bankers' *clearing house for paying and accepting funds. It is an electronic system operated through terminals in bank branches. Participating banks must be members of the New York Clearing House Association or affiliates of it, for example foreign banks operating in the USA can only take part through selected correspondents among the 12 New York Clearing Houses. Outside New York, similar transactions are undertaken through Fedwire, a clearing system for members of the *Federal Reserve System.

**client account**  A bank or building society account operated by a professional person (e.g. a solicitor, stockbroker, agent, etc.) on behalf of a client. A client account is legally required for any company handling investments on a client's behalf; it protects the client's money in case the company becomes insolvent and makes dishonest appropriation of the client's funds more difficult. For this reason money in client accounts should be quite separate from the business transactions of the company or the professional person. Client accounts can be current or deposit and usually attract higher rates of interest from banks because of their high value and short-term nature.

**close company**  A company resident in the UK that is under the control of five or fewer participators or any number of participators who are also directors. There is also an alternative asset-based test, which applies if five or fewer participators, or any number who are directors, would be entitled to more than 50% of the company's assets on a winding-up. The principal consequences of being a close company are that certain payments made to shareholders can be treated by the Inland Revenue as a *distribution, as can loans or quasi-loans. Close investment companies do not qualify for the reduced rate of *corporation tax. There are a number of other consequences. In the USA close companies are known as **closed companies**.

**closed-end fund**  A fund set up by an *investment company that issues a fixed number of shares to its investors. *Compare* open-end fund.

**close out**  To close an *open position, usually on a futures market by buying to cover a short sale or by selling a long purchase (*see* futures contract).

**close price**  The price of a share or commodity when the margin between the bid and offer prices is narrow.

**closing deal**  A transaction on a commodity market or stock exchange that closes a long or short position or terminates the liability of an *option holder.

**closing prices**  The buying and selling prices recorded at the end of a day's trading on a commodity market or stock exchange. *See* after-hours deals.

**club deal** *See* syndicated loan.

**CME** Abbreviation for *Chicago Mercantile Exchange.

**CMO** Abbreviation for *collateralized mortgage obligation.

**CNAR** Abbreviation for compound net annual rate. *See* compound annual return.

**CNMV** Abbreviation for Comisión del Mercado de Valores. *See* Madrid Stock Exchange.

**coemption** The act of buying up the whole stock of a commodity. *See* corner.

**Coffee, Sugar and Cocoa Exchange Inc. of New York (CSCE)** A major world market dealing in coffee, sugar, and cocoa *futures contracts and *options.

**Coffee Terminal Market Association of London Ltd** A former trading market in London dealing in *futures contracts for Robusta coffee. It is now incorporated into *London FOX.

**coinsurance** *See* facultative reinsurance.

**collar** Two interest-rate *options combined to protect an investor against wide fluctuations in interest rates. One, the **cap**, covers the investor if the interest rate rises against him or her; the other, the **floor**, covers the investor if the rate of interest falls too far.

**collateral** A form of *security, especially an impersonal form of security, such as life-assurance policies or shares, used to secure a bank loan. In some senses such impersonal securities are referred to as a secondary security, rather than a primary security, such as a guarantee.

**collateralized mortgage obligation (CMO)** A US bond secured by a portfolio of mortgages and offering a fixed *redemption date.

**collecting bank** *See* remitting bank.

**colón 1.** (₡) The standard monetary unit of Costa Rica, divided into 100 céntimos. **2.** (₡) The standard monetary unit of El Salvador, divided into 100 centavos.

**COMEX** Abbreviation for the *Commodity Exchange Inc. of New York.

**commercial bank** A privately owned UK bank, licensed under the Banking Act 1987 (*see* Banking Acts 1979 and 1987) to provide a wide range of financial services, both to the general public and to firms. The principal activities are operating cheque current accounts, receiving deposits, taking in and paying out notes and coin, and making loans. Additional services include trustee and executor facilities, the supply of foreign currency, the purchase and sale of securities, insurance, a credit-card system, and personal pensions. They also compete with the *finance houses and *merchant banks by providing venture capital and with *building societies by providing mortgages.

The number of commercial banks has gradually reduced following a series of mergers. The main banks with national networks of branches are the *Big Four (National Westminster, Barclays, Lloyds, and the Midland), the Royal Bank of Scotland, the Bank of Scotland, the Ulster Bank, and the TSB Group plc. They are also known as High-Street banks or *joint-stock banks. *See also* clearing bank.

**commercial banking**  Banking services offered to business customers rather than private individuals.

**commercial bill**  Any *bill of exchange other than a *Treasury bill. *See* bank bill; trade bill.

**commercial collection agency**  *See* debt collection agency.

**commercial credit company**  A US finance house that gives credit to businesses rather than individuals.

**commercial loan selling**  A transaction involving two banks and one business customer. Bank A grants a loan to the customer and then sells that loan agreement to Bank B. Bank A makes a profit on the sale; Bank B has a loan book it would not otherwise achieve; and the customer borrows at a favourable rate. Commercial loan selling is common in the USA.

**commercial paper**  A relatively low-risk short-term (maturing at 60 days or less in the US but longer in the UK) unsecured form of borrowing. Commercial paper is often regarded as a reasonable substitute for Treasury bills, certificates of deposit, etc. The main issuers are large creditworthy institutions, such as insurance companies, bank trust departments, and pension funds. In the UK, sterling commercial paper was first issued in 1986. Commercial paper is now available in Australia, France, Hong Kong, the Netherlands, Singapore, Spain, and Sweden.

**Commerzbank Index**  An arithmetically weighted index of 60 German shares representing 75% of the Bonn market. It has largely replaced the **Bonn Index FAZ**, which is based on 100 industrial shares.

**commission**  A payment made to an intermediary, such as an agent, salesman, broker, etc., usually calculated as a percentage of the value of the goods sold. Sometimes the whole of the commission is paid by the seller (e.g. an estate agent's commission in the UK) but in other cases (e.g. some commodity markets) it is shared equally between buyer and seller. In advertising, the commission is the discount (usually between 10% and 15%) allowed to an advertising agency by owners of the advertising medium for the space or time purchased on behalf of their clients. A **commission agent** is an agent specializing in buying or selling goods for a principal in another country for a commission.

**commission broker**  In the USA, a stock-exchange dealer who executes orders to buy or sell securities on payment of a fee or a commission based on the value of the deal.

**commitment fee**  An amount charged by a bank to keep open a line of credit or to continue to make unused loan facilities available to a potential borrower. *See* firm commitment.

**commodity**  **1.** A raw material traded on a *commodity market, such as grain, coffee, cocoa, wool, cotton, jute, rubber, pork bellies, or orange juice (sometimes known as **soft commodities** or **softs**) or metals and other solid raw materials (known as **hard commodities**). In some contexts soft commodities are referred to as **produce**. **2.** A *good regarded in economics as the basis of production and exchange.

**commodity broker**  A *broker who deals in *commodities, especially one who trades on behalf of principals in a *commodity market (*see also* futures contract). The rules governing the procedure adopted in each market vary from commodity to commodity and the function of brokers may also vary. In some markets brokers pass on the names of their principals, in others they do not, and in yet others they are permitted to act as principals. Commodity brokers, other than those dealing in metals, are often called **produce brokers**. *See* Securities and Futures Authority Ltd; London FOX; London Metal Exchange.

**commodity exchange**  *See* commodity market.

**Commodity Exchange Inc. of New York (COMEX)**  A *commodity exchange in New York that specializes in trading in metal *futures contracts and *options.

**Commodity Futures Trading Commission (CFTC)**  A US government body set up in 1975 in Washington to control trading in commodity futures (*see* futures contract) and *options.

**commodity market**  A market in which *commodities are traded. The main *terminal markets in commodities are in London and New York, but in some commodities there are markets in the country of origin. Some commodities are dealt with at auctions (e.g. tea), each lot being sold having been examined by dealers, but most dealers deal with goods that have been classified according to established quality standards. In these commodities both *actuals and futures (*see* futures contract) are traded on **commodity exchanges**, often with daily *callovers, in which dealers are represented by *commodity brokers. Many commodity exchanges offer *option dealing in futures and settlement of differences on futures through a *clearing house. As commodity prices fluctuate widely, commodity exchanges provide users and producers with *hedging facilities with outside speculators and investors helping to make an active market, although amateurs are advised not to gamble on commodity exchanges.

The fluctuations in commodity prices have caused considerable problems in developing countries, from which many commodities originate, as they are often important sources of foreign currency, upon which the economic welfare of the country depends. Various measures have been used to restrict price fluctuations but none have been completely successful. *See also* London Clearing House; London FOX; London Metal Exchange; United Nations Common Fund for Commodities.

**Common Agricultural Policy (CAP)**  A policy set up by the *European Economic Community to support free trade within the Common Market and to protect farmers in the member states. The *European Commission fixes a **threshold price**, below which cereals may not be imported into the European Community (EC), and also buys surplus cereals at an agreed **intervention price** in order to help farmers achieve a reasonable average price, called the **target price**. Prices are also agreed for meats, poultry, eggs, fruit, and vegetables, with arrangements similar to those for cereals. The European Commission is also empowered by the CAP to subsidize the modernization of farms within the community. The common policy for exporting agricultural products to non-member countries is laid down by the CAP. In the UK, the Intervention Board for Agricultural Produce is responsible for the implementation of EC regulations regarding the CAP. *See also* Common Budget; European Agricultural Guidance and Guarantee Fund.

**Common Budget**  The fund, administered by the *European Commission, into which all levies and customs duties on goods entering the European Community (EC) are paid and from which all subsidies due under the *Common Agricultural Policy are taken.

**Common External Tariff (CET)**  The tariff of import duties payable on certain goods entering any country in the European Community from non-member countries. Income from these duties is paid into the *Common Budget.

**Common Fisheries Policy**  A 20-year fishing policy agreed between members of the European Community (EC) in 1983. It lays down annual catch limits for major species of fish, a 12-mile exclusive fishing zone for each state, and an equal-access zone of 200 nautical miles from its coast, within which any member state is allowed to fish. There are some exceptions to these regulations.

**Common Market**  *See* European Community; European Economic Community.

**common stock**  The US name for *ordinary shares.

**community charge**  *See* poll tax.

**commutation**  The right to receive an immediate cash sum in return for accepting smaller annual payments at some time in the future. This is usually associated with a pension in which certain life-assurance policyholders can, on retirement, elect to take a cash sum from the pension fund immediately and a reduced annual pension.

**company**  A corporate enterprise that has a legal identity separate from that of its members; it operates as one single unit, in the success of which all the members participate. An **incorporated company** is a legal person in its own right, able to own property and to sue and be sued in its own name. A company may have limited liability (a *limited company), so that the liability of the members for the company's debts is limited. An **unlimited company** is one in which the liability of the members is not limited in any way. There are various different types of company: a **chartered company** is one formed under Royal Charter; a **joint-stock company** is a company in which the members pool their stock, trading on the basis of their joint stock.

A **registered company**, one registered under the Companies Acts, is the most common type of company. A company may be registered either as a public limited company or a private company. A **public limited company** must have a name ending with the initials 'plc' and have an authorized share capital of at least £50,000, of which at least £12,500 must be paid up. A **private company** is any registered company that is not a public company. The shares of a private company may not be offered to the public for sale. A **statutory company** is a company formed by special Act of Parliament.

**Company Bulletin Board Service**  An electronic market operated by the London Stock Exchange, for 100 smaller companies which had only one market maker, between April and November 1992. It was then replaced by the *Stock Exchange Alternative Trading Service (SEATS).

**company formation**  The procedure to be adopted for forming a company in the UK. The *subscribers to the company must send to the *Registrar of Companies a statement giving details of the registered address of the new company together with the names and addresses of the first directors and secretary, with their written consent to act in these capacities. They must also give a declaration (**declaration of compliance**) that the provisions of the Companies Acts have been complied with and provide the memorandum of association and the articles of association. Provided all these documents are in order the Registrar will issue a certificate of incorporation and a certificate enabling it to start business. In the case of a *public limited company additional information is required.

**compensation for loss of office**  A payment, often tax-free, made by a company to a director, senior executive, or consultant who is forced to retire before the expiry of a service contract, as a result of a merger, takeover, or any other reason. This form of **severance pay** (*see also* redundancy payment) may be additional to a retirement pension or in place of it; it must also be shown separately in the company's accounts. Because these payments can be very large, they are known as **golden handshakes**. *See also* golden parachute.

**compensation fund**  A fund set up by the *London Stock Exchange, to which member firms contribute. It provides compensation to investors who suffer loss as a result of a member firm failing to meet its financial obligations.

**competition and credit control**  The subject of an important paper issued in 1971 by the *Bank of England. It outlined a number of changes affecting the banking system and the means of controlling credit. From October 1971 a new system of reserve requirements was implemented, the banks agreed to abandon collusion on setting interest rates, and the Bank of England changed its operations in the gilt-edged securities market. The main aim of these changes was to stimulate more active competition between the banks and to move towards greater reliance upon interest rates as a means of credit control. Further changes were made in 1981 with the abolition of the *minimum lending rate and the reserve asset ratio.

**composite rate tax**  A special rate of tax (introduced in the UK in 1951 and abolished in 1991) that building societies and banks deducted from interest paid to investors; it was about 3% below the *basic rate of income tax. Since its abolition taxpayers have paid the full basic rate (which is deducted at source) and non-taxpayers have been able to opt to be paid gross interest or have been able to reclaim the tax.

**compound annual return (CAR)**  The total return available from an investment or deposit in which the interest is used to augment the investment. The more frequently the interest is credited, the higher the CAR. The CAR is usually quoted on a gross basis. The return, taking into account the deduction of tax at the basic rate on the interest, is known as the **compound net annual rate** (**CNAR**).

**compound interest**  *See* interest.

**compound net annual rate (CNAR)**  *See* compound annual return.

**comprehensive income tax**  An income tax for which the tax base consists not only of income but also of capital gains as well as other accretions of wealth, such as legacies. Although this is not a tax currently levied in the UK, tax theorists find it attractive since sometimes clear distinctions between income, capital gains, etc., are difficult to sustain.

**comptroller** The title of the financial director in some companies or chief financial officer of a group of companies. The title is more widely used in the USA than in the UK.

**compulsory liquidation (compulsory winding-up)** The winding-up of a company by a court. A petition must be presented both at the court and the registered office of the company. Those by whom it may be presented include: the company, the directors, a creditor, an official receiver, and the Secretary of State for Trade and Industry. The grounds on which a company may be wound up by the court include: a special resolution of the company that it be wound up by the court; that the company is unable to pay its debts; that the number of members is reduced below two; or that the court is of the opinion that it would be just and equitable for the company to be wound up. The court may appoint a *provisional liquidator after the winding-up petition has been presented; it may also appoint a *special manager to manage the company's property. On the grant of the order for winding-up, the official receiver becomes the *liquidator and continues in office until some other person is appointed, either by the creditors or the members. *Compare* members' voluntary liquidation.

**compulsory purchase annuity** An annuity that must be purchased with the fund built up from certain types of pension arrangements. When retirement age is reached, a person who has been paying premiums into this type of pension fund is obliged to use the fund to purchase an annuity to provide an income for the rest of his or her life. The fund may not be used in any other way (except for a small portion, which may be taken in cash).

**computer-to-computer interface (CTCI)** The link between a securities house in the USA and the *National Association of Securities Dealers Automated Quotation System (NASDAQ) computer, which allows the simultaneous reporting of a trade to NASDAQ and the recording of the same trade on the securities house's own data store.

**concert-party agreements** Secret agreements between apparently unconnected shareholders to act together to manipulate the share price of a company or to influence its management. The Companies Act 1981 laid down that the shares of the parties to such an agreement should be treated as if they were owned by one person, from the point of view of disclosing interests in a company's shareholding.

**conditionality** The terms under which the *International Monetary Fund (IMF) provides balance-of-payments support to member states. The principle is that support will only be given on the condition that it is accompanied by steps to solve the underlying problem. Programmes of economic reform are agreed with the member; these emphasize the attainment of a sustainable balance-of-payments position and boosting the supply side of the economy. The most recent review of general guidelines of conditionality principles was undertaken in 1988. Lending by commercial banks is frequently linked to IMF conditionality.

**confirmed letter of credit** *See* letter of credit.

**conflict of interests** A situation that can arise if a person (or firm) acts in two or more separate capacities and the objectives in these capacities are not identical. The conflict may be between self-interest and the interest of a company for which a person works or it could arise when a person is a director of two companies, which find themselves competing. The proper course of action in the case of a conflict of interests is for the persons concerned to declare their interests, to make known the way in which they conflict, and to abstain from voting or sharing in the decision-making procedure involving these interests.

**conglomerate** A group of companies merged into one entity, although they are active in totally different fields. A conglomerate is usually formed by a company wishing to diversify so that it is not totally dependent on one industry.

**consequential-loss policy** *See* business-interruption policy.

**consideration** **1.** A promise by one party to a *contract that constitutes the price for buying a promise from the other party to the contract. A consideration is essential if a contract, other than a *deed, is to be valid. It usually consists of a promise to do or not to do something or to pay a sum of money. **2.** The money value of a contract for the purchase or sale of securities on the London Stock Exchange, before commissions, charges, stamp duty, and any other expenses have been deducted.

**consolidated accounts** The combined accounts of a *group of companies. Although a parent company and its subsidiaries (the companies it owns and controls) are separate companies, it is customary to combine their results in a single set of accounts, which eliminates inter-company shareholdings and inter-company indebtedness; it also aggregates the assets and liabilities of all the companies. Parent companies of groups are required by law to prepare and file consolidated accounts in addition to individual accounts of the subsidiary companies. *See also* holding company.

**consolidated annuities** *See* Consols.

**Consolidated Fund** The Exchequer account, held at the Bank of England and controlled by the Treasury, into which taxes are paid and from which government expenditure is made. It was formed in 1787 by the consolidation of several government funds.

**Consolidated Quotation Service (CQS)** A service provided by the National Association of Securities Dealers Automated Quotation Service (NASDAQ) in the USA, offering all available quotations on stocks listed on the *New York Stock Exchange and *American Stock Exchange and selected securities on regional stock exchanges.

**consolidation** An increase in the *nominal price of a company's shares, by combining a specified number of lower-price shares into one higher-priced share. For example five 20p shares may be consolidated into one £1 share. In most cases this can be done by an ordinary resolution at a general meeting of the company.

**Consols** Government securities that pay interest but have no *redemption date. The present bonds, called **consolidated annuities** or **consolidated stock**, are the result of merging several loans at various different times going back to the 18th century. Their original interest rate was 3% on the nominal price of £100; most now pay 2½% and therefore stand at a price that makes their annual *yield comparable to long-dated *gilt-edged securities, e.g. at £27¾ they yield about 9%.

**consortium** A combination of two or more large companies formed on a temporary basis to quote for a large project, such as a new power station or dam. The companies would then work together, on agreed terms, if they were successful in obtaining the work. The purpose of forming a consortium may be to eliminate competition between the members or to pool skills, not all of which may be available to the individual companies. To qualify as a consortium in the UK, the minimum requirement is that UK companies, each with a 5% holding, own 75% or more of the consortium company, which must, itself, be a UK company. These percentage holdings refer to the beneficial ownership of the share capital.

**consortium relief** A means of enabling companies owned by a *consortium to transfer to members of the consortium (or vice versa) the benefit of their tax losses or certain other payments for which they are unable to obtain tax relief in their own right. The relief is not available for all losses and the requirements for consortium status are rigidly defined.

**constant-dollar plan** The US name for *pound-cost averaging, i.e. the investment of a specified sum of money at regular intervals in the acquisition of assets. It is sometimes called **dollar-cost averaging**.

**consumer credit** Short-term loans to the public for the purchase of goods. The most common forms of consumer credit are credit accounts at retail outlets, personal loans from banks and finance houses, *hire purchase, and *credit cards. Since the *Consumer Credit Act 1974, the borrower has been given greater protection, particularly with regard to regulations establishing the true rate of interest being charged when loans are made (*see* annual percentage rate). The Act also made it necessary for anyone giving credit in a business (with minor exceptions) to obtain a licence. *See* consumer-credit register.

**Consumer Credit Act 1974** A UK Act of Parliament aimed at protecting the borrower in credit agreements, loans, and mortgages. The Act requires full written details of the true interest rate (i.e. *annual percentage rate) to be quoted, a *cooling-off period to be given, during which borrowers may change their minds and cancel agreements, and all agreements to be in writing. The Act does not cover overdrafts.

**Consumer Credit Protection Act 1969** The US equivalent of the UK *Consumer Credit Act 1974.

**consumer-credit register** The register kept by the Director General of Fair Trading, as required by the Consumer Credit Act 1974, relating to the licensing or carrying on of consumer-credit businesses or consumer-hire businesses. The register contains particulars of undetermined applications, licences that are in force or have at any time been suspended or revoked, and decisions given by the Director under the Act as well as any appeal from them. The public is entitled to inspect the register on payment of a fee.

**consumer instalment loan** The US name for *hire purchase.

**consumer price index** The name for the *Retail Price Index in the USA and some other countries.

**Consumers' Association (CA)** A UK charitable organization formed in 1957 to provide independent and technically based guidance on the goods and services available to the public. The Consumers' Association tests and investigates products and services and publishes comparative reports on performance, quality, and value in its monthly magazine *Which?* It also publishes *Holiday Which?* and *Gardening From Which?* as well as various books, including *The Legal Side of Buying a House, Starting Your Own Business*, and *The Which? Book of Saving and Investing*. The US equivalent is the **Consumer Advisory Council**.

**contango 1.** (formerly) To carry over the purchase of securities from one account to the next on the London Stock Exchange. **2.** *See* forwardation.

**contingency insurance** An insurance policy covering financial losses occurring as a result of a specified event happening. The risks covered by policies of this kind are various and often unusual, such as a missing documents indemnity, the birth of twins, or pluvial insurance.

**contingent annuity (reversionary annuity)** An annuity in which the payment is conditional on a specified event happening. The most common form is an annuity purchased jointly by a husband and wife that begins payment after the death of one of the parties (*see* joint-life and last-survivor annuities).

**contingent liability** A liability that, at a balance sheet date, can be anticipated to arise if a particular event occurs. Typical examples include a court case pending against the company, the outcome of which is uncertain, or loss of earnings as a result of a customer invoking a penalty clause in a contract that may not be completed on time. Under the Companies Act 1985, such liabilities must be explained by a note on the company balance sheet.

**continuation** An arrangement between an investor and a stockbroker in which the broker reduces the *commission payable for a series of purchases by that investor of the same stock over a stated period.

**continuous net settlement** The daily settlement of securities transactions on a net basis by a *clearing house. It reduces the need for the delivery of certificates and cash payments to settle individual transactions, by producing daily net accounts in each security for each security firm as well as accounts recording the transaction of each firm with the clearing house.

**contract** A legally binding agreement. Agreement arises as a result of an *offer and *acceptance, but a number of other requirements must be satisfied for an agreement to be legally binding. There must be *consideration (unless the contract is by *deed); the parties must have an intention to create legal relations; the parties must have capacity to contract (i.e. they must be competent to enter a legal obligation, by not being a minor, mentally disordered, or drunk); the agreement must comply with any formal legal requirements; the agreement must be legal (*see* illegal contract); and the agreement must not be rendered void either by some common-law or statutory rule or by some inherent defect.

In general, no particular formality is required for the creation of a valid contract. It may be oral, written, partly oral and partly written, or even implied from conduct. However, certain contracts are valid only if made by deed (e.g. transfers of shares in statutory companies, transfers of shares in British ships, legal *mortgages, certain types of lease) or in writing (e.g. *hire-purchase agreements, *bills of exchange, promissory notes, contracts for the sale of land made after 21 September 1989), and certain others, though valid, can only be enforced if evidenced in writing (e.g. guarantees, contracts for the sale of land made before 21 September 1989).

**contract guarantee insurance** An insurance policy designed to guarantee the financial solvency of a contractor during the performance of a contract. If the contractor becomes financially insolvent and cannot complete the work the insurer makes a payment equivalent to the contract price, which enables another contractor to be paid to complete the work. *See also* credit insurance.

**contracting out** *See* State Earnings-Related Pension Scheme.

**contract note** A document sent by a stockbroker or commodity broker to a client as evidence that the broker has bought (in which case it may be called a **bought note**) or sold (a **sold note**) securities or commodities in accordance with the client's instructions. It will state the quantity of securities or goods, the price, the date (and sometimes the time of day at which the bargain was struck), the rate of commission, the cost of the transfer stamp and VAT (if any), and the amount due and the settlement date.

**contributory** Any person who is liable to contribute towards the assets of a company on liquidation. The list of contributories will be settled by the liquidator or by the court. This list will include all shareholders, although those who hold fully paid-up shares will not be liable to pay any more.

**contributory pension** A *pension in which the employee as well as the employer contribute to the pension fund. *Compare* non-contributory pension.

**controlling interest** An interest in a company that gives a person control of it. To have a controlling interest in a company, a shareholder would normally need to own or control more than half the voting shares. However, in practice, a shareholder might control the company with considerably less than half the shares, if the remaining shares are held by a large number of people. For legal purposes, a director is said to have a controlling interest in a company if that director alone, or together with his or her spouse, minor children, and the trustees of any settlement in which he or she has an interest, owns more than 20% of the voting shares in a company or in a company that controls that company.

**conversion premium** The cost of converting a share at the current market price into a *convertible security or warrant. It is normally expressed as a percentage of the market price of the convertible security.

**convertibility** The extent to which one currency can be freely exchanged for another. Since 1979 sterling has been freely convertible. The *International Monetary Fund encourages free convertibility, although many governments try to maintain some direct control over foreign-exchange transactions involving their own currency, especially if there is a shortage of hard-currency foreign-exchange reserves.

**convertible (conversion issue)** **1.** A security, usually a *bond or *debenture, that can be converted into the ordinary shares or preference shares of the company at a fixed date or dates at a fixed price. In effect, **convertible loan stock** is equivalent to a bond plus a stock *option. **2.** A government security in which the holder has the right to convert a holding into new stock instead of obtaining repayment.

**convertible adjusted-rate preferred stock**  *See* adjustable-rate preferred stock.

**convertible loan stock**  *See* convertible.

**convertible revolving credit**  A *revolving credit that can be converted by mutual agreement into a fixed-term loan.

**convertible term assurance**  A *term assurance that gives the policyholder the option to widen the policy to become a *whole (of) life policy or an *endowment assurance policy, without having to provide any further evidence of good health. All that is required is the payment of the extra premium.

**cooling-off period**  The 14 days that begins when a life-assurance policy, credit agreement, etc., is effected, during which new policyholders, borrowers, etc., can change their minds. During this period any policies or agreements entered into can be cancelled with a full refund of any premiums, arrangement fees, etc.

**córdoba**  (C$) The standard monetary unit of Nicaragua, divided into 100 centavos.

**CORES**  Abbreviation for Computerized Order Routing and Execution System. *See* Tokyo Stock Exchange.

**corner**  A monopoly established by an organization that succeeds in controlling the total supply of a particular good or service (often referred to as **cornering the market**). It will then force the price up until further supplies or substitutes can be found. This objective has often been attempted, but rarely achieved, in international *commodity markets. Because it is undesirable and has antisocial effects, a corner can now rarely be attempted as government restrictions on monopolies and antitrust laws prevent it. An example of an attempt to corner a market was Nelson Bunker Hunt's attack on the silver market in the USA in the early 1980s.

**corporate bond**  A bond or security representing a normal commercial loan in sterling which, if conversion is possible, can only be converted into a similar bond. In the UK, corporate bonds are exempt from *capital-gains tax.

**corporate finance**  The funding of businesses, usually by banks and involving large corporations.

**corporate raider**  A person or company that buys a substantial proportion of the equity of another company (the target company) with the object of either taking it over or of forcing the management of the target company to take certain steps to improve the image of the company sufficiently for the share price to rise enough for the raider's holding to be sold at a profit.

**corporate venturing**  The provision of venture capital by one company, either directly or by means of a venture-capital fund, for another company; the objectives are usually either to obtain information about the activities of the company requiring the venture capital or its markets or as a preliminary step towards acquiring that company. It may often be a means of moving into a fresh market cheaply and without needing to acquire the necessary expertise and personnel required to do so on its own.

**corporation tax**  A tax levied on the trading profits, chargeable gains, and other income of companies and other incorporated bodies. The rate of corporation tax is set in the UK in the Budget by the Chancellor; it is currently 33%, although companies with profits below a fixed amount (£250,000 in 1992–93) pay a reduced rate of 25%. For profits between £250,000 and £1,250,000 p.a. there is an increasing rate, until the full rate applies at the higher figure. Corporation tax is paid in two parts: *advance corporation tax and mainstream corporation tax. Of particular interest is the relationship between corporation taxes on companies and income taxes on their individual shareholders. In 'classical' corporation-tax systems, corporation tax is levied on the company and then, from what remains, dividends are paid to shareholders, who are again taxed in full by means of income tax. In *imputation systems of taxation, such as that used in the UK, part of the company's corporation tax is effectively treated as a payment on account of the shareholders' income tax on their dividends. *See also* franked investment income.

**correspondent bank** A bank in a foreign country that offers banking facilities to the customers of a bank in another country. These arrangements are usually the result of agreements, often reciprocal, between the two banks. The most frequent correspondent banking facilities used are those of money transmission.

**corset 1.** A restriction of the movements of currency exchange values imposed by certain formal market mechanisms. **2.** A restriction imposed, especially by a government, on borrowing or lending. Specifically, it was the colloquial name for the Supplementary Special Deposits scheme imposed by the UK government in 1973, abolished in 1980. The scheme was designed to limit the growth of bank deposits, i.e. interest-bearing eligible liabilities, and thus indirectly control bank lending and the money supply, which depended on them.

**cost accountant** An *accountant whose principal function is to gather and manipulate data on the costs and efficiency of industrial processes and thus to advise management on the profitability of ventures. It is the cost accountant who operates budgetary control of departments, estimates unit costs, and provides the information required for preparing *tenders.

**cost-benefit analysis** A method of deciding whether or not a particular project should be undertaken, by comparing the relevant economic costs and the potential benefits. It can be used for private investment projects, calculating outlays and returns, and estimating the *net present value of the project: if this is positive the project would be profitable. Cost-benefit analysis is also frequently used by governments in an attempt to evaluate all the social costs and benefits of a project (e.g. road building) that is much more problematic.

**cost effectiveness 1.** Achieving a goal with the minimum of expenditure. **2.** Achieving a goal with an expenditure that makes the achievement viable in commercial terms.

**cost of capital** The return that a company must earn on additional investment if the value of the existing equity is not to be reduced.

**cost of funds** The cost to banks of borrowing in the principal *money markets, which determines their rates of interest when lending to their customers.

**cost-push inflation** An increase in the prices of goods caused by increases in the cost of inputs (especially wages and raw materials). As an explanation of *inflation, cost-push theories became popular in the 1970s when they appeared to explain the rapid inflation of that period, which followed on from very rapid rises in wages and the increases in oil prices. However, the theory is also widely criticized as: (a) it describes only changes in relative prices (e.g. oil) rather than rises in the general price level (which is how inflation is defined); and (b) most economists would now agree that price rises can only continue if there is an accompanying increase in the *money supply.

**cote officielle  1.** The official price for a security as quoted on a French stock exchange.  **2.** The *Paris Bourse itself, to distinguish it from the *coulisse*.

**coulisse**  The unofficial market in securities attached to the Paris Bourse.

**council tax**  A UK local-government tax raised according to property valuation. Replacing the community charge from 1993–94, the tax is charged on the value of a property as defined by a series of bands. Different bands apply to different regions of the UK. Council tax will assume that two people live at the address, with rebates for single occupancy, and provides for a scale of earnings exemptions.

**counterparty**  A person who is a party to a contract.

**counterparty risk**  The risk that either of the parties to a contract (counterparties) will fail to honour their obligations under the contract. In commodity markets, for example, the buyer of a particular commodity faces the *market risk (that the market price will fall); there is also counterparty risk, that the seller will become insolvent or fail for some other reason to comply with the contract. In such organized markets as *London FOX and *London International Financial Futures and Options Exchange, this risk is reduced by the *London Clearing House (LCH) becoming counterparty to the contract, i.e. the buyer contracts to buy from LCH and the seller contracts to sell to LCH (*see* novation). The risk of default by either the buyer or the seller is thus assumed by LCH, the buyer and seller being left with the greatly reduced counterparty risk that LCH will fail.

**countervailing credit**  *See* back-to-back credit.

**coupon  1.** One of several dated slips attached to a bond, which must be presented to the agents of the issuer or the company to obtain an interest payment or dividend. *See also* coupon security. They are usually used with *bearer bonds; the **coupon yield** is the *yield provided by a bearer bond. **2.** The rate of interest paid by a fixed-interest bearer bond. A 5% coupon implies that the bond pays 5% interest.

**coupon security**  A US government stock (Treasury bond or Treasury note) that pays interest on a *coupon.

**Court of Auditors**  A body appointed by the Council of Ministers of the European Community to look into the income and expenditure of the Community. It has one representative of each of the 12 member states.

**covenant**  A promise made in a deed which may or may not be under seal. A covenant is frequently used as a means of providing funds to a body of persons or *trust established for charitable purposes. Such a deed has, initially, to be for a minimum period of four years. The payer covenants to pay an agreed sum to the charity, from which income tax at the *basic rate has been deducted. The charity can reclaim the tax so deducted and if the payer is a higher-rate taxpayer, a further claim for tax relief (currently 15% of the grossed up payment) can be made by the payer. For example, if the payment to a charity is £75, the gross payment would be £100, and the taxpayer could claim a further £15 in tax relief.

Covenants may be entered into concerning the use of land, frequently to restrict the activities of a new owner or tenant (e.g. a covenant not to sell alcohol or run a fish-and-chip shop). Such covenants may be enforceable by persons deriving title from the original parties. This is an exception to the general rule that a contract cannot bind persons who are not parties to it.

Covenants are also used in loan agreements to specify the criteria with which the borrower has to comply. If these are not met, the borrower is either in default or the loan ceases to be available.

**cover** **1.** The security provided by *insurance or *assurance against a specified risk. **2.** *See* dividend cover. **3.** Collateral given against a loan or credit, as in option dealing. **4.** A hedge purchased to safeguard an open position in commodity futures or currency dealing. *See also* hedging; covered bear. **5.** Money set aside from income to meet potential bad debts or losses. **6.** (or **covering bid**) The second bid in competitive bidding for bonds.

**covered bear (protected bear)** A person who has sold securities, commodities, or currency that they do not have, although they do have a hedge that they could sell at a profit if the market moves upwards, preventing them from covering their bear sale at a profit. *See also* hedging.

**covered call writing** Selling (writing) a call *option on equities one owns. Thus, if the manager of a portfolio expects the price of a certain holding in the portfolio to remain unchanged or to fall, he or she can increase the portfolio income by the amount of the premium received for the call option sold. If the shares rise in price the manager has to deliver them at the exercise price. *Compare* naked call writing.

**CP** Abbreviation for *commercial paper.

**CPA** Abbreviation for certified public accountant. *See* certified accountant.

**CPP accounting** Abbreviation for *current purchasing power accounting.

**CQS** Abbreviation for *Consolidated Quotation Service.

**crash** **1.** A rapid and serious fall in the level of prices in a market. **2.** A breakdown of a computer system. A program is said to crash if it terminates abnormally. A computer is said to crash either if it suffers a mechanical failure, or if one of the programs running on it misbehaves in a way that causes the computer to stop.

**crawling peg (sliding peg)** A method of exchange-rate control that accepts the need for stability given by fixed (or pegged) exchange rates, while recognizing that fixed rates can be prone to serious misalignments, which in turn can cause periods of financial upheaval. Under crawling peg arrangements, countries alter their pegs by small amounts at frequent intervals, rather than making large infrequent changes. This procedure provides flexibility and, in conjunction with the manipulation of interest rates, reduces the possibility of destabilizing speculative flows of capital. However, it is exposed to the criticism made against all fixed-rate regimes, that they are an inefficient alternative to the free play of market forces. At the same time, the crawling peg loses a major advantage of fixed rates, which is to inject certainty into the international trading system. The rates may move as frequently as daily under a crawling-peg policy.

**CRD** Abbreviation for *Central Registration Depository.

**creation price** The cost to the managers of a *unit trust of creating the units, i.e. the underlying cost of the securities plus the accrued income.

**credit** **1.** The reputation and financial standing of a person or organization. **2.** The sum of money that a trader or company allows a customer before requiring payment. **3.** The ability of members of the public to purchase goods with money borrowed from finance companies, banks, and other money lenders. **4.** An entry on the right-hand side of an *account in double-entry book-keeping, showing a positive asset.

**credit brokerage** *See* ancillary credit business.

**credit card** A plastic card issued by a bank or other finance institution. The cards are personal to the user, bear the user's name and signature, and are magnetized. They can be used to buy goods and services from retailers. The retailers are paid direct by the relevant credit-card company, less a service charge. Customers are charged monthly by the credit-card company and may pay no interest provided the full debt is settled each month. A minimum repayment is usually required each month, typically 5% of the outstanding debt. Interest is payable on the outstanding balances at a high rate compared with normal borrowing (usually between 24% and 30% p.a.). In the UK the main suppliers of cards are Barclaycard and Access (through the Visa and Mastercard systems).

**credit control** Any system used by an organization to ensure that its outstanding debts are paid within a reasonable period. It involves establishing a **credit policy**, *credit rating of clients, and chasing accounts that become overdue. *See also* factoring.

**credit guarantee** *See* credit insurance.

**credit insurance** **1.** An insurance policy that continues the repayments of a particular debt in the event of the policyholder being financially unable to do so because of illness, death, redundancy, or any other specified cause. **2.** A form of insurance or **credit guarantee** against losses arising from bad debts. This is not usually undertaken by normal insurance policies but by specialists known as factors (*see* factoring). *See also* Export Credits Guarantee Department.

**credit line** **1.** The extent of the credit available to a borrower or the user of a *credit card as set down in the initial credit agreement. **2.** The facility for borrowing money over a given period to a specified extent.

**creditor** One to whom an organization or person owes money. The *balance sheet of a company shows the total owed to creditors and a distinction has to be made between creditors who will be paid during the coming accounting period and those who will be paid later than this.

**creditors' committee** A committee of creditors of an insolvent company or a bankrupt individual, which represents all the creditors. They supervise the conduct of the administration of a company or the bankruptcy of an individual or receive reports from an administrative *receiver. If large debts are involved, the creditors' committees are often run by creditor banks.

**creditors' voluntary liquidation (creditors' voluntary winding-up)** The winding-up of a company by special resolution of the members when it is insolvent. A **meeting of creditors** must be held within 14 days of such a resolution and the creditors must be given seven days' notice of the meeting. Notices must also be posted in the *London Gazette* and two local newspapers. The creditors also have certain rights to information before the meeting. A *liquidator may be appointed by the members before the meeting of creditors or at the meeting by the creditors. If two different liquidators are appointed, an application may be made to the court to resolve the matter.

**credit rating** An assessment of the creditworthiness of an individual or a firm, i.e. the extent to which they can safely be granted credit. Traditionally, banks have provided confidential trade references, but recently **credit-reference agencies** (also known as **rating agencies**) have grown up, which gather information from a wide range of sources, including the county courts, bankruptcy proceedings, hire-purchase companies, and professional debt collectors. This information is then provided, for a fee, to interested parties. The consumer was given some protection from such activities in the Consumer Credit Act 1974, which allows an individual to obtain a copy of all the information held by such agencies relating to that individual, as well as the right to correct any discrepancies. There are also agencies that specialize in the corporate sector, giving details of a company's long-term and short-term debt. This can be extremely important to the price of the company's shares on the market, its ability to borrow, and its general standing in the business community.

**credit reference** An indication of a borrower's previous borrowing record, usually given by a bank or other lender to enable a borrower to extend an existing credit line or open new credit facilities. Such information is also provided by **credit-reference agencies**. *See* ancillary credit business; banker's reference; credit rating.

**credit sale agreement** *See* hire purchase.

**credit squeeze** A government measure, or set of measures, to reduce economic activity by restricting the money supply. Measures used include increasing the interest rate (to restrain borrowing), controlling moneylending by banks and others, and increasing down payments or making other changes to hire-purchase regulations.

**credit transfer** An electronic system of settling a debt by transferring money through a bank or post office. The payer completes written instructions naming the receiver and giving the receiver's address and acount number. Several receivers may be listed and settled by a single transaction. The popularity of this system led the banks to introduce a credit-clearing system in 1961 and the post office in 1968. *See also* giro.

**credit union** A US non-profitmaking cooperative that functions as a *savings bank, taking deposits from savers and lending to house buyers, etc. A *share account with a credit union pays a dividend rather than interest.

**creeping takeover** The accumulation of a company's shares, by purchasing them openly over a period on a stock exchange, as a preliminary to a takeover (*see* takeover bid). Under the Securities and Exchange Commission (SEC) regulations, in the USA once a 5% holding in another company has been acquired this must be disclosed to the SEC within 10 days (according to section 13(d) of the US Securities and Exchange Act). The **section-13(d) window**, however, enables more than 5% of the stock to be accumulated before a declaration is made.

**cross-border listing** The practice of listing shares in a company on the stock exchanges of different countries in order to create a larger market for the shares. This is a necessary procedure because the securities houses and stockbrokers of one country cannot normally deal through the exchanges of another. The practice has led to the creation of multinational securities houses.

**cross-currency interest-rate swap** An *interest-rate swap that exchanges one currency for another; the currencies revert to their original form at maturity. One of the two currencies will bear interest at a fixed rate and the other at a floating rate. *Compare* currency interest-rate swap.

**crossed** In the USA, denoting a situation in which one market maker's offer price is lower than the bid price of another. In UK markets this is referred to as *backwardation.

**crossed cheque** *See* cheque.

**crossing** A practice that occurs on the London Stock Exchange when the same broker or securities house buys and sells a block of securities, instead of allowing the sale to cross the market in accordance with Stock Exchange rules. In the USA, such a transaction is known as a **wash sale**.

**cruzeiro** (Cr$) The standard monetary unit of Brazil, divided into 100 centavos.

**CSCE** Abbreviation for *Coffee, Sugar and Cocoa Exchange Inc. of New York.

**CTCI** Abbreviation for *computer-to-computer interface.

**cum-** *See* ex-.

**cum-dividend** *See* ex-.

**cum-new** Denoting a share that is offered for sale with the right to take up any *scrip issue or *rights issue. *Compare* ex-new.

**cumulative preference share** A type of *preference share that entitles the owner to receive any dividends not paid in previous years. Companies are not obliged to pay dividends on preference shares if there are insufficient earnings in any particular year. Cumulative preference shares guarantee the eventual payment of these dividends in arrears before the payment of dividends on ordinary shares, provided that the company returns to profit in subsequent years.

**currency** **1.** Any kind of money that is in circulation in an economy. **2.** Anything that functions as a *medium of exchange, including coins, banknotes, cheques, *bills of exchange, promissory notes, etc. **3.** (or **legal tender**) The money in use in a particular country. *See* foreign exchange. **4.** The time that has to elapse before a bill of exchange matures.

**currency future** A *financial futures contract in which a currency for forward delivery is bought or sold at a particular exchange rate.

**currency interest-rate swap** A transaction involving the exchange of two currencies, both bearing interest at fixed rates or both bearing interest at floating rates. *See* interest-rate swap. *Compare* cross-currency interest-rate swap.

**currency option** A contract giving the right either to buy or to sell a specified currency at a fixed exchange rate within a given period. The price agreed is called the **strike price** or **exercise price**. This is the price at which the buyer has the right to buy or sell the currency.

**currency risk** *See* market risk.

**currency swap** A transaction in which specified amounts of one currency are exchanged for another currency at a fixed price.

**current account 1.** An active account at a bank or building society into which deposits can be paid and from which withdrawals can be made by cheque (*see also* cheque account), direct debit, standing order, or cash card through an automated teller machine. The bank or building society issues cheque books free of charge and supplies regular statements listing all transactions and the current balance. Banks sometimes make charges for current accounts, based on the number of transactions undertaken, but modern practice is to waive these charges if a certain credit balance has been maintained for a given period. Building societies usually make no charges and pay interest on balances maintained in a current account. Banks, in order to remain competitive, are following this practice, although they have traditionally not paid interest on current-account balances. In the UK current accounts can be overdrawn but usually then incur additional bank charges. **2.** The part of the *balance of payments account that records non-capital transactions. **3.** An account in which intercompany or interdepartmental balances are recorded. **4.** An account recording the transactions of a partner in a partnership that do not relate directly to that partner's capital in the partnership (*see* capital account).

**current assets** Assets that form part of the circulating capital of a business and are turned over frequently in the course of trade. The most common current assets are stock in trade, debtors, and cash. *Compare* capital asset.

**current-cost accounting (CCA)** A method of accounting, recommended by the Sandilands Committee (1975), to deal with the problem of showing the effects of inflation on business profits. Instead of showing assets at their historical cost (i.e. their original purchase price), less depreciation where appropriate, the assets are shown at their current cost (*see* replacement cost) at the time of producing the accounts. This method of accounting was used considerably in the UK in the late 1970s and early 1980s, when inflation was high; it was not popular, however, and as inflation reduced many companies abandoned it.

**current liabilities** Amounts due to the creditors of an organization that are due to be paid within 12 months.

**current purchasing power accounting (CPP accounting)** A method of accounting designed to deal with the problem of showing the effects of inflation on business profits. In this method the historical cost of an asset (i.e. its original purchase price) is increased by *indexation using, for example, the Retail Price Index. The method was not adopted because the Sandilands Committee recommended *current-cost accounting as preferable. However, current-cost accounting does not strictly show the effects of inflation because it can confuse the effects of inflation with price changes caused by other factors.

**current ratio**  The proportion of the *current assets to the *current liabilities of an organization. This ratio is used in the analysis of *balance sheets to gauge the likelihood that an organization can pay its debts regularly. There is no absolute figure for the ratio that is desirable, although clearly an excess of current liabilities over current assets would be a cause for concern; different ratios might be appropriate to different sorts of business. In analysing successive balance sheets, trends might be more important than the absolute figures.

**current yield**  *See* yield.

**Customs and Excise**  *See* Board of Customs and Excise.

**customs union**  A union of two or more states to form a region in which there are no import or export duties between members but goods imported into the region bear the same import duties. The *European Community is an example.

**DA** **1.** Abbreviation for *deposit account. **2.** Abbreviation for *discretionary account.

**D/A** Abbreviation for *documents against acceptance.

**Daily Official List** A publication issued daily by the London Stock Exchange to summarize transactions in listed securities.

**daimyo bond** A *bearer bond issued on the Japanese markets and in the *eurobond market by the *World Bank.

**dalasi** (D) The standard monetary unit of the Gambia, divided into 100 bututs.

**damages** Compensation, in monetary form, for a loss or injury, breach of contract, tort, or infringement of a right. Damages refers to the compensation awarded, as opposed to damage, which refers to the actual injury or loss suffered. The legal principle is that the award of damages is an attempt, as far as money can, to restore the position of the injured party to what it was before the event in question took place. In general, damages capable of being quantified in monetary terms are known as **liquidated damages**. In particular, liquidated damages include instances in which a genuine pre-estimate can be given of the loss that will be caused to one party if a contract is broken by the other party. However, liquidated damages must be distinguished from a *penalty. Another form of liquidated damages is that expressly made recoverable under a statute. These may also be known as **statutory damages** if they involve a breach of statutory duty or are regulated or limited by statute. **Unliquidated damages** are those fixed by a court rather than those that have been estimated in advance.

**dated security** A stock that has a fixed *redemption date.

**dawn raid** An attempt by one company or investor to acquire a significant holding in the equity of another company by instructing brokers to buy all the shares available in that company as soon as the stock exchange opens, usually before the target company knows that it is, in fact, a target. The dawn raid may provide a significant stake from which to launch a *takeover bid. The conduct of dawn raids is now restricted by the *City Code on Takeovers and Mergers.

**Dax** Abbreviation for *Deutsche Aktienindex.

**day order** An order to a stockbroker, commodity broker, etc., to buy or sell a specified security or commodity at a fixed price or within fixed limits; the order is valid for the day on which it is given and automatically becomes void at the close of trading on that day.

**days of grace** The extra time allowed for payment of a *bill of exchange or insurance premium after the actual due date. With bills of exchange the usual custom is to allow 3 days of grace (not including Sundays and *Bank Holidays) and 14 days for insurance policies.

**day-to-day money (overnight money)**   Money lent, often by one bank to another, for one trading day and repayable 24 hours later.

**DCF**   Abbreviation for *discounted cash flow.

**dead-cat bounce**   A temporary recovery on a stock exchange, caused by *short covering after a substantial fall. It does not imply a reversal of the downward trend.

**deadweight debt**   A debt that is incurred to meet current needs without the security of an enduring asset. It is usually a debt incurred by a government; the *national debt is a deadweight debt incurred by the UK government during the two World Wars.

**dealer**   **1.** A trader of any kind.   **2.** A person who deals as a principal, such as a *market maker on a stock exchange, a commodity merchant, etc., rather than as a broker or agent.

**dear money (tight money)**   A monetary policy in which loans are difficult to obtain and only available at high rates of interest. *Compare* cheap money.

**death duties**   Taxes levied on a person's estate at the time of death. The principal death duty in the UK was *estate duty, which was introduced in 1894. This became *capital-transfer tax in 1974, which itself became *inheritance tax in 1986. Both these taxes also tax life-time gifts, which estate duty itself had begun to do; otherwise any form of death duty can be avoided by giving away all or part of one's estate before death.

**death-valley curve**   A curve on a graph showing how the venture capital invested in a new company falls as the company meets its start-up expenses before its income reaches predicted levels. This erosion of capital makes it difficult for the company to interest further investors in providing additional venture capital. *See also* maximum slippage.

**debenture**   **1.** The most common form of long-term loan taken by a company. It is usually a loan repayable at a fixed date, although some debentures are *irredeemable securities; these are sometimes called *perpetual debentures. Most debentures also pay a fixed rate of interest, and this interest must be paid before a *dividend is paid to shareholders. Most debentures are also secured on the borrower's assets, although some, known as **naked debentures** or *unsecured debentures, are not. In the USA debentures are usually unsecured, relying only on the reputation of the borrower. In a *secured debenture, the bond may have a *fixed charge (i.e. a charge over a particular asset) or a *floating charge. If debentures are issued to a large number of people (for example in the form of **debenture stock** or **loan stock**) trustees may be appointed to act on behalf of the debenture holders. There may be a premium on redemption and some debentures are *convertible, i.e. they can be converted into ordinary shares on a specified date, usually at a specified price. The advantage of debentures to companies is that they carry lower interest rates than, say, overdrafts and are usually repayable a long time into the future. For an investor, they are usually saleable on a stock exchange and involve less risk than *equities.   **2.** A *deed under seal setting out the main terms of such a loan.

**3.** A form of bank security covering corporate debt, either fixed or floating; in either case the bank ranks as a preferred creditor in the event of a liquidation.

**debit card** A plastic card issued by a bank or building society to enable its customers with cheque accounts to pay for goods or services at certain retail outlets by using the telephone network to debit their cheque accounts directly. It is also known as a **payment card**. The retail outlets, such as petrol stations and some large stores, need to have the necessary computerized input device, into which the card is inserted; the customer may be required to tap in a *personal identification number before entering the amount to be debited. Some debit cards also function as *cheque cards and *cash cards. In the USA these cards are sometimes called **Asset cards**.

**debt** A sum owed by one person to another. In commerce, it is usual for debts to be settled within one month of receiving an invoice, after which *interest may be incurred. A long-term debt may be covered by a *bill of exchange, which can be a *negotiable instrument. *See also* debenture.

**debt adjusting** *See* ancillary credit business.

**debt collection agency** An organization that specializes in collecting the outstanding debts of its clients, charging a commission for doing so. Because of the historical stigma attached to the phrase 'debt collection', these agencies prefer to be called **commercial collection agencies**. *See also* ancillary credit business.

**debt counselling** *See* ancillary credit business.

**debt discounting** The purchase of a *debt from a trader, especially an exporter at a discount. *See* debt collection agency; forfaiting.

**debt instrument** A document used to raise a short-term loan consisting of a *promissory note, *bill of exchange, or any other legally binding *bond.

**debtor** One who owes money to another. In *balance sheets, debtors are those who owe money to the organization and a distinction has to be made between those who are expected to pay their debts during the next accounting period and those who will not pay until later.

**debt rescheduling** A negotiation concerning outstanding loans in which the debtor has repayment difficulties. The rescheduling can take the form of an entirely new loan or an extension of the existing loan repayment period, deferring interest or principal repayments. When debt rescheduling concerns less developed countries, the new agreement may involve a lowering of interest rates or an offer of an aid package of foreign investment to the country to offset some of the existing debt. In the late 1980s the major UK commercial banks wrote off or made provision for nearly £10 billion of debt to less developed countries — often Latin American countries who had simply stopped repaying their earlier loans. In the late 1980s and early 1990s a wide range of rescheduling schemes were adopted, including some in which the debt, or part of it, is converted into internal aid programmes.

**debt service ratio (DSR)** The proportion of annual export earnings needed to service a country's external debts, including both interest payments and repayment of principal. The DSR is an important statistic, indicating the severity of a country's indebtedness. The effect of *debt rescheduling programmes can be examined by comparing pre- and post-rescheduling DSRs.

**debt swap**  The exchange of an outstanding loan to a third party between one bank and another. The loans are usually to governments of third-world countries and are often expressed in the local currency.

**decimal currency**  A currency system in which the standard unit is subdivided into 100 parts. Following the example of the USA in 1792, most countries have introduced a decimal system. However, it was not until 15 February 1971 that decimalization was introduced in the UK, following the recommendations of the Halesbury Committee of 1961. The UK now has eight decimal coins, the 1p, 2p, 5p, 10p, 20p, 50p, £1 (introduced in 1983), and £2 (introduced in 1989). The ½p was introduced to ease the transition from a system based on 240 units to one based on 100 units but was abandoned in 1984.

**decision tree**  A diagram used to map the various possible courses of action that flow from a decision and the subsequent decisions that have to be made as a result of it. It consists of a series of levels at each of which the possible courses of action are represented by branches arising from decision points. It is often used in analysing financial situations and possible investments.

**declaration day**  The last day but one of an account on the London Stock Exchange, on which traditional *options must be declared, i.e. the owner of the option must state whether or not the option to purchase (call) or sell (put) the securities concerned will be exercised.

**declaration of solvency**  A declaration made by the directors of a company seeking voluntary liquidation that it will be able to pay its debts within a specified period, not exceeding 12 months from the date of the declaration. It must contain a statement of the company's assets and liabilities, and a copy must be sent to the Registrar of Companies. A director who participates in a declaration of solvency without reasonable grounds will be liable to a fine or imprisonment on conviction. *See* members' voluntary liquidation.

**decreasing term assurance**  A form of *term assurance in which the amount to be paid in the event of the death of the *life assured reduces with the passage of time. These policies are usually arranged in conjunction with a cash loan or mortgage.

**deductions at source**  A method of tax collection in which a person paying income to another deducts the tax on the income and is responsible for paying it to the authorities. Tax authorities have found that, in general, it is easier to collect tax from the payer rather than the recipient of income, especially if paying the tax is made a condition of the payer's obtaining tax relief for the payment. The payee receives a credit against the liability for the tax already suffered. Examples of this under the UK tax system are interest payments (bank, building society, government stocks, and other securities), payments under deed of covenant, trust income, sub-contractors in the building industry, mortgage interest payments (*see* Mortgage Interest Relief at Source), and rent paid to a non-resident. In these instances income tax is always deducted at the *basic rate, with the exception of discretionary and accumulation trusts in which *additional rate tax is also deducted. In addition, all employers in the UK operate the *PAYE system, which endeavours to ensure that income tax for all employees is deducted at source on a weekly or monthly basis and accounted for to the Inland Revenue.

**deed** A document that has been signed, sealed, and delivered. The seal and the delivery make it different from an ordinary written agreement. The former use of sealing wax and a signet to effect the seal is now usually replaced by using a small paper disc; delivery may now be informal, i.e. by carrying out some act to show that the deed is intended to be operative. Some transactions, such as conveyances of land, must be carried out by deed to be effective.

**deed of covenant** A legal document, which must be in a specified form, used to transfer income from one person to another with a view to making a saving in tax. It authorizes regular annual payments to be made, which must normally be at least six (except in the case of payments to charities, when it can be three). The person making the payment deducts income tax at the basic rate from the payment, in most cases obtaining tax relief on it. Any recipient who is exempt from tax (e.g. a charity) can reclaim the tax deducted. In certain cases, such as payments to charities, tax relief at higher rates may be available to the payer; this does not apply to student children.

**deed of partnership** *See* partnership.

**deed poll** A *deed having a straight edge at the top, as opposed to an indenture. A deed poll was used when only one party was involved in an action, e.g. when a person declared the wish to be known by a different name. Deeds commonly now have straight edges and are used for all purposes.

**deep-discount bond** A fixed-interest security paying little or no interest (in the latter case it may be called a *zero-coupon bond). Because it provides little or no income it is offered at a substantial discount to its *redemption value, providing a large capital gain in place of income. This may have tax advantages in certain circumstances.

**default 1.** Failure to do something that is required by law, especially failure to comply with the rules of legal procedure. **2.** Failure to comply with the terms of a contract.

**deferred annuity** An *annuity in which payments do not start at once but either at a specified later date or when the policyholder reaches a specified age.

**deferred asset** An asset the realization of which is likely to be considerably delayed. An example might be a payment of *advance corporation tax (ACT), which can be used to offset a future payment of *corporation tax. If there is no possibility of a liability to corporation tax in the near future, the ACT is a deferred asset rather than an actual asset.

**deferred coupon note** A bond on which no interest is paid until after a set date. In the USA such bonds are called **deferred interest bonds**.

**deferred liability** A prospective liability that will only become a definite liability if some future event occurs. *See also* contingent liability.

**deferred ordinary share 1.** A type of ordinary share, formerly often issued to founder members of a company, in which dividends are only paid after all other types of ordinary share have been paid. They often entitle their owners to a large share of the profit. **2.** A type of share on which little or no dividend is paid for a fixed number of years, after which it ranks with other ordinary shares for dividend.

**deferred-payment agreement** *See* hire purchase.

**deferred taxation** A sum set aside for tax in the *accounts of an organization that will become payable in a period other than that under review. It arises because of timing differences between tax rules and accounting conventions. The principle of **deferred-tax accounting** is to re-allocate a tax payment to the same period as that in which the relevant amount of income or expenditure is shown. Historically, the timing difference has arisen in company accounts because the percentages used for the calculation of capital allowances have differed from those used for depreciation.

**deficit financing** The creation of a government *budget deficit for the purpose of influencing economic activity.

**deflation** A general fall in the price level; the opposite of *inflation. As with inflation, a general change in the price level should, in theory, have no real effect. However, if traders are holding goods whose prices fall, they may suffer such large losses that they are forced into bankruptcy. However, agents holding money are simultaneously better off, although there may be a lag in increasing expenditure, during which a *recession may occur. The only major deflation in this century occurred during the Great Depression in the 1920s and 1930s. Since then, governments have avoided deflation wherever possible. *See also* disinflation.

**degearing** The process in which some of the fixed-interest loan stock of a company is replaced by *ordinary share capital. *See* capital gearing.

**delivery date** **1.** The day in the month that commodities on a futures contract have to be delivered. **2.** The maturity date for foreign exchange in a forward exchange contract. **3.** The date that a buyer of securities receives the relevant certificates.

**delivery month** The month in which commodities on a futures contract must be handed over to the buyer. A month is specified but usually any day within that month will fulfil the contract obligations.

**delta stocks** The least liquid stocks on the London Stock Exchange, whose prices did not have to be displayed under the former classification system. This system has now been replaced by *Normal Market Size. *See also* alpha stocks.

**demand deposit** An instant-access current account (or check account) in the USA; normally defined as one in which funds are payable within 30 days. Bank demand deposit drafts are negotiable. In the UK it is called a *sight deposit.

**demand for money** The existence of a stable demand for money has been the core of *monetarism. If this is accepted, it can be shown that *fiscal policy is neutral, i.e. when government expenditure pushes up interest rates, private investment is reduced accordingly. Furthermore, changes in the supply of money are a necessary and sufficient condition for changes in the nominal value of the *gross domestic product or for inflation. However, econometric evidence has failed to establish whether or not the demand for money is, in fact, stable.

**demand-pull inflation** A rise in prices caused by an excess of demand over supply in the economy as a whole. When the labour force and all resources are fully employed extra demand will only disappear as a result of rising prices. Popular in the 1960s and 1970s as a 'Keynesian theory' of *inflation, it lost support to monetarist theories of inflation in the 1980s. *See also* cost-push inflation; quantity theory of money.

**denomination   1.** The face value of a security, i.e. the sum to be paid on its redemption.   **2.** The act of nominating a currency in which an international transaction is to take place.

**Department of Trade and Industry** The UK government department responsible for: international trade policy; the promotion of exports (under the direction of the British Overseas Trade Board); industrial policy; competition policy and consumer protection, including relations with the *Office of Fair Trading and the *Monopolies and Mergers Commission; policy on scientific research and development; company legislation and the Companies Registration Office; patents and the *Patent Office; the insolvency service; and the regulation of the insurance industry.

**deposit   1.** A sum of money paid by a buyer as part of the sale price of something in order to reserve it. Depending on the terms agreed, the deposit may or may not be returned if the sale is not completed.   **2.** A sum of money left with an organization, such as a bank, for safekeeping or to earn interest or with a broker, dealer, etc., as a security to cover any trading losses incurred. **3.** A sum of money paid as the first instalment on a *hire-purchase agreement. It is usually paid when the buyer takes possession of the goods.

**deposit account (DA)** An *account with a bank from which money cannot be withdrawn by cheque (*compare* cheque account). The interest paid will depend on the current rate of interest and the notice required by the bank before money can be withdrawn, but it will always be higher than that on a *current account. Tax on the interest is normally deducted at source, but it can be paid net of tax for overseas and business customers.

**deposit bonds** National Savings Deposit Bonds, introduced by the Department for *National Savings in 1983 and withdrawn from sale in 1989, offering a premium rate of interest on lump sums between £100 and £100,000. The bonds will continue to earn interest until the tenth anniversary of their purchase; interest is taxable, but not deducted at source.

**deposit insurance** Protection against loss of deposits by a customer, in case a bank or other financial institution fails. In the UK, depositors are protected by the **Deposit Protection Fund** up to a specified percentage of their deposits. In the USA, the *Federal Deposit Insurance Corporation provides similar protection, through the Bank Insurance Fund.

**deposit-taking institution** An institution whose main function is to take deposits. This is the basis of the legal definition of a bank as laid down in the *Banking Acts 1979 and 1987. In the UK deposit-taking institutions are regulated by the Bank of England.

**depreciation   1.** An amount charged to the *profit and loss account of an organization to represent the wearing out or diminution in value of an asset. The amount charged is normally based on a percentage of the value of the asset as shown in the books; however, the way in which the percentage is used reflects different views of depreciation. **Straight-line depreciation** allocates a given percentage of the cost of the asset each year, thus suggesting an even spread of the cost of the asset over its useful life. **Reducing- (or diminishing-) balance depreciation** applies a constant percentage reduction first to the cost of the asset and subsequently to the cost as reduced by previous depreciations. In this way reducing amounts are charged periodically to the profit and loss account; by this method the depreciated value of the asset in the balance sheet may approximate more closely to its true value. *See also* accumulated depreciation.   **2.** A fall in the value of a currency with a *floating exchange rate relative to another. Depreciation can refer both to day-to-day movements and to long-term realignments in value. For currencies with a *fixed exchange rate a *devaluation or *revaluation of currency is required to change the relative value. *Compare* appreciation.

**depression**   *See* recession.

**deregulation**   The removal of controls imposed by governments on the operation of markets. Many economists and politicians believe that during this century governments have imposed controls over markets that have little or no justification. However, most economists still argue that certain markets should be regulated (*see* regulation), particularly if a monopoly is involved.

**derivative instrument (derivative)**   A financial instrument that is valued according to the expected price movements of an underlying asset, which may be a commodity, a currency, or a security. Derivatives can be used either to hedge a position or to establish a synthetic open position. Examples of derivatives are futures, warrants, options, swaps, etc.

**derivative market**   A futures or options market derived from a cash market. For example, the market in traded options or equities which are bought and sold on the *London International Financial Futures and Options Exchange is a derivative market of the *London Stock Exchange.

**designated order turn-around (DOT)**   An electronic system on the New York Stock Exchange that enables members to place orders to buy or sell stocks within a specified range of prices for automatic execution.

**Deutsche Aktienindex (Dax)**   A share index on the Frankfurt Stock Exchange. Introduced in mid-1988, it was the first real-time German index of 30 leading stocks.

**Deutsche Terminbörse**   A futures and options exchange based in Frankfurt. It opened in 1990 and trades in *financial futures and stock options.

**Deutschmark**   (DM) The standard monetary unit of Germany, divided into 100 pfennige.

**devaluation**   A fall in the value of a currency relative to gold or to other currencies. Governments engage in devaluation when they feel that their currency has become overvalued, for example through high rates of inflation making exports uncompetitive or because of a substantially adverse *balance of trade. The intention is that devaluation will make exports cheaper and imports dearer, although the loss of confidence in an economy forced to devalue invariably has an adverse effect. Devaluation is a measure that need only concern governments with a *fixed exchange rate for their currency. With a *floating exchange rate, devaluation or revaluation takes place continuously and automatically (*see* depreciation; realignment; revaluation of currency).

**dilution of equity**   An increase in the number of ordinary shares in a company without a corresponding increase in its assets or profitability. The result is a fall in the value of the shares as a result of this dilution.

**diminishing-balance depreciation**  *See* depreciation.

**dinar  1.** (DA) The standard monetary unit of Algeria, divided into 100 centimes.  **2.** The standard monetary unit of Bahrain (BD), Iraq (ID), Jordan (JD), Kuwait (KD), and Yemen (YD), divided into 1000 fils.  **3.** (TD) The standard monetary unit of Tunisia, divided into 1000 millimes.  **4.** (Din.) The standard monetary unit of Yugoslavia and Croatia, divided into 100 paras.  **5.** (LD) The standard monetary unit of Libya, divided into 1000 dirhams.  **6.** An Iranian monetary unit, worth one hundredth of a *rial.

**direct debit**  A form of *standing order given to a bank by an account holder to pay regular amounts from a cheque account to a third party. Unlike a normal standing order, however, the amount to be paid is not specified; the account holder trusts the third party to claim an appropriate sum from the bank. The amount to be paid can be varied. In the USA this arrangement is known as **reverse wire transfer**.

**direct investment**  The investment by some US banks in the equity of certain kinds of company, e.g. real estate and property development. Savings and loans companies suffered heavy losses and failures in the late 1980s as a result of such direct investments. National banks are prohibited from making direct investments and many other institutions are now wary of doing so.

**directive  1.** An instruction to carry out certain money-market operations, particularly instructions given by the US *Federal Reserve System.  **2.** A legislative decision by the European Community's Council of Ministers and Parliament, which is binding on member states but allows them to decide how to enact the required legislation.

**director**  A person appointed to carry out the day-to-day management of a company. A public company must have at least two directors, a private company at least one. The directors of a company, collectively known as the **board of directors**, usually act together, although power may be conferred (by the articles of association) on one or more directors to exercise executive powers; in particular there is often a **managing director** with considerable executive power.
    Directors may be discharged from office by an ordinary resolution with special notice at a general meeting, whether or not they have a *service contract in force. They may be disqualified for *fraudulent trading or *wrongful trading or for any conduct that makes them unfit to manage the company.
    Directors' remuneration consists of a salary and in some cases **directors' fees**, paid to them for being a director, and an expense allowance to cover their expenses incurred in the service of the company. Directors' remuneration must be disclosed in the company's accounts and shown separately from any pension payments or *compensation for loss of office.

**directors' report**  An annual report by the directors of a company to its shareholders, which forms part of the company's *accounts required to be filed with the Registrar of Companies under the Companies Act 1985. The information that must be given includes the principal activities of the company, a fair review of the developments and position of the business with likely future developments, details of research and development, significant issues on the sale, purchase, or valuation of assets, recommended dividends, transfers to reserves, names of the directors and their interests in the company during the period, employee statistics, and any political or charitable gifts made during the period. *See also* medium-sized company; small company.

**direct participation program (DPP)** A US investment plan enabling investors to make tax benefits; the investments are in real estate, oil, gas, and agriculture but exclude real-estate investment trusts.

**direct placing** A *placing of shares in a company direct to investors, without recourse to underwriters to back the deal or to public subscription.

**direct quotation** The quotation of a rate of exchange of currency based on a single unit of the home currency, e.g. £1 = $1.75.

**direct taxation** Taxation, the effect of which is intended to be borne by the person or organization that pays it. Economists distinguish between direct taxation and indirect taxation. The former is best illustrated by *income tax, in which the person who receives the income pays the tax, thereby suffering a reduction in income. The latter is illustrated by *VAT, in which the tax is paid by traders but the effects are borne by the consumers who buy the trader's goods. In practice these distinctions are rarely clear-cut. Corporation tax is a direct tax but there is evidence that its incidence can be shifted to consumers by higher prices or to employees by lower wages. Inheritance tax could also be thought of as a direct tax on the deceased, although its incidence falls on the heirs of the estate.

**dirham 1.** (DH) The standard monetary unit of Morocco, divided into 100 centimes. **2.** (Dh) The standard monetary unit of the United Arab Emirates, divided into 100 fils. **3.** A Qatari monetary unit, worth one hundredth of a *riyal. **4.** A Libyan monetary unit, worth one thousandth of a *dinar.

**dirty float** A technique for managing the exchange rate in which a government publicly renounces direct intervention in the foreign exchange markets while continuing to engage in intervention surreptitiously. This technique was widely used after the collapse of the Bretton Woods fixed exchange rate system in the early 1970s as governments were unable to agree programmes of explicitly managed floating, but were not prepared to accept fully floating rates.

**disbursement** A payment made by a professional person, such as a solicitor or banker, on behalf of a client. This is claimed back when the client receives an account for the professional services.

**discharge** To release a person from a binding legal obligation by agreement, by the performance of an obligation, or by law. For example, the payment of a debt discharges the debt; similarly, a judicial decision that a contract is frustrated discharges the parties from performing it.

**discount 1.** A deduction from a *bill of exchange when it is purchased before its maturity date. The party that purchases (discounts) the bill pays less than its face value and therefore makes a profit when it matures. The amount of the discount consists of interest calculated at the *bill rate for the length of time that the bill has to run. *See* discount market. **2.** A reduction in the price of goods below list price, for buyers who pay cash (**cash discount**), for members of the trade (**trade discount**), for buying in bulk (**bulk** or **quantity discount**), etc. **3.** The amount by which the market price of a security is below its *par value. A

£100 par value loan stock with a market price of £95 is said to be at a 5% discount.

**discount broker**   *See* bill broker.

**discounted cash flow (DCF)**   A method of appraising capital-investment projects by comparing their income in the future and their present and future costs with the current equivalents. The current equivalents take account of the fact that future receipts are less valuable than current receipts, in that interest can be earned on current receipts; on the other hand future payments are less onerous than current payments, as interest can be earned on money retained for future payments. Accordingly, future receipts and payments are discounted to their present values by applying **discount factors**, taking account of interest that could be earned for the relevant number of years to the date of payment or receipt. *See also* net present value.

**discount factor**   *See* discounted cash flow.

**discount house**   **1.** A shop open to members of the public, or in some cases to members of a trade, that sells goods, usually consumer durables, at prices that are close to wholesale prices.   **2.** A company or bank on the *discount market that specializes in discounting *bills of exchange, especially *Treasury bills.

**discounting back**   Reducing a future payment or receipt to its present equivalent by taking account of the interest, which when added to the present equivalent for the relevant number of years would equate to the future payment or receipt. *See also* discounted cash flow.

**discount market**   The part of the *money market consisting of banks, *discount houses, and *bill brokers. By borrowing money at short notice from commercial banks or discount houses, bill brokers are able to *discount bills of exchange, especially Treasury bills, and make a profit. The loans are secured on unmatured bills.

**discount market deposit**   A short-term deposit made with a *discount house, usually by a *clearing bank, earning a rate of interest known as the **discount market deposit rate**. These deposits provide the discount houses with their main source of funds.

**discount rate**   **1.** *See* bill rate.   **2.** The rate of interest charged by the US Federal Reserve Banks when lending to other banks.

**discount window**   A method by which a central bank supplies a banking system with short-term funds, either by purchasing *Treasury bills or by making secured loans. The term arose in the USA when banks with insufficient funds sent a cashier to the counter window of the Federal Reserve Bank to ask for additional money.

**discretionary account (DA)**   An account placed with a stockbroker, securities house, or commodity broker in which the broker is empowered to carry out transactions on this account without referring back for approval to the principal. Principals normally set parameters for their accounts, but with a discretionary account the broker has more discretion, only reporting back on purchases, sales, profits and losses, and the value of the portfolio.

**discretionary order  1.** An order given to a stockbroker, commodity broker, etc., to buy or sell a stated quantity of specified securities or commodities, leaving the broker discretion to deal at the best price.  **2.** A similar order given to a stockbroker in which the sum of money is specified but the broker has discretion as to which security to buy.

**discretionary trust**  A trust in which the shares of each beneficiary are not fixed by the settlor in the trust deed but may be varied at the discretion of some person or persons (often the trustees). In an **exhaustive discretionary trust** all the income arising in any year must be paid out during that year, although no beneficiary has a right to any specific sum. In a **nonexhaustive discretionary trust** (or **accumulation trust**), income may be carried forward to subsequent years and no beneficiary need receive anything. Such trusts are useful when the needs of the beneficiaries are likely to change, for example when they are children.

**dishonour  1.** To fail to accept (*see* acceptance) a *bill of exchange (**dishonour by non-acceptance**) or to fail to pay a bill of exchange (**dishonour by non-payment**). A dishonoured foreign bill must be protested (*see* protest). **2.** To fail to pay a cheque when the account of the drawer does not have sufficient funds to cover it. When a bank dishonours a cheque it marks it 'refer to drawer' and returns it to the payee through his or her bank.

**disinflation**  A gentle form of *deflation, to restrain *inflation without creating unemployment. Disinflationary measures include restricting consumer spending by raising the *interest rate, imposing restrictions on *hire-purchase agreements, and introducing price controls on commodities in short supply.

**disintermediation**  The elimination of financial intermediaries, such as brokers and bankers, from transactions between borrowers and lenders or buyers and sellers in financial markets. An example of disintermediation is the *securitization of debt. Disintermediation has been a consequence of improved technology and *deregulation (*see also* globalization). Disintermediation allows both parties to a financial transaction to reduce costs by eliminating payments of commissions and fees. Disintermediation often occurs when governments attempt to impose direct controls on the banking system, such as reserve asset ratios and lending ceilings. In response, the market develops new instruments and institutions that are not covered by the direct controls. When these controls are relaxed, funds may return to the normal banking system, i.e. there may be **reintermediation**.

**disposable income  1.** The income a person has available to spend after payment of taxes, National Insurance contributions, and other deductions, such as pension contributions.  **2.** In *national income accounts, the total value of income of individuals and households available for consumer expenditure and savings, after deducting income tax, National Insurance contributions, and remittances overseas.

**distributable profits**  The profits of a company that are legally available for distribution as *dividends. They consist of a company's accumulated realized profits after deducting all realized losses, except for any part of these net realized profits that have been previously distributed or capitalized. *Public companies, however, may not distribute profits to such an extent that their net assets are reduced to less than the sum of their called-up capital (*see* share capital) and their undistributable reserves (*see* capital reserves).

**distributable reserves**  The retained profits of a company that it may legally distribute by way of *dividends. *See* distributable profits.

**distribution**  **1.** A payment by a company from its *distributable profits, usually by means of a *dividend.  **2.** A dividend or quasi-dividend on which *advance corporation tax is payable. For UK tax purposes a distribution includes, in addition to dividends, any payment, whether in cash or kind, out of the assets of a company in respect of shares of that company, except repayments of capital.  **3.** The allocation of goods to consumers by means of wholesalers and retailers.  **4.** The division of property and assets according to law, e.g. of a bankrupt person or a deceased person.

**divergence indicator**  The amount by which individual national currencies of member states of the European Community are allowed to move away from the agreed central parity of these currencies in relation to each other and to the *European Currency Unit.

**diversification**  **1.** The spreading of an investment portfolio over a wide range of companies to avoid serious losses if a recession is localized to one sector of the market.  **2.** The movement of a manufacturer, trader, etc., into a wider field of products or services.

**dividend**  The distribution of part of the earnings of a company to its shareholders. The dividend is normally expressed as an amount per share on the *par value of the share. Thus a 15% dividend on a £1 share will pay 15p. However, investors are usually more interested in the **dividend yield**, i.e. the dividend expressed as a percentage of the share value; thus if the market value of these £1 shares is now £5, the dividend yield would be $1/5 \times 15\% = 3\%$. The size of the dividend payment is determined by the board of directors of a company, who must decide how much to pay out to shareholders and how much to retain in the business; these amounts may vary from year to year. In the UK it is usual for companies to pay a dividend every six months, the largest portion (the **final dividend**) being announced at the company's AGM together with the annual financial results. A smaller **interim dividend** usually accompanies the interim statement of the company's affairs, six months before the AGM. Dividends are paid by *dividend warrant. In the USA dividends are usually paid quarterly by **dividend check**. *See also* dividend cover; yield.
     Interest payments on *gilt-edged securities are also sometimes called dividends although they are fixed.

**dividend check**  *See* dividend.

**dividend cover**  The number of times a company's *dividends to ordinary shareholders could be paid out of its *net profits after tax in the same period. For example, a net dividend of £400,000 paid by a company showing a net profit of £1M is said to be covered 2½ times. Dividend cover is a measure of the probability that dividend payments will be sustained (low cover might make it difficult to pay the same level of dividends in a bad year's trading) and of a company's commitment to investment and growth (high cover implies that the company retains its earnings for investment in the business). Negative dividend cover is unusual, and is taken as a sign that a company is in difficulties. In the USA, the dividend cover is expressed as the **pay-out ratio**, the total dividends paid as a percentage of the net profit. *See also* price–dividend ratio.

**dividend equalization reserve** A reserve formerly created to smooth out fluctuations in the incidence of taxation so that dividends could be maintained. Such reserves are now normally referred to as **deferred-tax accounts** (*see* deferred taxation).

**dividend limitation (dividend restraint)** An economic policy in which the dividends a company can pay to its shareholders are limited by government order. It is usually part of a *prices and income policy to defeat *inflation, providing a political counterpart to a wage freeze.

**dividend mandate** A document in which a shareholder of a company notifies the company to whom dividends are to be paid.

**dividend stripping (bond washing)** The practice of buying *gilt-edged securities after they have gone ex-dividend (*see* ex-) and selling them cum-dividend just before the next dividend is due. This procedure enables the investor to avoid receiving dividends, which in the UK are taxable as income, and to make a tax-free *capital gain. This activity has mainly been indulged in by high-rate taxpayers but has now become of little interest since the rules regulating the taxation of accrued interest were changed.

**dividend waiver** A decision by a major shareholder in a company not to take a dividend, usually because the company cannot afford to pay it.

**dividend warrant** The cheque issued by a company to its shareholders when paying *dividends. It states the tax deducted (*see* advance corporation tax) and the net amount paid. This document must be sent by non-taxpayers to the Inland Revenue when claiming back the tax.

**dividend yield** *See* dividend.

**dobra** (Db) The standard monetary unit of São Tomé e Príncipe, divided into 100 centavos.

**documentary bill** A *bill of exchange attached to the shipping documents of a parcel of goods. These documents include the bill of lading, insurance policy, dock warrant, invoice, etc.

**documentary credit** *See* letter of credit.

**documents against acceptance (D/A)** A method of payment for goods that have been exported in which the exporter sends the shipping documents with a *bill of exchange to a bank or agent at the port of destination. The bank or agent releases the goods when the bill has been accepted by the consignee. *Compare* cash against documents.

**documents against presentation (D/P)** *See* cash against documents.

**dollar** The standard monetary unit of Antigua and Barbuda (EC$), Australia ($A), Bahamas (B$), Barbados (BDS$), Belize (BZ$), Bermuda (Bd$), the British Virgin Islands (US$), Brunei (B$), Canada (Can$), Cayman Islands (CI$), Dominica (EC$), Fiji (F$), Grenada (EC$), Guam (US$), Guyana (G$), Hong Kong (HK$), Jamaica (J$), Kiribati ($A), Liberia (L$), Micronesia (US$), New Zealand ($NZ), Puerto Rico (US$), Saint Kitts and Nevis (EC$), Singapore (S$), the Solomon Islands (SI$), Taiwan (NT$), Trinidad and Tobago (TT$), Tuvalu ($A), the USA (US$), the Virgin Islands (US$), and Zimbabwe (Z$), in all cases divided into 100 cents.

**dollar-cost averaging** *See* constant-dollar plan.

**dollar pool**  The fund of dollars and other currencies held to enable UK residents to buy foreign securities, domestic property, etc. It was abolished in 1979 when UK exchange control was abandoned.

**dollar stocks**  US or Canadian securities.

**domicile (domicil)**  **1.** The country or place of a person's permanent home, which may differ from that person's nationality or place of *residence. Domicile is determined by both the physical fact of residence and the continued intention of remaining there. For example, a citizen of a foreign country who is resident in the UK is not necessarily domiciled there unless there is a clear intention to make the UK a permanent home. Under the common law, it is domicile and not residence or nationality that determines a person's civil status, including the capacity to marry. A corporation may also have a domicile, which is determined by its place of registration.  **2.** In banking, an account is said to be domiciled at a particular branch and the customer treats that branch as his or her main banking contact. Customers may be charged for using other branches as if they were their own. Computer technology, however, now allows customers to use many branches as if their account was domiciled there.

**dông**  (D) The standard monetary unit of Vietnam, divided into 10 hao, or 100 xu, or 1000 trinh.

**DOT**  Abbreviation for *designated order turn-around.

**double auction**  A method of trading in certain *commodity markets in which open outcry (*see* callover) is used. Buyers and sellers shout out the prices at which they are willing to trade. If a buyer and a seller shout out the same price a deal is concluded and subsequently confirmed by written contract.

**double option**  A combination of a put *option and a call option. *See* butterfly; straddle.

**double taxation**  Taxation that falls on the same source of income in more than one country. Taxation is normally levied on a person's worldwide income in the country of residence but, in addition, most countries also levy a charge on income that arises within that country whether it is from interest or a business. As a result a large number of treaties (**double-taxation agreements**) have been concluded between countries to ensure that their own residents are not doubly taxed. The agreements also attempt to cover fiscal evasion.

As a result there are several different kinds of relief from double taxation available:

(i) relief by agreement, providing for exemption, in whole or in part, of certain categories of income;

(ii) credit agreement, in which tax charged in one country is allowed as a credit in the other;

(iii) deduction agreement, in which the overseas income is reduced by the foreign tax paid on it;

(iv) if there is no agreement the UK tax authorities will allow the foreign tax paid as a credit up to the amount of the corresponding UK liability.

*See* unilateral relief.

**Dow Jones Industrial Average**  An index of security prices issued by Dow Jones & Co. (a US firm providing financial information), used on the New York Stock Exchange. It is a narrowly based index, comparable to the London Financial Times Ordinary Share Index (*see* Financial Times Share Indexes), having 30 constituent companies. The index was founded in 1884, based then on 11 stocks (mostly in railways), but was reorganized in 1928 when it was given the value of 100. Its lowest point was on 2 July 1932, when it reached 41. In 1987 it exceeded 2400. There are three other Dow Jones indexes, representing price movements in US home bonds, transportation stocks, and utilities. *Compare* Standard and Poor's 500 Stock Index.

**downstream** **1.** To borrow funds for use by a subsidiary company at the better rates appropriate to the parent company, which would not have been available to the subsidiary company. *Compare* upstream. **2.** Denoting the respondent bank (**downstream bank**) in an arrangement with a *correspondent bank.

**D/P** Abbreviation for documents against presentation. *See* cash against documents.

**DPP** Abbreviation for *direct participation program.

**drachma** (Dr) The standard monetary unit of Greece, divided into 100 lepta.

**draft** **1.** *See* bank draft. **2.** Any order in writing to pay a specified sum, e.g. a *bill of exchange. **3.** A preliminary version of a document, before it has been finalized.

**dragon markets** A colloquial name for the emerging markets and economies in the Pacific basin, including Indonesia, Malaysia, the Philippines, and Thailand. They are characterized by dynamic growth and high savings ratios.

**drawdown** **1.** The drawing of funds against a *line of credit, often a *eurocredit. *See also* flexible drawdown. **2.** The movement of a customer's funds from one account to another account, which may be in another bank.

**drawee** **1.** The person on whom a *bill of exchange is drawn (i.e. to whom it is addressed). The drawee will accept it (*see* acceptance) and pay it on maturity. **2.** The bank on whom a cheque is drawn, i.e. the bank holding the account of the individual or company that wrote it. **3.** The bank named in a *bank draft. *Compare* drawer.

**drawer** **1.** A person who signs a *bill of exchange ordering the *drawee to pay the specified sum at the specified time. **2.** A person who signs a cheque ordering the drawee bank to pay a specified sum of money on demand.

**drawing rights** *See* Special Drawing Rights.

**drip-feed** To fund a new company in stages rather than by making a large capital sum available at the start.

**drop-dead fee** A fee paid by an individual or company that is bidding for another company to the organization lending the money required to finance the bid. The fee is only paid if the bid fails and the loan is not required. Thus, for the price of the drop-dead fee, the bidder ensures that the interest charges are only incurred if the money is required.

**drop lock** A new form of issue in the bond market that combines the benefits of a bank loan with the benefits of a bond. The borrower arranges a variable-rate bank loan on the understanding that if long-term interest rates fall to a specified level, the bank loan will be automatically refinanced by a placing of fixed-rate long-term bonds with a group of institutions. They are most commonly used on the international market.

**DSR** Abbreviation for *debt service ratio.

**DTB** Abbreviation for *Deutsche Terminbörse.

**dual-capacity system** A system of trading on a stock exchange in which the functions of *stockjobber and *stockbroker are carried out by separate firms. In a **single-capacity system** the two functions can be combined by firms known as *market makers. Dual capacity existed on the *London Stock Exchange prior to October 1986 (see Big Bang), since when a single-capacity system has been introduced, bringing London into line with most foreign international stock markets. The major advantage of single capacity is that it cuts down on the costs to the investor, although it can also create more opportunity for unfair dealing (see Chinese wall).

**due date** The date on which a debt is due to be settled, such as the maturity date of a *bill of exchange.

**EAGGF**  Abbreviation for *European Agricultural Guidance and Guarantee Fund.

**early bargains**  *See* after-hours deals.

**earned income**  Income generally acquired by the personal exertion of the taxpayer as distinct from such passive income as dividends from investments. It is often thought by tax theorists that earned income should be taxed at a lower rate than unearned income, since the latter accrues without the expenditure of the taxpayer's time and effort. This has been reflected in different ways in the UK over the years, with such measures as earned-income relief, wife's earned-income relief, and investment-income surcharge. Earned income consists primarily of wages and salaries, business profits, royalties, and some pensions. There are currently no differences in the UK between the rates of taxation for earned and unearned income. *See* income-tax allowances.

**earnings per share (eps)**  The earnings of a company over a stated period (usually one year) divided by the number of ordinary shares issued by the company. The earnings (sometimes called **available earnings**) are calculated as annual profits, after allowing for tax and any exceptional items. **Fully diluted earnings per share** include any shares that the company is committed to issuing but has not yet issued (e.g. through *convertibles). *See also* price–earnings ratio.

**earnings-related pension**  *See* pension; State Earnings-Related Pension Scheme.

**earnings yield**  *See* yield.

**easy money**  *See* cheap money.

**EC**  Abbreviation for *European Community.

**ECGD**  Abbreviation for *Export Credits Guarantee Department.

**ECP**  Abbreviation for *euro-commercial paper.

**ECU**  Abbreviation for *European Currency Unit.

**EDF**  Abbreviation for *European Development Fund.

**EDI**  Abbreviation for *electronic data interchange.

**EDSP**  Abbreviation for Exchange Delivery Settlement Price. *See* settlement price.

**EEC**  Abbreviation for *European Economic Community.

**EFTA**  Abbreviation for *European Free Trade Association.

**EIB** Abbreviation for *European Investment Bank.

**electronic data interchange (EDI)** The exchange by electronic means between banks and their customers and between suppliers and purchasers in industry of invoices, payment instructions, and funds.

**electronic funds transfer at point of sale (EFTPOS)** The automatic debiting of a purchase price from the customer's bank or credit-card account by a computer link between the checkout till and the bank or credit-card company. The system is used in the UK by most large reputable UK retailers and also operates in Scandinavia and many parts of Europe. The system depends on a magnetic strip on the customer's plastic card which is 'wiped' through a terminal reader machine at the point of sale. This gives authorization and prints a voucher for the customer to sign. Transfer of funds to the retailer can take place within 48 hours.

**electronic transfer of funds (ETF)** The transfer of money from one bank account to another by means of computers and communications links. Banks routinely transfer funds between accounts using computers; another variety of ETF is the telebanking service enabling the Viewdata network to be used for banking in a customer's home. In the USA, the Electronic Transfer of Funds Act 1978 limits customer liability for unauthorized transfers to $50M. *See also* electronic funds transfer at point of sale.

**eligibility** Criteria that determine which bills the Bank of England will discount, as *lender of last resort. Such bills, known as *eligible paper, include Treasury bills, short-dated gilts, and first-class trade bills.

**eligible list** A listing of the names of banks entitled to discount acceptances at the Bank of England.

**eligible paper** **1.** Treasury bills, short-dated gilts, and any first-class security, accepted by a British bank or an accepting house and thus acceptable by the Bank of England for rediscounting, or as security for loans to discount houses. The Bank of England's classification of eligible paper influences portfolios because of the ability to turn them into quick cash, and thus reinforces the Bank's role as *lender of last resort. **2.** Acceptances by US banks available for rediscounting by the *Federal Reserve System.

**eligible reserves** Cash held in a US bank plus the money held in its name at its local Federal Reserve Bank.

**EMA** Abbreviation for *European Monetary Agreement.

**EMCOF** Abbreviation for *European Monetary Cooperation Fund.

**employee buyout** The acquisition of a controlling interest in the equity of a company by its employees. This may occur if the company is threatened with closure and the employees wish to secure their jobs. By obtaining financial backing, the employees acting as a group of individuals, or by means of a trust, can acquire a majority of the shares by offering existing shareholders more than their *break-up value.

**employee participation** **1.** The encouragement of motivation in a workforce by giving shares in the company to employees. Employee shareholding (*see* employee share-ownership plan) is now an important factor in improving industrial relations. **2.** The appointment to a board of directors of a representative of the employees of a company, to enable the employees to take part in the direction of the company.

**Employee Retirement Income Security Act 1974 (ERISA)** US legislation setting guidelines for the running of private pension plans and employee profit-sharing schemes. The act also set up an insurance fund, the Pension Benefit Guaranty Corporation, to protect employees' contributions if the scheme failed or ended before its term.

**employee share-ownership plan (ESOP)** A method of giving employees shares in the business for which they work. Various such plans came into existence in the UK after their announcement in 1989; in 1990, in order to encourage their growth, company owners were given *roll-over relief from capital-gains tax for sales of shares through ESOPs.

**EMS** Abbreviation for *European Monetary System.

**EMU** Abbreviation for *European Monetary Union.

**endorsement (indorsement)** **1.** A signature on the back of a *bill of exchange or cheque, making it payable to the person who signed it. A bill can be endorsed any number of times, the presumption being that the endorsements were made in the order in which they appear, the last named being the holder to receive payment. If the bill is **blank endorsed**, i.e. no endorsee is named, it is payable to the bearer. In the case of a **restrictive endorsement** of the form 'Pay X only', it ceases to be a *negotiable instrument. A **special endorsement**, when the endorsee is specified, becomes payable **to order**, which is short for 'in obedience to the order of'. **2.** A signature required on a document to make it valid in law. **3.** An amendment to an *insurance policy or cover note, recording a change in the conditions of the insurance.

**endowment assurance** An assurance policy that pays a specified amount of money on an agreed date or on the death of the *life assured, whichever is the earlier. As these policies guarantee to make a payment (either on death or on matrimony) they offer both life cover and a reasonable investment. A *with-profits policy will also provide bonuses in addition to the sum assured. These policies are often used in the repayment of a personal *mortgage or as a form of saving, although they lost their tax relief on premiums in the Finance Act 1984.

**endowment mortgage** *See* mortgage.

**entrepreneur** An individual who undertakes (from the French *entreprendre* to undertake) to supply a good or service to the market for profit. The entrepreneur will usually invest capital in the business and take on the risks associated with the investment. In most modern capitalist economies the initiative of entrepreneurs is regarded as an important element in creating a society's wealth; governments are therefore encouraged to establish conditions in which they will thrive.

**EOE** Abbreviation for *European Options Exchange.

**EPP** Abbreviation for *executive pension plan.

**eps** Abbreviation for *earnings per share.

**EPU** Abbreviation for *European Payments Union.

**equitable interest**  An interest in, or ownership of, property that is recognized by equity but not by the common law. A beneficiary under a trust has an equitable interest. Any disposal of an equitable interest (e.g. a sale) must be in writing. Some equitable interests in land must be registered or they will be lost if the legal title to the land is sold. Similarly, equitable interests in other property will be lost if the legal title is sold to a bona fide purchaser for value who has no notice of the equitable interest. In such circumstances the owner of the equitable interest may claim damages from the person who sold the legal title.

**equities**  The ordinary shares of a company, especially those of a publicly owned quoted company. In the event of a liquidation, the ordinary shareholders are entitled to share out the asssets remaining after all other creditors (including holders of *preference shares) have been paid out. Investment in equities on a stock exchange represents the best opportunity for capital growth, although there is a high element of risk as only a small proportion (if any) of the investment is secured. Although equities pay relatively low profit-related dividends, unlike *fixed-interest securities, they are popular in times of low interest rates or inflation, as they tend to rise in value as the value of money falls.

**equity**  **1.** A beneficial interest in an asset. For example, a person having a house worth £100,000 with a mortgage of £20,000 may be said to have an equity of £80,000 in the house.  **2.** The net assets of a company after all creditors (including the holders of *preference shares) have been paid off.  **3.** The amount of money returned to a borrower in a mortgage or hire-purchase agreement, after the sale of the specified asset and the full repayment of the lender of the money.  **4.** The ordinary share capital of a company (*see* equities; equity capital).

**equity accounting**  The practice of showing in a company's accounts a share of the undistributed profits of another company in which it holds a share of the *equity (usually a share of between 20% and 50%). The share of profit shown by the equity-holding company is usually equal to its share of the equity in the other company. Although none of the profit may actually be paid over, the company has a right to this share of the undistributed profit.

**equity capital**  The part of the share capital of a company owned by ordinary shareholders, although for certain purposes, such as *pre-emption rights, other classes of shareholders may be deemed to share in the equity capital and therefore be entitled to share in the profits of the company or any surplus assets on winding up. *See also* A shares.

**equity dilution**  A reduction in the percentage of the *equity owned by a shareholder as a result of a new issue of shares in the company, which rank equally with the existing voting shares.

**equity gearing**  *See* capital gearing.

**equity-linked policy**  An insurance or assurance policy in which a proportion of the premiums paid are invested in equities. The surrender value of the policy is therefore the selling price of the equities purchased; as more premiums are paid the portfolio gets larger. Although investment returns may be considerably better on this type of policy than on a traditional endowment policy, the risk is greater, as the price of equities can fall dramatically reducing the value of the policy. With *unit-linked policies, a much wider range of investments can be achieved and the risk is correspondingly reduced.

**ERDF** Abbreviation for *European Regional Development Fund.

**ERISA** Abbreviation for *Employee Retirement Income Security Act 1974.

**ERM** Abbreviation for Exchange Rate Mechanism. *See* European Monetary System.

**escrow** A *deed that has been signed and sealed but is delivered on the condition that it will not become operative until some stated event happens. It will become effective as soon as that event occurs and it cannot be revoked in the meantime. Banks often hold escrow accounts, in which funds accumulate to pay taxes, insurance on mortgaged property, etc.

**escudo** The standard monetary unit of Cape Verde (CV Esc) and Portugal (Esc); it is divided into 100 centavos.

**ESOP** Abbreviation for *employee share-ownership plan.

**estate** **1.** The sum total of a person's assets less liabilities (usually as calculated at death for the purposes of *inheritance tax). **2.** A substantial piece of land, usually attached to a large house.

**estate duty** A former tax on the estate of a deceased person at the time of death. This tax applied in the UK from 1894 to 1974, when it was converted to *capital-transfer tax. The latter tax became *inheritance tax in 1986, when it reverted to a form of taxation similar to the former estate duty. The tax is levied on the assets less the liabilities of the deceased, taking into account (to forestall avoidance) certain gifts made in a defined period before the death.

**eurobond** A *bond issued in a *eurocurrency, which is now one of the largest markets for raising money (it is much larger than the UK stock exchange). The reason for the popularity of the eurobond market is that *secondary market investors can remain anonymous, usually for the purpose of avoiding tax. For this reason it is difficult to ascertain the exact size and scope of operation of the market. Issues of new eurobonds normally take place in London, largely through syndicates of US and Japanese investment banks; they are *bearer securities, unlike the shares registered in most stock exchanges, and interest payments are free of any *withholding taxes. There are various kinds of eurobonds. An ordinary bond, called a **straight**, is a fixed-interest loan of 3 to 8 years duration; others include **floating-rate notes**, which carry a variable interest rate based on the *London Inter Bank Offered Rate; and perpetuals, which are never redeemed. Some carry *warrants and some are *convertible. *See also* Centrale de Livraison de Valeurs Mobilières; Euroclear; note issuance (or purchase) facility; swap; zero-coupon bond.

**eurocheque** A cheque drawn on a European bank, available in 39 countries, which can be cashed at any bank or bureau de change in the world that displays the EC sign (of which there are some 200 000). It can also be used to pay for goods and services in shops, hotels, restaurants, garages, etc., that display the EC sign (over 4 million). The cheques are blank and are made out for any amount as required, usually in the local currency. They have to be used with a **Eurocheque Card**, which guarantees cheques for up to about £100. In most cases, a commission of 1.25% is added to the foreign currency value of the cheque before it is converted to sterling and there is a cheque charge (for cheques drawn on UK banks).

**Euroclear** One of two settlement houses for the clearance of *eurobonds. Based in Brussels, it was set up in 1968 by a number of banks. The other settlement house is *Centrale de Livraison de Valeurs Mobilières.

**euro-commercial paper (ECP)** *Commercial paper issued in a *eurocurrency, the market for which is centred in London. It provides a quick way of obtaining same-day funds by the issue of unsecured notes, for example in Europe for use in New York.

**eurocredit** A loan in a *eurocurrency.

**eurocurrency** A currency held in a European country other than its country of origin. For example, dollars deposited in a bank in Switzerland are *eurodollars, yen deposited in Germany are **euroyen**, etc. Eurocurrency is used for lending and borrowing; the **eurocurrency market** often provides a cheap and convenient form of liquidity for the financing of international trade and investment. The main borrowers and lenders are the commercial banks, large companies, and the central banks. By raising funds in eurocurrencies it is possible to secure more favourable terms and rates of interest, and sometimes to avoid domestic regulations and taxation. Most of the deposits and loans are on a short-term basis but increasing use is being made of medium-term loans, particularly through the raising of *eurobonds. This has to some extent replaced the syndicated loan market, in which banks lent money as a group in order to share the risk. *Euromarkets emerged in the 1950s.

**eurocurrency market** *See* eurocurrency.

**eurodeposit** A deposit using the currency of another country, i.e. a transaction in the *eurocurrency market.

**eurodollars** Dollars deposited in financial institutions outside the USA. The eurodollar market evolved in London in the late 1950s when the growing demand for dollars to finance international trade and investment coincided with a greater supply of dollars. The prefix 'euro' indicates the origin of the practice but it now refers to all dollar deposits made anywhere outside the USA. *See also* eurocurrency.

**euroequity** A capital issue in a country foreign to that of the issuing company.

**euromarket** **1.** A market that emerged in the 1950s for financing international trade. Its principal participants are *commercial banks, large companies, and the *central banks of members of the EC. Its main business is in *eurobonds, *euro-commercial paper, *euronotes, and *euroequities issued in *eurocurrencies. The largest euromarket is in London, but there are smaller ones in Paris, Brussels, and Frankfurt. **2.** The European Community, regarded as one large market for goods.

**euronote** A form of *euro-commercial paper consisting of short-term negotiable *bearer *notes. They may be in any currency but are usually in dollars or ECUs. The **euronote facility** is a form of *note issuance facility set up by a syndicate of banks, which underwrites the notes.

**European Agricultural Guidance and Guarantee Fund (EAGGF)** A fund set up under the *Common Agricultural Policy to buy produce from farmers in

EC member states at pre-arranged minimum prices and to sell when prices have risen. Criticism of various uses of the fund to create the 'butter mountain' and 'wine lake' have been widespread.

**European Commission (Commission of the European Communities)**
The single executive body formed in 1967 from the three separate executive bodies of the European Coal and Steel Community, the European Atomic Energy Community, and the *European Economic Community. It now consists of 17 Commissioners: two each from the UK, France, Germany, Spain, and Italy; and one each from Belgium, the Netherlands, Luxembourg, Ireland, Denmark, Greece, and Portugal. The Commissioners accept joint responsibility for their decisions, which are taken on the basis of a majority vote. The Commission initiates action in the *European Community and mediates between member governments.

**European Community (EC)**  The 12 nations (Belgium, Denmark, France, Germany (originally West Germany), Greece, Ireland, Italy, Luxembourg, the Netherlands, Portugal, Spain, and the UK) that form an economic community, with some common monetary, political, and social aspirations. The community grew from the European Coal and Steel Community, the European Atomic Energy Community, and the *European Economic Community. The Commission of the European Communities (see European Commission) was formed in 1967 with the Council of the European Communities. The community policy emerges from a dialogue between the Commission, which initiates and implements the policy, and the Council, which takes the major policy decisions. The European Parliament, formed in 1957, exercises democratic control over policy, and the European Court of Justice imposes the rule of law on the community, as set out in its various treaties.

**European Currency Unit (ECU)**  A currency medium and unit of account created in 1979 to act as the reserve asset and accounting unit of the *European Monetary System. The value of the ECU is calculated as a weighted average of a basket of specified amounts of *European Community (EC) currencies; its value is reviewed periodically as currencies change in importance and membership of the EC expands. It also acts as the unit of account for all EC transactions. It has some similarities with the *Special Drawing Rights of the *International Monetary Fund; however, ECU reserves are not allocated to individual countries but are held in the *European Monetary Cooperation Fund. Private transactions using the ECU as the denomination for borrowing and lending have proved popular. It has been suggested that the ECU will be the basis for a future European currency to replace all national currencies.

**European Development Fund (EDF)**  A fund administered by the *European Community; it gives grant aid and makes loans to developing countries for specific infrastructure projects.

**European Economic Community (EEC; Common Market)**  The European common market set up by the six member states of the European Coal and Steel Community (ECSC) in 1957. At the same time the European Atomic Energy Community (Euratom) was set up; the controlling bodies of these three communities were merged in 1967 to form the Commission of European Communities (see European Commission) and the Council of European Communities (see European Community). The European Parliament and the European Court of Justice were formed in accordance with the Treaty of Rome

in 1957. The treaty aimed to forge a closer union between the countries of
Europe by removing the economic effects of their frontiers. This included the
elimination of customs duties and quotas between members, a common trade
policy to outside countries, the abolition of restrictions on the movement of
people and capital between member states, and a *Common Agricultural
Policy. In addition to these trading policies, the treaty envisaged a
harmonization of social and economic legislation to enable the Common
Market to work (see also European Investment Bank). The UK, Ireland, and
Denmark joined in 1973, Greece joined in 1979, and Portugal and Spain became
members in 1986, making a total of 12 nations. See also European Monetary
System.

**European Free Trade Association (EFTA)**  A trade association formed in
1960 between Austria, Denmark, Norway, Portugal, Sweden, Switzerland, and
the UK. Finland and Iceland joined later while the UK, Denmark, and Portugal
left on joining the *European Community (EC). EFTA is a looser association
than the EC, dealing only with trade barriers rather than generally coordinating
economic policy. All tariffs between EFTA and EC countries were abolished
finally in 1984 and the establishment of a European Economic Area (EEA),
comprising all EFTA and EC countries, is planned. EFTA is governed by a
council in which each member has one vote; decisions must normally be
unanimous and are binding on all member countries.

**European Investment Bank (EIB)**  A bank set up under the Treaty of Rome
in 1958 to finance capital-investment projects in the *European Economic
Community (EEC). It grants long-term loans to private companies and public
institutions for projects that further the aims of the Community. The 12
members of the *European Community subscribed to the Bank's capital of
28,000M ECU but most of the funds lent by the bank are borrowed on the
international capital markets. The bank is non-profit making and charges
interest at a rate that reflects the rate at which it borrows. Its headquarters are in
Luxembourg.

**European Monetary Agreement (EMA)**  An agreement made in 1958 by the
then members of the *Organization for European Economic Cooperation (now
known as *Organization for Economic Cooperation and Development). The
agreement enabled currencies of member states to be bought, sold, and
exchanged without restriction and allowed for certain credit funds to be
established.

**European Monetary Cooperation Fund (EMCOF)**  A fund that contains
deposits from the 12 member states of the *European Community in gold and
currency. The purpose of the fund is to help keep the European currencies in
the *European Monetary System aligned, pending full *European Monetary
Union.

**European Monetary System (EMS)**  A European system of exchange-rate
stabilization involving the countries of the *European Community. There are
two elements: the **Exchange Rate Mechanism** (**ERM**), under which
participating countries commit themselves to maintaining the value of their
currencies within agreed narrow limits, and a *balance of payments support
mechanism, organized through the *European Monetary Cooperation Fund.
The ERM is generally regarded as having helped to maintain exchange-rate
stability and to have encouraged the coordination of macroeconomic policy. It

operates by giving each currency a value in ECUs and drawing up a **parity grid** giving exchange values in ECUs for each pair of currencies. If market rates differ from this parity by more than a permitted percentage (currently 2.25%), the relevant governments have to take action to correct the disparity. The ultimate goal of the EMS is controversial: to some its function is to facilitate monetary cooperation; to others, it is the first step towards a single European currency and *European Monetary Union (EMU) with a European *central bank. In 1992 the ERM failed and the Italian, British, and Spanish governments were unable to support their currencies above their floor values (*see* realignment); they then had to be allowed to float, enabling critics of the EMS to claim that the system was flawed and that EMU was therefore unattainable. *See also* European Currency Unit.

**European Monetary Union (EMU)** The controversial planned merger of the currencies of the member states of the *European Community. This would involve coordinating their monetary policies, to which some political opposition remains. It is planned to come into being progressively and to be achieved by 1997. It would be controlled by a European *central bank to which all member states would send representatives. *See also* European Monetary System.

**European Options Exchange (EOE)** A market based in Amsterdam that deals in traded *options, mostly in currencies but also in some securities and precious metals. It is affiliated to the *Amsterdam Stock Exchange.

**European Payments Union (EPU)** The original arm of the *Organization for European Economic Cooperation (OEEC), formed to look after payments for international trade. In 1958 the EPU was replaced by the *European Monetary Agreement.

**European Regional Development Fund (ERDF)** A fund set up by the *European Community to allocate money for specific projects in member states for work on the infrastructure, usually in regions of high unemployment or social deprivation. Each country has a quota and has to undertake works approved by the EC before grant aid is given.

**euroyen** Japanese currency deposited in a bank in another country, e.g. Germany. *See* eurocurrency.

**ex-** (Latin: without) A prefix used to exclude specified benefits when a security is quoted. A share is described as **ex-dividend** (xd or ex-div) when a potential purchaser will no longer be entitled to receive the company's current dividend, the right to which remains with the vendor. Government stocks go ex-dividend 36 days before the interest payment. Similarly, **ex-rights**, **ex-scrip**, **ex-coupon**, **ex-capitalization** (**ex-cap**), and **ex-bonus** mean that each of these benefits belongs to the vendor rather than the buyer. **Ex-all** means that all benefits belong to the vendor. **Cum-** (Latin: with) has exactly the opposite sense, meaning that the dividend or other benefits belong to the buyer rather than the seller. The price of a share that has gone ex-dividend will usually fall by the amount of the dividend, while one that is **cum-dividend** will usually rise by this amount. However, in practice market forces usually mean that these falls and rises are often slightly less than expected.

**ex-all** *See* ex-.

**ex-bonus** *See* ex-.

**ex-capitalization (ex-cap)** *See* ex-.

**excess   1.** An initial sum which the holder of an insurance policy must bear before any claim is met by the insurer. It is most often used in car insurance, e.g. the first £50 of any claim has to be borne by the insured party.   **2.** A bank or other financial institution's margin of assets over liabilities. *See also* excess reserves.   **3.** *See* excess shares.

**excess reserves**   Higher reserves than required, held by banks. This usually undesirable state occurs as a result of poor demand for loans or high interest rates. Banks often sell excess reserves to one another.

**excess shares**   Shares not taken up by other shareholders in a *rights issue, for which an invitation to purchase is sent to shareholders with their standard letters of *allotment.

**exchange   1.** The trading of goods, stocks, shares, commodities, paper currencies, etc.   **2.** The place in which such trading occurs, e.g. a stock exchange or commodities exchange.

**exchange control**   Restrictions on the purchase and sale of foreign exchange. It is operated in various forms by many countries, in particular those who experience shortages of *hard currencies; sometimes different regulations apply to transactions that would come under the capital account of the *balance of payments. There has been a gradual movement towards dismantling exchange controls by many countries in recent years. The UK abolished all form of exchange control in 1979.

**Exchange Delivery Settlement Price (EDSP)**   *See* settlement price.

**exchange equalization account**   An account set up in 1932 and managed by the Bank of England on behalf of the government. It contains the official gold and foreign-exchange reserves (including *Special Drawing Rights) of the UK and is used as a buyer of foreign exchange to support the value of sterling. Although all *exchange controls were abolished in 1979, the Bank of England still makes use of this account to help to stabilize rates of exchange.

**exchange rate**   *See* rate of exchange.

**Exchange Rate Mechanism (ERM)**   *See* European Monetary System.

**exchequer**   The account held by the *Bank of England for all government funds.

**Exchequer stocks**   *See* gilt-edged security.

**ex-coupon**   *See* ex-.

**ex-dividend**   *See* ex-.

**executive pension plan (EPP)**   A pension for a senior executive or director of a company in which the company provides a tax-deductible contribution to the premium. An executive pension plan may be additional to any group pension scheme provided by the company, as long as the pension limit of two thirds of the working salary is not exceeded.

**executive share options**   A form of profit-sharing scheme in which the executives of a company are given options to purchase shares at preferential rates.

**executor** A person named in a will of another person to gather in the assets of that person's estate, paying any outstanding liabilities and distributing any residue to the beneficiaries in accordance with the instructions contained in the will.

**exempt gilts** Government gilt-edged securities that pay interest gross, unlike ordinary gilts, on which tax is deducted from interest payments. These gilts are of particular interest to foreign buyers and others, such as institutions, who do not pay income tax.

**exempt unit trust** A *unit trust in which only institutional investors who are not subject to taxation are allowed to invest, i.e. it is restricted to charities and pension funds.

**exercise date** The date on which the holder of a traded *option can be called on to implement the option contract. It is normally after three, six, or nine months.

**exercise notice** Formal notification from the owner of a traded *option to the person or the firm that has written it that the owner wishes to exercise the option to buy (for a call option) or sell (for a put option) at the *exercise price on the *exercise date.

**exercise price (striking price)** The price per share at which a traded *option entitles the owner to buy the underlying security in a call option or to sell it in a put option. *See also* exercise notice.

**ex gratia** (Latin: as of grace) Denoting a payment made out of gratitude, moral obligation, kindness, etc., rather than to fulfil a legal obligation. When an ex gratia payment is made, no legal liability is admitted by the payer.

**ex growth** (of a share or a company) Having had substantial growth in the past but now not holding out prospects for immediate growth of earnings or value.

**Eximbank** *See* Export-Import Bank.

**ex-new** Describing a share that is offered for sale without the right to take up any *scrip issue or *rights issue. *Compare* cum-new.

**expenditure tax (outlay tax)** A tax on the expenditure of individuals or households. This form of taxation, of which VAT is an example, is often preferred by tax theorists to income taxes, as it does not distort the incentive to work.

**expiry date** **1.** The date on which a contract expires. **2.** The last day on which an *option expires. In a European option the option must be taken up or allowed to lapse on this date. In an American option the decision can be taken at any time up to the expiry date.

**Export Credits Guarantee Department (ECGD)** A UK government department, responsible to the Secretary of State for Trade and Industry, that was set up under the Export Guarantees and Overseas Investment Act 1978. It encourages exports from the UK by making export credit insurance available to exporters and guaranteeing repayment to UK banks that provide finance for exports on credit terms of two years or more. It also insures British private investment overseas against war risk, expropriation, and restrictions on the making of remittances. The department was largely privatized in 1991 but some of its overseas functions are still supervised by the government.

**Export-Import Bank (Eximbank)** A US bank established by the US government to foster trade with the USA. It provides export credit guarantees and guarantees loans made by commercial banks to US exporters.

**Export-Import Bank of Japan** A Japanese bank that funds export credits from a variety of sources, including foreign-exchange loans from commercial banks.

**ex-rights** *See* ex-; ex-new.

**ex-scrip** *See* ex-; ex-new.

**external account** A UK bank account held by someone who resides outside the sterling area.

**eyrir** (plural **aurar**) A monetary unit of Iceland worth one hundredth of a króna.

**face value** **1.** The nominal value (*see* nominal price) printed on the face of a security. This is known also as the *par value. It may be more or less than the market value. **2.** The value printed on a banknote or coin.

**factoring** The buying of the trade debts of a manufacturer, assuming the task of debt collection and accepting the credit risk, thus providing the manufacturer with working capital. A firm that engages in factoring is called a **factor**. **With service factoring** involves collecting the debts, assuming the credit risk, and passing on the funds as they are paid by the buyer. **With service plus finance factoring** involves paying the manufacturer up to 90% of the invoice value immediately after delivery of the goods, with the balance paid after the money has been collected. This form of factoring is clearly more expensive than with service factoring. In either case the factor, which may be a bank or finance house, has the right to select its debtors. In the UK, the High-Street banks have well over 60% of the factoring market, run by factoring subsidiary companies owned by the banks. *See also* undisclosed factoring.

**facultative reinsurance** A form of *reinsurance in which the terms, conditions, and reinsurance premium are individually negotiated between the insurer and the reinsurer. There is no obligation on the reinsurer to accept the risk or on the insurer to reinsure it if it is not considered necessary. The main differences between facultative reinsurance and **coinsurance** is that the policyholder has no indication that reinsurance has been arranged. In coinsurance, the coinsurers and the proportion of the risk they are covering are shown on the policy schedule. Also, coinsurance involves the splitting of the premium charged to the policyholder between the coinsurers, whereas the reinsurers charge entirely separate reinsurance premiums.

**fall-back price** *See* Common Agricultural Policy.

**fallen angel** A security in the US market that has dropped below its original value; it may be sold for its increased *yield.

**Fannie Mae** Colloquial name in the USA for the *Federal National Mortgage Association (FNMA).

**fate** Whether or not a cheque or bill has been paid or dishonoured. A bank requested by another bank to **advise fate** of a cheque or bill is being asked if it has been paid or not.

**FCA** Abbreviation for Fellow of the *Institute of Chartered Accountants.

**FCCA** Abbreviation for Fellow of the Chartered Association of Certified Accountants. *See* certified accountant; chartered accountant.

**FCIA**  Abbreviation for *Foreign Credit Insurance Association.

**FCII**  Abbreviation for Fellow of the *Chartered Insurance Institute.

**FDIC**  Abbreviation for *Federal Deposit Insurance Corporation.

**FECDBA**  Abbreviation for the *Foreign Exchange and Currency Deposit Brokers' Association.

**FED**  Abbreviation for the *Federal Reserve System.

**Federal Deposit Insurance Corporation (FDIC)**  A corporation that provides *deposit insurance for US banks through the Bank Insurance Fund. It operates throughout the *Federal Reserve System and also for other banks outside it (*see* state banks).

**federal funds rate**  The highly volatile and sensitive interest rate charged between member banks of the *Federal Reserve System. As the overnight rate paid on federal funds, it is a key indicator of money-market interest rates. Every transaction can alter the level at which the rate is fixed.

**Federal Home Loan Bank**  12 regional organizations in the USA that supply credit for *savings and loans associations (the US equivalent of *building societies) and other organizations providing domestic mortgages. They are independent organizations but since legislation passed in 1989 they have been supervised by a five-member **Federal Housing Finance Board**. The legislation also made it a duty for district banks to provide cheap mortgage finance for borrowers on low incomes.

**Federal Home Loan Mortgage Corporation (FHLMC)**  A corporation established in the USA in 1970 to buy mortgages from *savings and loans associations in order to resell them in the secondary market. The stock of the corporation is held by the *Federal Home Loan Bank Board, the regulatory body for the savings and loans associations established in the 1930s to provide reserves for the mortgage lending institutions. The FHLMC is usually referred to in market reports as 'Freddie Mac'.

**Federal National Mortgage Association (FNMA)**  A government sponsored quoted company formed in the USA to trade in *mortgages, guaranteed by the Federal Housing Finance Board (*see* Federal Home Loans Bank). It is the largest source of housing finance in the USA. FNMA is often referred to in market reports as 'Fannie Mae'.

**Federal Open Market Committee (FOMC)**  The policy committee of the *Federal Reserve System, which sets the level of money and credit in the US banking system. Its members, the governors of the Federal Reserve Board and some of the presidents of the 12 *Federal Reserve Banks, meet monthly and regulate the money supply by instructing the federal banks to buy or sell securities.

**Federal Reserve Bank**  Any of the 12 banks that together form the *Federal Reserve System in the USA; they are situated in Boston, New York, Philadelphia, Cleveland, Richmond, Atlanta, Chicago, St Louis, Minneapolis, Kansas City, Dallas, and San Francisco. They provide *central bank services and are involved with the Federal Reserve Board of Governors in developing and enacting monetary policy, as well as regulating local commercial and savings banks. Each Federal Reserve Bank is owned by the local banks in its district.

**federal reserve float** Fictitious money created when a *Federal Reserve Bank credits an account in another bank with the value of a cheque before it has collected payment from the paying bank. A float is not created when the transaction involves a paying bank in the same city as the Federal Reserve Bank. Processing and transport delays cause the creation of most floats.

**Federal Reserve System** The organization, consisting of the 12 *Federal Reserve Banks, that functions as the *central bank of the USA. Created by the Federal Reserve Act 1913, the system controls monetary policy, regulates the cost of money and the money supply to local banks, and supervises international banking by means of its agreement with the central banks of other countries. The system is administered centrally by the **Federal Reserve Board**, based in Washington DC.

**Fédération Internationale des Bourses de Valeurs (FIBV)** A world federation of stock exchanges, formed in 1961 by a number of stock markets as a means of exchanging information and opinions.

**Fed funds** Funds that are immediately available at the US *Federal Reserve Banks, for use overnight or sometimes longer (when they are known as **Term Fed Funds**) by another Federal Reserve Bank. Rates fluctuate daily.

**fedwire** A high-speed electronic link in the USA between the 12 *Federal Reserve Banks and the Treasury, used to move large sums of money for themselves and their customers. The transactions are often completed within minutes of being initiated.

**fen** A monetary unit of China, worth one hundredth of a *yuan.

**FHLMC** Abbreviation for *Federal Home Loan Mortgage Corporation.

**fiat money** Money that a government has declared to be legal tender, although it has no intrinsic value and is not backed by reserves. Most of the world's paper money is now fiat money. *Compare* fiduciary issue.

**FIBV** Abbreviation for *Fédération Internationale des Bourses de Valeurs.

**fidelity guarantee** An insurance policy covering employers for any financial losses they may sustain as a result of the dishonesty of employees. Policies can be arranged to cover all employees or specific named persons. Because of the nature of the cover, insurers require full details of the procedure adopted by the organization in recruiting and vetting new employees and they usually reserve the right to refuse to cover a particular person without giving a reason.

**fiduciary 1.** Denoting a person who holds property in trust or as an executor. Persons acting in a fiduciary capacity do so not for their own profit but to safeguard the interests of some other person or persons. **2.** Denoting a loan that is made on trust, rather than against some security.

**fiduciary issue 1.** In the UK, the part of the issue of banknotes by the Bank of England that is backed by government securities, rather than by gold. Nearly the whole of the note issue is now fiduciary. *Compare* fiat money. **2.** Formerly, in the UK, banknotes issued by a bank without backing in gold, the value of the issues relying entirely on the reputation of the issuing bank.

**FIFO** Abbreviation for *first in, first out.

**fillér** A monetary unit of Hungary, worth one hundredth of a *forint.

**fils  1.** A monetary unit of the United Arab Emirates, worth one hundredth of a *dirham. **2.** A monetary unit of Bahrain, Iraq, Jordan, and Kuwait, worth one thousandth of a *dinar. **3.** A monetary unit of Yemen, worth one hundredth of a *riyal and one thousandth of a *dinar.

**FIMBRA** Abbreviation for Financial Intermediaries, Managers and Brokers Regulatory Association Ltd. *See* Self-Regulating Organization.

**final dividend** *See* dividend.

**finance  1.** The practice of manipulating and managing money. **2.** The capital involved in a project, especially the capital that has to be raised to start a new business. **3.** A loan of money for a particular purpose, especially by a *finance house.

**Finance Act** The annual UK Act of Parliament that changes the law relating to taxation, giving the rates of income tax, corporation tax, etc., proposed in the preceding Budget.

**finance bill** A *bill of exchange used for short-term credit. It cannot be sold on to another party in the same way as a *banker's acceptance.

**finance house** An organization, many of which are owned by *commercial banks, that provides finance for *hire-purchase agreements. A consumer, who buys an expensive item (such as a car) from a trader and does not wish to pay cash, enters into a hire-purchase contract with the finance house, who collects the deposit and instalments. The finance house pays the trader the cash price in full, borrowing from the commercial banks in order to do so. The finance house's profit is the difference between the low rate of interest it pays to the commercial banks to borrow and the high rate it charges the consumer. Most finance houses are members of the *Finance Houses Association.

**finance-house base rate** The rate of interest charged by a *finance house for *hire purchase, *leasing, and other borrowings. It is based on the *London Inter Bank Offered Rate plus a margin.

**Finance Houses Association** A UK organization of *finance houses, set up in 1945 to regulate the trade of hire purchase and to negotiate with the government on acceptable terms and conditions. Its members control most UK hire-purchase agreements.

**finance lease** A lease in which the lessee acquires all the financial benefits and risks attaching to ownership of whatever is being leased. *Compare* operating lease.

**financial accountant** An accountant whose primary responsibility is the management of the finances of an organization and the preparation of its annual accounts. *Compare* cost accountant.

**financial adviser  1.** Anyone who offers financial advice to someone else, especially one who advises on *investments. *See also* independent financial adviser. **2.** An organization, usually a merchant bank, that advises the board of a company during a takeover (*see* takeover bid).

**Financial and Operational Combined Uniform Single (FOCUS)** A monthly or quarterly financial report filed by a broker-dealer with its *Self-Regulating Organization.

**financial futures** A *futures contract in currencies or interest rates (*see* interest-rate futures). Unlike simple forward contracts, futures contracts themselves can be bought and sold on specialized markets. Until about 1970 trading in financial futures did not exist, although futures and options were dealt in widely on *commodity markets. However, instantaneous trading across the world coupled with accelerated international capital flows combined to produce great volatility in interest rates, stock-market prices, and currency exchanges. The result has been an environment in which organizations and individuals responsible for managing large sums need a financial futures and options market both to manage risks effectively and as a source of additional profit. In the UK financial futures and options are traded on the *London International Financial Futures and Options Exchange (LIFFE). *See also* hedging; index futures; portfolio insurance.

**financial institution** Any organization, such as a bank, building society, or finance house, that collects funds from individuals, other organizations, or government agencies and invests these funds or lends them on to borrowers. Some financial institutions are non-deposit-taking, e.g. brokers and life insurance companies, who fund their activities and derive their income from selling securities or insurance policies, or undertaking brokerage services. At one time there was a clear distinction and regulatory division between deposit-taking and non-deposit-taking financial institutions. This is no longer the case; brokers and other companies now often invest funds for their clients with banks and in the money markets.

**financial instrument** *See* instrument; negotiable instrument.

**Financial Intermediaries, Managers and Brokers Regulatory Association Ltd (FIMBRA)** *See* Self-Regulating Organization.

**financial intermediary** **1.** A bank, building society, finance house, insurance company, investment trust, etc., that holds funds borrowed from lenders in order to make loans to borrowers. **2.** In the *Financial Services Act 1986, a person or organization that sells insurance but is not directly employed by an insurance company (e.g. a broker, insurance agent, bank). *See also* independent intermediary.

**financial investment** *See* investment.

**Financial Ombudsman** **1.** (**Banking Ombudsman**) An official in charge of a service set up in 1986 by 19 banks, which fund the service, to investigate complaints from individual bank customers against the service provided by member banks. In January 1993 the service was extended to deal with complaints from small businesses (turnover less than £1 million). **2.** (**Building Societies Ombudsman**) An official in charge of a service set up in 1987 by all the UK building societies, who fund the service, to investigate complaints from building-society customers against the services provided by the building societies. **3.** (**Insurance Ombudsman**) An official in charge of a service set up in 1981 by some 200 insurance companies, who fund the service, to settle disputes between insurance policyholders and member insurance companies. **4.** (**Investment Ombudsman**) An official in charge of a service set up in 1989 by IMRO (*see* Self-Regulating Organization) to settle disputes between IMRO members and their customers. Although the service provided is funded by IMRO it is independent of it. **5.** (**Pensions Ombudsman**) An official, appointed by the Secretary of State for Social Services under the Social Security

Act 1990, who is responsible for resolving disputes between individuals and their pension schemes. The Pensions Ombudsman is responsible to Parliament.

**Financial Reporting Council (FRC)**  A UK company limited by guarantee, set up in 1989 to oversee and support the work of the *Accounting Standards Board and the *Financial Reporting Review Panel to encourage good financial reporting generally. Its chairman and three deputies are appointed jointly by the Secretary of State for Trade and Industry and the Governor of the Bank of England. It first met in May 1990.

**Financial Reporting Review Panel (FRRP)**  A UK company limited by guarantee; it is a subsidiary of the *Financial Reporting Council, which acts as its sole director. The panel investigates departures from the accounting requirements of the Companies Act 1985 and is empowered to take legal action to remedy any such departures. Its remit covers the financial reports of public companies and large private companies. All other companies are subject to scrutiny by the Department of Trade and Industry. The panel does not look at all company accounts but has doubtful cases drawn to its attention.

**Financial Services Act 1986**  A UK Act of Parliament that came into force in April 1988. Its purpose was to regulate investment business in the UK by means of the *Securities and Investment Board and its *Self-Regulating Organizations. It provided legislation for many of the recommendations of the *Gower Report.

**Financial Statement and Budget Report (FSBR)**  The document published by the Chancellor of the Exchequer on Budget Day. It summarizes the provisions of the Budget as given in the Chancellor's speech to the House of Commons.

**Financial Times Share Indexes**  A number of share indexes published by the *Financial Times,* daily except Sundays and Mondays, as a barometer of share prices on the London Stock Exchange. The **Financial Times Actuaries Share Indexes** are calculated by the Institute of Actuaries and the Faculty of Actuaries as weighted arithmetic averages for 54 sectors of the market (capital goods, consumer goods, etc.) and divided into various industries. They are widely used by investors and portfolio managers. The widest measure of the market comes from the **FTA All-Share Index** of some 800 shares and fixed-interest stocks (increased from 657 in October 1992), which includes a selection from the financial sector. Calculated after the end of daily business, it covers 98% of the market and 90% of turnover by value. The **FTA World Share Index** was introduced in 1987 and is based on 2400 share prices from 24 countries. The **Financial Times Industrial Ordinary Share Index** (or FT-30) represents the movements of shares in 30 leading industrial and commercial shares, chosen to be representative of British industry rather than of the Stock Exchange as a whole; it therefore excludes banks, insurance companies, and government stocks. The index is an unweighted geometric average, calculated hourly during the day and closing at 4.30 pm. The index started from a base of 100 in 1935 and for many years was the main day-to-day market barometer. It continues to be published but it has been superseded as the main index by the **Financial Times-Stock Exchange 100 Share Index** (FT-SE 100 or **FOOTSIE**), a weighted arithmetic index representing the price of 100 securities with a base of 1000 on 3 January 1984. This index is calculated minute-by-minute and its constituents, whose membership is by market capitalization, above £1 billion, are reviewed quarterly. The index was created to help to support a UK equity-market base for a futures contract. In 1992 the index series was extended to create two further real-time indexes, the **FT-SE Mid 250**, comprising companies capitalized between £150 million and £1 billion, and the **FT-SE Actuaries 350**, both based on 31 December 1985. These indexes are further broken down into Industry Baskets, comprising all the shares of the industrial sectors, to provide an instant view of industry performance across the market, and corresponding roughly to sectors defined by markets in New York and Tokyo. A **FT-SE Small Cap Index** covers 500–600 companies capitalized between £20 million and £150 million, calculated at the end of the day's business, both including and excluding investment trusts. The **Financial Times Government Securities Index** measures the movements of Government stocks (gilts). The newest indexes measure the performance of securities throughout the European market. The **Financial Times-Stock Exchange Eurotrack 100 Index** (FT-SE Eurotrack 100) is a weighted average of 100 stocks in Europe, which started on 29 October 1990, with a base of 1000 at the close of business on 26 October 1990. Quoted in Deutschmarks, the index combines prices from *SEAQ and SEAQ International with up-to-date currency exchange rates. On 25 February 1991 the **Financial Times-Stock Exchange Eurotrack 200 Index** was first quoted, with the same base as the Eurotrack 100 to combine the constituents of the FT-SE 100 and the Eurotrack 100.

**financial year   1.** Any year connected with finance, such as a company's accounting period or a year for which budgets are made up.   **2.** A specific period relating to corporation tax, i.e. the year beginning 1 April (the year beginning 1 April 1994 is the financial year 1994). Corporation-tax rates are fixed for specific financial years by the Chancellor in the Budget; if a company's accounting period falls into two financial years the profits have to be apportioned to the relevant financial years to find the rates of tax applicable. *Compare* fiscal year.

**financier**   A person who finances a business deal or venture or who makes arrangements for such a deal or venture to be financed by a merchant bank or other *financial institution.

**financing gap**   The difference between a country's foreign exchange requirements, for imports and the servicing of its debts, and what it has available from export receipts and overseas earnings. This gap must be filled either by raising further foreign exchange (donor aid, loans, etc.) or by cutting back the requirements, either by reducing imports or rescheduling the repayment of debts. Forecasting the financing gap and negotiating means of bridging it are major elements in helping countries with balance of payments problems.

**fine paper**   *See* first-class paper.

**fine trade bill**   A *bill of exchange that is acceptable to the Bank of England as security, when acting as *lender of last resort. It will be backed by a first-class bank or finance house.

**FINEX   1.** Abbreviation for Financial Instrument Exchange. *See* New York Cotton Exchange.   **2.** The name for certain Brazilian export finance programmes.

**firm commitment   1.** An undertaking by a bank to lend up to a maximum sum over a period at a specified rate; a *commitment fee usually has to be paid by the borrower, which is not returned if the loan is not taken up. **2.** An agreement in which an underwriter of a flotation in the USA assumes the risk that not all the securities issued will be sold, by guaranteeing to buy all the excess securities at the offer price.

**first-class paper (fine paper)** A *bill of exchange, cheque, etc., drawn on or accepted or endorsed by a first-class bank, *finance house, etc.

**first in, first out (FIFO)** A method of charging homogeneous items of stock to production when the cost of the items has changed. It is assumed, both for costing and stock valuation purposes, that the earliest items taken into stock are those used in production, although this may not necessarily correspond with the physical movement of the stock items. *Compare* last in, first out.

**first-loss policy** A property insurance policy in which the policyholder arranges cover for an amount below the full value of the items insured and the insurer agrees not to penalize the policyholder for under-insurance. The main use of these policies is in circumstances in which a total loss is virtually impossible. For example, a large warehouse may contain £2.5M worth of wines and spirits but the owner may feel that no more than £500,000 worth could be stolen at any one time. The solution is a first-loss policy that deals with all claims up to £500,000 but pays no more than this figure if more is stolen. First-loss policies differ from coinsurance agreements with the policyholders because the insured is not involved in claims below the first-loss level and the premiums are not calculated proportionately. In the above example, the premium might be as much as 80–90% of the premium on the full value.

**first notice day** **1.** The date on which a seller in a futures market informs the *clearing house of an intention to deliver according to the terms of a particular *futures contract. **2.** The date on which the clearing house notifies the buyer of such an arrangement.

**first of exchange** *See* bills in a set.

**fiscal agent** **1.** A third party who acts on behalf of a bond issuer to pay subscribers to the issue and generally assist the issuer. **2.** An agent for one of the national *financial institutions in the USA who acts as an adviser, for example, to the National Mortgage Association for its debt securities. **3.** In the USA, an agent empowered to collect taxes, revenues, and duties on behalf of the government. For example, the *Federal Reserve Banks perform this function for the US Treasury.

**fiscal policy** The use of government spending to influence macroeconomic conditions. Fiscal policy was actively pursued to sustain full employment in the post-war years; however, monetarists and others have claimed that this set off the inflation of the 1970s. Fiscal policy has remained 'tight' in most western countries since the 1980s, with governments actively attempting to reduce the level of public expenditure.

**fiscal year** In the UK, the year beginning on 6 April in one year and ending on 5 April in the next (the fiscal year 1992/93 runs from 6 April 1992 to 5 April 1993). This will change in 1994 so that it coincides with the calendar year, running from 1 January to 31 December. Income tax, capital-gains tax, and annual allowances for inheritance tax are calculated for fiscal years, and the UK Budget estimates refer to the fiscal year. In the USA it runs from 1 July to the following

30 June. The fiscal year is sometimes called the **tax year** or the **year of assessment.** *Compare* financial year.

**fixed asset** *See* capital asset.

**fixed capital** The amount of capital tied up in the *capital assets of an organization.

**fixed capital formation** An investment over a given period, as used in the *national income accounts. It consists primarily of investment in manufacturing and housing. **Gross fixed capital formation** is the total amount of expenditure on investment, while **net fixed capital formation** includes a deduction for the *depreciation of existing capital.

**fixed charge (specific charge)** A *charge in which a creditor has the right to have a specific asset sold and applied to the repayment of a debt if the debtor defaults on any payments. The debtor is not at liberty to deal with the asset without the charge-holder's consent. *Compare* floating charge.

**fixed debenture** A *debenture that has a *fixed charge as security. *Compare* floating debenture.

**fixed exchange rate** A *rate of exchange between one currency and another that is fixed by government and maintained by that government buying or selling its currency to support or depress its currency. *Compare* floating exchange rate.

**fixed-interest security** A type of *security that gives a fixed stated interest payment once or twice per annum. They include *gilt-edged securities, *bonds, *preference shares, and *debentures; as they entail less risk than *equities they offer less scope for capital appreciation. They do, however, often give a better *yield than equities.

　　The prices of fixed-interest securities tend to move inversely with the general level of interest rates, reflecting changes in the value of their fixed yield relative to the market. Fixed-interest securities tend to be particularly poor investments at times of high inflation as their value does not adjust to changes in the price level. To overcome this problem some gilts now give index-linked interest payments.

**fixed rate currency swap** *See* currency interest rate swap.

**fixed-rate mortgage** A *mortgage in which the rate of interest paid by the borrower is fixed, usually for the first few years of the loan.

**flat yield** *See* yield.

**flexible drawdown** The *drawdown in stages of funds available under a credit agreement.

**flip-flop FRN** A perpetual *floating-rate note (i.e. one without redemption), which can be converted into a short-term note of up to four years' maturity and back again into a perpetual FRN.

**float 1.** In the USA, the proportion of a corporation's stocks that are held by the public rather than the corporation. **2.** Money created as a result of a delay in processing cheques, e.g. when one account is credited before the paying bank's account has been debited. *See* federal reserve float. **3.** Money set aside as a contingency fund or an advance to be reimbursed. **4.** *See* flotation.

**floater** A colloquial name for a *floating-rate note.

**floating capital** Funds available for carrying on a business, including funds employed in marketable investments.

**floating charge** A *charge over the assets of a company; it is not a legal charge over its fixed assets but floats over the charged assets until crystallized by some predetermined event. For example, a floating charge may be created over all the assets of a company, including its trading stock. The assets may be freely dealt with until a crystallizing event occurs, such as the company going into liquidation. Thereafter no further dealing may take place but the debt may be satisfied from the charged assets. Such a charge ranks in priority after legal charges and after preferred creditors in the event of a winding-up. It must be registered (*see* register of charges).

**floating debenture** A *debenture that has a *floating charge as security. *Compare* fixed debenture.

**floating debt** The part of the *national debt that consists primarily of short-term *Treasury bills. *See also* funding operations.

**floating exchange rate** A *rate of exchange between one currency and others that is permitted to float according to market forces. Most major currencies and countries now have floating exchange rates but governments and central banks intervene, buying or selling currencies when rates become too high or too low. *Compare* fixed exchange rate.

**floating policy** An insurance policy that has only one sum insured although it may cover many items. No division of the total is shown on the policy and the policyholder is often able to add or remove items from the cover without reference to the insurers, provided that the total sum insured is not exceeded.

**floating-rate certificate of deposit (FRCD)** A certificate of deposit with a variable interest rate, normally for interbank lending purposes. Commonly bearing a one-year maturity, these certificates have interest rates that may be adjusted (e.g. every 90 days); they are usually expressed in eurodollars at a rate linked to LIBOR.

**floating-rate interest** An *interest rate on certain bonds, certificates of deposit, etc., that changes with the market rate in a predetermined manner, usually in relation to the *base rate.

**floating-rate note (FRN)** A *eurobond with a *floating-rate interest, usually based on the *London Inter Bank Offered Rate. They first appeared in the 1970s and have a maturity of between 7 and 15 years. They are usually issued as negotiable *bearer bonds. A **perpetual FRN** has no *redemption. *See also* flip-flop FRN.

**floating warranty** A guarantee given by one person to another that induces this other person to enter into a contract with a third party. For example, a car dealer may induce a customer to enter into a hire-purchase contract with a finance company. If the car does not comply with the dealer's guarantee, the customer may recover damages from the dealer, on the basis of the hire-purchase contract, even though the dealer is not a party to that contract.

**floor   1.** The room in a stock exchange, commodity exchange, Lloyd's, etc., in which dealing takes place. Dealings are invariably restricted to *floor traders.

With the increased use of computers floor trading is becoming less frequent.
**2.** *See* collar.

**floor broker** A person who deals on the *floor of an exchange for a third party.

**floor trader** A member of a stock exchange, commodity market, Lloyd's, etc.,
who is permitted to enter the dealing room of these institutions and deal with
other traders, brokers, underwriters, etc. Each institution has its own rules of
exclusivity, but in many, computer dealing is replacing face-to-face floor trading.

**florin** (Af) The standard monetary unit of Aruba, divided into 100 cents.

**flotation** The process of launching a public company for the first time by
inviting the public to subscribe in its shares (also known as 'going public'). It
applies both to private and nationalized share issues, and can be carried out by
means of an *introduction, *issue by tender, *offer for sale, *placing, or *public
issue. After flotation the shares can be traded on a stock exchange. Flotation
allows the owners of the business to raise new capital or to realize their
investments. In the UK, flotation can be either on the *main market through a
full listing or on the *unlisted securities market, where less stringent regulations
apply. Some countries allow flotation on *over-the-counter markets.

**flotation cost** The total cost incurred by a company in offering its securities
to the public.

**flurry** A burst of activity on a speculative market, especially on a financial
market.

**FNMA** Abbreviation for *Federal National Mortgage Association.

**FOCUS** Abbreviation for *Financial and Operational Combined Uniform Single.

**FOMC** Abbreviation for *Federal Open Market Committee.

**FOOTSIE** Colloquial name for the Financial Times-Stock Exchange 100 share
index. *See* Financial Times Share Indexes.

**forced sale** A sale that has to take place because it has been ordered by a
court or because it is necessary to raise funds to avoid bankruptcy or liquidation.

**forced saving** A government measure imposed on an economy with a view to
increasing savings and reducing expenditure on consumer goods. It is usually
implemented by raising taxes, increasing interest rates, or raising prices.

**force majeure** (French: superior force) An event outside the control of either
party to a contract (such as a strike, riot, war, act of God) that may excuse either
party from fulfilling contractual obligations in certain circumstances, provided
that the contract contains a force majeure clause.

**foreclosure** The legal right of a lender of money if the borrower fails to repay
the money or part of it on the due date. The lender must apply to a court to be
permitted to sell the property that has been held as security for the debt. The
court will order a new date for payment in an order called a **foreclosure nisi**. If
the borrower again fails to pay, the lender may sell the property. This procedure
can occur when the security is the house in which the mortgagor lives and the
mortgagor fails to pay the mortgagee (bank, building society, etc.) the mortgage
instalments. The bank, etc., then forecloses the mortgage, dispossessing the
mortgagor.

**foreign bill** *See* inland bill.

**foreign bond** A bond held by a resident of one country denominated in the currency of another country. *See* bulldog bond; Yankee bond.

**Foreign Credit Insurance Association (FCIA)** A consortium operated on voluntary lines by 50 US insurance companies to underwrite export credits for US exporters. It is run under the aegis of the *Export-Import Bank.

**foreign exchange** The currencies of foreign countries. Foreign exchange is bought and sold in *foreign-exchange markets. Firms or organizations require foreign exchange to purchase goods from abroad or for purposes of investment or speculation.

**Foreign Exchange and Currency Deposit Brokers' Association (FECDBA)** The UK trade association for brokers dealing in *foreign exchange.

**Foreign Exchange and Trade Central Law** A Japanese law regulating import controls; it has been somewhat relaxed due to Western pressure, particularly since Japan joined the *Organization for Economic Cooperation and Development.

**foreign-exchange broker** A *broker who specializes in arranging deals in foreign currencies on the *foreign-exchange markets. Most transactions are between commercial banks and governments. Foreign-exchange brokers do not normally deal direct with the public or with firms requiring foreign currencies for buying goods abroad (who buy from commercial banks). Foreign-exchange brokers earn their living from the *brokerage paid on each deal.

**foreign-exchange dealer** A person who buys and sells *foreign exchange on a *foreign-exchange market, usually as an employee of a *commercial bank. Banks charge fees or commissions for buying and selling foreign exchange on behalf of their customers; dealers may also be authorized to speculate in forward exchange rates.

**foreign-exchange market** An international market in which foreign currencies are traded. It consists primarily of foreign-exchange dealers employed by *commercial banks (acting as principals) and *foreign-exchange brokers (acting as intermediaries). Although tight *exchange controls have been abandoned by many governments, including the UK government, the market is not entirely free in that it is to some extent manipulated by the Bank of England on behalf of the government, usually by means of the *exchange equalization account. Currency dealing has a *spot currency market for delivery of foreign exchange within two days and a forward-exchange market (*see* forward-exchange contract) in which transactions are made for foreign currencies to be delivered at agreed dates in the future. This enables dealers, and their customers who require foreign exchange in the future, to hedge their purchases and sales. Options and futures on forward-exchange rates can also be traded on various world markets, including the *London International Financial Futures and Options Exchange and the *Deutsche Terminbörse in Frankfurt.

**foreign investment** Investment in the domestic economy by foreign individuals or companies. Foreign investment takes the form of either direct investment in productive enterprises or investment in *financial instruments, such as a portfolio of shares. Countries receiving foreign investment tend to have a mixed attitude towards it. While the creation of jobs and wealth is welcome, there is frequently antagonism on the grounds that the country is being 'bought by foreigners'. Similarly, there is frequently resentment in the country whose nationals invest overseas, especially if there is domestic unemployment. Nevertheless, foreign investment is increasingly important in the economy of the modern world.

**foreign sector** The part of a country's economy that is concerned with external trade (imports and exports) and capital flows (inward and outward).

**foreign trade multiplier** The effect that an increase in home demand has on a country's foreign trade. The primary effect is to increase that country's imports of raw materials. A secondary effect may be an increase in exports because the increased home demand enables manufacturers to be more competitive and also because the countries supplying the increased quantities of imports have more foreign exchange available to increase *their* imports.

**forfaiting** A form of *debt discounting for exporters in which a forfaiter accepts at a discount, and without recourse, a *promissory note, *bill of exchange, *letter of credit, etc., received from a foreign buyer by an exporter. Maturities are normally from one to three years. Thus the exporter receives payment without risk at the cost of the discount.

**forfeited share** A partly paid share in a company that the shareholder has to forfeit because of failure to pay a subsequent part or final payment.

**forgery** The legal offence of making a false instrument in order that it may be accepted as genuine, thereby causing harm to others. Under the Forgery and Counterfeiting Act 1981, an instrument may be a document or any device (e.g. magnetic tape) on which information is recorded. An instrument is considered false, for example, if it purports to have been made or altered by someone who did not do so, on a date or at a place when it was not, or by someone who does not exist.

**forint** (Ft) The standard monetary unit of Hungary, divided into 100 fillér.

**for the account** Denoting a transaction on the *London Stock Exchange, either a purchase or a sale, that the investor intends to close out with an equivalent sale or purchase within the same *account. In dealing for the account the investor will only be called upon for any losses and not for the total cost of a purchase.

**forwardation** A situation in a *commodity market in which spot goods can be bought more cheaply than goods for forward delivery, enabling a dealer to buy spot goods and carry them forward to deliver them against a forward contract. *Compare* backwardation.

**forward-dated** *See* post-date.

**forward dealing** Dealing in commodities, securities, currencies, freight, etc., for delivery at some future date at a price agreed at the time the contract (called a **forward contract**) is made. This form of trading enables dealers and manufacturers to cover their future requirements by *hedging their more immediate purchases. Strictly, a forward contract differs from a *futures contract in that the former cannot be closed out by a matching transaction, whereas a futures contract can, and often is. However, this distinction is not always adhered to and the two words are sometimes used synonymously.

**forward delivery** Terms of a contract in which goods are purchased for delivery at some time in the future (*compare* spot goods). Commodities may be sold for forward delivery up to one year or more ahead, often involving shipment from their port of origin. *See also* forward dealing.

**forward-exchange contract** An agreement to purchase *foreign exchange at a specified date in the future at an agreed exchange rate. In international trade, with floating rates of exchange, the forward-exchange market provides an important way of eliminating risk on future transactions that will require foreign exchange. The buyer on the forward market gains by the certainty such a contract can bring; the seller, by buying and selling exchanges for future delivery, makes a market and earns a living partly from the profit made by selling at a higher price than the buying price and partly by speculation. There are also active options and futures markets in forward foreign-exchange rates. *See* financial futures; foreign-exchange market.

**forward price** The fixed price at which a given amount of a commodity, currency, or a financial instrument is to be delivered on a fixed date in the future. A forward contract differs from a *futures contract in that each forward deal stands alone.

**forward rate agreement (FRA)** An agreement between two parties on an interest rate to be paid at a specified time in the future; for example, a contract on interest rates to be paid for a three-month period, starting in six months' time. In such transactions the parties take a risk on the difference between what they expect the interest rates will be in the period and what they actually are.

**founders' shares** Shares issued to the founders of a company. They often have special rights to dividends. *See also* deferred ordinary share.

**FRA** Abbreviation for *forward rate agreement.

**fractional banking** A banking practice that some governments impose on their banks, calling for a fixed fraction between cash reserves and total liabilities. If governments increase the ratio of reserves to deposits, this indicates a tighter credit policy. In the USA large banks have to keep up to 12% of their deposits with their regional *Federal Reserve Bank.

**franc** **1.** (F) The standard monetary unit of France, French dependencies, Andorra, and Monaco, divided into 100 centimes. **2.** The standard monetary unit of Belgium (BF), Benin (Communauté Financière Africaine franc; CFAF), Burkina-Faso (CFAF), Burundi (FBu), Cameroon (CFAF), the Central African Republic (CFAF), Chad (CFAF), Comoros (CF), the Congo (CFAF), Djibouti (DF), Equatorial Guinea (CFAF), Gabon (CFAF), Guinea (GF), Cote d'Ivoire, (CFAF), Liechtenstein (SwF), Luxembourg (LuxF), Madagascar (FMG), Mali (CFAF), Niger (CFAF), Senegal (CFAF), Switzerland (SwF), Togo (CFAF), and Rwanda (RF). In all countries it is divided into 100 centimes.

**franked investment income** Dividends and other distributions from UK companies that are received by other companies. The principle of the *imputation system of taxation is that once one company has paid corporation tax, any dividends it pays can pass through any number of other companies without carrying a further corporation-tax charge, hence the term 'franked'. The amount of tax credit included in the franked investment income can reduce the amount of *advance corporation tax that the recipient company has to pay on its own dividends. Where franked investment income exceeds franked payments, the excess is carried forward to future accounting periods and can be set off against future franked payments (e.g. dividends). If the company has unused trading losses that could be carried back, a terminal loss, unused capital allowances, or a deduction for charges on income (e.g. debenture interest) then a claim can be made for the repayment of any unused tax credit.

**franked payment**  A dividend or other distribution from a UK company together with the amount of *advance corporation tax (ACT) attributable to the dividend. Thus, if the basic rate of income tax is 25%, a franked payment is the dividend actually paid plus ⅓ of it, i.e. it is a grossed-up dividend. In any accounting period ACT is actually paid on franked payments less *franked investment income at the basic rate of income tax.

**Frankfurt Stock Exchange (Frankfurt Wertpapierbörse)**  The oldest and largest of eight regional stock exchanges in Germany, accounting for more than 75% of equity trading in Germany. It first recorded trading in 1820 (of shares in the Austrian National bank) and was subsequently recognized as a centre for dealing in bonds. Trading is now on three markets; the *Amlichter Handel* for Government bonds and major companies, the *Geregelter Markt* for smaller companies, and the *Freiverkehr*, the third market. Prices are determined on an auction basis by the official brokers (*Kursmakler*) and free brokers (*Freimakler*), who base them on buying and selling orders from the banks. The main market indicator is the *Deutsche Aktienindex (Dax index).

**fraud**  A false representation by means of a statement or conduct, in order to gain a material advantage. A contract obtained by fraud is voidable on the grounds of fraudulent *misrepresentation. If a person uses fraud to induce someone to part with money that he or she would not otherwise have parted with, this may amount to theft. *See also* fraudulent conveyance; fraudulent preference; fraudulent trading.

**fraudulent conveyance**  The transfer of property to another person for the purposes of putting it beyond the reach of creditors. For example, if a man transfers his house into the name of his wife because he realizes that his business is about to become insolvent, the transaction may be set aside by the court under the provisions of the Insolvency Act 1986.

**fraudulent preference**  Paying money to a creditor of a company, or otherwise improving a creditor's position, at a time when the company is unable to pay its debts. If this occurs because of an act of the company within six months of winding-up (or two years if the preference is given to a person connected with the company), an application to the court may be made to cancel the transaction. The court may make any order that it thinks fit, but no order may prejudice the rights of a third party who has acquired property for value without notice of the preference.

**fraudulent trading**  The carrying on of the business of a company with intent to defraud creditors or for any other fraudulent purpose. This includes accepting money from customers when the company is unable to pay its debts and cannot meet its obligations under the contract. The liquidator of a company may apply to the court for an order against any person who has been a party to fraudulent trading to make such contributions to the assets of the company as the court thinks fit. Thus an officer of the company may be made personally liable for some of its debts. 'Fraudulent' in this context implies actual dishonesty or real moral blame; this definition has limited the usefulness of the remedy as fraud is notoriously difficult to prove. *See* wrongful trading.

**FRC** Abbreviation for *Financial Reporting Council.

**FRCD** Abbreviation for *floating-rate certificate of deposit.

**Freddie Mac** Colloquial name in the USA for the *Federal Home Loan Mortgage Corporation (FHLMC).

**free capital 1.** Capital in the form of cash. *See also* liquid assets. **2.** The shares in a public company that are available to the general public, i.e. those not held by controlling shareholders. In the USA it is known as the **free float**.

**free depreciation** A method of granting tax relief to organizations by allowing them to charge the cost of fixed assets against taxable profits in whatever proportions and over whatever period they choose. This gives businesses considerable flexibility, enabling them to choose the best method of depreciation depending on their anticipated cash flow, profit estimates, and taxation expectations.

**free float** *See* free capital.

**free issue** *See* scrip issue.

**free market 1.** A market that is free from government interference, prices rising and falling in accordance with supply and demand. **2.** A security that is widely traded on a stock exchange, there being sufficient stock on offer for the price to be uninfluenced by availability. **3.** A *foreign-exchange market that is free from pegging of rates by governments, rates being free to rise and fall in accordance with supply and demand.

**free reserves** The amount of money a bank is free to lend; the level of its funds above the amounts it owes to others. In the USA this includes what it owes to the relevant *Federal Reserve Bank.

**freeze-out** Pressure applied to minority shareholders of a company that has been taken over, to sell their stock to the new owners.

**Friendly Society** A UK non-profitmaking association registered as such under the Friendly Society Acts 1896–1955. Mutual insurance societies, dating back to the 17th century, were widespread in the 19th and 20th centuries, until many closed in 1946 after the introduction of National Insurance. Some developed into trade unions and some large insurance companies are still registered as Friendly Societies. They now offer tax-free investment plans normally over a 10-year period, with the policies including a life-assurance element. Investment in the tax-free plans are limited by government regulations (in 1992–93 investors could put up to £18 a month or £240 a year in a plan).

**FRN** Abbreviation for *floating-rate note.

**front-door method** *See* back door.

**front-end load** The initial charge made by a unit trust, life-assurance company, or other investment fund to pay for administration and commission for any introducing agent. The investment made on behalf of the investor is, therefore, the total initial payment less the front-end load. *Compare* back-end load.

**front running** The practice by *market makers of dealing on advance information provided by brokers and the investment analysis department in the same firm, before their clients have been given the information. *See also* Chinese wall.

**frozen assets**  Assets that for one reason or another cannot be used or realized. This may happen when a government refuses to allow certain assets to be exported.

**FRRP**  Abbreviation for *Financial Reporting Review Panel.

**FSBR**  Abbreviation for *Financial Statement and Budget Report.

**FT Cityline**  A telephone service giving information on the Financial Times Ordinary Share Index (*see* Financial Times Share Indexes). The information is updated seven times each day.

**FT-SE 100**  *See* Financial Times Share Indexes.

**FT-SE Eurotrack Indexes**  *See* Financial Times Share Indexes.

**FT Share Indexes**  *See* Financial Times Share Indexes.

**full consolidation**  A method of accounting that allows a parent company to show in its balance sheet the assets and liabilities of subsidiaries at full market value and to allow for such items as *goodwill.

**full listing**  A description of a company whose shares appear on the *Official List of the *main market of the *London Stock Exchange. *See* listing requirements.

**fully paid share capital**  *See* share capital.

**functions of money**  In economics, money fulfils the functions of acting as a *medium of exchange, a *unit of account, and a store of value. None of the functions occur in an economy based on barter.

**fund**  A reserve of money or investments held for a specific purpose, e.g. to provide a source of pensions (*see* pension funds) or to sell as units (*see* fund manager; unit trust).

**fundamental analysis**  *See* investment analyst.

**funded debt**  The part of the *national debt that the government is under no obligation to repay by a specified date. This consists mostly of *Consols. *See also* funding operations.

**funded pension scheme**  A pension scheme that pays benefits to retired people from a *pension fund invested in securities. The profits produced by such a fund are paid out as pensions to the members of the scheme.

**funding**  Paying short-term debt by arranging long-term borrowing. *See* funding operations.

**funding operations**  **1.** The replacement of short-term fixed-interest debt (*floating debt) by long-term fixed-interest debt (*funded debt). This is normally associated with the government's handling of the national debt through the operations of the Bank of England. The bank buys Treasury bills and replaces them with an equal amount of longer-term government bonds, thus lengthening the average maturity of government debt. This has the effect of tightening the monetary system, as Treasury bills are regarded by the commercial banks as liquid assets while bonds are not. *See also* overfunding.

**2.** A change in the *capital gearing of a company, in which short-term debts, such as overdrafts, are replaced by longer-term debts, such as *debentures.

**fund manager (investment manager)** An employee of one of the larger institutions, such as an insurance company, *investment trust, or *pension fund, who manages its investment fund. The fund manager decides which investments the fund shall hold, in accordance with the specified aims of the fund, e.g. high income, maximum growth, etc.

**fund of funds** A *unit trust belonging to an institution in which most of its funds are invested in a selection of other unit trusts owned by that institution. It is designed to give maximum security to the small investor by spreading the investments across a wide range.

**funds broker** In the USA, a broker who arranges short-term loans between banks.

**fungibles** **1.** Interchangeable goods, securities, etc., that allow one to be replaced by another without loss of value. Bearer bonds and banknotes are examples. **2.** Perishable goods the quantity of which can be estimated by number or weight.

**FUTOP** Abbreviation for *Guarantee Fund for Danish Options and Futures.

**futures** *See* futures contract.

**Futures and Options Exchange** *See* London FOX.

**futures contract** An agreement to buy or sell a fixed quantity of a particular commodity, currency, or security for delivery at a fixed date in the future at a fixed price. Unlike an *option, a futures contract involves a definite purchase or sale and not an option to buy or sell; it therefore may entail a potentially unlimited loss. However, **futures** provide an opportunity for those who must purchase goods regularly to hedge against changes in price. For *hedging to be possible there must be speculators willing to offer these contracts; in fact trade between speculators usually exceeds the amount of hedging taking place by a considerable amount. In London, futures are traded in a variety of markets. *Financial futures are traded on the *London International Financial Futures and Options Exchange; the *Baltic Exchange deals with shipping and agricultural products; *London FOX deals with cocoa, coffee, and other foodstuffs; the *London Metal Exchange with metals; and the *International Petroleum Exchange with oil. In these **futures markets**, in many cases actual goods (*see* actuals) do not pass between dealers, a bought contract being cancelled out by an equivalent sale contract, and vice versa; money differences arising as a result are usually settled through a *clearing house (*see also* London Clearing House). In some futures markets only brokers are allowed to trade; in others, both dealers and brokers are permitted to do so. *See also* forward-exchange contract.

**futures market** *See* futures contract.

**future value** The value that a sum of money (the **present value**) invested at compound interest will have in the future. If the future value is $F$, and the present value is $P$, at an annual rate of interest $r$, compounded annually for $n$ years, $F = P(1 + r)^n$. Thus a sum with a present value of £1000 will have a future value of £1973.82 at 12% p.a., after six years.

**G3; G5; G7; G10** Abbreviations for *Group of Three; *Group of Five; *Group of Seven; Group of Ten.

**GAB** Abbreviation for *general arrangements to borrow.

**GAFTA** Abbreviation for *Grain and Feed Trade Association.

**game theory** A mathematical theory, developed by J. von Neumann (1903–57) and O. Morgenstern (1907–  ) in 1944, concerned with predicting the outcome of games of strategy (rather than games of chance) in which the participants have incomplete information about the others' intentions. Under perfect competition there is no scope for game theory, as individual actions are assumed not to influence others significantly; under oligopoly, however, this is not the case. Game theory has been increasingly applied to economics in recent years, particularly in the theory of industrial organizations.

**gaming contract** A contract involving the playing of a game of chance by any number of people for money. A **wagering contract** involves only two people. In general, both gaming contracts and wagering contracts are by statute null and void and no action can be brought to recover money paid or won under them.

**gamma stocks** Stocks in relatively small companies in which trade was infrequent. It was used in the former classification system on the London Stock Exchange, but has now been replaced by *Normal Market Size. *See also* alpha stocks.

**garnishee order** An order made by a judge on behalf of a *judgment creditor restraining a third party (often a bank), called a **garnishee**, from paying money to the judgment debtor until sanctioned to do so by the court. The order may also specify that the garnishee must pay a stated sum to the judgment creditor, or to the court, from the funds belonging to the judgment debtor.

**Garn-St Germain Act 1982** US legislation that enabled banks to compete for customers on equal terms with other money-market funds, allowed *savings and loans associations to make business loans and increase their consumer lending, gave the federal authorities powers to allow for mergers and acquisitions of failed banks and savings institutions, and increased the lending limits for national banks.

**GATT** Abbreviation for *General Agreement on Tariffs and Trade.

**GDP** Abbreviation for *gross domestic product.

**GDP deflator** The factor by which the value of GDP (*see* gross domestic product) at current prices must be reduced (deflated) to express GDP in terms of the prices of some base year (e.g. 1980). The GDP deflator is thus a measure of *inflation.

**geared investment trust**  An *investment trust that borrows money, usually to increase its investment in equities. The shares of a geared investment trust tend to rise faster in rising markets and fall faster in falling markets than ungeared trusts.

**gearing**  *See* capital gearing; degearing; leverage.

**gearing adjustment**  An adjustment in *current-cost accounting to allow for the fact that in inflationary times profits may accrue to a company from its fixed-interest capital, so that the whole cost of capital maintenance need not fall on the profits available to the ordinary shareholders.

**gearing effect**  The way in which the *capital gearing of a company affects its shareholders' dividends.

**General Agreement on Tariffs and Trade (GATT)**  A trade treaty that has been in operation since 1948, to which 95 nations are party and a further 28 nations apply its rules de facto; thus some 90% of world trade is governed by GATT regulations. Its objectives are to expand world trade and to provide a permanent forum for international trade problems. Special attention is given to the trade problems of developing countries. The **Tokyo round**, concluded in 1979, agreed many tariff reductions, non-tariff measures, and a revised anti-dumping code. The **Uruguay round**, begun in 1986, is conducting negotiations on non-tariff measures, subsidies, safeguards, etc. The Uruguay round reached stalemate several times in 1991 and 1992. The GATT office is in Geneva.

**general arrangements to borrow (GAB)**  The special arrangements made by the *Group of Ten (G10) to enable the *International Monetary Fund to increase its lending to members of G10. They came into effect in 1962 and were augmented in 1983 when Switzerland, though not a member of the IMF, joined the GAB, enabling it to extend its loan facilities to non-members.

**General Commissioners**  An unpaid local body of persons of good standing appointed by the Lord Chancellor or, in Scotland, by the Secretary of State for Scotland, to hear appeals against income tax, corporation tax, and capital-gains tax assessments or matters of dispute arising from them. General Commissioners can appoint their own clerk, often a lawyer, who can advise them on procedure and legal matters. *Compare* Special Commissioners.

**general undertaking**  The undertaking given by the directors of a UK company setting out their obligations to the London Stock Exchange when their shares are to be traded on the *unlisted securities market. It is equivalent to the listing agreement (*see* listing requirements) of the *main market.

**Gensaki**  The Japanese money market for the resale and repurchase of medium- and long-term government securities.

**geometric mean**  An average obtained by calculating the $n$th root of a set of $n$ numbers. For example the geometric mean of 7, 100, and 107 is $^3\sqrt{74\ 900} = 42.15$, which is considerably less than the *arithmetic mean of 71.3.

**German Futures and Options Market**  *See* Deutsche Terminbörse.

**German stock exchanges**  Stock exchanges in Berlin, Bremen, Dusseldorf, Frankfurt, Hamburg, Hanover, Munich, and Stuttgart. As a result of reunification, other exchanges may be re-established in the east. Frankfurt is the largest exchange, handling more than 75% of German equity trading (*see* Frankfurt Stock Exchange).

**Gesellschaft**  The German name for a limited company. *See Aktiengesellschaft; Gesellschaft mit beschränkter Haftung.*

**Gesellschaft mit beschränkter Haftung (GmbH)**  The German name for a private limited company. The letters GmbH after the name of a company is equivalent to Ltd in the UK. *Compare Aktiengesellschaft.*

**gift**  The transfer of an asset from one person to another for no consideration. Gifts have importance for tax purposes; if they are sufficiently large they may give rise to charges under *inheritance tax if given within seven years prior to death. *See* lifetime transfers.

**gift with reservation**  A gift in which the donor retains some benefit (e.g. the gift of a house in which the donor continues to reside). In general, the donor is treated as not having parted with the asset until any reservation has been removed.

**gilt-edged dealer**  *See* primary dealer.

**gilt-edged security (gilt)**  A *fixed-interest security or stock issued by the British government in the form of **Exchequer stocks** or **Treasury stocks**. Gilts are among the safest of all investments, as the government is unlikely to default on interest or on principal repayments. They may be irredeemable (*see* Consols) or redeemable. **Redeemable gilts** are classified as: **long-dated gilts** or **longs** (not redeemable for 15 years or more), **medium-dated gilts** or **mediums** (redeemable in 5 to 15 years), or **short-dated gilts** or **shorts** (redeemable in less than 5 years).

   Like most fixed-interest securities, gilts are sensitive not only to interest rates but also inflation rates. This led the government to introduce **index-linked gilts** in the 1970s, with interest payments moving in a specified way relative to inflation.

   Most gilts are issued in units of £100. If they pay a high rate of interest (i.e. higher than the current rate) a £100 unit may be worth more than £100 for a period of its life, even though it will only pay £100 on *redemption. Gilts bought through a stockbroker or bank are entered on the *Bank of England Stock Register. Gilts can, however, be bought direct by post through the *National Savings Stock Register.

**gilt unit trust**  A *unit trust that invests in *gilt-edged securities only.

**Ginnie Mae**  **1.** Colloquial US name for the *Government National Mortgage Association (GNMA).  **2.** Colloquial US name for a mortgage-supported bond issued by the Government National Mortgage Association. A **Ginnie Mae pass-through** is a bond backed by mortgages guaranteed by the GNMA, entitling the buyer to part of a pool of residential mortgages. These securities are called 'pass-throughs' because the investor receives both the principal and interest from the bank or originating mortgage supplier, who retains no margin or profit.

**giro** **1.** A banking arrangement for settling debts that has been used in Europe for many years. In 1968 the Post Office set up the UK **National Girobank** (now **Girobank plc**) based on a central office in Bootle, Merseyside. Originally a system for settling debts between people who did not have bank accounts, it now offers many of the services provided by *commercial banks, with the advantage that there are many more post offices, at which Girobank services are provided, than there are bank branches. Also the post offices are open for longer hours than banks. Girobank also offers banking services to businesses, including an **automatic debit transfer** system, enabling businesses to collect money from a large number of customers at regular intervals for a small charge. **Bank Giro** is a giro system operated in the UK, independently of Girobank, by the clearing banks. It has no central organization, being run by bank branches. The service enables customers to make payments from their accounts by *credit transfer to others who may or may not have bank accounts. **Bancogiro** is a giro system in operation in Europe, enabling customers of the same bank to make payments to each other by immediate book entry. **2.** A colloquial name for a payment made by the UK Department of Social Security to a person in need of financial support.

**globalization**  The process that has enabled investment in financial markets to be carried out on an international basis. It has come about as a result of improvements in technology and *deregulation; as a result of globalization, for example, investors in London can buy shares or bonds directly from Japanese brokers in Tokyo rather than passing through intermediaries. *See also* disintermediation.

**GmbH**  Abbreviation for *Gesellschaft mit beschränkter Haftung. Compare* AG.

**GNMA**  Abbreviation for *Government National Mortgage Association, often referred to colloquially as *Ginnie Mae.

**GNP**  Abbreviation for *gross national product.

**godfather offer**  A *tender offer pitched so high that the management of the target company is unable to discourage shareholders from accepting it.

**going-concern concept**  A principle of accounting practice that assumes businesses to be going concerns, unless circumstances indicate otherwise. It assumes that an enterprise will continue in operation for the foreseeable future, i.e. that the accounts assume no intention or necessity to liquidate or significantly curtail the scale of the enterprise's operation. The implications of this principle are that assets are shown at cost, or at cost less depreciation, and not at their break-up values; it also assumes that liabilities applicable only on liquidation are not shown. The **going-concern value** of a business is higher than the value that would be achieved by disposing of its individual assets, since it is assumed that the business has a continuing potential to earn profits.

**gold card**  A *credit card that entitles its holder to various benefits (e.g. an unsecured overdraft, some insurance cover, a higher limit) in addition to those offered to standard card holders. Higher annual fees are charged by credit-card companies. The cards are available only to those on higher-than-average incomes. Some of the costs are offset to the customer by offering lower interest rates on outstanding debts.

**gold clause**  A clause in a loan agreement between governments stipulating that repayments must be made in the gold equivalent of the currency involved at the time either the agreement or the loan was made. The purpose is to protect the lender against a fall in the borrower's currency, especially in countries suffering high rates of inflation.

**gold coins**  Coins made of gold ceased to circulate after World War I. At one time it was illegal to hold more than four post-1837 gold coins and there have been various restrictions on dealing in and exporting gold coins at various times. Since 1979 (Exchange Control, Gold Coins Exemption, Order) gold coins may be imported and exported without restriction, except that gold coins more than 50 years old with a value in excess of £8000 cannot be exported without authorization from the Department of Trade and Industry. *See also* Britannia coins; Krugerrand.

**golden handcuffs**  *See* golden hello.

**golden handshake**  *See* compensation for loss of office.

**golden hello**  A financial incentive paid by a securities firm (e.g. a *market maker) to a newly employed specialist, such as a dealer or investment analyst, who leaves another firm. **Golden handcuffs** are financial inducements used to persuade specialists to stay in a particular firm. Golden hellos and golden handcuffs became popular at the time of *Big Bang, when the major stockbroking firms were attempting to gain a large share of the market by employing the leading specialists.

**golden parachute**  A clause in the employment contract of a senior executive in a company that provides for financial and other benefits if the executive is sacked or decides to leave as the result of a takeover or change of ownership.

**golden share**  A share in a company that controls at least 51% of the voting rights. A golden share has been retained by the UK government in some *privatization issues to ensure that the company does not fall into foreign or other unacceptable hands.

**gold market**  *See* bullion.

**gold pool**  An organization of eight countries (Belgium, France, Italy, Netherlands, Switzerland, UK, USA, and West Germany) that between 1961 and 1968 joined together in an attempt to stabilize the price of gold.

**gold standard**  A former monetary system in which a country's currency unit was fixed in terms of a specific quantity of gold bullion. In this system currency was freely convertible into gold and free import and export of gold was permitted. The UK was on the gold standard from the early 19th century until it finally withdrew in 1931. Most other countries ceased to peg their currencies to the value of gold soon after. *See also* International Monetary Fund.

**gold tranche**  *See* reserve tranche.

**good**  A *commodity or *service regarded by economists as satisfying a human need. An **economic good** is one that is both needed and sufficiently scarce to command a price.

**goodwill**  An *intangible asset that normally represents the excess of the value of a business over the value of its *tangible assets. This excess value is largely attributable to the fact that the business generates profits in excess of the return to be expected from investing a sum equivalent to the value of the tangible assets alone. The goodwill is a saleable asset when a business is sold and is sometimes shown as such in the balance sheet. However, for limited companies, the Companies Act 1981 stipulates that goodwill purchased in this way must be written off by charges to the *profit and loss account over a period not exceeding its economic life. *See* amortization.

**go public** To apply to a stock exchange to become a *public limited company. *See* flotation.

**gourde** (G) The standard monetary unit of Haiti, divided into 100 centimes.

**government actuary** A government officer who, with a small team of *actuaries, has the responsibility of estimating future expenditure on the basis of observed population trends. The government actuary provides a consulting service to government departments and to Commonwealth governments, advising on social security schemes and superannuation arrangements and on government supervision of insurance companies and *Friendly Societies.

**government broker** The stockbroker formerly appointed by the government to sell government securities on the London Stock Exchange, under the instructions of the Bank of England. The government broker is also the broker to the National Debt Commissioners (*see* national debt). Until October 1986 (*see* Big Bang) the government broker was traditionally the senior partner of Mullins & Co. Since then, when the Bank of England started its own gilt-edged dealing room, the government broker has been appointed from the gilt-edged division of the Bank of England, although some of the functions formerly carried out by the government broker are now undertaken by the *primary dealers.

**Government National Mortgage Association (GNMA)** A US government agency that guarantees payment on securities backed by mortgages granted by such national organizations as the Federal Housing Association. *See also* Ginnie Mae.

**government security** *See* gilt-edged security.

**Government Statistical Service (GSS)** A service of statistical information and advice provided to the UK government by specialist staffs employed in the statistics divisions of individual government departments. The statistics collected are made generally available through such publications as *Social Trends*, published for the Central Statistical Office by HM Stationery Office.

**government stock** Stocks issued by a government, e.g. US Treasury bonds or UK Treasury stock and Exchequer stock (*see* gilt-edged security).

**Gower Report** A report on the protection of investors delivered to the UK government in 1984 by Professor J. Gower. Many of its recommendations were adopted in the subsequent *Financial Services Act 1986.

**Grain and Feed Trade Association (GAFTA)** A commodity association that provides contracts for transaction in grain, rice, and animal feeds. It no longer provides a futures or options market, which has now moved to *London FOX.

**granny bond** An index-linked savings certificate (*see* National Savings). They were formerly only available to persons over retirement age, hence the name.

**granter** The seller of an *option.

**grant-in-aid** Any grant from central government to a local authority for particular services, other than the rate-support grant.

**grant of probate**  An order from the High Court in the UK authorizing the
executors of a will to deal with and distribute the property of the deceased
person. If the person died intestate or did not appoint executors, the
administrator of the estate has to obtain *letters of administration.

**Green Book**  An informal name for the book entitled *Unlisted Securities
Market*, issued by the London Stock Exchange. It sets out the terms and
conditions for admission to the USM and the subsequent obligations of the
companies involved.

**green currencies**  The currencies of members of the European Community
using artificial rates of exchange for the purposes of the *Common Agricultural
Policy (CAP). Their object is to protect farm prices in the member countries
from the wide variations due to fluctuations in the real rates of exchange. Green
currencies used as their bases the European Unit of Account (EUA); this was
later replaced by the *European Currency Unit (ECU).
    The **green pound** is the popular name for the British pound sterling used as
a green currency. It is used to calculate payments due by or to the UK to or from
the fund of the CAP, i.e. when the value of the pound sterling differs from the
value of the green pound.

**greenmail**  The purchase of a large block of shares in a company, which are
then sold back to the company at a premium over the market price in return for
a promise not to launch a bid for the company. This practice is not uncommon
in the USA, where companies are much freer than in the UK to buy their own
shares. Although the morality of greenmail is dubious, it can be extremely
profitable. It is also sometimes called **greymail**.

**green pound**  *See* green currencies.

**grey knight**  In a takeover battle, a counterbidder whose ultimate intentions
are undeclared. The original unwelcome bidder is the *black knight, the
welcome counterbidder for the target company is the *white knight. The grey
knight is an ambiguous intervener whose appearance is unwelcome to all.

**greymail**  *See* greenmail.

**grey market**  **1.** Any market for goods that are in short supply. It differs from a
black market in being legal; a black market is usually not. **2.** A market in shares
that have not been issued, although they are due to be issued in a short time.
Market makers will often deal with investors or speculators who are willing to
trade in anticipation of receiving an allotment of these shares or are willing to
cover their deals after flotation. This type of grey market provides an indication
of the market price (and premium, if any) after flotation. An investor who does
not receive the anticipated allocation has to buy the shares on the open market,
often at a loss.

**grey wave**  A company that is thought to be potentially profitable and
ultimately a good investment, but that is unlikely to fulfil expectations in the
near future. The fruits of an investment in the present should be available when
the investor has grey hair.

**groschen**  **1.** An Austrian monetary unit, worth one hundredth of a
*schilling. **2.** A German coin, worth 10 pfennige.

**gross domestic product (GDP)** The monetary value of all the goods and services produced by an economy over a specified period. It is measured in three ways:

(i) on the basis of expenditure, i.e. the value of all goods and services bought, including consumption, capital expenditure, increase in the value of stocks, government expenditure, and exports less imports;

(ii) on the basis of income, i.e. income arising from employment, self-employment, rent, company profits (public and private), and stock appreciation;

(iii) on the basis of the value added by industry, i.e. the value of sales less the costs of raw materials.

In the UK, statistics for GDP are published monthly by the government on all three bases, although there are large discrepancies between each measure. Economists are usually interested in the real rate of change of GDP to measure the performance of an economy, rather than the absolute level of GDP. *See also* GDP deflator; gross national product (GNP); net national product (NNP).

**gross income 1.** The income of a person or an organization before the deduction of the expenses incurred in earning it. **2.** Income that is liable to tax but from which the tax has not been deducted. For many types of income, tax may be deducted at source (*see* deductions at source) leaving the taxpayer with a net amount.

**gross interest** The amount of interest applicable to a particular loan or deposit before tax is deducted. Interest rates may be quoted gross (as they are on government securities) or net (as in most building society deposits or bank deposits). The gross interest less the tax deducted at the basic rate of income tax gives the net interest. Any tax suffered is usually, but not always, available as a credit against tax liabilities. Since 1991 low wage-earners and non-taxpayers have been able to apply to have interest on bank and building-society accounts paid gross.

**gross national product (GNP)** The *gross domestic product (GDP) with the addition of interest, profits, and dividends received from abroad by UK residents. The GNP better reflects the welfare of the population in monetary terms, although it is not as accurate a guide as to the productive performance of the economy as the GDP. *See also* net national product (NNP).

**gross profit** The total sales revenue of an organization, less the cost of the goods sold. The cost of the goods sold includes their purchase price and costs of bringing them to a state to be sold but not the costs of distribution, general administration, or finance costs.

**gross receipts** The total amount of money received by a business in a specified period before any deductions for costs, raw materials, taxation, etc. *Compare* net receipts.

**gross yield** The *yield on a security calculated before tax is deducted. This yield is often quoted for the purpose of comparison even on ordinary shares, where dividends have tax deducted before they are paid. The yield after tax is called the **net yield**.

**groszy** A monetary unit of Poland, worth one hundredth of a *zloty.

**group accounts** *See* group of companies.

**group income** A means of enabling dividends and other payments to be made between members of groups of companies in specified circumstances without accounting for *advance corporation tax. The dividends when received are not *franked investment income but are referred to as group income. Like franked investment income they are not liable to corporation tax in the recipient company.

**group life assurance** A life-assurance policy that covers a number of people, usually a group of employees or the members of a particular club or association. Often a single policy is issued and premiums are deducted from salaries or club-membership fees. In return for an agreement that all employees or members join the scheme, insurers are prepared to ask only a few basic questions about the health of a person joining. However, with the advent of AIDS insurers are no longer prepared to waive all health enquiries.

**group of companies** A holding (parent) company together with its subsidiaries. A company is a **subsidiary** of another company if the parent company holds more than half of the nominal value of its *equity capital or holds some shares in it and controls the composition of its board of directors. If one company has subsidiaries, which themselves have subsidiaries, all the companies involved are members of the same group. Groups of companies are required by the UK Companies Act 1985 to file **group accounts**, which normally consist of a consolidated balance sheet and a consolidated profit and loss account for the whole group. In certain circumstances the Department of Trade and Industry will permit groups to publish separate accounts for each subsidiary without consolidation or to omit certain subsidiaries from group accounts. The reasons for doing so, however, have to be bona fide.

**Group of Five (G5)** The five countries France, Japan, UK, USA, and Germany who have agreed to stabilize their exchange rates by acting together to overcome adverse market forces. The agreement was made at the Plaza Hotel, New York and is known as the **Plaza Agreement**.

**Group of Seven (G7)** The seven leading industrial nations: USA, Japan, Germany, France, UK, Italy, and Canada. This group evolved from the first economic summit held in 1976 and now holds an annual meeting attended by heads of state. The original aim was to discuss economic coordination but the agenda has since broadened to include political issues. However, increasing enthusiasm for international economic cooperation in the 1980s led to collective action, for example on exchange rates as a result of meetings of G7 finance ministers.

**Group of Ten (G10; The Paris Club)** The ten relatively prosperous industrial nations that agreed in 1962 to lend money to the *International Monetary Fund (IMF). They are Belgium, Canada, France, Italy, Japan, Netherlands, Sweden, Germany, UK, and USA. They inaugurated *Special Drawing Rights. Switzerland, although not a member of the IMF, is a party to the *general arrangements to borrow, which the G10 countries established to provide additional credit facilities.

**Group of Three (G3)** The three largest industrialized economies, i.e. the USA, Germany, and Japan.

**group relief** A means of enabling a company within a group of companies to transfer to another company in the same group the benefit of its own tax losses or certain other payments for which it is unable to obtain tax relief in its own right. This relief is not available for all losses and the requirements for group status are rigidly defined. There are other possible tax reliefs available within groups, e.g. surrender of *advance corporation tax, group roll-overs (*see* roll-over relief), and *group income, although none of these qualify as group relief.

**growth** **1.** An increase in the value of an asset. If growth is sought in an investment, it is an increase in its capital value that is required. *See also* growth stocks. **2.** The expansion of an economy, usually expressed in terms of an increase of national income.

**growth industry** Any industry that is expected to grow faster than others.

**growth stocks** Securities that are expected to offer the investor sustained *capital growth. Investors and investment managers often distinguish between growth stocks and income stocks. The former are expected to provide *capital gains; the latter, high income. The investor will usually expect a growth stock to be an ordinary share in a company whose products are selling well and whose sales are expected to expand, whose capital expenditure on new plant and equipment is high, whose earnings are growing, and whose management is strong, resourceful, and investing in product development and long-term research.

**GSS** Abbreviation for *Government Statistical Service.

**guarani** (₡) The standard monetary unit of Paraguay, divided into 100 céntimos.

**guarantee** **1.** *See* warranty. **2.** A promise made by a third party (**guarantor**), who is not a party to a contract between two others, that the guarantor will be liable if one of the parties fails to fulfil the contractual obligations. For example, a bank may make a loan to a person, provided that a guarantor is prepared to repay the loan if the borrower fails to do so. The banker may require the guarantor to provide some *security to support the guarantee. *See also* bank guarantee.

**guaranteed-income bond** A bond issued by a life-assurance company that guarantees the purchaser a fixed income for a specified period as well as a guaranteed return of capital at the end of the term or on prior death. *See also* single-premium assurance.

**guaranteed minimum pension** The earnings-related component of a state pension that a person would have been entitled to as an employee of a company, had that person not contracted out of the *State Earnings-Related Pension Scheme (SERPS). Any private pension contract must pay at least the guaranteed minimum pension if it is to be an acceptable replacement of a SERPS pension.

**guaranteed stocks** Stocks issued by UK nationalized industries on which the income is guaranteed by the government.

**Guarantee Fund for Danish Options and Futures (FUTOP)** An options and futures exchange, based in Copenhagen, that opened in September 1988 and trades as an exchange in Danish government bond futures, options, and mortgage credits.

**guarantor** A person who guarantees to pay a debt incurred by someone else if that person fails to repay it. A person who acts as a guarantor for a bank loan, for example, must repay the loan if the borrower fails to repay it when it becomes due.

**guilder** The standard monetary unit of the Netherlands (f), the Antilles (NAf), and Surinam (Sf), divided into 100 cents.

**haircut**  *See* margin.

**halala**  A monetary unit of Saudi Arabia, worth one hundredth of a *riyal.

**haler**  A monetary unit of the Czech Republic and Slovakia, worth one hundredth of a *koruna.

**half-commission man**  A person who is not a member of a stock exchange but works for a *stockbroker, introducing clients in return for half, or some other agreed share, of the commission.

**hammering**  An announcement on the *London Stock Exchange that a broker is unable to meet his or her obligations. It was formerly (until 1970) introduced by three blows of a hammer by a waiter and followed by the broker's name.

**Hang Seng Index**  An arithmetically weighted index based on the capital value of 33 stocks on the Hong Kong Stock Exchange. It was first quoted in 1964 and takes its name from the Hang Seng Bank. The number of stocks, 33, was chosen because the bank was founded in 1933 and 33 is a lucky number in Chinese astrology.

**hao**  A monetary unit of Vietnam, worth one tenth of a *dông.

**harakiri swap**  A swap made without a profit margin; the term derives from the Japanese word for ritual suicide.

**hard commodities**  *See* commodity.

**hard currency**  A currency that is commonly accepted throughout the world; they are usually those of the western industrialized countries although other currencies have achieved this status, especially within regional trading blocs. Holdings of hard currency are valued because of their universal purchasing power. Countries with *soft currencies go to great lengths to obtain and maintain stocks of hard currencies, often imposing strict restrictions on their use by the private citizen.

**hard dollars**  A fee paid to a US stockbroker, investment adviser, etc., for research, analysis, or advice, as opposed to **soft dollars**, which refers to the commission earned on purchases made.

**heavy share**  A share that has a high price relative to the average price of shares on the market. As investors tend to prefer to buy larger numbers of low-priced shares, heavy shares are often split, i.e. the par value is divided by two or four, which has the same effect on the market price.

**hedging**  An operation undertaken by a trader or dealer who wishes to protect an *open position, especially a sale or a purchase of a commodity, currency, security, etc., that is likely to fluctuate in price over the period that the position remains open. For example, a manufacturer may contract to sell a large quantity of a product for delivery over the next six months. If the product depends on a raw material that fluctuates in price, and if the manufacturer does not have sufficient raw material in stock, an open position will result. This open position can be hedged by buying the raw material required on a *futures contract; if it has to be paid for in a foreign currency the manufacturer's currency needs can be hedged by buying that foreign currency forward or on an *option. Operations of this type do not offer total protection because the prices of *spot goods and futures do not always move together, but it is possible to reduce the vulnerability of an open position substantially by hedging.

Buying futures or options as a hedge is only one kind of hedging; it is known as **long hedging**. In **short hedging**, something is sold to cover a risk. For example, a fund manager may have a large holding of long-term fixed income investments and is worried that an anticipated rise in interest rates will reduce the value of the *portfolio. This risk can be hedged by selling interest-rate futures on a *financial futures market. If interest rates rise the loss in the value of the portfolio will be offset by the profit made in covering the futures sale at a lower price.

**hedging against inflation** Protecting one's capital against the ravages of inflation by buying *equities or making other investments that are likely to rise with the general level of prices.

**hidden reserve** Funds held in reserve but not disclosed on the balance sheet (they are also known as **off-balance-sheet reserves** or **secret reserves**). They arise when an asset is deliberately either undisclosed or undervalued. Such hidden reserves are permitted for some banking institutions but are not permitted for limited companies as they reduce profits and therefore the corporation-tax liability of the company.

**hidden tax** A tax, the *incidence of which may be hidden from the person who is suffering it. An example could be a tax levied on goods at the wholesale level, which increases the retail price in such a way that the final customer cannot detect either that it has happened or the amount of the extra cost. Again, a government might introduce a hidden tax by artificially causing the price of a certain utility to be raised above its usual commercial value.

**higher rates** Rates of taxation above the *basic rate in the UK income tax schedule of rates. The higher rate may apply to all income above a specified figure or there may be a series of higher-rate bands, the tax rate in each band being higher than its predecessor. The higher-rate tax for all income above a specified figure is 15%, i.e. all income above the specified figure is taxed at 40% (25% basic rate and 15% higher rate). *See also* progressive tax.

**high yielder** A stock or share that gives a high yield but is more speculative than most, i.e. its price may fluctuate.

**hire purchase (HP)** A method of buying goods in which the purchaser takes possession of them as soon as an initial instalment of the price (a **deposit**) has been paid; ownership is obtained when all the agreed number of subsequent instalments have been completed. A **hire-purchase agreement** differs from a **credit-sale agreement** and **sale by instalments** (or a **deferred payment agreement**) because in these transactions ownership passes when the contract is signed. It also differs from a contract of hire, because in this case ownership never passes. Hire-purchase agreements in the UK were formerly controlled by government regulations stipulating the minimum deposit and the length of the repayment period. These controls were removed in 1982. Hire-purchase agreements were also formerly controlled by the Hire Purchase Act 1965, but most are now regulated by the Consumer Credit Act 1974. In this Act a hire-purchase agreement is regarded as one in which goods are bailed in return for periodical payments by the bailee; ownership passes to the bailee if the terms of the agreement are complied with and the option to purchase is exercised.

A hire-purchase agreement often involves a *finance company as a third party. The seller of the goods sells them outright to the finance company, which enters into a hire-purchase agreement with the hirer.

**historical-cost accounting**  The traditional form of accounting, in which assets are shown in balance sheets at their cost to the organization (historical cost), less any appropriate depreciation. In times of high inflation this method tends to overstate profits; as a result other forms of accounting (*see* current-cost accounting; current purchasing power accounting) were used. Most organizations have now reverted to historical-cost accounting.

**holder**  The person in possession of a *bill of exchange or promissory note. This person may be the payee, the endorsee, or the bearer. When value (which includes a past debt or liability) has at any time been given for a bill, the holder is a **holder for value**, as regards the acceptor and all who were parties to the bill before value was given. A **holder in due course** is one who has taken a bill of exchange in good faith and for value, before it was overdue, and without notice of previous dishonour or of any defect in the title of the person who negotiated or transferred the bill. This person holds the bill free from any defect of title of prior parties and may enforce payment against all parties liable on the bill.

**holding company (parent company)**  A company in a *group of companies that holds shares in other companies (usually, but not necessarily, its subsidiaries).

**home banking**  Carrying out normal banking transactions by means of a home computer linked to a bank's computer. Payment of telephone bills was the first major use of the service in the USA, where it is largely restricted to New York and other major cities. In the UK limited experiments have been conducted but only a small minority of High-Street bank customers have access to the service; it is more common among business customers who make use of electronic banking services between business premises and the bank.

**home service assurance**  *See* industrial life assurance.

**Hong Kong Commodities Exchange Ltd**  A commodity exchange in Hong Kong founded in 1977. It deals in sugar futures and other commodities.

**Hong Kong stock exchanges**  Two exchanges were established in 1891 and 1921, which were merged into the Hong Kong Stock Exchange in 1947. This took over the Far East Stock Exchange (founded 1969), the Kam Ngam Stock Exchange (founded 1971), and the Kowloon Stock Exchange (founded 1972) to become the **Stock Exchange of Hong Kong** in April 1986. *See also* Hang Seng Index.

**honour policy** A marine insurance policy which covers the risk of a person who has an interest in a voyage in circumstances in which the interest may be difficult to establish.

**horizontal spread** A combination of *options with different expiry dates, such as a long put option combined with a short put option.

**hostile bid** A *takeover bid that is unwelcome either to the board of directors of the target company or to its shareholders.

**hot money** **1.** Money that moves at short notice from one financial centre to another in search of the highest short-term interest rates, for the purposes of *arbitrage, or because its owners are apprehensive of some political intervention in the money market, such as a *devaluation. Hot money can influence a country's *balance of payments. **2.** Money that has been acquired dishonestly and must therefore be untraceable.

**HP** Abbreviation for *hire purchase.

**hypothecation** **1.** An authority given to a banker, usually as a **letter of hypothecation**, to enable the bank to sell goods that have been pledged (*see* pledge) to them as security for a loan. It applies when the bank is unable to obtain the goods themselves. The goods have often been pledged as security in relation to a documentary bill, the banker being entitled to sell the goods if the bill is dishonoured by non-acceptance or non-payment. **2.** A mortgage granted by a ship's master to secure the repayment with interest, on the safe arrival of the ship at her destination, of money borrowed during a voyage as a matter of necessity (e.g. to pay for urgent repairs). The hypothecation of a ship itself, with or without cargo, is called **bottomry** and is effected by a **bottomry bond**; that of its cargo alone is **respondentia** and requires a **respondentia bond**. The bondholder is entitled to a maritime *lien.

**IBBR** Abbreviation for Inter Bank Bid Rate. *See* London Inter Bank Bid Rate.

**IBEL** Abbreviation for *interest-bearing eligible liabilities.

**IBMBR** Abbreviation for Inter Bank Market Bid Rate. *See* London Inter Bank Bid Rate.

**IBNR claims reserve** A reserve held by an insurance company for claims 'incurred but not yet reported'.

**IBRD** Abbreviation for *International Bank for Reconstruction and Development.

**ICC** Abbreviation for *International Chamber of Commerce.

**ICCH** Abbreviation for International Commodities Clearing House. *See* London Clearing House.

**IDA** Abbreviation for *International Development Association.

**IFA** Abbreviation for *independent financial adviser.

**IFC** Abbreviation for *International Finance Corporation.

**Ifox** Abbreviation for *Irish Futures and Options Exchange.

**illegal contract** A contract prohibited by statute (e.g. one between traders providing for minimum resale prices) or illegal at common law on the grounds of *public policy. An illegal contract is totally void, but neither party (unless innocent of the illegality) can recover any money paid or property transferred under it, according to the maxim *ex turpi causa non oritur actio* (a right of action does not arise out of an evil cause). Related transactions may also be affected. A related transaction between the same parties (e.g. if X gives Y a promissory note for money due under an illegal contract) is equally tainted with the illegality and is therefore void. The same is true of a related transaction with a third party (e.g. if Z lends X the money to pay Y) if the original illegality is known to the third party.

**illegal partnership** A partnership formed for an illegal purpose and therefore disallowed by law. A partnership of more than 20 partners is illegal, except in the case of certain professionals, e.g. accountants, solicitors, and stockbrokers.

**IMF** Abbreviation for *International Monetary Fund.

**immediate annuity** An *annuity contract that begins to make payments as soon as the contract has come into force.

**immediate holding company** A company that has a *controlling interest in another company, even though it is itself controlled by a third company, which is the *holding company of both companies.

**immigrant remittances** Money sent by immigrants from the country in which they work to their families in their native countries. These sums can be a valuable source of foreign exchange for the native countries.

**impact day** The day on which the terms of a *new issue of shares are made public.

**implied term** A provision of a contract not agreed to by the parties in words but either regarded by the courts as necessary to give effect to their presumed intentions or introduced into the contract by statute (as in the case of contracts for the sale of goods). An implied term may constitute either a condition of the contract or a *warranty; if it is introduced by statute it often cannot be expressly excluded.

**imprest account** A means of controlling petty-cash expenditure in which a person is given a certain sum of money (float or imprest). When some of it has been spent that person provides the appropriate vouchers for the amounts spent and is then reimbursed so that the float is restored. Thus at any given time the person should have either vouchers or cash to a total of the amount of the float.

**imputation system of taxation** A system of *corporation tax in which some, or all, of the corporation tax is treated as a tax credit on account of the income tax payable by the shareholders on their dividends. Such a system was introduced into the UK in 1972 and the imputation works through the system of *advance corporation tax.

**IMRO** Abbreviation for Investment Management Regulatory Organization. *See* Self-Regulating Organization.

**incestuous share dealing** The buying and selling of shares in companies that belong to the same group, in order to obtain an advantage of some kind, usually a tax advantage. The legality of the transaction will depend on its nature.

**inchoate instrument** A *negotiable instrument in which not all the particulars are given. The drawer of an inchoate instrument can authorize a third party to fill in a specified missing particular.

**incidence of taxation** The impact of a tax on those who bear its burden, rather than those who pay it. For example, *VAT is paid by traders, but the ultimate burden of it falls on the consumer of the trader's goods or services. Again, a company may pay corporation tax but if it then raises its prices or reduces its employees' wages to recoup the tax it may be said to have shifted the incidence.

**income** Any sum that a person or organization receives either as a reward for effort (e.g. salary or trading profit) or as a return on investments (e.g. rents or interest). From the point of view of taxation, income has to be distinguished from *capital. *See also* income profit.

**income and expenditure account** An account, similar to a *profit and loss account, prepared by an organization whose main purpose is not the generation of profit. It records the income and expenditure of the organization and results in either a surplus of income over expenditure or of expenditure over income. Such an organization's accounts do not use the *accrual concept.

**income bond** **1. (National Savings Income Bond)** A type of bond introduced by the UK Department for *National Savings in 1982. It is designed to pay out a regular monthly income on lump-sum investments. Interest is taxable but not deducted at source; the interest rate is variable. The minimum investment is £2000; larger purchases and additions can be made to existing holdings in multiples of £1000. The maximum holding is £50,000 for each holder (£100,000 can be held jointly). Indexed income bonds were withdrawn in 1987. **2.** *See* guaranteed-income bond.

**income distribution** The payment by a *unit trust of its half-yearly income to unit holders, in proportion to their holdings. The income distributed is the total income less the manager's service charge and income tax at the standard rate.

**income profit** Any sum accruing to a person or organization that represents pure income and is not partly a payment of capital. This term is especially used in a legal sense, when deciding whether annual payments are assessable to Schedule D Case III for income tax purposes. If they are pure income profit they are so assessable; if not there may be a capital element to be disentangled.

**income shares** *See* investment trust.

**incomes policy** A government policy aimed at controlling inflation and maintaining full employment by holding down increases in wages and prices by statutory or other means. In the 1960s and 1970s incomes policies were widely pursued in the developed world. This reflected the strong belief that inflation and unemployment were closely connected, although incomes policies were unpopular with workers, whose wages were held down, often to an extent that caused a fall in the purchasing power of their incomes, as a result of inflation. With the rise of *monetarism and the increasing popularity of laissez-faire government in the 1980s, incomes policies became much less attractive.

**income stock** A stock or share bought primarily for the steady and relatively high income it can be expected to produce. This may be a fixed-interest gilt or an ordinary share with a good *yield record.

**income tax** A direct tax on income. The principal direct tax in most countries, it is levied on the incomes of either individual taxpayers or households. It lends itself particularly well to levying ability-to-pay taxes and to progressive taxation. Its defects are that it may discourage work and risk-bearing investment. In the UK, the tax is calculated on the taxpayer's *taxable income, i.e. gross income less any *income-tax allowances and deductions. If the allowances and deductions exceed the gross income in a *fiscal year, no income tax is payable; if tax has been deducted at source it will normally be repayable (*see* deductions at source). In the UK, from 6 April 1992 the first £2000 of taxable income is charged at a reduced rate of 20% after which tax at the *basic rate applies. For those on high incomes, higher-rate tax is also charged (*see* higher rates). *See also* PAYE.

**income-tax allowances** Allowances and deductions that may be made from a taxpayer's gross income before calculating the income-tax liability. In general, these can be divided into two groups. **Personal reliefs** are primarily concerned with the individual circumstances of the taxpayer – whether the taxpayer is a single person, a married man or a married woman (or in some countries, a married couple); the age and dependants of the taxpayer are also taken into account (*see* personal allowances). **Deductions**, on the other hand, are certain payments that can be used to reduce a tax liability. In the UK, for example, these would include interest on a loan to buy property (subject to a ceiling of £30,000), contributions to a pension scheme, medical insurance for those over 65, charitable donations, and investment through the *Business Expansion Scheme.

**income-tax year** *See* fiscal year.

**inconvertible paper money** Paper money that is not convertible into gold. Most paper money now falls into this category, although until 1931, in the UK, the Bank of England had an obligation to supply any holder of a banknote with the appropriate quantity of gold.

**incorporated company** *See* company.

**increasing capital** An increase in the number or value of the shares in a company to augment its authorized *share capital. If the articles of association of the company do not permit this to be done (with the agreement of the members), the articles will need to be changed. A company cannot increase its share capital unless authorized to do so by its articles of association.

**indemnity  1.** An agreement by one party to make good the losses suffered by another, usually by payment of money, repair, replacement, or reinstatement. This is the function of *indemnity insurance. In some professions indemnities exist to protect the insured against damage caused to a third party by the insured's actions; for example, doctors may have a professional indemnity to cover any mistakes in treatment or incorrect diagnosis.  **2.** An undertaking by a bank's client, who has lost a document (such as a share certificate or bill of lading), that the bank will be held harmless against any consequences of the document's absence if it proceeds to service the documents that have not been mislaid. The bank usually requires a *letter of indemnity to make sure that it suffers no loss.

**indemnity insurance** Any insurance designed to compensate a policyholder for a loss suffered, by the payment of money, repair, replacement, or reinstatement. In every case the policyholder is entitled to be restored to the same financial position as that immediately before the loss-causing event occurred. There must be no element of profit to the policyholder nor any element of loss. Most – but not all – insurance policies are *indemnity contracts. For example, personal accident and life-assurance policies are not contracts of indemnity as it is impossible to calculate the value of a lost life or limb (as the value of a car or other property can be calculated).

**independent financial adviser (IFA)** A person defined under the *Financial Services Act 1986 as an adviser who is not committed to the products of any one company or organization. Such a person is licensed to operate by one of the *Self-Regulating Organizations or *Recognized Professional Bodies. With no loyalties except to the customer, the IFA must offer **best advice** from the whole market place. Eight categories of IFA exist, grouped into four main areas: advising on investments; arranging and transacting life assurance, pensions, and unit trusts; arranging and transacting other types of investments; and management of investments. All licensed independent financial advisers contribute to a compensation fund for the protection of their customers.

**independent intermediary**  A person who acts as a representative of a prospective policyholder in the arrangement of an insurance or assurance policy. In *life assurance and *pensions it is a person who represents more than one insurer and is legally bound to offer advice to clients on the type of assurance or investment contracts best suited to their needs. In general insurance the independent intermediary can represent more than six insurers and is responsible for advising clients on policies that best suit their needs. They must, themselves, have *professional-indemnity insurance to cover any errors that they may make. Although, in both cases, intermediaries are the servants of the policyholder (and the insurer is therefore not responsible for their errors), they are paid by the insurer in the form of a commission, being an agreed percentage of the first or renewal premium paid by the policyholder.

**independent taxation**  A system of personal taxation introduced in the UK in the fiscal year 1990–91 in which a husband and wife are treated as completely separate and independent taxpayers for both *income tax and *capital-gains tax. The change affects a number of reliefs, primarily the personal allowance, to which every taxpayer is entitled: it also introduced a new married couples allowance. Moreover under this system each spouse is entitled to their own capital-gains tax exemption and wives will pay tax on their own income, including their share arising from jointly held property.

**indexation**  The policy of connecting such economic variables as wages, taxes, social-security payments, annuities, or pensions to rises in the general price level (*see* inflation) This policy is often advocated by economists in the belief that it mitigates the effects of inflation. In practice, complete indexation is rarely possible, so that inflation usually leaves somebody worse off (e.g. lenders, savers) and somebody better off (borrowers). *See* Retail Price Index.

**indexation allowance**  An amount that can be deducted from capital gains in the UK since 1982 to offset the effects of inflation for *capital-gains tax purposes. It involves indexing items of allowable expenditure by reference to the *Retail Price Index. The rules for indexation are contained in the Finance Acts 1982 and 1985.

**index futures**  A *futures contract on a *financial futures market, such as the *London International Financial Futures and Options Exchange, which offers facilities for trading in futures and *options on the FT-SE 100 Index and the FT-SE Eurotrack 100 Index (*see* Financial Times Share Indexes). On the FT-SE 100 Index the trading unit is £25 per index point; thus if a futures contract is purchased when the index stands at 2400, say, the buyer is covering an equivalent purchase of equities of £60,000 (£25 × 2400). If the index rises 100 points the purchaser can sell a matching futures contract at this level, making a profit of £2500 (£25 × 100). On the FT-SE Eurotrack 100 Index the trading unit is DM100 per index point. *See also* portfolio insurance.

**index-linked annuity**  *See* indexation.

**index-linked gilts**  *See* gilt-edged security; indexation.

**index-linked savings certificates**  *See* indexation; National Savings.

**index number**  A number used to represent the changes in a set of values between a *base year and the present. *See* Financial Times Share Indexes; Retail Price Index.

**indirect taxation** Taxation that is intended to be borne by persons or organizations other than those who pay the tax (*compare* direct taxation). The principal indirect tax in the UK is *VAT, which is paid by traders as goods or services enter into the chain of production, but which is ultimately borne by the consumer of the goods or services. One of the advantages of indirect taxes is that they can be collected from comparatively few sources while their economic effects can be widespread.

**individual retirement account (IRA)** A US pension plan that allows annual sums to be set aside from earnings free of tax and accumulated in a fund, which pays interest. Basic-rate tax is payable once the saver starts to withdraw from the account, which must be done no later than the participant's 70th birthday. The concession is not available to employees in a company-pension scheme or profit-sharing scheme.

**industrial bank** A relatively small *finance house that specializes in *hire purchase, obtaining its own funds by accepting long-term deposits, largely from the general public. Industrial banks were pioneered in the early years of this century in the USA by Arthur Morris, a US businessman.

**industrial life assurance** A life-assurance policy, usually for a small amount, the premiums for which are paid on a regular basis (weekly or monthly) and collected by an official of the assurance company, who calls at the policyholder's home. Records of the premium payments are kept in a book, which – together with the policy document – has to be produced to make a claim. This type of assurance began in industrial areas (hence its name), where small weekly policies were purchased to help pay the funeral expenses of the policyholder. The company official who calls to collect the premium is called an agent or, in certain areas, a tally man (*see also* agency). This type of insurance is now more widely known as **home service assurance**.

**inflation** A persistent rise in the level of prices and wages throughout an economy. If the rises in wages are sufficient to raise production costs, further rises in prices inevitably occur, creating an **inflationary spiral** in which the rate of inflation increases continuously and in some cases alarmingly (**hyperinflation**). The causes of inflation are not simple and probably cannot be ascribed to any single factor, although according to *monetarism it is an inevitable consequence of too rapid an increase in the *money supply, a view proposed by the US economist Milton Friedman (1912–    ). Monetarists therefore believe that inflation can be restricted by judicious control of the money supply. They also tend to support the view that high unemployment is a deterrent to persistent wage claims (those in work being grateful for being paid at all) and therefore provides a curb on the inflationary spiral. It also reduces the total demand in the economy. Followers of the British economist John Maynard Keynes (1883–1946), on the other hand, believe that factors other than the money supply create inflation. According to this theory, low inflation and low unemployment can both be maintained by a rigidly enforced *incomes policy. *See also* cost-push inflation; demand-pull inflation.

The rate of inflation in an economy is usually measured by means of price indexes, notably the *Retail Price Index.

**inflation accounting** A method of accounting that, unlike *historical-cost accounting, attempts to take account of the fact that a monetary unit (e.g. the pound sterling) does not have a constant value; because of the effects of inflation, successive accounts expressed in that unit do not necessarily give a fair view of the trend of profits. The principal methods of dealing with inflation have been *current-cost accounting and *current purchasing power accounting.

**inflationary gap** **1.** The difference between the total spending in an economy (both private and public) and the total spending that would be needed to maintain full employment. **2.** Government expenditure in excess of taxation income and borrowing from the public. This excess will be financed by increasing the money supply, by printing paper money, or by borrowing from banks.

**inflationary spiral** *See* inflation.

**inheritance tax** A form of wealth tax on amounts inherited, usually in excess of a specified amount that is free of tax (£150,000 in the UK, from the tax year 1992–93). A true inheritance tax would be based on the amounts inherited by an individual or possibly by a household. The inheritance tax introduced in 1986 in the UK is not strictly such a tax since it taxes the total estate left by a deceased person together with a tapered charge on *gifts that that person may have made up to seven years before his or her death. This charge is added to the cumulative total used to calculate the amount of inheritance tax due. For the purposes of working out any inheritance tax due, the estate is said to be comprised of chargeable assets only, such as houses and stocks and shares.

**initial charge** The charge paid to the managers of a *unit trust by an investor when units are first purchased. For most trusts the initial charge ranges between 5% and 6%, as laid down in the trust deed. *Money-market unit trusts and *exempt unit trusts have lower initial charges and in some cases no initial charge.

**initial public offering (IPO)** The US name for a *flotation.

**injunction** An order by a court that a person shall do, or refrain from doing, a particular act. This is an equitable remedy that may be granted by the High Court wherever 'just and convenient'. The county court also has a limited jurisdiction to grant injunctions. An **interlocutory injunction** lasts only until the main action is heard. **Interim injunctions**, lasting a short time only, may be granted on the application of one party without the other being present (an **ex parte interim injunction**) if there is great urgency. **Prohibitory injunctions** forbid the doing of a particular act; **mandatory injunctions** order a person to do some act. Failure to obey an injunction is contempt of court and punishable by a fine or imprisonment.

**inland bill (agency bill)** A *bill of exchange that is both drawn and payable in the UK. Any other bill is classed as a **foreign bill**.

**Inland Revenue** *See* Board of Inland Revenue.

**input tax** The VAT included in the price a trader pays for the goods and services acquired during the course of trading. This tax can be deducted from the *output tax in arriving at the amount to be accounted for to the Customs and Excise.

**inscribed stock (registered stock)** Shares in loan stock, for which the names of the holders are kept in a register rather than by the issue of a certificate of ownership. On a transfer, a new name has to be registered, which makes them cumbersome and unpopular in practice.

**insider dealing (insider trading)** Dealing in company securities with a view to making a profit or avoiding a loss while in possession of information that, if generally known, would affect their price. Under the Companies Securities (Insider Dealing) Act 1985 those who are or have been connected with a company (e.g. the directors, the company secretary, employees, and professional advisers) are prohibited from such dealing on or, in certain circumstances, off the stock exchange if they acquired the information by virtue of their connection and in confidence. The prohibition extends to certain unconnected persons to whom the information has been conveyed.

**insolvency** The inability to pay one's debts when they fall due. In the case of individuals this may lead to *bankruptcy and in the case of companies to *liquidation. In both of these cases the normal procedure is for a specialist, a trustee in bankruptcy or a liquidator, to be appointed to gather and dispose of the assets of the insolvent and to pay the creditors. Insolvency does not always lead to bankruptcy and liquidation, although it often does. An insolvent person may have valuable assets that are not immediately realizable.

**insolvency practitioner** *See* liquidator.

**Insolvency Practitioners Association** A professional body whose members act as *liquidators, receivers, and trustees in *insolvency and are identified by the letters MIPA (membership) or FIPA (fellowship).

**inspection and investigation of a company** An inquiry into the running of a company made by inspectors appointed by the Department of Trade and Industry. Such an inquiry may be held to supply company members with information or to investigate fraud, unfair prejudice, nominee shareholdings, or *insider dealing. The inspectors' report is usually published.

**Inspector of Taxes** A civil servant responsible to the *Board of Inland Revenue for issuing tax returns and assessments, the conduct of appeals, and agreeing tax liabilities with taxpayers.

**instalment** One of a series of payments, especially when buying goods on *hire purchase, settling a debt, or buying a new issue of shares.

**Institute of Actuaries** One of the two professional bodies in the UK to which actuaries belong. To become an actuary it is necessary to qualify as a fellow of one or the other. The roots of the profession go back to 1756, when a Fellow of the Royal Society, James Dodson, produced the first table of premiums for life assurance, after having been turned down for an assurance policy on the grounds of his age. The Institute is in London; the other organization, the **Faculty of Actuaries**, is based in Edinburgh.

**Institute of Chartered Accountants** Any of the three professional accountancy bodies in the UK, the **Institute of Chartered Accountants in England and Wales**, the **Institute of Chartered Accountants of Scotland**, and the **Institute of Chartered Accountants in Ireland**. The institutes are separate but recognize similar codes of practice. The largest is the England and Wales institute, with some 90 000 members, who are identified by the letters ACA or FCA (as are members of the Ireland institute; in Scotland members use the letters CA). The institutes ensure high standards of education and training in accountancy, provide qualification by examination, and supervise professional conduct in the service of clients and of the public. They are members of the Consultative Committee of Accountancy Bodies, whose Accounting Standards

Committee is responsible for drafting accounting standards. *See also* chartered accountant.

**institutional investor (institution)**  A large organization, such as an insurance company, unit trust, bank, trade union, or a pension fund of a large company, that has substantial sums of money to invest on a stock exchange. Institutions usually employ their own investment analysts and advisors; they are usually able to influence stock exchange sentiment more profoundly than private investors and their policies can often affect share prices. Because institutions can build up significant holdings in companies, they can also influence company policy, usually by making their opinions known at shareholders' meetings, especially during *takeover-bid negotiations.

**instrument**  **1.** A formal document. *See* negotiable instrument.  **2.** A tool that is used by a government in achieving its macroeconomic targets. For example, interest rates and the *money supply may be considered instruments in the pursuit of stable prices, while government expenditure and taxation may be considered instruments in the pursuit of full employment.

**insurable interest**  The legal right to enter into an insurance contract. A person is said to have an insurable interest if the event insured against could cause that person a financial loss. For example, anyone may insure their own property as they would incur a loss if an item was lost, destroyed, or damaged. If no financial loss would occur, no insurance can be arranged. For example, a person cannot insure a next-door neighbour's property. The limit of an insurable interest is the value of the item concerned, although there is no limit on the amount of life assurance a person can take out, because the financial effects of death cannot be accurately measured.

Insurable interest was made a condition of all insurance by the Life Assurance Act 1774. Without an insurable interest, an insured person is unable to enforce an insurance contract (or life-assurance contract) as it is the insurable interest that distinguishes insurance from a bet or wager. A marine insurance policy requires that the insurable interest must exist at the time of the loss. Other general forms of insurance require that the insurable interest exists both at the time of contracting and at the time of loss.

**insurable risk**  *See* risk.

**insurance**  A legal contract in which an *insurer promises to pay a specified amount to another party, the *insured, if a particular event (known as the *peril), happens and the insured suffers a financial loss as a result. The insured's part of the contract is to promise to pay an amount of money, known as the **premium**, either once or at regular intervals. In order for an insurance contract to be valid, the insured must have an *insurable interest. It is usual to use the word 'insurance' to cover events (such as a fire) that may or may not happen, whereas *assurance refers to an event (such as death) that must occur at some time (*see also* life assurance). *See also* reinsurance.

**insurance broker**  A person who is registered with the *Insurance Brokers Registration Council to offer advice on all insurance matters and arrange cover, on behalf of the client, with an *insurer. Insurance brokers act as intermediaries and their income comes from commission paid to them by insurers, usually in the form of an agreed percentage of the first premium or on subsequent premiums. Insurance brokers are regulated by *FIMBRA in accordance with the Financial Services Act 1986. *See also* Lloyd's.

**Insurance Brokers Registration Council** A statutory body established under the Insurance Brokers Registration Act 1977. It is responsible for the registration and training of insurance brokers and for laying down rules relating to such matters as accounting practice, staff qualifications, advertising, and the orderly conduct and discipline of broking businesses.

**Insurance Ombudsman** *See* Financial Ombudsman.

**insurance policy** A document that sets out the terms and conditions of an insurance contract, stating the benefits payable and the *premium required. *See also* life assurance.

**insurance premium** *See* insurance; premium.

**insurance tied agent** An agent who represents a particular insurance company or companies. In life and pensions insurance, a tied agent represents only one insurer and is only able to advise the public on the policies offered by that one company. In general insurance (motor, household, holiday, etc.), a tied agent represents no more than six insurers, who are jointly responsible for the financial consequences of any failure or mistake the agent makes. In both cases the agent receives a commission for each policy that is sold and a further commission on each subsequent renewal of the policy. The commission is calculated as an agreed percentage of the total premium paid by the policyholder. The distinction between the two forms of insurance tied agent was a consequence of the Financial Services Act 1986 and the General Insurance Selling Code 1989 of the *Association of British Insurers.

**insured** A person or company covered by an *insurance policy. In some policies that cover death, the alternative word *assured may be used for the person who receives the payment in the event of the assured's death.

**insurer** A person, company, syndicate, or other organization that underwrites an insurance risk.

**intangible asset (invisible asset)** An asset that can neither be seen nor touched. The most common of these are *goodwill, *patents, *trademarks, and copyrights. Goodwill is probably the most intangible and invisible of all assets as no document provides evidence of its existence and its commercial value is difficult to determine. However, it frequently does have very substantial value as the capitalized value of future profits, not attributable purely to the return on *tangible assets. While goodwill is called either an intangible asset or an invisible asset, such items as insurance policies and less tangible overseas investments are usually called invisible assets.

**integration** The combination of two or more companies under the same control for their mutual benefit, by reducing competition, saving costs by reducing overheads, capturing a larger market share, pooling technical or financial resources, cooperating on research and development, etc. In **horizontal** (or **lateral**) **integration** the businesses carry out the same stage in the production process or produce similar products or services; they are therefore competitors. In a monopoly, horizontal integration is complete, while in an oligopoly there is considerable horizontal integration. In **vertical integration** a company obtains control of its suppliers (sometimes called **backward integration**) or of the concerns that buy its products or services (**forward integration**).

**intellectual property**  An *intangible asset, such as a copyright, *patent, or *trademark. *See also* royalty.

**inter-account dealing**  Speculative transactions on the *London Stock Exchange in which all individual purchases and sales within an *account cancel each other out, so that only differences have to be settled. *See also* cash and new.

**interbank market  1.** The part of the London *money market in which banks lend to each other and to other large financial institutions. The *London Inter Bank Offered Rate (LIBOR) is the rate of interest charged on interbank loans. Trading is over-the-counter and usually through brokers and dealers. The sums are large but the periods of the loans are very short, often overnight.  **2.** The market between banks in foreign currencies, including spot currencies and forward *options.

**inter-dealer broker**  A member of the *London Stock Exchange who is only permitted to deal with *market makers, rather than the public.

**interdict**  An *injunction in Scottish law.

**interest**  The charge made for borrowing a sum of money. The *interest rate is the charge made, expressed as a percentage of the total sum loaned, for a stated period of time (usually one year). Thus, a rate of interest of 15% per annum means that for every £100 borrowed for one year, the borrower has to pay a charge of £15, or a charge in proportion for longer or shorter periods. In **simple interest**, the charge is calculated on the sum loaned only, thus $I = Prt$, where $I$ is the interest, $P$ is the principal sum, $r$ is the rate of interest, and $t$ is the period. In **compound interest**, the charge is calculated on the sum loaned plus any interest that has acrued in previous periods. In this case $I = P[(1 + r)^n - 1]$, where $n$ is the number of periods for which interest is separately calculated. Thus, if £500 is loaned for two years at a rate of 12% per annum, compounded quarterly, the value of $n$ will be $4 \times 2 = 8$ and the value of $r$ will be $12/4 = 3\%$. Thus, $I = 500[(1.03)^8 - 1] = £133.38$, whereas on a simple-interest basis it would be only £120. These calculations of interest apply equally to deposits that attract income in the form of interest.

    In general, rates of interest depend on the money supply, the demand for loans, government policy, the risk of nonrepayment as assessed by the lender, the period of the loan, and relative levels of foreign-exchange rates into other currencies.

**interest arbitrage**  Transactions between financial centres in foreign currencies that take advantage of differentials in interest rates between the two centres and the difference between the forward and spot exchange rates. In some circumstances it is possible to make a profit by buying a foreign currency, changing it into the currency of the home market, lending it for a fixed period, and buying back the foreign currency on a forward basis.

**interest-bearing eligible liabilities (IBEL)**  Liabilities recognized by the Bank of England as being held by UK banks, e.g. net deposits. In times of strict monetary control the Bank of England requires other UK banks to deposit a percentage of these liabilities with it.

**interest cover**  A measure of the extent to which a company's earnings (profits before tax) cover interest paid on its loan capital. It is expressed as the ratio of earnings to interest due.

**interest-only mortgage** A *mortgage for those who have an asset, e.g. a *personal equity plan (PEP), which can be used to repay the capital at the end of the loan period. During the loan period the borrower pays the interest on the mortgage.

**interest rate** The amount charged for a loan, usually expressed as a percentage of the sum borrowed. Conversely, the amount paid by a bank, building society, etc., to a depositor on funds deposited, again expressed as a percentage of the sum deposited. *See* annual percentage rate; base rate; London Inter Bank Bid Rate; London Inter Bank Offered Rate.

**interest-rate futures** A form of *financial futures that enables investors, *portfolio managers, borrowers, etc., to obtain protection against future movements in interest rates. Interest-rate futures also enable dealers to speculate on these movements. In the UK, interest-rate futures are dealt in on the *London International Financial Futures and Options Exchange, using contracts for three-month sterling, eurodollars, ECUs, etc., in the short term and long gilts, US Treasury bonds, ECU bonds, etc., in the long term. For long gilts, for example, the standard contract is for £50,000 of nominal value and the *tick size is 0.01% of the nominal value. *See* hedging.

**interest-rate margin** **1.** The amount charged to borrowers over and above the base rate. This margin is the bank's profit on the transaction but has to take account of risk of loss or default by the borrower. **2.** The difference between the rate at which banks lend and the rate they pay for deposits. It may be a major indicator of banks' profitability.

**interest-rate option** A form of *option enabling traders and speculators to hedge themselves against future changes in interest rates.

**interest-rate policy** The policy by which governments influence *interest rates through the supply of bonds. Higher rates of interest will discourage *investment and reduce the *demand for money, giving a downward impetus to both employment and prices. Lower interest rates will have the opposite effect.

**interest-rate swap** A form of dealing between banks, security houses, and companies in which borrowers exchange fixed-interest rates for floating-interest rates, or vice versa. Swaps can be in the same currency (*see* currency interest-rate swap) or cross-currency (*see* cross-currency interest-rate swap). *See also* rate anticipation swap.

**interest-sensitive** Denoting an activity that is sensitive to changes in the general level of interest rates. For example, consumer goods usually bought on some form of *hire-purchase basis are interest-sensitive because they cost more as interest rates rise.

**interest yield** *See* yield.

**interim dividend** *See* dividend.

**interim report** Any report other than a final report. In commercial terms, an interim report normally refers to the statements that a company makes halfway through its financial year, setting out the state of its profits for the first half year. It may or may not be used to justify its interim *dividend. An interim report is a requirement for a company seeking a quotation on the London Stock Exchange.

**intermarket spread swap**  Swapping securities in the hope of improving the spread between the yields of the securities.

**intermediary**  Any person or organization that acts as an agent (*see* agency) or *broker between the parties to a transaction. *See also* financial intermediary; independent intermediary.

**intermediation**  The process of acting as an *intermediary between a borrower and a lender or between a seeker and a provider of some other financial service. *See also* disintermediation.

**internal audit**  An *audit that an organization carries out on its own behalf, normally to ensure that its own internal controls are operating satisfactorily. Whereas an external audit is almost always concerned with financial matters, this may not necessarily be the case with an internal audit; internal auditors may also concern themselves with such matters as the observation of the safety and health at work regulations or of the equal opportunities legislation. It may also be used to detect any theft or fraud.

**internal capital generation rate**  The rate at which a bank creates equity in its balance sheet by increasing retained earnings as a proportion of its shareholders' equity.

**internal rate of return (IRR)**  The rate of return that discounts the *net present value of a project to zero. This is a method used in conjunction with *discounted cash flow in order to discover what rate of return on the outlay is represented by the cash flows from the project. If the IRR exceeds the market rate of interest then the project is profitable. The IRR is usually considered less reliable than the actual net present value as a means of appraising a project. First, if returns in different periods fluctuate from positive to negative, a unique IRR will not exist. Secondly, the IRR tends to favour projects with large returns early on, even if they have a low net present value. *See also* payback period.

**Internal Revenue Service (IRS)**  The US federal organization that assesses and collects all personal and business federal taxes. It is the equivalent of the Inland Revenue in the UK.

**International Bank for Reconstruction and Development (IBRD)**  A specialized agency working in coordination with the United Nations, established in 1945 to help finance post-war reconstruction and to help raise standards of living in developing countries, by making loans to governments or guaranteeing outside loans. It lends on broadly commercial terms, either for specific projects or for more general social purposes; funds are raised on the international capital markets. The Bank and its affiliates, the *International Development Association and the *International Finance Corporation, are often known as the **World Bank**; it is owned by the governments of 151 countries. Members must also be members of the *International Monetary Fund. The headquarters of the Bank are in Washington, with a European office in Paris and a Tokyo office.

**International Chamber of Commerce (ICC)**  An international business organization that represents business interests in international affairs. Its office is in Paris.

**International Commodities Clearing House (ICCH)**  *See* London Clearing House.

**international commodity agreements** Agreements between governments
that aim to stabilize the price of commodities. This is often important for
producing nations, for whom the revenue from commodity sales may make a
major contribution to the national income. Methods tried include government-
financed buffer stocks and the imposition of price limits between which the
price of the commodity is allowed to fluctuate.

**International Development Association (IDA)** An affiliate of the
*International Bank for Reconstruction and Development (IBRD) established in
1960 to provide assistance to poorer developing countries (those with a GNP of
less than $835 per head). With the IBRD it is known as the **World Bank**. It is
funded by subscription and transfers from the net earnings of IBRD. The
headquarters of the IDA are in Washington, with offices in Paris and Tokyo,
administered by IBRD staff.

**International Finance Corporation (IFC)** An affiliate of the *International
Bank for Reconstruction and Development (IBRD) established in 1956 to
provide assistance for private investment projects. Although the IFC and IBRD
are separate entities, both legally and financially, the IFC is able to borrow from
the IBRD and reloan to private investors. The headquarters of the IFC are in
Washington. Its importance increased in the 1980s after the emergence of the
debt crisis and the subsequent reliance on the private sector.

**International Monetary Fund (IMF)** A specialized agency of the United
Nations established in 1945 to promote international monetary cooperation
and expand international trade, stabilize exchange rates, and help countries
experiencing short-term balance of payments difficulties to maintain their
exchange rates. The Fund assists members by supplying the amount of foreign
currency it wishes to purchase in exchange for the equivalent amount of its own
currency. The member repays this amount by buying back its own currency in a
currency acceptable to the Fund, usually within three to five years (*see also*
Special Drawing Rights). The Fund is financed by subscriptions from its
members, the amount determined by an estimate of their means. Voting power
is related to the amount of the subscription – the higher the contribution the
higher the voting rights. The head office of the IMF is in Washington. *See also*
conditionality.

**International Petroleum Exchange (IPE)** An exchange, founded in London
in 1980, that deals in *futures contracts and *options (including traded options)
in oil (gas oil, Brent crude oil, and heavy fuel oil) with facilities for making an
exchange of futures for physicals (*see* actuals). There are 35 floor members of
the exchange, which is located in St Katharine Dock and shared with *London
FOX. The exchange makes use of the services provided by the *London Clearing
House.

**International Stock Exchange of the UK and Republic of Ireland Ltd**
*See* London Stock Exchange.

**International Union of Credit and Investment Insurers** *See* Berne Union.

**intervention mechanism** The action by central banks and governments to
stabilize exchange rates of currencies in the *European Monetary System by
buying or selling currencies on the open market or by initiating *currency swaps.

**intervention price** *See* Common Agricultural Policy.

**inter vivos gifts** Gifts made between living people. *See* lifetime transfers.

**intestacy** The state of a person who has died without having left a valid will. Such a person is said to have died **intestate**. Intestacy can be either total (if no will is left at all) or partial (if not all the deceased's property is left by will). The Administration of Estates Act contains a table showing the destination of the property in an intestacy. If the intestate has no close relatives but a spouse survives, then the spouse takes everything. If children or grandchildren survive, the spouse takes £40,000 plus a life interest in half of the remaining estate. The children or grandchildren take the rest. If a person is survived by a spouse and other close relatives but not by children or grandchildren, the spouse receives £85,000 plus half the rest of the estate, and the remainder goes to the nearest of the surviving relatives. If there are no relatives, the estate goes to the Crown as *bona vacantia*.

**in-the-money option** *See* intrinsic value.

**intrinsic value** **1.** The value something has because of its nature, before it has been processed in any way. **2.** The difference between the market value of the underlying security in a traded *option and the *exercise price. An option with an intrinsic value is said to be **in the money**; an option with zero intrinsic value is **at the money**; one with less intrinsic value than zero is **out of the money**. *See also* time value.

**introduction** A method of issuing shares on the *London Stock Exchange in which a broker or issuing house takes small quantities of the company's shares and issues them to clients at opportune moments. It is also used by existing public companies that wish to issue additional shares. *Compare* issue by tender; offer for sale; placing; public issue.

**investment** **1.** The purchase of capital goods, such as plant and machinery in a factory in order to produce goods for future consumption. This is known as **capital investment**; the higher the level of capital investment in an economy, the faster it will grow. **2.** The purchase of assets, such as securities, works of art, bank and building-society deposits, etc., with a primary view to their financial return, either as income or capital gain. This form of **financial investment** represents a means of saving. The level of financial investment in an economy will be related to such factors as the rate of interest, the extent to which investments are likely to prove profitable, and the general climate of business confidence.

**investment analyst** A person employed by stockbrokers, banks, insurance companies, unit trusts, pension funds, etc., to give advice on the making of investments, especially investments in securities, commodities, etc. Many pay special attention to the study of *equities in the hope of being able to advise their employers to make profitable purchases of ordinary shares. To do this they use a variety of techniques, including a comparison of a company's present profits with its future trading prospects; this enables the analyst to single out the companies likely to outperform the general level of the market. This form of **technical analysis** is often contrasted with **fundamental analysis**, in which predicted future market movements are related to the underlying state of an economy and its expected trends. Analysts who rely on past movements to predict the future are called *chartists.

**investment bank**  A US bank that fulfils many of the functions of a UK
*merchant bank. It is usually one that advises on mergers and acquisitions and
provides finance for industrial corporations by buying shares in a company and
selling them in relatively small lots to investors. Capital provided to companies
is usually long-term and based on fixed assets. In the USA, commercial banks
were excluded from selling securities for many years but the law was relaxed in
the late 1980s, when certain safeguards were introduced, including a ceiling on
the value of transactions.

**investment bond**  A single-premium life-assurance policy in which an
investment of a fixed amount is made (usually over £1000) in an *asset-backed
fund. Most policies are open-ended but can be surrendered at any time.
Investment bonds confer attractive tax benefits in some circumstances. *See also*
single-premium assurance; top slicing.

**investment club**  A group of investors who, by pooling their resources, are
able to make more frequent and larger investments on a stock exchange, often
being able to reduce brokerage and to spread the risk of serious loss. The
popularity of investment clubs has waned with the rise of *unit trusts and
*investment trusts, both of which have the advantages of professional
management.

**investment company**  *See* investment trust.

**investment currency pool**  *See* dollar pool.

**investment income**  **1.** A person's income derived from investments.  **2.** The
income of a business derived from its outside investments rather than from its
trading activities.

**Investment Management Regulatory Organization (IMRO)**  *See*
Self-Regulating Organization.

**investment manager**  *See* fund manager.

**Investment Ombudsman**  *See* Financial Ombudsman.

**investment portfolio**  *See* portfolio.

**investment trust (investment company)**  A company that invests the funds
provided by shareholders in a wide variety of securities. It makes its profits from
the income and capital gains provided by these securities. The investments
made are usually restricted to securities quoted on a stock exchange, but some
will invest in unquoted companies. The advantages for shareholders are much
the same as those with *unit trusts, i.e. spreading the risk of investment and
making use of professional managers. Investment trusts, which are not usually
*trusts in the usual sense, but private or public limited companies, differ from
unit trusts in that in the latter the investors buy units in the fund but are not
shareholders. Some investment trusts aim for high capital growth (**capital
shares**), others for high income (**income shares**). *See also* accumulation unit;
geared investment trust; split-capital investment trust; unitization.

**invisible asset**  *See* intangible asset.

**invisible balance**  The *balance of payments between countries that arises as
a result of transactions involving services, such as insurance, banking, shipping,
and tourism (often known as **invisibles**), rather than the sale and purchase of
goods. Invisibles can play an important part in a nation's current account,

although they are often difficult to quantify. The UK relies on a substantial invisible balance in its balance of payments.

**invisibles**  *See* invisible balance.

**IOSCO**  Abbreviation for International Organization of Securities Commissions.

**IOU**  A written document providing evidence of a debt, usually in the form 'I owe you…'. It is not a *negotiable instrument or a *promissory note and requires no stamp (unless it includes a promise to pay). It can, however, be used as legal evidence of a debt.

**IPE**  Abbreviation for *International Petroleum Exchange.

**IPO**  Abbreviation for *initial public offering.

**IRA**  Abbreviation for *individual retirement account.

**Irish Futures and Options Exchange (Ifox)**  An exchange that opened in Dublin in 1989; it trades principally in short-term and long-term Irish gilt futures in conjunction with the Irish Stock Exchange.

**IRR**  Abbreviation for *internal rate of return.

**irredeemable securities (irredeemables)**  Securities, such as some government loan stock (*see* Consols) and some *debentures, on which there is no date given for the redemption of the capital sum. The price of fixed-interest irredeemables on the open market varies inversely with the level of interest rates.

**irrevocable documentary acceptance credit**  A form of irrevocable confirmed *letter of credit in which a foreign importer of UK goods opens a credit with a UK bank or the UK office of a local bank. The bank then issues an irrevocable letter of credit to the exporter, guaranteeing to accept *bills of exchange drawn on it on presentation of the shipping documents. Once the letter of credit has been drawn up, the importer has to 'accept' that he or she will pay, by signing the acceptance.

**irrevocable letter of credit**  *See* letter of credit.

**IRS**  Abbreviation for *Internal Revenue Service.

**ISE**  Abbreviation for International Stock Exchange. *See* London Stock Exchange.

**Islamic finance**  A form of business that is bound by strict religious rules; these rules normally prevent the making of a profit in association with non-Islamic organizations or individuals. It is now acceptable, however, for internal profits to be generated, which may be achieved using an Islamic investment company and any of the following. **Murabaha** is a good vehicle for temporary idle funds, which are used to purchase goods from a supplier for immediate sale and delivery to the buyer, who pays a predetermined margin over cost on a deferred payment date. The term can be as short as seven days. **Musharaka transactions** involve participation with other parties in trade financing, leasing, real estate, and industrial projects. Net profits are shared in proportions agreed at the outset. **Ijarah** involves profit from rental income on real estate. **Ijarawa-Iktina** is leasing of large capital items, such as property or plant and machinery. Leasing is achieved by the equivalent of monthly rental payments, and at the expiry the lessee purchases the equipment.

**issue  1.** The number of shares or the amount of stock on offer to the public at a particular time. *See also* new issue; rights issue; scrip issue.  **2.** The number of banknotes distributed by the Bank of England at a particular time.

**issue by tender (sale by tender)**  A method of issuing shares on the *London Stock Exchange in which an *issuing house asks investors to *tender for them. The stocks or shares are then allocated to the highest bidders. It is usual for the tender documents to state the lowest price acceptable. This method may be used for a *new issue or for loan stock (*see* debenture), but is not frequently employed. *Compare* introduction; offer for sale; placing; public issue.

**issued (or subscribed) share capital**  *See* share capital.

**issue date**  The date from which interest accrued on a security is calculated.

**issue price**  The price at which a *new issue of shares is sold to the public. Once the issue has been made the securities will have a market price, which may be above (at a premium on) or below (at a discount on) the issue price (*see also* stag). In an *introduction, *offer for sale, or *public issue, the issue price is fixed by the company on the advice of its stockbrokers and bankers; in an *issue by tender the issue price is fixed by the highest bidder; in a *placing the issue price is negotiated by the *issuing house or broker involved.

**issuing house**  A financial institution, usually a *merchant bank, that specializes in the *flotation of private companies on a *stock exchange. In some cases the issuing house will itself purchase the whole issue (*see* underwriter), thus ensuring that there is no uncertainty in the amount of money the company will raise by flotation. It will then sell the shares to the public, usually by an *offer for sale, *introduction, *issue by tender, or *placing. In the USA this function is performed by an *investment bank.

**itayose**  The Japanese concept for stock-exchange dealing in which all orders that arrive at a broker's or dealer's office before the exchange has opened are treated as having arrived at the same time, i.e. the time the exchange opened.

**Jakarta Stock Exchange** A stock exchange in Indonesia that originally opened in 1912 but was closed during World War II and from 1958 to 1977, when the modern market reopened. It issues a composite share index.

**jiao** A monetary unit of China, worth one tenth of a *yuan.

**jobber** **1.** A former dealer in stocks and shares, who had no contact with the general public, except through a *stockbroker. Jobbers were replaced by *market makers on the *London Stock Exchange in the Big Bang of October 1986. **2.** A dealer who buys and sells commodities, etc., for his or her own account.

**jobber's turn** The difference between the price at which a former jobber on the London Stock Exchange was prepared to buy and the price at which the jobber was prepared to sell. *See also* spread.

**jobbing backwards** Looking back on a transaction or event and thinking about how one might have acted differently, had one known then what one knows now.

**job lot** A collection of diverse things, such as stocks or shares, sold together as one lot at one all-inclusive price.

**joint account** **1.** A *bank account or a building-society account held in the names of two or more people, often husband and wife. On the death of one party the balance in the account goes to the survivor(s), except in the case of partnerships, executors' accounts, or trustees' accounts. It is usual for any of the holders of a joint account to operate it alone. **2.** In the USA, a syndicate of *investment banks acting together in an underwriting venture.

**joint and several liability** A liability that is entered into by a group, on the understanding that if any of the group fail in their undertaking the liability must be shared by the remainder. Thus, if two people enter into a joint and several guarantee for a bank loan, if one becomes bankrupt the other is liable for repayment of the whole loan.

**joint investment** A security purchased by more than one person. The certificate will bear the names of all the parties, but only the first named will receive notices. To dispose of the holding all the parties must sign the *transfer deed.

**joint-life and last-survivor annuities** Annuities that involve two people (usually husband and wife). A joint-life annuity begins payment on a specified date and continues until both persons have died. A last-survivor annuity only begins payment on the death of one of the two people and pays until the death of the other. *Compare* single-life pension.

**joint-stock bank** A UK bank that is a *public limited company rather than a private bank (which is a partnership). During the 19th century many private banks failed; the joint-stock banks became stronger, however, largely as a result of amalgamations and careful investment. In the present century, they became known as *commercial banks or High-Street banks.

**joint-stock company** A *company in which the members pool their stock and trade on the basis of their joint stock. This differs from the earliest type of company, the merchant corporations or regulated companies of the 14th century, in which members traded with their own stock, subject to the rules of the company. Joint-stock companies originated in the 17th century and some still exist, although they are now rare.

**judgment creditor** The person in whose favour a court decides, ordering the **judgment debtor** to pay the sum owed. If the judgment debtor fails to pay, the judgment creditor must return to the court asking for the judgment to be enforced.

**judgment debtor** *See* judgment creditor.

**junk bond** A *bond that offers a high rate of interest because it carries a higher than usual probability of default. The issuing of junk bonds to finance the takeover of large companies in the USA is a practice that developed in the 1970s and subsequently spread elsewhere. *See* leveraged buyout.

**kaffirs** An informal name for shares in South African gold-mining companies on the London Stock Exchange.

**kamikaze pricing** The practice of offering loans at exceptionally low interest rates to capture a larger share of the corporate banking market. It is named after the Japanese suicide pilots of World War II.

**kangaroos** An informal name for Australian shares, especially in mining, land, and tobacco companies, on the London Stock Exchange.

**Kansas City Board of Trade** A US grain market in Kansas City that also trades in futures and options.

**Keogh plan** A US savings scheme to create a pension plan for self-employed people, in which tax is deferred until withdrawals are made. It can be held at the same time as a corporate pension or *individual retirement account. Keogh plans originated with the Self-Employment Individuals Retirement Act 1982.

**kerb market** **1.** The former practice of trading on the street after the formal close of business of the London Stock Exchange. **2.** Dealing on the London Metal Exchange in any metal, outside the normal hours for formal ring trading (*see* callover). **3.** Any informal market, such as one for dealing in securities not listed on a stock exchange.

**key-person assurance** An insurance policy on the life of a key employee (male or female) of a company, especially the life of a senior executive in a small company, whose death would be a serious loss to the company. In the event of the key man or woman dying, the benefit is paid to the company. In order that there should be an *insurable interest, a loss of profit must be the direct result of the death of the key person.

**khoum** A monetary unit of Mauritania, worth one fifth of an *ouguiya.

**kina** (k) The standard monetary unit of Papua New Guinea, divided into 100 toea.

**kip** (KN) The standard monetary unit of Laos, divided into 100 at.

**KISS** Abbreviation for *Kurs Information Service System.

**kite** An informal name for an *accommodation bill. **Kite-flying** or **kiting** is the discounting of a kite (accommodation bill) at a bank, knowing that the person on whom it is drawn will dishonour it.

**kiting** **1.** *See* kite. **2.** An informal US name for the dishonest practice of improving the apparent cash position in a company's accounts by paying a large cheque on the last day of the accounting period from one of its current accounts into a second current account. Because the first account will not have been debited, but the second account will have been credited, the overall cash position is temporarily overstated.

**kobo** A monetary unit of Nigeria, worth one hundredth of a *naira.

**Korea Stock Exchange** A securities trading market in Seoul that dates from 1911; the present system was set up in 1956 and the exchange is now one of Asia's largest and most modern.

**koruna** (Kčs) The standard monetary unit of the Czech Republic and Slovakia, divided into 100 haleru.

**krona** (Skr) The standard monetary unit of Sweden, divided into 100 öre.

**króna** (ISk) The standard monetary unit of Iceland, divided into 100 aurar.

**krone** The standard monetary unit of Denmark (Dkr), the Faeroe Islands (Fkr), Greenland (Dkr), and Norway (Nkr), divided into 100 øre.

**kroon** The standard monetary unit of Estonia, divided into 100 centes.

**Krugerrand** A South African coin containing 1 troy ounce of gold. Minted since 1967 for investment purposes, it enables investors to evade restrictions on holding gold. Since 1975 an import licence has been required to bring them into the UK. In the 1980s their popularity waned for political reasons and because other countries have produced similar coins. *See* Britannia coins.

**Kuala Lumpur Commodity Exchange** A commodity market trading in rubber and palm oil in Malaysia. It provides hedging facilities for consumers and traders in natural rubber.

**Kurs Information Service System (KISS)** The share information system on the *Frankfurt Stock Exchange. Among other uses, it provides information for the *Deutsche Aktienindex.

**kuru** A monetary unit of Turkey, worth one hundredth of a *lira.

**kwacha** **1.** (Mk) The standard monetary unit of Malawi, divided into 100 tambala. **2.** (k) The standard monetary unit of Zambia, divided into 100 ngwee.

**kwanza** (Nkz) The standard monetary unit of Angola, divided into 100 lwei.

**kyat** (k) The standard monetary unit of Myanmar, divided into 100 pyas.

**laari** A monetary unit of the Maldives, worth one hundredth of a *rufiyaa.

**Lady Macbeth strategy** A strategy used in takeover battles in which a third party makes a bid that the target company would favour, i.e. it appears to act as a *white knight, but subsequently changes allegiance and joins the original bidder.

**lagged reserve requirement (LRR)** A requirement of the US Federal Reserve Banks from the 1960s to the mid-1980s in which local banks had to leave with them deposits reflecting the local banks' own deposits two weeks earlier. This was a crude method of monetary control, which has now been superseded by the system of contemporaneous reserves (excluding time deposits, which are still subject to the two-week lag).

**land bank   1.** The amount of land a developer owns that is awaiting development.   **2.** *See* Agricultural Bank.

**last in, first out (LIFO)** A method of charging homogeneous items of stock to production when the cost of the items has changed. It is assumed, both for costing and stock valuation purposes, that the latest items taken into stock are those used in production although this may not necessarily correspond with the physical movement of the goods. The LIFO method is not acceptable to the Inland Revenue in the UK. *Compare* first in, first out.

**last-survivor policy   1.** An assurance policy on the lives of two or more people, the sum assured being paid on the death of the last to die. *See also* joint-life and last-survivor annuities.   **2.** A contract (formerly called a **tontine**) in which assurance is arranged by a group of people, who all pay premiums into a fund while they are alive. No payment is made until only one person from the group is left alive. At that point the survivor receives all the policy proceeds. Contracts of this kind are not available in the UK because of the temptation they provide to members to murder their fellows, in order to be the last survivor.

**last trading day** The last day on which commodity trading for a particular delivery period can be transacted.

**laundering money** Processing money acquired illegally (as by theft, drug dealing, etc.) so that it appears to have come from a legitimate source. This is often achieved by paying the illegal cash into a foreign bank and transferring its equivalent to a bank with a good name in a hard-currency area.

**LAUTRO** Abbreviation for Life Assurance and Unit Trust Regulatory Organization. *See* Self-Regulating Organization.

**LBO** Abbreviation for *leveraged buyout.

**LCH**  Abbreviation for *London Clearing House.

**LDP**  Abbreviation for *London daily prices.

**lean back**  A period of cautious inaction by a government agency before intervening in a market. For example, a central bank might allow a lean-back period to elapse to allow exchange rates to stabilize, before intervening in the foreign-exchange market.

**lease-back (renting back)**  A method of raising finance in which an organization sells its land or buildings to an investor (usually an insurance company) on condition that the investor will lease the property back to the organization for a fixed term at an agreed rental. This releases capital for the organization, enabling it to be used for other purposes.

**leasing**  Hiring equipment, such as a car or a piece of machinery, to avoid the capital cost involved in owning it. In some companies it is advantageous to use capital for other purposes and to lease some equipment, paying for the hire out of income. The equipment is then an asset of the leasing company rather than the lessor. Sometimes a case can be made for leasing rather than purchasing, on the grounds that some equipment quickly becomes obsolete.

**legal reserve**  The minimum amount of money that building societies, insurance companies, etc., are bound by law to hold as security for the benefit of their customers.

**legal tender**  Money that must be accepted in discharge of a debt. It may be **limited legal tender**, i.e. it must be accepted but only up to specified limits of payment; or **unlimited legal tender**, i.e. acceptable in settlement of debts of any amount. Bank of England notes and the £2 and £1 coins are unlimited legal tender in the UK. Other Royal Mint coins are limited legal tender; i.e. debts up to £10 can be paid in 50p and 20p coins; up to £5 by 10p and 5p coins; and up to 20p by bronze coins.

**lek**  (Lk) The standard monetary unit of Albania, divided into 100 qindar.

**lempira**  (L) The standard monetary unit of Honduras, divided into 100 centavos.

**lender of last resort**  A country's central bank with responsibility for controlling its banking system. In the UK, the Bank of England fulfils this role, lending to *discount houses, either by repurchasing *Treasury bills, lending on other paper assets, or granting direct loans, charging the *base rate of interest. *Commercial banks do not go directly to the Bank of England; they borrow from the discount houses.

**leone**  (Le) The standard monetary unit of Sierra Leone, divided into 100 cents.

**lepta**  A monetary unit of Greece, worth one hundredth of a *drachma.

**letter of allotment**  See allotment.

**letter of comfort**  A letter to a bank from the parent company of a subsidiary that is trying to borrow money from the bank. The letter gives no guarantee for the repayment of the projected loan but offers the bank the comfort of knowing that the subsidiary has made the parent company aware of its intention to borrow; the parent also usually supports the application, giving, at least, an assurance that it intends that the subsidiary should remain in business and that it will give notice of any relevant change of ownership.

**letter of credit (documentary credit)** A letter from one banker to another authorizing the payment of a specified sum to the person named in the letter on certain specified conditions (*see* letter of indication). Commercially, letters of credit are widely used in the international import and export trade as a means of payment. In an export contract, the exporter may require the foreign importer to open a letter of credit at the importer's local bank (the issuing bank) for the amount of the goods. This will state that it is to be negotiable at a bank (the negotiating bank) in the exporter's country in favour of the exporter; often, the exporter (who is called the beneficiary of the credit) will give the name of the negotiating bank. On presentation of the shipping documents (which are listed in the letter of credit) the beneficiary will receive payment from the negotiating bank.

An **irrevocable letter of credit** cannot be cancelled by the person who opens it or by the issuing bank without the beneficiary's consent, whereas a **revocable letter of credit** can. In a **confirmed letter of credit** the negotiating bank guarantees to pay the beneficiary, even if the issuing bank fails to honour its commitments (in an **unconfirmed letter of credit** this guarantee is not given). A confirmed irrevocable letter of credit therefore provides the most reliable means of being paid for exported goods. However, all letters of credit have an expiry date, after which they can only be negotiated by the consent of all the parties.

A **circular letter of credit** is an instruction from a bank to its correspondent banks to pay the beneficiary a stated sum on presentation of a means of identification. It has now been replaced by *traveller's cheques.

Although the term 'letter of credit' is still widely used, in 1983 the International Chamber of Commerce recommended **documentary credit** as the preferred term for these instruments.

**letter of hypothecation** *See* hypothecation.

**letter of indemnity 1.** A letter stating that the organization issuing it will compensate the person to whom it is addressed for a specified loss. *See also* indemnity. **2.** A letter written to a company registrar asking for a replacement for a lost share certificate and indemnifying the company against any loss that it might incur in so doing. It may be required to be countersigned by a bank.

**letter of indication (letter of identification)** A letter issued by a bank to a customer to whom a *letter of credit has been supplied. The letter has to be produced with the letter of credit at the negotiating bank; it provides evidence of the bearer's identity and signature. It is used particularly with a circular letter of credit carried by travellers, although *traveller's cheques are now more widely used.

**letter of intent** A letter in which a person formally sets out an intention to do something, such as signing a contract in certain circumstances, which is often specified in detail in the letter. The letter does not constitute either a contract or a promise to do anything, but it does indicate the writer's serious wish to pursue a particular course.

**letter of licence** A letter from a creditor to a debtor, who is having trouble raising the money to settle the debt. The letter states that the creditor will allow the debtor a stated time to pay and will not initiate proceedings before that time. *See also* arrangement.

**letter of regret** A letter from a company, or its bankers, stating that an application for an allotment from a *new issue of shares has been unsuccessful.

**letter of renunciation** **1.** A form, often attached to an *allotment letter, on which a person who has been allotted shares in a *new issue renounces the rights to them, either absolutely or in favour of someone else (during the **renunciation period**). **2.** A form on the reverse of some unit-trust certificates, which the holder completes when wishing to dispose of the holding. The completed certificate is sent to the trust managers.

**letters of administration** An order authorizing the person named (the *administrator) to distribute the property of a deceased person, who has not appointed anyone else to do so. The distribution must be in accordance with the deceased's will, or the rules of *intestacy in the absence of one.

**leu** (plural **lei**) The standard monetary unit of Romania, divided into 100 bani.

**lev** (plural **leva**) The standard monetary unit of Bulgaria, divided into 100 stotinki.

**leverage** **1.** The US word for *capital gearing. **2.** The use by a company of its limited assets to guarantee substantial loans to finance its business.

**leveraged buyout (LBO)** A takeover ploy (*see* takeover bid) in which, for example, a small company, whose assets are limited, borrows heavily on these assets and the assets of the target company in order to finance a takeover of a larger company, often making use of *junk bonds. An LBO means that the company emerging as a result of an acquisition has a high ratio of debt to equity. This could be caused by various circumstances or as a result of a deliberate strategy in order to give current equity holders a beneficial payout, unrelated to the size of the company or its assets.

**liability** *See* contingent liability; current liabilities; deferred liability; long-term liability; secured liability.

**liability insurance** A form of insurance policy that promises to pay any compensation and court costs the policyholder becomes legally liable to pay because of claims for injury to other people or damage to their property as a result of the policyholder's negligence. Policies often define the areas in which they will deal with liability, e.g. personal liability or employers' liability.

**liability management** The management of a bank's deposits, especially by increasing deposits from customers, attracting funds from *institutional investors through timed *certificates of deposit, hedging liabilities against interest-rate movements, and ensuring that a gap exists between the maturity of its assets and those liabilities that the bank must pay out. It can also be achieved by the purchase or sale of funds on the *interbank market.

**LIBID** Abbreviation for *London Inter Bank Bid Rate.

**LIBOR** Abbreviation for *London Inter Bank Offered Rate.

**licensed dealer** A dealer licensed by the Department of Trade and Industry to provide investment advice and deal in securities, either as an agent or principal. Licensed dealers are not members of the *London Stock Exchange and are not covered by its compensation fund.

**licensed deposit taker** A category of financial institutions as defined by the Banking Act 1979, which divided banking into recognized banks, licensed deposit takers, and exempt institutions. To qualify for authorization, the licensed deposit taker had to satisfy the Bank of England that it conducted its business in a prudent manner. The aim of the Act was to bring more institutions under the supervision of the Bank of England. As the Banking Act 1987 established a single category of authorized institutions eligible to carry out banking business the distinction has now disappeared.

**lien** The right of one person to retain possession of goods owned by another until the possessor's claims against the owner have been satisfied. The lien may be **general**, when the goods are held as security for all outstanding debts of the owner, or **particular**, when only the claims of the possessor in respect of the goods held must be satisfied. A **banker's lien** applies to certain financial documents held by a bank on behalf of a customer who owes money to the bank.

**life assurance** An *insurance policy that pays a specified amount of money on the death of the *life assured or, in the case of an *endowment assurance policy, on the death of the life assured or at the end of an agreed period, whichever is the earlier. Life assurance grew from a humble means of providing funeral expenses to a means of saving for oneself or one's dependants, with certain tax advantages.

**Life Assurance and Unit Trust Regulatory Organization (LAUTRO)** *See* Self-Regulating Organization.

**life assured** The person upon whose death a life-assurance policy makes an agreed payment. The life assured need not be the owner of the policy.

**life annuity** An *annuity that ceases to be paid on the death of a specified person, which may or may not be the *annuitant.

**lifeboat** **1.** A fund set up to rescue dealers on an exchange in the event of a market collapse and the ensuing insolvencies. **2.** The rescue of a company that is in financial difficulty by new or restructured loans from its group of bankers.

**life office** A company that provides *life assurance.

**lifetime transfers** The name for *inter vivos gifts that was adopted when *inheritance tax replaced the former *capital-transfer tax in the UK in 1986. For inheritance tax, lifetime transfers have to be taken into account; however, certain transfers are exempt, e.g. transfers between spouses, certain marriage, charitable, or political gifts, and annual gifts of less than a specified sum. A tapering relief is given for lifetime transfers made over the seven years prior to the donor's death, while gifts made seven years before death escape tax.

**LIFFE** Abbreviation for *London International Financial Futures and Options Exchange.

**LIFO** Abbreviation for *last in, first out.

**likuta** (plural **makuta**) A monetary unit of Zaïre, worth one hundredth of a *zaïre.

**lilangeni** (plural **emalangeni**; E) The standard monetary unit of Swaziland, divided into 100 cents.

**LIMEAN** Abbreviation for *London Inter Bank Mean Rate.

**limit 1.** An order given by an investor to a broker restricting a particular purchase to a stated maximum price or a particular sale to a stated minimum price. Such a **limit order** will also be restricted as to time; it may be given firm for a stated period or firm until cancelled. **2.** The *maximum fluctuations (up or down) allowed in certain markets over a stated period (usually one day's trading). In some volatile circumstances the market moves the limit up (or down). The movement of prices on the *Tokyo Stock Exchange is limited in this way as it is on certain US commodity markets.

**limitation of actions** Statutory rules limiting the time within which civil actions can be brought.

**limited by guarantee** *See* limited company.

**limited company** A *company in which the liability of the members in respect of the company's debts is limited. It may be **limited by shares**, in which case the liability of the members on a winding-up is limited to the amount (if any) unpaid on their shares. This is by far the most common type of registered company. The liability of the members may alternatively be **limited by guarantee**; in this case the liability of members is limited by the memorandum to a certain amount, which the members undertake to contribute on winding-up. These are usually societies, clubs, or trade associations. Since 1980 it has not been possible for such a company to be formed with a share capital, or converted to a company limited by guarantee with a share capital. *See also* public limited company.

**limited liability** *See* limited company.

**limited market** A market for a particular security in which buying and selling is difficult, usually because a large part of the issue is held by very few people or institutions.

**limit order** *See* limit.

**line 1.** The acceptance of a risk by an insurance *underwriter. **2.** A large quantity of something, such as a block of shares. *See also* credit line.

**line of credit** *See* credit line.

**liquid assets (liquid capital; quick assets; realizable assets)** Assets held in cash or in something that can be readily turned into cash (e.g. deposits in a bank current account, trade debts, marketable investments). The ratio of these assets to current liabilities provides an assessment of an organization's *liquidity or solvency. *See also* liquid ratio.

**liquidate** To wind up or dissolve a *limited company. This may be undertaken by either the directors or the shareholders. If the company is solvent, i.e. its assets exceed its liabilities, the assets will be distributed to the shareholders. *See* liquidation; liquidator.

**liquidation (winding-up)** The distribution of a company's assets among its creditors and members prior to its dissolution. This brings the life of the company to an end. The liquidation may be voluntary (*see* creditors' voluntary liquidation; members' voluntary liquidation) or by the court (*see* compulsory liquidation). *See also* liquidate; liquidator.

**liquidation committee** A committee set up by the creditors of a company being wound up in order to consent to the *liquidator exercising certain powers.

When the company is unable to pay its debts, the committee is usually composed of creditors only; otherwise it consists of creditors and *contributories.

**liquidator**  A person appointed by a court, or by the members of a company or its creditors, to regularize the company's affairs on a *liquidation (winding-up). In the case of a *members' voluntary liquidation, it is the members of the company who appoint the liquidator. In a *creditors' voluntary liquidation, the liquidator may be appointed by company members before the **meeting of creditors** or by the creditors themselves at the meeting; in the former case the liquidator can only exercise his or her powers with the consent of the court. If two liquidators are appointed, the court resolves which one is to act. In a *compulsory liquidation, the court appoints a *provisional liquidator after the winding-up petition has been presented; after the order has been granted, the court appoints the *official receiver as liquidator, until or unless another officer is appointed.

The liquidator is in a relationship of trust with the company and the creditors as a body; a liquidator appointed in a compulsory liquidation is an officer of the court, is under statutory obligations, and may not profit from the position. A liquidator must be a qualified **insolvency practitioner**, according to the Insolvency Act 1986. Under this Act, insolvency practitioners must meet certain statutory requirements, including membership of an approved professional body (such as the Insolvency Practitioners' Association or the Institute of Chartered Accountants). On appointment, the liquidator assumes control of the company, collects the assets, pays the debts, and distributes any surplus to company members according to their rights. In the case of a compulsory liquidation, the liquidator is supervised by the court, the *liquidation committee, and the Department of Trade and Industry. The liquidator receives a *statement of affairs from the company officers and must report on these to the court.

**liquid capital**  *See* liquid assets.

**liquidity**  The extent to which an organization's assets are liquid (*see* liquid assets), enabling it to pay its debts when they fall due and also to move into new investment opportunities.

**liquidity ratio**  *See* cash ratio.

**liquid ratio (acid-test ratio)**  The ratio of the liquid assets of an organization to its *current liabilities. The liquid assets are normally taken to be trade debt and cash and any other assets that are readily marketable. The ratio gives an indication of the organization's ability to pay its debts without needing to make further sales. It therefore provides the ultimate (acid-test) proof of its solvency.

**lira**  **1.** (l; lit) The standard monetary unit of Italy and San Marino, divided into 100 centesimi. **2.** (IT) The standard monetary unit of Turkey, divided into 100 kurus. **3.** (Lm) The standard monetary unit of Malta, divided into 100 cents.

**Lisbon Stock Exchange**  Portugal's main stock exchange, regulated by Portugal's central bank, the Bank of Portugal.

**lisente**  A monetary unit of Lesotho, worth one hundredth of a *loti.

**listed company**  A company that has a **listing agreement** (*see* listing requirements) with the London Stock Exchange and whose shares therefore have a *quotation on the *main market. These companies were formerly called **quoted companies**.

**listed security 1.** In general, a security that has a *quotation on a recognized *stock exchange. **2.** On the *London Stock Exchange, a security that has a quotation in the Official List of Securities of the *main market, as opposed to the unlisted securities market or the *third market. *See also* flotation; listing requirements; Yellow Book.

**listing requirements** The conditions that must be satisifed before a security can be traded on a stock exchange. To achieve a quotation in the Official List of Securities of the *main market of the *London Stock Exchange, the requirements contained in a **listing agreement** must be signed by the company seeking quotation. The two main requirements of such a listing are usually:
(i) that the value of the company's assets should exceed a certain value;
(ii) that the company publish specific financial information, both at the time of *flotation and regularly thereafter (*see* accounts; directors' report).
  Listing requirements are generally more stringent the larger the market. For example, the main market in London demands considerably more information from companies than the *unlisted securities market. The listing requirements are set out in the *Yellow Book. *See also* unlisted securities.

**lists closed** The closing of the application lists for a *new issue on the London Stock Exchange, after a specified time or after the issue has been fully subscribed.

**Little Board** The colloquial name for the *American Stock Exchange, the New York market for smaller company stocks and bonds. *Compare* Big Board.

**Liverpool Cotton Association** A major world market in cotton, set up originally in 1841. It now trades in both actuals and futures.

**Lloyd's** A corporation of underwriters (**Lloyd's underwriters**) and insurance brokers (**Lloyd's brokers**) that developed from a coffee shop in Tavern Street in the City of London in 1689. It takes its name from the proprietor of the coffee shop, Edward Lloyd. By 1774 it was established in the Royal Exchange and in 1871 was incorporated by Act of Parliament. It now occupies a new (1986) building in Lime Street (built by Sir Richard Rogers). As a corporation, Lloyd's itself does not underwrite insurance business; all its business comes to it from some 260 Lloyd's brokers, who are in touch with the public, and is underwritten by some 350 *syndicates of Lloyd's underwriters, who are approached by the brokers and who do not, themselves, contact the public.
  The 30 000 or so Lloyd's underwriters must each deposit a substantial sum of money with the corporation and accept unlimited liability before they can become members. They are grouped into syndicates, run by a syndicate manager or agent, but most of the members of syndicates are **names**, underwriting members of Lloyd's who take no part in organizing the underwriting business, but who share in the profits or losses of the syndicate and provide the risk capital. Lloyd's has long specialized in marine insurance but now covers almost all insurance risks.

**Lloyd's broker** *See* Lloyd's.

**Lloyd's underwriter** *See* Lloyd's.

**LME** Abbreviation for *London Metal Exchange.

**loading  1.** The addition of a charge to cover incidental expenses, administrative costs, profit, etc., on an insurance policy, bank account, or purchases of unit trusts. **2.** The charging of interest on a loan.

**loan** Money lent on condition that it is repaid, either in instalments or all at once, on agreed dates and usually that the borrower pays the lender an agreed rate of interest (unless it is an **interest-free loan**). *See also* balloon; bank loan; bridging loan; bullet; local loan; personal loan.

**loan account** An account opened by a bank in the name of a customer to whom it has granted a loan, rather than an *overdraft facility. The amount of the loan is debited to this account and any repayments are credited; interest is charged on the full amount of the loan less any repayments. The customer's current account is credited with the amount of the loan. With an overdraft facility, interest is only charged on the amount of the overdraft, which may be less than the full amount of the loan.

**loanback** An arrangement in which an individual can borrow from the accumulated funds of his or her pension scheme. Usually a commercial rate of interest has to be credited to fund for the use of the capital. Some life assurance companies offer loan facilities on this basis of up to fifteen times the annual pension premium.

**loan capital** Money required to finance the activities of an organization that is raised by loans (*see* debenture), as distinct from its *share capital. The principal advantages of loan capital over share capital are that it can be readily repaid when the company has funds, interest charges are deductible for tax purposes, and there is no capital duty on the issue of loan stock. Unlike the share capital, which has a right to share in the organization's profits, loan capital earns a fixed-interest return.

**Loan Guarantee Scheme** A UK government scheme introduced in 1980 that guarantees 70% of a company's overdraft for a 3% premium. The bank must accept the risk for the balance of 30%. Its purpose is to support small businesses.

**loan note** A form of loan stock (*see* debenture) in which an investor takes a note rather than cash as the result of a share offer to defer tax liability. The yield is often variable and may be linked to the *London Inter Bank Offered Rate. Loan notes are not usually marketable but are usually repayable on demand.

**loan selling** The sale of bank loans by one bank to another. For example, Third World debt may be sold at a discount to the market value in order to reduce the burden of the debt on a particular bank. Loans to individuals may also be sold in this way, from one financial institution to another, often without the borrower knowing that the lender has changed. *See also* eurobond.

**loan stock** *See* debenture.

**local** A person who has a seat on a commodity futures market and who deals for his or her own account.

**local authority bill** A *bill of exchange drawn on a UK local government authority.

**local authority stock** A bond issued by a UK local government authority.

**local loan**  A loan obtained by a UK local government authority for financing capital expenditure.

**local taxation**  A form of taxation levied by a local government authority rather than by a central government. It can take various forms, including a local sales tax, local income tax, a property tax (e.g. UK rates), or a poll tax (e.g. the former UK community charge).

**lock-up**  An investment in an asset that is not readily realizable or one that is specifically intended to be held for a long period (e.g. over ten years).

**loco**  The location in which a particular commodity has been traded, e.g. a contract in rubber futures may have been traded **loco KL** (in Kuala Lumpur).

**Lombard rate  1.** The rate of interest at which the German central bank, the *Bundesbank, lends to German commercial banks, usually ½% above the *discount rate.  **2.** The interest rate charged by a German commercial bank lending against security. *See also* special Lombard rate.

**Lombard Street**  The street in the City of London that is the centre of the banking market. Many commercial banks have offices in or near Lombard Street, as do many bill brokers and discount houses. The Bank of England and the Royal Exchange are round the corner.

**Lomé Convention**  The convention which, in 1976, set up the *European Development Fund to aid developing countries outside the European Community.

**London acceptance credit**  A method of providing immediate cash for a UK exporter of goods. On shipment of the goods the exporter draws a *bill of exchange on the foreign buyer. The accepted bill is then pledged to a *merchant bank in London, which accepts an *accommodation bill drawn by the exporter. The acceptance can be discounted on the bank's reputation, to provide the exporter with immediate finance, whereas the foreign buyer's acceptance would be difficult, or impossible, to discount in London.

**London and New Zealand Futures Association**  A UK commodity market in Bradford, established in 1953 to trade in New Zealand wool.

**London Bankers' Clearing House**  The organization that daily sets off all cheques drawn for and against the *clearing banks in the UK. It has been housed in 10 Lombard Street, in the City of London, since the 1770s. *See also* Association for Payment Clearing Services.

**London Chamber of Commerce and Industry**  The largest chamber of commerce in the UK. It provides the normal services of a chamber of commerce and in addition runs courses and examinations in business subjects.

**London Clearing House (LCH)**  A *clearing house established in 1888 (known before 1991 as the International Commodities Clearing House and originally as the London Produce Clearing House). LCH is an independent body, owned by six major UK commercial banks. It provides futures and options markets with *netting and settlement services as well as becoming a counterparty (*see* counterparty risk) to every transaction between its members. In this capacity LCH takes the risk of its members defaulting, which it covers by collecting *margins from members; it also provides an independent guarantee of £200 million from its shareholders and from the insurance market. Exchanges making use of LCH facilities include the *London International Financial Futures and Options Exchange, *London FOX, the *London Metal Exchange, and the *International Petroleum Exchange.

**London Cocoa Terminal Market**  A former market now incorporated into *London FOX.

**London Commodity Exchange**  *See* London FOX.

**London daily prices (LDP)**  The price fixed each day for trading in white sugar.

**London FOX (Futures and Options Exchange)**  A commodity exchange formed in 1987 from the **London Commodity Exchange**, which itself emerged after World War II as a successor to the London Commercial Sale Rooms. London FOX is located in a purpose-built exchange in St Katharine Dock, which it shares with the *International Petroleum Exchange. The commodities dealt in on the exchange are cocoa, coffee, raw sugar, and white sugar as well as the agricultural products potatoes, soya-bean meal, wheat, barley, pigs, and lamb. The market also includes the **Baltic International Freight Futures Market** (BIFFEX). The market is in futures and traded options and it makes use of the services provided by the *London Clearing House.

**London Grain Futures Market**  A former market now incorporated into *London FOX.

**London Inter Bank Bid Rate (LIBID)**  The rate of interest at which banks bid for funds to borrow from each other. *See* London Inter Bank Offered Rate.

**London Inter Bank Mean Rate (LIMEAN)**  The median average between the London Inter Bank Offered Rate (LIBOR) and the London Inter Bank Bid Rate (LIBID).

**London Inter Bank Offered Rate (LIBOR)**  The rate of interest in the short-term wholesale market (*see* interbank market) in which banks offer to lend money to each other. The loans are for a minimum of £250,000 for periods from overnight up to five years. The importance of the market is that it allows individual banks to adjust their liquidity positions quickly, covering shortages by borrowing from banks with surpluses. This reduces the need for each bank to hold large quantities of liquid assets, thus releasing funds for more profitable lending transactions. LIBOR is the most significant interest rate for international banks. It is officially fixed at 11 am each day by five major London banks, but fluctuates during the day. It is also used as a benchmark for lending to bank customers. *See also* London Inter Bank Bid Rate.

**London International Financial Futures and Options Exchange (LIFFE)**
A *financial futures market opened in 1982, in London's Royal Exchange, to provide facilities within the European time zone for dealing in options and futures contracts, including those in government bonds, stock-and-share indexes, foreign currencies, and interest rates. In 1991 LIFFE moved into its own premises in the City of London. A client wishing to buy or sell options or futures telephones a LIFFE broker, who instructs the booth run by that broker on the floor of the exchange. The booth clerk hands a slip to the broker's trader in the *pit of the market who executes the transaction with another trader. The bargain details are passed to the *London Clearing House, which acts as guarantor. Automated (electronic) pit trading was introduced in 1989, though this only

operates after the close of live pit trading. The *London Traded Options Market merged with LIFFE in 1992, when the words 'and Options' was added to its name, although the acronym remains unchanged.

**London Meat Futures Exchange**   A former market now incorporated into *London FOX.

**London Metal Exchange (LME)**   A central market for non-ferrous metals, established in London in 1877 to supply a central market for the import of large quantities of metal from abroad. The Exchange deals in copper, lead, zinc, aluminium (all in minimum lots of 25 tonnes), tin (minimum 5 tonnes), and nickel (minimum 6 tonnes). The official prices of the LME are used by producers and consumers worldwide for their long-term contracts. Dealings on the LME include *futures and *options contracts. Bargains are guaranteed by the *London Clearing House.

**London Potato Futures Market**   A former market now incorporated into *London FOX.

**London Soya-Bean Meal Futures Market**   A former market now incorporated into *London FOX.

**London Stock Exchange**   The market in London that deals in securities. Dealings in securities began in London in the 17th century. The name Stock Exchange was first used for New Jonathan's Coffee House in 1773, although it was not formally constituted until 1802. The development of the industrial revolution encouraged many other share markets to flourish throughout the UK, all the remnants of which amalgamated in 1973 to form The Stock Exchange of Great Britain and Ireland. After the *Big Bang in 1986 this organization became the **International Stock Exchange of the UK and Republic of Ireland Ltd (ISE)** in an attempt to stress the international nature of the main UK securities market, although it is still widely known as the London Stock Exchange. Its major reforms included:
(i) allowing banks, insurance companies, and overseas securities houses to become members and to buy existing member firms;
(ii) abolishing scales of commissions, allowing commissions to be negotiated;
(iii) abolishing the division of members into jobbers and brokers, enabling a member firm to deal with the public, to buy and sell shares for their own account, and to act as *market makers;
(iv) the introduction of the *Stock Exchange Automated Quotations System, a computerized dealing system that has virtually abolished face-to-face dealing on the floor of exchange.
     In merging with members of the international broking community in London, the International Stock Exchange became a registered investment exchange and The Securities Association Ltd became a *Self-Regulating Organization (SRO) complying with the Financial Services Act 1986. In 1991 The Securities Association Ltd merged with the *Association of Futures Brokers and Dealers Ltd to form the *Securities and Futures Authority (SFA), which is now the Self-Regulating Organization responsible for the Stock Exchange.
     The International Stock Exchange provides two markets for companies: the *main market for *listed companies and the *unlisted securities market (USM). A *third market, formed in 1987, merged with the USM in 1990. The International Stock Exchange formerly offered a market in traded options in

equities, currencies, and indexes but this has now moved to the *London International Financial Futures and Options Exchange.

**London Sugar Futures Market** A former market now incorporated into *London FOX.

**London Traded Options Market (LTOM)** A former subsidiary company of the London Stock Exchange. In 1992 this market, dealing in traded options in equities, merged with the *London International Financial Futures and Options Exchange.

**long-dated gilt** *See* gilt-edged security.

**long hedging** *See* hedging.

**long position** A position held by a dealer in securities (*see* market maker), commodities, currencies, etc., in which holdings exceed sales, because the dealer expects prices to rise enabling a profit to be made by selling at the higher levels. *Compare* short position.

**longs 1.** *See* gilt-edged security. **2.** Securities, commodities, currencies, etc., held in a *long position.

**long-term bond** A bond that does not mature in less than one year.

**long-term debt** Loans and debentures that are not due for repayment for at least ten years.

**long-term liability** A sum owed that does not have to be repaid within the next accounting period of a business. In some contexts a long-term liability may be regarded as one not due for repayment within the next three, or possibly ten, years.

**loss adjuster** A person appointed by an insurer to negotiate an insurance claim. The loss adjuster, who is independent of the insurer, discusses the claim with both the insurer and the policyholder, producing a report recommending the basis on which the claim should be settled. The insurer pays a fee for this service based on the amount of work involved for the loss adjuster, not on the size of the settlement. *Compare* loss assessor.

**loss assessor** A person who acts on behalf of the policyholder in handling a claim. A fee is charged for this service, which is usually a percentage of the amount received by the policyholder. *Compare* loss adjuster.

**loss-of-profits policy** *See* business-interruption policy.

**loss ratio** The total of the claims paid out by an insurance company, underwriting *syndicate, etc., expressed as a percentage of the amount of premiums coming in during the same period. For example, if claims total £2M and premiums total £4M, the result is a 50% loss ratio. Insurers use this figure as a guide to the profitability of their business when they are reconsidering premium rates for a particular risk.

**loti** (plural **maloti**; Ml) The standard monetary unit of Lesotho, divided into 100 lisente.

**lower of cost or market (LCM)** A method of valuing a current *asset of an organization in which the value taken is either its purchase (or production) price or the cost of replacing it (by purchase or manufacture), whichever is the lower. The Companies Act 1985 requires that a current asset be valued at either its purchase (or production) price or its *net realizable value, whichever is the lower.

**lower rate**   A rate of income tax in the UK below the *basic rate.

**LRR**   Abbreviation for *lagged reserve requirement.

**Ltd**   The usual abbreviation for *limited*. This (or the Welsh equivalent) must appear in the name of a private *limited company. *Compare* plc.

**LTOM**   Abbreviation for London Traded Options Market. *See* London International Financial Futures and Options Exchange.

**lump sum**   **1.** A sum of money paid all at once, rather than in instalments. **2.** An insurance benefit, such as a sum of money paid on retirement or redundancy or to the beneficiaries on the death of an insured person. Retirement *pensions can consist of a lump sum plus a reduced pension.   **4.** A form of *damages; a **lump-sum award** is given in tort cases.

**Luxembourg Stock Exchange**   A small stock exchange in Luxembourg; it functions as a settlement centre for trading in *eurobonds.

**lwei**   A monetary unit of Angola, worth one hundredth of a *kwanza.

**M0; M1; M2; M3; M4; M5** *See* money supply.

**Madrid Stock Exchange** The largest of four stock exchanges in Spain, the others being in Barcelona, Bilbao, and Valencia. They all now use a centralized settlement system, with the markets modelled on the London system (after the *Big Bang). The markets are overseen by a national securities commission, the Comisión del Mercado de Valores (CNMV).

**main market** The premier market for the trading of *equities on the *London Stock Exchange. For this market the *listing requirements are the most stringent and the liquidity of the market is greater than in the *unlisted securities market and the other junior markets. A company wishing to enter this market must have audited trading figures covering at least five years and must place 25% of its shares in public hands. The main market currently deals in some 7000 securities. *Compare* over-the-counter market; third market; unlisted-securities market.

**mainstream corporation tax (MCT)** The liability for *corporation tax of a company for an accounting period after the relevant *advance corporation tax (ACT) has been deducted. In the imputation system of corporation tax in the UK, payments on account of ACT are paid when dividends are paid to shareholders. Mainstream corporation tax is the balance remaining to be paid.

**making a price** On the *London Stock Exchange, the quoting by a *market maker of a selling price and a buying price for a specified security without knowing whether the enquirer wishes to buy or sell. Having made a price, the market maker is bound to buy or sell at the quoted prices, though the quantity may be limited by saying so when the price is made.

**making-up price** The price at which securities that have not been paid for on *account day (on the London Stock Exchange) are carried forward to the next account.

**managed currency** A currency in which the government controls, or at least influences, the exchange rate. This control (known as **managed floating**) is usually exerted by the central bank buying and selling in the foreign-exchange market. *See also* clean floating.

**managed fund** A fund, made up of investments in a wide range of securities, that is managed by a life-assurance company to provide low risk investments for the smaller investor, usually in the form of *investment bonds, *unit trusts, or unit-linked saving plans (*see* unit-linked policy). The *fund managers will have a stated investment policy favouring a specific category of investments.

**managed PEP** *See* personal equity plan.

**managed unit trust** *See* managed fund.

**management audit** An independent review of the management of an organization, carried out by a firm of management consultants specializing in this type of review. The review will cover all aspects of running the organization, including the control of production, marketing, sales, finance, personnel, warehousing, etc.

**management buy-in** The acquisition of a company by a team of managers, usually specially formed for the purpose, often backed by a venture-capital organization. Their normal target is the small family-owned company, which the owners wish to sell, or occasionally an unwanted subsidiary of a public company.

**management buyout** The acquisition of a company by its managers, often in the face of closure, after the acquisition of the company by another group that wishes to dispose of it, or occasionally as a result of its owners wishing to dispose of the business through a trade sale. In some cases a management buyout occurs when a large corporate group of companies wishes to divest itself of an operating division. Financial backers tend to like managers who know the company's business intimately, staking their own assets and taking full control of the company with the aim of boosting its profitability. Popularized in the early 1980s, management buyouts have occasionally failed, but many have continued to profit and a few have been sold on to major groups.

**management company** A company that manages *unit trusts. Its fees, known as **management charges**, are usually stated in the agreement setting up the trust; they are paid by the unit holders.

**mandate** A written authority given by one person (the **mandator**) to another (the **mandatory**) giving the mandatory the power to act on behalf of the mandator. It comes to an end on the death, mental illness, or bankruptcy of the mandator. *See also* dividend mandate.

**mandatory quote period** The period between Monday and Friday when all *market makers registered in a security on the *London Stock Exchange must display their prices. For *SEAQ the period is 8.30 a.m. to 4.30 p.m., and on SEAQ International 9.30 a.m. to 4.00 p.m.

**Manila Stock Exchange (MSE)** One of three stock exchanges in the Philippines. Manila Stock Exchange dates from 1927 and was modelled on the New York Stock Exchange; the other two are the Makati Stock Exchange (1965) and the Metropolitan Stock Exchange (1974), which is now inactive.

**Marché à Terme des Instruments Financiers (MATIF)** The French international *financial futures exchange. It opened in 1986 and competes with the *London International Financial Futures and Options Exchange.

**Marché des Options Négotiables de Paris (MONEP)** The French traded *options market founded in 1987.

**Mareva injunction** An order of the court preventing the defendant from dealing with specified assets. Such an order will be granted in cases in which the plaintiff can show that there will be a substantial risk that any judgment obtained against the defendant will be worthless, because the defendant will dissipate any assets to avoid paying. It is usually granted to prevent assets leaving the jurisdiction of the English courts, but may in exceptional circumstances extend to assets abroad. It is named after the 1975 case *Mareva Compañía Naviera SA* v *International Bulkcarriers SA*.

**margin 1.** The percentage of the cost of goods that has to be added to the cost to arrive at the selling price. **2.** The difference between the prices at which a *market maker or commodity dealer will buy and sell. This is often known colloquially as a **haircut**. **3.** In banking, the price added to a market rate of interest or subtracted from a market rate of deposit to provide a return for the bank. **4.** In commodity and currency dealing, the amount advanced by a speculator or investor to a broker or dealer, when buying futures. **5.** Money or securities deposited with a stockbroker to cover any possible losses a client may make. *See also* margin call; profit margin.

**marginal cost** The additional cost of producing an additional unit of output. In conditions of perfect competition, marginal cost would be equal to the market price.

**marginal costing** The process of costing products or activities by taking account only of the direct costs of the product or activity. The normal procedure of marginal costing is to compare the direct costs with the selling price of the product or service in order to see what contribution the item makes towards fixed overheads and profit. *Compare* absorption costing.

**marginal relief** Relief given by a tax authority if a marginal increase in a person's earnings brings that person's income into a higher tax bracket and results in an unfair tax burden. One option for the taxpayer would be to pay tax at the lower rate, adding to the tax the amount by which the increased income exceeds the limit for this lower rate. For example, if the rate of tax is 25% up to £30,000 and 30% for incomes that exceed this figure, a taxpayer earning, say, £30,100 might opt to pay tax at 25% on the £30,000 and pay over to the tax authorities the additional £100. Another option that occurs in the UK is to reduce the personal allowance, gradually, when the taxpayer's income is over a certain figure, until the excess over the basic allowance is lost.

**marginal tax rate** The additional tax paid for each unit increase in income. In the UK, for example, a taxpayer paying tax at the *higher rate of 40% will pay tax at this rate on all additional earnings and also on all taxable capital gains (*see* capital-gains tax). Under a *progressive tax system there is a tendency for the marginal tax rates of the poor and the rich to be very high, giving rise to the *poverty trap for the poor and, it is claimed, work disincentives for the rich.

**margin call** A call to a client from a commodity broker, financial futures broker, or stockbroker to increase the *margin, i.e. the amount of money or securities deposited with the broker as a safeguard. This usually happens if the client has an *open position in a market that is moving adversely for this position.

**marked cheque** A cheque that the bank on which it is drawn has marked 'good for payment'. This practice has been replaced in the UK by *bank drafts, although it is still used in the USA, where such cheques are called **certified checks**.

**marker barrel** A standard oil price based on one barrel of Saudi Arabian oil or some other internationally recognized oil (e.g. North Sea Brent crude). It sets standard prices for oil in the rest of the world.

**market 1.** The arena in which buyers and sellers meet to exchange items of value. A physical market in which traders haggle for the best price is one of the basic concepts of trade. The absence of a physical market for some goods is usually seen as one of the major sources of economic inefficiency. **2.** An organized gathering in which trading in securities (*see* stock exchange), commodities (*see* commodity market), currencies, etc., takes place. **3.** The demand for a particular product or service, often measured by sales during a specified period.

**marketable security** A security (stock, share, bond, etc.) that can be bought or sold on a *stock exchange. *See also* London Stock Exchange. *Compare* non-marketable securities.

**market capitalization (market valuation)** The value of a company obtained by multiplying the number of its issued shares by their *market price.

**market forces** The forces of supply and demand that in a *free market determine the quantity available of a particular product or service and the price at which it is offered. In general, a rise in demand will cause both supply and price to increase, while a rise in supply will cause both a fall in price and a drop in demand, although many markets have individual features that modify this simple analysis. In practice, most markets are not free, being influenced either by restrictions on supply or by government intervention that can affect demand, supply, or price.

**market instrument** A *negotiable instrument used for short-term debt.

**market maker** A dealer in securities on the *London Stock Exchange who undertakes to buy and sell securities as a principal and is therefore obliged to announce buying and selling prices for a particular security at a particular time. Before October 1986 (*see* Big Bang) this function was performed by a *stockjobber, who was then obliged to deal with the public through a *stockbroker. However since October 1986, when the rules changed, market makers attempt to make a profit by dealing in securities as principals (selling at a higher price than that at which they buy; *see* margin) as well as acting as agents, working for a commission. While this dual role may create a conflict of interest for market makers (*see* Chinese wall; front running), it avoids the restrictive trade practice of the former system and reduces the cost of dealing in the market.

**market order** An order given to a stockbroker, commodity broker, dealer, etc., to buy or sell specified securities or commodities immediately at the prevailing *market price. *Compare* limit order (*see* limit).

**market portfolio** *See* Markowitz model.

**market price 1.** The price of a raw material, product, service, security, etc., in an open market. In a formal market, such as a stock exchange, commodity market, foreign-exchange market, etc., there is often a *margin between the buying and selling price; there are, therefore, two market prices. In these circumstances the market prices often quoted are the average of the buying and selling price (*see* middle price). **2.** The economic concept of the price at which commodities are exchanged in a market, either for money or for each other.

**market rate of discount** *See* bill rate.

**market risk** One of the risks inherent in dealing on a market (*compare* counterparty risk). The obvious market risks are buying on a market that subsequently falls and selling on a market that rises; these risks can be reduced by *hedging, especially by means of the *futures contracts or *options, but they can never be eliminated. These forms of market risk are the obverse of the market opportunities that provide speculators with the chance of making a profit. The **currency risk** may be an element of the market risk. For example, a buyer of US securities in London, paying in sterling, faces not only the risk that the price of the securities will fall in the USA, but also the risk that there will be an unfavourable change in the rate of exchange between dollars and pounds.

**market-risk premium** *See* risk premium.

**market valuation** *See* market capitalization.

**market value** The value of an asset if it were to be sold on the open market at its current *market price. When land is involved it may be necessary to distinguish between the market value in its present use and that in some alternative use; for example, a factory site may have a market value as a factory site, and be so valued in the company's accounts, which may be less than its market value as building land.

**markings** The official number of bargains that have taken place during a working day on the *London Stock Exchange.

**marking up** The raising of prices by *market makers on the *London Stock Exchange in anticipation of an increased demand for a particular security.

**markka** (Fmk) The standard monetary unit of Finland, divided into 100 penniä.

**Markowitz model** A method of selecting the optimum investment *portfolio, devised by H. M. Markowitz (1927–   ). It makes use of the concepts of a **market portfolio** (containing all available investments in amounts proportional to the total market value of each individual security) and a graph (the **capital market line**) of alternative combinations of risk and return, resulting from investing fixed sums in the market portfolio.

**master trust** A name sometimes used by unit-trust managers for their *fund of funds.

**match** A purchase contract and a sales contract that cancel each other out.

**matched bargain** A transaction in which a sale of a particular quantity of stock is matched with a purchase of the same quantity of the same stock. Transactions of this kind are carried out on the *London Stock Exchange by **matching brokers**.

**matched sale–purchase agreement (MSP)** A device used by the US Federal Reserve in which it sells money-market instruments for immediate effect and couples the sale with the forward purchase of the same instrument, to facilitate the distribution of reserves of the banking system.

**material facts** Information pertinent to an insurance policy or claim that an insured person is obliged to provide for the insurer. The policy can be declared invalid if material facts are shown to have been deliberately withheld or incorrectly stated.

**materiality** The state of having sufficient significance to require separate disclosure in accounting. A statement issued by the Institute of Chartered

Accountants in England and Wales says 'a matter is material if its nondisclosure, misstatement, or omission would be likely to distort the view given by the accounts or other statement under consideration'.

**MATIF** Abbreviation for *Marché à Terme des Instruments Financiers.

**maturity balance** The combination of securities, both federal and national, held by the US Federal Reserve.

**maturity date** The date on which a document, such as a *bond, *bill of exchange, or insurance policy, becomes due for payment. In some cases, especially for redeemable government stocks, the maturity date is known as the **redemption date**. *See also* redemption.

**maturity yield** *See* yield.

**maximum fluctuation** The maximum daily price fluctuation that is permitted in some markets. *See* limit.

**maximum investment plan (MIP)** A unit-linked endowment policy marketed by a life-assurance company that is designed to produce maximum profit rather than life-assurance protection. It calls for regular premiums, usually over ten years, with options to continue. These policies normally enable a tax-free fund to be built up over ten years and, because of the regular premiums, *pound cost averaging can be used, linked to a number of markets.

**maximum slippage** The period between the date on which a new company expects to start earning income and the date up to which it can survive on its venture capital. After this date has passed, the company would be unable to raise further funds and would sink into insolvency. *See also* death-valley curve.

**MCT** Abbreviation for *mainstream corporation tax.

**mean** An average. *See* arithmetic mean; geometric mean; median.

**mean deviation** In statistics, the *arithmetic mean of the deviations (all taken as positive numbers) of all the numbers in a set of numbers from their arithmetic mean. For example, the arithmetic mean of 5, 8, 9, and 10 is 8, and therefore the deviations from this mean are 3, 0, 1, and 2, giving a mean deviation of 1.5.

**mean price** *See* middle price.

**median** A form of *mean in which a set of numbers is arranged in an ascending or descending scale and the middle number (if the set comprises an odd number) or the arithmetic mean of the middle two numbers (if it comprises an even number) is taken as the median. This can give a more representative average in some circumstances than an *arithmetic mean or a *geometric mean.

**medium-dated gilt** *See* gilt-edged security.

**medium of exchange** A substance or article of little intrinsic value that is used to pay for goods or services. In primitive economies various articles, such as sea shells, have been used for this purpose but *money is now used universally.

**mediums** *See* gilt-edged security.

**medium-sized company** A company, as defined by the UK Companies Act 1981, that falls below any two of the following three size criteria: (1) gross assets

£2,800,000; (2) turnover £5,750,000; (3) average number of employees 250. If these companies are not *public limited companies or banking, insurance, or shipping companies, they may file abbreviated *profit and loss accounts with the Registrar of Companies (*see* modified accounts), although they must provide their own shareholders with the full statutory information. *Compare* small company.

**medium-term financial assistance (MTFA)**  A loan available to member states of the European Community experiencing monetary difficulties due to adverse balance of payments. The donor countries may attach conditions on granting these loans, which usually have a term of two to five years. *Compare* short-term monetary support.

**medium-term liabilities**  Liabilities falling due in, say, more than one but less than ten years.

**medium-term note (MTN)**  An unsecured *note issued in a eurocurrency with a maturity of about three to six years.

**meeting of creditors**  *See* bankruptcy; creditors' voluntary liquidation; liquidator.

**MEFF Renta Fija (MEFF RF)**  A *financial futures and *options exchange in Barcelona. Until December 1991, when it merged with MOFEX, the Madrid options exchange, it was known as MEFF (Mercado de Futuros Financieros) and dealt exclusively in financial futures (both fixed income and variable income). Since the merger MEFF RF deals in fixed income products (interest-rate and currency futures and options), while the Madrid exchange, known as **MEFF Renta Variable** (**MEFF RV**), handles variable income derivatives (equity and stock index futures and options).

**MEFF Renta Variable (MEFF RV)**  *See* Meff Renta Fija.

**meltdown**  A disastrous and uncontrolled fall in share prices. *Black Monday has also been called Meltdown Monday, for example. The expression is, of course, derived from the disaster that results when the core of a nuclear reactor melts uncontrollably.

**member bank**  A bank that belongs to a central banking or clearing system. In the UK a member bank is a *commercial bank that is a member of the *Association for Payment Clearing Services. In the USA it is a commercial bank that is a member of the *Federal Reserve System.

**member firm**  A firm of brokers or *market makers that is a member of the *London Stock Exchange (International Stock Exchange). There are some 360 member firms with some 5300 individual members. Banks, insurance companies, and overseas securities houses can now become corporate members.

**member of a company**  A shareholder of a company whose name is entered in the *register of members. Founder members (*see* founders' shares) are those who sign the memorandum of association; anyone subsequently coming into possession of the company's shares becomes a member.

**members' voluntary liquidation (members' voluntary winding-up)**  The winding-up of a company by a special resolution of the members in circumstances in which the company is solvent. Before making the winding-up resolution, the directors must make a *declaration of solvency. It is a criminal offence to make such a declaration without reasonable grounds for believing that it is true. When the resolution has been passed, a *liquidator is appointed; if, during the course of the winding-up, the liquidator believes that the company will not be able to pay its debts, a meeting of creditors must be called and the winding-up is treated as a members' *compulsory liquidation.

**memorandum of satisfaction**  A document stating that a mortgage or charge on property has been repaid. It has to be signed by all the parties concerned and a copy sent to the *Registrar of Companies, if the mortgage or charge was made by a company.

**merchant bank**  A bank that formerly specialized in financing foreign trade, an activity that often grew out of its own merchanting business. This led them into accepting *bills of exchange and functioning as *accepting houses. More recently they have tended to diversify into the field of *hire-purchase finance, the granting of long-term loans (especially to companies), providing venture capital, advising companies on flotations and *takeover bids, underwriting new issues, and managing investment portfolios and unit trusts. Many of them are old-established and some offer a limited banking service. Their knowledge of international trade makes them specialists in dealing with the large *multinational companies. They are most common in Europe, but some merchant banks have begun to operate in the USA.

**merger**  The combination of two or more organizations for the benefit of all of them. The objective is invariably to increase efficiency and sometimes to avoid competition, although in the UK approval of the *Monopolies and Mergers Commission may be required and the merger must be conducted on lines sanctioned by the *City Code on Takeovers and Mergers. Mergers are normally amicably arranged by all the parties concerned, unlike some takeovers.

**merger accounting**  A method of accounting in which the assets of a merged subsidiary company are shown in the accounts of the parent company using the *historical-cost accounting principle. This is based on their value at the time of acquisition, which may be less than their present value.

**metical**  (plural **meticais**; Mt) The standard monetary unit of Mozambique, divided into 100 centavos.

**mezzanine**  Denoting an intermediate stage in some financial process. **Mezzanine funding** is an intermediate level in the funding of a new company, lying between the provision of a loan and the taking of a share in its equity.

**Mid-America Commodity Exchange**  An exchange in Chicago that deals in *futures and *options contracts in a variety of commodities as well as in *financial futures.

**middleman**  A person or organization that makes a profit by trading in goods or services as an intermediary. Middlemen include agents, brokers, dealers, merchants, factors, wholesalers, distributors, and retailers. They earn their profit by providing a variety of different services, including finance, bulk buying, holding stocks, breaking bulk, risk sharing, making a market and stabilizing prices, providing information about products (to consumers) and about markets (to producers), providing a distribution network, and introducing buyers to sellers.

**middle price (mean price)** The average of the *offer price of a security, commodity, currency, etc., and the *bid price. It is the middle price that is often quoted in the financial press.

**mil** A monetary unit of Malta, worth one thousandth of a *lira.

**Milan Stock Exchange** A relatively small stock exchange in Italy, which in 1992 was in the throes of reorganization.

**millième** A monetary unit of Egypt, worth one thousandth of a *pound.

**millime** A Tunisian monetary unit, worth one thousandth of a *dinar.

**minimum lending rate (MLR)** The successor, between 1971 and 1981, of the *bank rate. In this decade it was the minimum rate at which the Bank of England would lend to the *discount houses. This was a published figure; the present more informal *base rate does not have the same status. When the government suspended MLR in 1981 it reserved the right to reintroduce it at any time, which it did for one day in January 1985.

**minimum subscription** The minimum sum of money, stated in the *prospectus of a new company, that the directors consider must be raised if the company is to be viable.

**minority interest** The interest of individual shareholders in a company more than 50% of which is owned by a holding company. For example, if 60% of the ordinary shares in a company are owned by a holding company, the remaining 40% will represent a minority interest. These shareholders will receive their full share of profits in the form of dividends although they will be unable to determine company policy as they will always be outvoted by the majority interest held by the holding company.

**minority protection** Remedies evolved to safeguard a minority of company members from the abuse of majority rule. They include just and equitable winding-up, applying for relief on the basis of unfair prejudice, bringing a derivative or representative action, and seeking an inspection and investigation of the company.

**mint par of exchange** The rate of exchange between two currencies that were on the *gold standard. The rate was then determined by the gold content of the basic coin.

**MIP** **1.** Abbreviation for monthly investment plan. **2.** Abbreviation for marine insurance policy. **3.** Abbreviation for *maximum investment plan.

**MIRAS** Abbreviation for *mortgage interest relief at source.

**misfeasance** **1.** The negligent or otherwise improper performance of a lawful act. **2.** An act by an officer of a company in the nature of a breach of trust or breach of duty, particularly if it relates to the company's assets.

**misfeasance summons** An application to the court by a creditor, contributory, liquidator, or the official receiver during the course of winding up a company. The court is asked to examine the conduct of a company officer who is suspected of a breach of trust or duty and it can order this officer to make restitution to the company.

**mismatch** **1.** A *floating-rate note in which the coupon is paid monthly but the interest rate paid is that applicable to a note of longer maturity. **2.** The state of the typical books of a bank that borrows short-term and lends long-term, creating a condition in which assets and liabilities are not matched. This is acceptable as long as deposits keep coming in.

**misrepresentation** An untrue statement of fact, made by one party to the other in the course of negotiating a contract, that induces the other party to enter into the contract. The person making the misrepresentation is called the **representor**, and the person to whom it is made is the **representee**. A false statement of law, opinion, or intention does not constitute a misrepresentation; nor does a statement of fact known by the representee to be untrue. Moreover, unless the representee relies on the statement so that it becomes an inducement to enter into the contract, it is not a misrepresentation. The remedies for misrepresentation vary according to the degree of culpability of the representor. If the representor is guilty of **fraudulent misrepresentation** (i.e. not honestly believing in the truth of any statement made) the representee may, subject to certain limitations, set the contract aside and may also sue for *damages. If the representor is guilty of **negligent misrepresentation** (i.e. believing a statement made without reasonable grounds for doing so) the representee may also rescind (*see* rescission) the contract and sue for damages. If the representor has committed merely an **innocent misrepresentation** (reasonably believing a statement to be true) the representee is restricted to rescinding the contract.

**mitigation of damage** Minimizing the loss incurred by the person who suffered a loss and is claiming *damages as a result of it. The injured party has a duty to take all reasonable steps to mitigate any loss and the courts will not, therefore, award damages to compensate for a loss that could have been avoided by reasonable action.

**MLR** Abbreviation for *minimum lending rate.

**MMC** Abbreviation for *Monopolies and Mergers Commission.

**MMDA** Abbreviation for *money-market deposit account.

**mock auction** An auction during which a lot is sold to someone at a price lower than the highest bid, part of the price is repaid or credited to the bidder, the right to bid is restricted to those who have bought or agreed to buy one or more articles, or articles are given away or offered as gifts. Under the Mock Auction Act 1961 it is an offence to promote or conduct a mock auction.

**modified accounts** A form of statutory *annual accounts for small companies and medium-sized companies in the UK. Currently all companies have to submit full accounts to their shareholders, although consideration is being given to shortened accounts even for large companies. However, the small and medium-sized companies need file only modified accounts with the *Registrar of Companies. For small companies, modified accounts consist only of a balance sheet, certain specified notes, and a copy of the auditors' report. In the case of medium-sized companies the profit and loss account may omit some information but otherwise full information must be filed.

**MONEP** Abbreviation for *Marché des Options Négotiables de Paris.

**monetarism** A school of thought in economics that places money at the centre of macroeconomic policy. Based on the *quantity theory of money, it relates the price level to the quantity of money in the economy. It claims that monetary factors are a major influence on the economy and that, in particular, government expansion of the money supply will tend to generate inflation rather than employment. This view is now associated with Milton Friedman (1912–  ) of Chicago University.

**monetarist** A person who supports *monetarism.

**monetary aggregate** Any of several measures of the *money supply from the narrow M0 to the broad M5.

**monetary assets and liabilities** Amounts receivable (assets) or payable (liabilities) that appear in a company's accounts as specific sums of money, e.g. cash and bank balances, loans, debtors, and creditors. These are to be distinguished from such non-monetary items as plant and machinery, stock in trade, or equity investments, which, although they are also expressed in accounts at a value (frequently cost), are not necessarily realizable at that value.

**monetary compensatory amount** Subsidies and taxes on farm products produced within the EC that form part of the *Common Agricultural Policy. They are used to bridge the gap between the green pound (*see* green currencies), and foreign exchange rates to prevent fluctuation in these rates from altering the farm prices. The object is to enable agricultural products to cost the same in all member countries and to prevent trading between countries in these products purely to make a profit as a result of changes in the exchange rate.

**monetary control** The use of the *central bank of a country by its government to control the *money supply. In the UK, the Bank of England acts in this way but in the USA the Federal Reserve Bank is largely independent of government policy.

**Monetary Control Act 1980** The US legislation that made all US banks members of the *Federal Reserve System.

**monetary inflation** The theory that *inflation is related to the expansion of the *money supply. *See* monetary policy; quantity theory of money.

**monetary policy** A means by which governments try to affect macroeconomic conditions by increasing or decreasing the supply of money. Three main options are available: (i) printing more money (now rarely used in practice); (ii) direct controls over money held by the monetary sector; (iii) *open-market operations. The traditional Keynesian view has been that monetary policy is at best a blunt instrument, while *monetarism expresses the opposite view. In practice, governments have tended to employ 'tight' monetary policies, in the belief that this restrains inflation. *Compare* fiscal policy.

**monetary reform** The revision of a country's currency by the introduction of a new currency unit or a substantial change to an existing system. Examples include decimalization of the UK currency (1971) and the change from the austral to the peso in Argentina (1992).

**monetary system 1.** The system used by a country to provide the public with money for internal use and to control the exchange of its own currency with those of foreign countries. It also includes the system used by a country for implementing its *monetary policy. **2.** A system used to control the exchange rate of a group of countries. *See* European Monetary System.

**monetary theory** Any theory concerned with the influence of the quantity of money in an economic system. *See* monetary policy; quantity theory of money.

**monetary unit** The standard unit of currency in a country. The monetary unit of each country is related to those of other countries by a *foreign exchange rate. In the European Community, the aim of one faction is the introduction of a single currency, the *European Currency Unit (ECU), which would come about by European Monetary Union.

**monetization** The sale of *Treasury bills to banks by the UK government to finance a budgetary deficit.

**money** A *medium of exchange that functions as a unit of account and a store of value. Originally it enhanced economic development by enabling goods to be bought and sold without the need for barter. However, throughout history money has been beset by the problem of its debasement as a store of value as a result of *inflation. Now that the supply of money is a monopoly of the state, most governments are committed in principle to stable prices. The central debate in economics over the past 50 years has been whether *fiscal policy and *monetary policy can have any effect other than to create inflation. The word *money* is derived from the Latin *moneta*, which was one of the names of Juno, the Roman goddess whose temple was used as a mint.

**money at call and short notice** One of the assets that appears in the balance sheet of a bank. It includes funds lent to discount houses, money brokers, the stock exchange, bullion brokers, corporate customers, and increasingly to other banks. 'At call' money is repayable on demand, whereas 'short notice' money implies that notice of repayment of up to 14 days will be given. After cash, money at call and short notice are the banks' most liquid assets. They are usually interest-earning secured loans but their importance lies in providing the banks with an opportunity to use their surplus funds and to adjust their cash and liquidity requirements.

**money broker** In the UK, a broker who arranges short-term loans in the *money market, i.e. between banks, discount houses, and dealers in government securities. Money brokers do not themselves lend or borrow money; they work for a commission arranging loans on a day-to-day and overnight basis. Money brokers also operate in the eurobond markets.

**moneylender** A person whose business it is to lend money, other than pawnbrokers, friendly or building societies, corporate bodies with special powers to lend money, banks, or insurance companies. The Consumer Credit Act 1974 replaces the earlier Moneylenders Acts and requires all moneylenders to be registered, to obtain an annual licence to lend money, and to state the true *annual percentage rate (APR) of interest at which a loan is made.

**money market 1.** The UK market for short-term loans in which *money brokers arrange for loans between the banks, the government, the *discount houses, and the *accepting houses, with the Bank of England acting as *lender of last resort. The main items of exchange are *bills of exchange, Treasury bills, and trade bills. The market takes place in and around Lombard Street in the City of London. Private investors, through their banks, can place deposits in the money market at a higher rate of interest than bank deposit accounts, for sums usually in excess of £10,000. **2.** The foreign-exchange market and the bullion market in addition to the short-term loan market.

**money-market deposit account (MMDA)** A high-yielding savings account introduced in the USA in 1982 to allow deposit-taking institutions to compete for savers' funds with the money markets. As long as the account has a balance of more than $1000 there is no regulatory limit on the account. Balances below $1000 attract a lower rate of interest. Restrictions on the account apply to withdrawals (three a month) and transfers for bill payment (three a month).

**money-market mutual fund** A US *open-end fund that invests in short-term debt instruments and sells its shares to investors.

**money-market unit trust (cash unit trust)** A *unit trust that invests in money-market instruments in order to provide investors with a risk-free income.

**money-purchase pension scheme** A pension scheme in which payment is based directly on contributions made during the retired person's working life, rather than a percentage of his or her final salary. *See* personal pension scheme.

**money supply** The quantity of money issued by a country's monetary authorities (usually the central bank). If the demand for money is stable, the widely accepted *quantity theory of money implies that increases in the money supply will lead directly to an increase in the price level, i.e. to inflation. Since the 1970s most western governments have attempted to reduce inflation by controlling the money supply. This raises two issues:
(i) how to measure the money supply;
(ii) how to control the money supply (*see* interest-rate policy).
   In the UK various measures of the money supply have been used, from the very narrow M0 to the very broad M5. They are usually defined as:
M0 — notes and coins in circulation plus the banks' till money and the banks' balances with the Bank of England;
M1 — notes and coins in circulation plus private-sector current accounts and deposit accounts that can be transferred by cheque;
M2 — notes and coins in circulation plus non-interest-bearing bank deposits plus building society deposits plus National Savings accounts;
M3 — M1 plus all other private-sector bank deposits plus certificates of deposit;
M3c — M3 plus foreign currency bank deposits;
M4 — M1 plus most private-sector bank deposits plus holdings of money-market instruments (e.g. Treasury bills);
M5 — M4 plus building society deposits.

**money-supply rules** A policy in which a government states in advance the extent to which it intends to expand the *money supply. It is based on the belief that *fiscal policy and *monetary policy cannot affect the real variables in an economic situation but that uncertainty concerning government intentions can destabilize markets. In these circumstances a stable-policy rule is the best a government can achieve.

**möngö** A Mongolian monetary unit worth one hundredth of a *tugrik.

**Monopolies and Mergers Commission (MMC)** A commission established in 1948 as the Monopolies and Restrictive Practices Commission and reconstructed under its present title by the Fair Trading Act 1973. It investigates questions referred to it on unregistered monopolies relating to the supply of goods in the UK, the transfer of newspapers, mergers qualifying for investigation under the Fair Trading Act, and uncompetitive practices and restrictive labour practices, including public-sector monopolies as laid down in the provisions of the Competition Act 1980.

**Monthly Digest of Statistics** A monthly publication of the UK Central Statistical Office providing statistical information on industry, national income, and the UK population.

**moonlighting** Having two jobs, one a full-time daytime job, the other a part-time evening job. Often the second job is undertaken on a self-employed basis and income is not returned for tax purposes.

**moratorium** **1.** An agreement between a creditor and a debtor to allow additional time for the settlement of a debt. **2.** A period during which one government permits a government of a foreign country to suspend repayments of a debt. **3.** A period during which all the trading debts in a particular market are suspended as a result of some exceptional crisis in the market. In these circumstances, not to call a moratorium would probably lead to more insolvencies than the market could stand. The intention of such a moratorium is, first, that firms should be given a breathing space to find out exactly what their liabilities are and, secondly, that they should be given time to make the necessary financial arrangements to settle their liabilities.

**mortality table (life table)** An actuarial table prepared on the basis of mortality rates for males and females. It provides life-assurance companies with the information they require to quote for life-assurance policies, annuities, etc.

**mortgage** An interest in property created as a security for a loan or payment of a debt and terminated on payment of the loan or debt. The borrower, who offers the security, is the **mortgagor**; the lender, who provides the money, is the **mortgagee**. *Building societies and banks are the usual mortgagees for house purchasers, although there are other providers. A mortgage is generally repaid by monthly instalments, usually over a period of 25 years. Repayments may consist of capital and interest (**repayment mortgage**) or of interest only, with arrangements being made to repay the capital, generally from the proceeds of an *endowment assurance policy (**endowment mortgage**) or a pension policy (**pension mortgage**). Business uses of the mortgage include using property to secure a loan to start a business. Virtually any property may be mortgaged (though land is the most common).

Under the Law of Property Act 1925, which governs mortgage regulations in the UK, there are two types of mortgage, legal and equitable. A **legal mortgage** confers a legal estate on the mortgagee; the only valid mortgages are (a) a lease granted for a stated number of years, which terminates on repayment of the loan at or before the end of that period; and (b) a deed expressed to be a *charge by way of legal mortgage. An **equitable mortgage** can be created if the mortgagee has only an equitable interest in the property (for example, when the mortgagee is a beneficiary under a trust of the property). Provided that this is done by *deed, the rights of the parties are very similar to those under a legal mortgage. An equitable mortgage can also be created of a legal or equitable interest by an informal agreement, e.g. the mortgagor hands the title deeds to the mortgagee as security for a loan. Such a mortgagee has the remedies of possession and foreclosure only (see below). A *second mortgage or subsequent mortgage may be taken out on the same property, provided that the value of the property is greater than the amount of the previous mortgage(s). All mortgages of registered land are noted in the *register of charges on application by the mortgagee, and a charge certificate is issued. When mortgaged land is unregistered, a first legal mortgagee keeps the title deeds. A subsequent legal mortgagee and any equitable mortgagee who does not have the title deeds should protect their interests by registration.

If the mortgaged property is the mortgagor's main residence, the mortgagor is entitled to **mortgage interest relief**, an income-tax allowance on the value of the interest paid on mortgages up to a specified figure (currently £30,000). For mortgages made on or after 1 August 1988, the limit of mortgage relief applies to the property rather than to the borrower. Thus when two or more people share a residence, the relief is allocated between them in equal shares. Previously, each occupant (except when couples were married) was entitled to the full relief. Under the MIRAS (*mortgage interest relief at source) scheme, interest payments made by a borrower to a bank, building society, etc., are made after deduction of an amount equivalent to the relief of income tax due at the basic rate, and therefore no other relief is necessary, unless the person paying the mortgage pays tax at a higher rate.

Under the **equity of redemption**, the mortgagor is allowed to redeem the property at any time on payment of the loan together with interest and costs; any provisions in a mortgage deed to prevent redemption (known as **clogs**) are void.

In theory, the mortgagee always has the right to take possession of mortgaged property even if there has been no default. This right is usually excluded by building-society mortgages until default, and its exclusion may be implied in any instalment mortgage. Where residential property is concerned, the court has power to delay the recovery of possession if there is a realistic possibility that the default will be remedied in a reasonable time. In case of default, the mortgagor has a statutory right to sell the property, but this will normally be exercised after obtaining possession first. Any surplus left after the debt and the mortgagee's expenses have been met must be paid to the mortgagor. The mortgagee also has a statutory right to appoint a *receiver to manage mortgaged property in the event of default; this power is useful where business property is concerned. As a final resort, a mortgage may be brought to an end by *foreclosure, in which the court orders the transfer of the property to the mortgagee. This is not common in times of rising property prices, as the mortgagor would lose more than the value of the debt, so the court will not order foreclosure where a sale would be more appropriate. However, when property values are falling the mortgagor may have *negative equity and the only recourse of the courts is foreclosure. *See also* amortizing mortgage; balloon mortgage; PEP mortgage; securitized mortgage.

**mortgage-backed security**  A bond (or note) in which the collateral is provided by a *mortgage or portfolio of mortgages, usually insured to cover any defaults.

**mortgage debenture**  A loan made to a company by an investor, secured on the real property of the company. *See* debenture.

**mortgagee**  A lender who provides a *mortgage.

**mortgagee in possession**  A *mortgagee (lender) who has exercised the right to take possession of a mortgaged property; this may happen at any time, even if there has been no default by the mortgagor. However, the mortgage deed may contain an agreement not to do this unless the borrower defaults on the loan. In the case of a dwelling house, a court order will be required before the lender can take possession. The court may adjourn the hearing to allow the mortgagor time to pay. The mortgagee will either receive the rents and profits if the property has been let or be empowered to manage the property. The mortgagee is not entitled to reap any personal benefit beyond repayment of the interest and the principal debt, must carry out reasonable repairs, and must not damage the property.

**mortgage interest relief at source (MIRAS)** A relief introduced into UK tax legislation in 1983, enabling a 'qualifying borrower' to deduct basic-rate tax from interest payments in respect of borrowing for house purchase. There is limit of £30,000 borrowing on which relief may be given. Only certain providers of funds are eligible to operate the scheme. No relief on higher-rate tax is available under this scheme.

**mortgagor** A borrower who takes out a *mortgage.

**mountain** A surplus of agricultural produce. Mountains of butter, meat, etc., have accumulated in the EC as a result of the *Common Agricultural Policy. According to this, farmers are guaranteed a minimum price for their produce, which the EC has to buy. Unable to sell the mountain within the EC, which would depress prices, the EC have to dispose of mountains to charitable causes or sell them outside the EC at very low prices. See Common Agricultural Policy.

**MSP** Abbreviation for *matched sale–purchase agreement.

**MTFA** Abbreviation for *medium-term financial assistance.

**MTN** Abbreviation for *medium-term note.

**multi-component euronote facility** A *euronote issued in a variety of currencies.

**multifunctional card** A plastic card issued by a bank or building society to its customers to function as a *cheque card, *debit card, and *cash card. Multifunctional cards operate in conjunction with a *personal identification number.

**multinational company** A company with sales and manufacturing centres in more than one country, especially with centres outside its native country or the country of its registered headquarters.

**multiple application** The submission of more than one application form for a new issue of shares that is likely to be oversubscribed (see allotment). In many countries it is illegal to do so either if the applications are made in the same name or if false names are used.

**multiple exchange rate** An exchange rate quoted by a country that has more than one value, depending on the use to which the currency is put. For example, some countries have quoted a specially favourable rate for tourists or for importers of desirable goods.

**multiple taxation** Taxation of the same income by more than two countries. Compare double taxation.

**multiplier** The feedback effect generated by a change in an economic variable. For example, an increase in total *investment will raise national income by an amount equal to its monetary value, but in addition it will have a wider positive feedback effect by stimulating other parts of the economy, thus creating new jobs and additional demand for goods. The effect of the multiplier is greatest in the construction industry: investment made in this industry has wide effects throughout the economy. Multipliers may be negative as well as positive.

**municipal bond**   A bond issued by a local government authority, especially one in the USA.

**mutual fund**   *See* open-end fund.

**mutual life-assurance company**   A type of life-assurance company that grew out of the Friendly Societies; there are no shareholders and apart from benefits and running expenses there are no other withdrawals from the fund; thus any profits are distributed to policyholders.

**mutual savings banks**   US institutions that take deposits and make domestic mortgage loans. They are owned by the depositors but do not have shareholders. *See also* thrifts.

**naira** (₦) The standard monetary unit of Nigeria, divided into 100 kobo.

**Nakasone bond** A bond issued by the Japanese government in a foreign currency. It is named after the prime minister in office when it was introduced (1982).

**naked call writing** Selling (writing) a call *option on equities that one does not own. A person may do this if he or she expects the price of a particular share to fall or remain unchanged. It is, however, a dangerous strategy because if the price rises the shares will have to be purchased at the market price in order to deliver them, thus involving an unlimited risk. *Compare* covered call writing.

**naked debenture** An unsecured *debenture.

**name** *See* Lloyd's; syndicate.

**narrow money** An informal name for M0, or sometimes M1: the part of the *money supply that can directly perform the function of a *medium of exchange. *Compare* broad money.

**narrow-range securities** *See* trustee investments.

**NASD** Abbreviation for *National Association of Securities Dealers Inc.

**NASDAQ** Abbreviation for *National Association of Securities Dealers Automated Quotation System.

**NASDAQ index** The price index of the *National Association of Securities Dealers Automated Quotation System for over-the-counter trading. The index is market-value-weighted. There are six indexes covering different sectors of the market, all of which were based on 5 February 1971. Two newer indexes are the NASDAQ-100 and the NASDAQ-Financial, operating from 1 February 1985, valued at 250.

**NASDAQ International** An international service based on NASDAQ that came into operation in January 1992. It provides a screen-based quotation system to support market-making in US registered equities from 8.30 am until 2 pm London time (i.e. between 3.30 am and 9 am Eastern Standard Time) on US business days. Most US and Canadian equity securities are available on the system.

**NASDIM** Abbreviation for *National Association of Securities Dealers and Investment Managers.

**National Association of Securities Dealers and Investment Managers (NASDIM)** A former association of some 800 licensed securities dealers. It was formed in 1979 from the Association of Licensed Dealers and disbanded in 1987 on the establishment of the statutory *Self-Regulating Organizations.

**National Association of Securities Dealers Automated Quotation System (NASDAQ)** A US computer system for trading in over-the-counter securities that began operations on 8 February 1971, when it was the first screen-based trading system with no market floor. It is now the second largest stock market in the USA, share traded in 1991 being worth $694,000 million. In 1991 NASDAQ had 425 active market makers, with an average of 10.5 market makers per security; it had 179 939 terminals in the USA and some 25 453 terminals operating in Canada, Switzerland, the UK, Germany, and France (*see also* NASDAQ International). NASDAQ provided the basis for the *SEAQ system on the *London Stock Exchange.

**National Association of Securities Dealers Inc. (NASD)** A US self-regulating organization of the securities industry responsible for operating and regulating the NASDAQ and over-the-counter securities markets. It is based in Washington, DC.

**national banks** US commercial banks established by federal charter, which requires them to be members of the *Federal Reserve System. They were created by the National Bank Act 1863 and formerly issued their own banknotes. Only some 30% of US banks are national banks (*compare* state banks), but the national banks hold over 65% of all deposits.

**National Chamber of Trade (NCT)** A non-profitmaking UK organization founded in 1897, with headquarters in Henley-on-Thames, that links and represents local *chambers of trade and commerce, national trade associations, and individual businesses in the UK. It maintains lobbies scrutinizing legislation in both Westminster and Brussels and provides expert advice for affiliated chambers and members.

**national debt** The debts of a central government, both internal and overseas. Net government borrowing each year is added to the national debt. By the end of the financial year 1990, the UK national debt amounted to £192.6 billion of which £6.7 billion was non-sterling and £185.9 was in sterling. The non-sterling debt is important because interest on it adversely affects the *balance of payments. Management of the national debt, which can be an important aspect of government monetary policy, is in the hands of the **National Debt Commissioners** of the Bank of England.

**National Economic Development Office** A former UK government organization whose council, the National Economic Development Council (**NEDC** *or* **Neddy**) of which the Chancellor of the Exchequer was chairman, brought together members of the government (including the secretaries of state for Education and Science, Employment, Energy, Environment, and Trade and Industry), management, and the unions to consider issues concerning employment and economic growth.

**National Girobank** *See* giro.

**national income accounts** Accounts that provide figures for the main macroeconomic variables, such as *gross national product, consumption, and *investment. Almost all countries produce national income accounts, which are widely used for evaluating national economic performances. Although the UN provides a standard system for measurement of national income accounts, many countries do not follow these and many disagreements remain as to how they should be measured.

**National Insurance** A levy in the UK for social security purposes, notionally intended to fund sickness and unemployment benefits and national retirement pensions. There are four classes of payment: Class 1 primary and secondary, paid by employees and employers respectively, based on the wages and salaries of employees; Class 2, a weekly sum paid by the self-employed; Class 3, voluntary contributions to keep up contribution requirements; Class 4, a further levy on the self-employed based on levels of profit. *See also* State Earnings-Related Pension Scheme (SERPS).

**nationalization** The process of bringing the assets of a company into the ownership of the state. Examples of nationalized industries in the UK are the British Coal Corporation (formerly the National Coal Board) and British Rail. Nationalization has often been pursued as much for political as economic ends and the economic justifications themselves are varied. One argument for nationalization is that if a company possesses a natural monopoly, the *profits it earns should be shared by the whole population through state ownership. Another argument might be that particular industries are strategically important for the nation and therefore cannot be entrusted to private enterprise. In the 1980s and 1990s Conservative governments have tended to reverse Labour's nationalization of the 1950s, 1960s, and 1970s with a series of *privatization measures.

**National Market System (NMS)** The segment of the *National Association of Securities Dealers Automated Quotation System (NASDAQ) in which securities are subject to real-time trade reporting. It encompasses approximately half of all NASDAQ securities and accounts for more than two thirds of NASDAQ share volume and more than 90% of aggregate NASDAQ market value.

**national plan** An economic plan formulated by a government as a blueprint for its economic development over a stated period, usually five or ten years.

**National Savings** The UK Department for National Savings was established in 1969, having previously been known as the Post Office Savings Department. It is responsible for administering a wide range of schemes for personal savers, including *premium bonds, *income bonds, *capital bonds, and *yearly savings plans. In addition the department has offered a range of **National Savings Certificates (NSC)**, costing either £10 (up to 1985) or £25 (from 1985), some of which have been index-linked (*see* indexation). The income they pay is income-tax free and the element of capital gain is free of capital-gains tax. *See also* National Savings Bank; National Savings Stock Register.

**National Savings Bank (NSB)** A savings bank founded in 1861, now operated by the Department for *National Savings through the agency of the Post Office (it was formerly called the Post Office Savings Bank). It offers ordinary accounts with a minimum deposit of £5 and a maximum of £10,000, and investment accounts paying a higher rate of interest for deposits of between £5 and £25,000.

**National Savings Certificates** *See* National Savings.

**National Savings Stock Register** An organization run by the Department for *National Savings from the Bonds and Stock Office in Blackpool. It enables members of the public to buy certain Treasury stocks and other *gilt-edged securities without going through a stockbroker; it thus provides an alternative to the main *Bank of England Stock Register. Purchases and sales are made by post and the interest paid is taxable, but is paid before deduction of tax (unlike the Bank of England Register). Because transactions are carried out by post, this method does not provide the maximum flexibility in a moving market. The maximum amount that can be invested in any one stock on any one day is £10,000, although there is no limit to the amount of stock that an investor may hold.

**National Securities Clearing Corporation (NSCC)**  A US securities *clearing house formed in 1977 by the merger of the National Clearing Corporation, owned by the *National Association of Securities Dealers Inc., and the clearing facilities of the *New York Stock Exchange (NYSE) and the *American Stock Exchange (AMEX). Purchases and sales in both markets are settled through the NSCC.

**National Stock Exchange**  See US stock exchanges.

**natural justice**  The minimum standard of fairness to be applied when resolving a dispute. The main rules of natural justice include: (1) the right to be heard – each party to the dispute should be given an opportunity to answer any allegations made by the other party; (2) the rule against bias – the person involved in settling the dispute should act impartially, in particular by disclosing any interest he or she may have in the outcome of the dispute. The rules of natural justice apply equally in judicial as well as in administrative proceedings. Alleging a breach of natural justice is the method commonly used to challenge an administrative decision before the courts.

**NAV**  Abbreviation for *net asset value.

**NBV**  Abbreviation for *net book value.

**NCI**  Abbreviation for *New Community Instrument.

**NCT**  Abbreviation for *National Chamber of Trade.

**NDP**  Abbreviation for *net domestic product.

**near money**  An asset that is immediately transferable and may be used to settle some but not all debts, although it is not as liquid as banknotes and coins. *Bills of exchange are examples of near money. Near money is not included in the *money supply indicators.

**NEDC (Neddy)**  Abbreviation for National Economic Development Council. See National Economic Development Office.

**negative cash flow**  A *cash flow in which the outflows exceed the inflows.

**negative equity**  An asset that has a market value below the sum of money borrowed to purchase it. It may refer to a house, bought at a time of high prices on a *mortgage, which now has a current market value below the sum still outstanding on the mortgage. Compare negative net worth.

**negative income tax (NIT)**  A means of targeting social security benefits to those most in need. The payments would be made through the income-tax system by granting personal allowances to taxpayers so that the *basic rate of income tax on these allowances would constitute a minimum amount required for living. Those with high incomes would obtain that amount as an income-tax relief, while those with incomes lower than the allowance would have a negative income-tax liability and be paid the appropriate sums. The principal objection to the system is that to cover the needs of the disadvantaged the wealthier would obtain excessively high allowances.

**negative interest** A charge made by a bank or other deposit taker for looking after a sum of money for a given period.

**negative net worth** The value of an organization that has liabilities in excess of its assets.

**negligence** A tort in which a breach of a **duty of care** results in damage to the person to whom the duty is owed. Such a duty is owed by manufacturers to the consumers who buy their products, by professional persons to their clients, by a director of a company to its shareholders, etc. A person who has suffered loss or injury as a result of a breach of the duty of care can claim damages in tort.

**negotiability** The ability of a document to change hands thereby entitling its owner to some benefit, so that legal ownership of the benefit passes by delivery or endorsement of the document. For a document to be negotiable it must also entitle the holder to bring an action in law if necessary. *See* negotiable instrument.

**negotiable instrument** A document of title that can be freely negotiated (*see* negotiability). Such documents are *cheques and *bills of exchange, in which the stated payee of the instrument can negotiate the instrument by either inserting the name of a different payee or by making the document 'open' by endorsing it (signing one's name), usually on the reverse. Holders of negotiable instruments cannot pass on a better title than they possess. Bills of exchange, including cheques, in which the payee is named or that bear a restrictive endorsement, such as 'not negotiable', are **non-negotiable instruments**.

**negotiable order of withdrawal (NOW)** A type of cheque used in US savings accounts that are interest-bearing and from which sums can be withdrawn. If no interest is paid the account is called a **NINOW**.

**negotiate 1.** To confer with a view to arriving at mutually acceptable terms for a contract or agreement. **2.** To transfer a *bill of exchange or cheque to another for consideration (*see* negotiability; negotiable instrument).

**net assets** The assets of an organization less its *current liabilities. The resultant figure is equal to the *capital of the organization. Opinion varies as to whether long-term liabilities should be treated as part of the capital and are therefore not deductible in arriving at net assets, or whether they are part of the liabilities and therefore deductible. The latter view is probably technically preferable. *See also* net current assets.

**net asset value (NAV)** The total assets of an organization less all liabilities and all capital charges (including debentures, loan stocks, and preference shares). It is called the **shareholder's equity** or the **net worth** of the organization. The **net asset value per share** is the NAV divided by the total number of ordinary shares issued.

**net book value (NBV)** The value at which an asset appears in the books of an organization (usually as at the date of the last balance sheet) less any depreciation that has been applied since its purchase or its last revaluation.

**net borrowed reserves** The amount that a US bank has borrowed from the *Federal Reserve System less the reserves they hold in excess of the required minimum. It is used as an indicator of interest-rate tendencies. If the banks have more money on loan than is covered by their reserves, interest rates will tend to rise.

**net current assets** *Current assets less *current liabilities. The resultant figure is also known as *working capital, as it represents the amount of the organization's capital that is constantly being turned over in the course of its trade. *See also* net assets.

**net dividend** The dividend paid by a company to its shareholders, after excluding the *tax credit received by the shareholders.

**net domestic product (NDP)** The *gross domestic product of a country less *capital consumption (i.e. depreciation).

**net income** **1.** The income of a person or organization after the deduction of the appropriate expenses incurred in earning it. **2.** *Gross income from which tax has been deducted.

**net interest** Interest paid into a savings or current account at a UK bank or building society after the deduction of tax at source. Interest on bank and building society accounts has been taxed at the basic rate, currently 25%, since April 1991.

**net investment** The addition to the stock of capital goods in an economy during a particular period (the **gross investment**) less *capital consumption (i.e. depreciation).

**net liquid funds** The cash available to an organization (including investments shown as *current assets) less any overdrafts or short-term loans.

**net national product (NNP)** The *gross national product less *capital consumption (i.e. depreciation) during the period. NNP is therefore equal to the national income, i.e. the amount of money available in the economy for expenditure on goods and services. However, NNP cannot be considered a very accurate measure, as it is difficult to calculate depreciation reliably.

**net premium** The annual payment received by an insurance company for an insurance policy after any charges (e.g. commission, brokerage, etc.) have been deducted.

**net present value (NPV)** The economic value of a project calculated by summing its costs and revenues over its full life and deducting the former from the latter. If the calculation yields a positive NPV then the project should be profitable. Future costs and revenues should be discounted by the relevant interest rate (e.g. the organization's cost of capital). *See* discounted cash flow. *Compare* accounting rate of return (ARR). Calculating NPVs can be difficult and often involves highly subjective judgments (such as estimating future interest rates). Frequently, therefore, simpler calculations, such as *payback period, are used. *See also* internal rate of return.

**net price** The price paid for something after all discounts, commissions, etc., have been deducted.

**net profit** **1.** (**net profit before taxation**) The profit of an organization when all receipts and expenses have been taken into account. In trading organizations, net profit is arrived at by deducting from the *gross profit all the expenses not already taken into account in arriving at the gross profit.   **2.** (**net profit after taxation**) The final profit of an organization, after all appropriate taxes have been deducted from the net profit before taxation. *See also* profit and loss account.

**net-profit ratio**  The proportion that *net profit bears to the total sales of an organization. This ratio is used in analysing the profitability of organizations and is an indicator of the extent to which sales have been profitable.

**net realizable value (NRV)**  The net value of an asset if it were to be sold, i.e. the sum received for it less the costs of the sale and of bringing it into a saleable condition.

**net receipts**  The total amount of money received by a business in a specified period after deducting costs, raw materials, taxation, etc. *Compare* gross receipts.

**net relevant earnings**  A person's non-pensionable earned income before personal allowances have been deducted but after deduction of expenses, capital allowances, losses, or any stock relief agreed with the Inland Revenue.

**net reproduction rate**  The number of female children in a population divided by the number of female adults in the previous generation. This figure gives a good guide to population trends; if it exceeds unity the population is expanding.

**net return**  The profit made on an investment after the deduction of all expenses, either before or after deduction of capital-gains tax.

**net tangible assets**  The *tangible assets of an organization less its current liabilities. In analysing the affairs of an organization the net tangible assets indicate its financial strength in terms of being solvent, without having to resort to such nebulous (and less easy-to-value) assets as *goodwill. *See also* price–net tangible assets ratio.

**netting**  The process of setting off matching sales and purchases against each other, especially sales and purchases of futures, options, and forward foreign exchange. This service is usually provided for an exchange or market by a *clearing house. *See also* novation.

**net worth**  The value of an organization when its liabilities have been deducted from the value of its assets. Often taken to be synonymous with *net asset value (i.e. the total assets as shown by the balance sheet less the current liabilities), net worth so defined can be misleading in that balance sheets rarely show the real value of assets; in order to arrive at the true net worth it would normally be necessary to assess the true market values of the assets rather than their *book values. It would also be necessary to value *goodwill, which may not even appear in the balance sheet. *See also* negative net worth; net tangible assets.

**net yield**  *See* gross yield.

**New Community Instrument (NCI)**  Loans organized on the international money market by the *European Investment Bank.

**new for old**  The basis for household insurance policies in which payments of claims are not subject to a deduction for wear and tear. As a result, a claim for an old and worn-out table would be met by the payment of the price of a new table of a similar type.

**new issue** **1.** A share being offered on a \*stock exchange for the first time. *See* flotation. **2.** A company that has entered its shares onto the stock exchange for the first time, or which is issuing additional shares.

**new-issue market** The section of the stock market that provides new long-term capital for investment by offering \*new issues.

**new shares** Shares that have been newly issued by a company on the \*new-issue market of a stock exchange.

**new time** The purchase or sale of securities on the \*London Stock Exchange during the last two dealing days of an account, for settlement during the following account. When making a bargain for new time this must be clearly understood between investor, broker, and market maker.

**New York Clearing House Association** A US \*clearing house for bankers in New York City. *See* Clearing House Inter-Bank Payments System.

**New York Cotton Exchange** The oldest commodity exchange in New York (founded in 1870) and the world's premier market for cotton futures and options trading. Since 1966 it has expanded into frozen concentrated orange juice (fcoj) through the Citrus Associates of the New York Cotton Exchange Inc. It also created FINEX, the Financial Instrument Exchange, which trades in US dollar index futures and options, five-year Treasury note futures and options, two-year US Treasury note futures, and ECU futures. The Cotton Exchange also houses the trading operations of the New York Futures Exchange.

**New York Mercantile Exchange (NYMEX)** A futures exchange in New York dealing in oil products and some rare metals.

**New York Stock Exchange (NYSE)** The main US stock exchange, though no longer the only one (*see* American Stock Exchange; National Association of Securities Dealers Automated Quotation System). It was founded in 1792 under the Buttonwood Agreement (the name of the tree under which 24 merchants agreed to give each other preference in their dealings); it moved to Wall Street in 1793. The New York Stock & Exchange Board was formally established in 1817; it was renamed the New York Stock Exchange in 1983.

**ngultrum** (Nu) The standard monetary unit of Bhutan, divided into 100 chetrum.

**ngwee** A monetary unit of Zambia, worth one hundredth of a \*kwacha.

**NIF** Abbreviation for \*note issuance (or purchase) facility.

**Nikkei Dow Jones Index** *See* Nikkei Stock Average.

**Nikkei Stock Average** An index of prices on the \*Tokyo Stock Exchange. It was originally known as the **Nikkei Dow Jones Index** and first calculated on 16 May 1949, based at 176.21. The Nikkei Stock Average is a price-weighted index of 225 Japanese companies representing 19% of first section issues, and accounting for about 51% of market value. It was restructured for the first time in its history in late 1991 by its administrator, the Nikon Keizai Shimbun financial newspaper group, to try to reduce the impact of futures-related trading on the index (Nikkei is a shortening of the full name of the newspaper group). Membership of the index is now reviewed annually, when up to six members can be replaced if their shares become illiquid or unrepresentative. Previous changes only occurred when companies were taken over or liquidated.

**nil paid** Denoting a share issue that has been made without payment, usually as a result of a *rights issue.

**NINOW** *See* negotiable order of withdrawal.

**NIT** Abbreviation for *negative income tax.

**NL** Abbreviation for no liability. It appears after the name of an Australian company, being equivalent to the British abbreviation *plc (denoting a public limited company).

**NMS** **1.** Abbreviation for *Normal Market Size. **2.** Abbreviation for *National Market System.

**N/N** Abbreviation for 'not to be noted', which may be written on a *bill of exchange to indicate that the collecting bank should not incur the expense of *noting it, if it is dishonoured.

**NNP** Abbreviation for *net national product.

**no-claim bonus** A reward, in the form of a premium discount, given to policyholders if they complete a year or more without making a claim. The system is mostly used in motor insurance, in which discounts of 33% for one claim-free year can rise to 60% of a premium for four successive years. In every case, the bonus is allowed for remaining claim-free and is not dependent on blame for a particular accident. So, for example, a no-claim bonus is lost if a vehicle is stolen through no fault of the insured.

**nominal capital (authorized capital)** *See* share capital.

**nominal interest rate** The interest rate on a fixed-interest security calculated as a percentage of its par value rather than its market price.

**nominal price** **1.** A minimal price fixed for the sake of having some consideration for a transaction. It need bear no relation to the market value of the item. **2.** The price given to a security when it is issued, also called the **face value**, **nominal value**, or *par value. For example, XYZ plc 25p ordinary shares have a nominal price of 25p, although the market value may be quite different. The nominal value of a share is the maximum amount the holder can be required to contribute to the company.

**nominal value** *See* par value.

**nominal yield** *See* yield.

**nomination** The person to whom the proceeds of a life-assurance policy should be paid as specified by the policyholder. *See* assignment of life policies.

**nominee** A person named by another (the **nominator**) to act on his or her behalf, often to conceal the identity of the nominator. *See* nominee shareholding.

**nominee shareholding** A shareholding held in the name of a bank, stockbroker, company, individual, etc., that is not the name of the beneficial owner of the shares. A shareholding may be in the name of nominees to facilitate dealing or to conceal the identity of the true owner. Although this cover was formerly used in the early stages of a takeover, to enable the bidder clandestinely to build up a substantial holding in the target company, this is now prevented by the Companies Act 1981, which makes it mandatory for anyone holding 5% or more of the shares in a public company to declare that interest to the company. The earlier Companies Act 1967 made it mandatory for directors to openly declare their holdings, and those of their families, in the companies of which they are directors.

**non-acceptance** The failure by the person on whom a *bill of exchange is drawn to accept it on presentation.

**non-amortizing mortgage** *See* balloon mortgage.

**non-assented stock** *See* assented stock.

**non-borrowed reserves** The reserves that a US bank has acquired by banking business and not through borrowing from the Federal Reserve. The Federal Reserve Bank calculates these figures on a weekly basis.

**non-business days** *See* Bank Holidays.

**non-contributory pension** A *pension in which the full premium is paid by an employer or the state and the pensioner makes no contribution. *Compare* contributory pension.

**non-cumulative preference share** A *preference share that does not have a right to a dividend from the profits of a subsequent year to make up for the non-payment of a dividend in a year in which profits were low. *Compare* cumulative preference share.

**non-domiciled** Denoting a person whose country of *domicile is not the same as his or her country of residence for tax purposes.

**non-marketable securities** UK government securities that cannot be bought and sold on a stock exchange (*compare* marketable security). Non-marketable securities include savings bonds and National Savings Certificates, tax-reserve certificates, etc., all of which form part of the *national debt.

**non-negotiable instruments** *See* negotiable instrument.

**non-obligatory expenditure** Expenditure which has been initiated by the European Parliament as an amendment to European Community budgets; it is not covered in the annual legislation affecting spending. *Compare* obligatory expenditure.

**non-qualifying policy** A UK life-assurance policy that does not satisfy the qualification rules contained in Schedule 15 of the Income and Corporation Taxes Act 1988. *Compare* qualifying policy.

**non-recourse finance** A bank loan in which the lending bank is only entitled to repayment from the profits of the project the loan is funding and not from other resources of the borrower.

**non-resident** The status of an individual who formerly lived in one country for fiscal purposes but who has moved to another country, either for employment or permanently. This person's liability to tax in the first country is restricted to income from sources within that country. *See also* residence; double taxation.

**non-taxable income** Income that is exempt from taxation. In the UK this includes interest from *National Savings Certificates and income arising from a *personal equity plan (PEP) or a *Tax Exempt Special Savings Account (Tessa).

**non-underwritten** Denoting a *euronote that has not been underwritten; such notes are a form of *euro-commercial paper.

**non-voting shares** See A shares.

**no-par-value (NPV)** Denoting a share issued by a company that has no *par value (see also nominal price). Dividends on such shares are quoted as an amount of money per share rather than as a percentage of the nominal price. No-par-value shares are not allowed by UK law but they are issued by some US and Canadian companies.

**Normal Market Size (NMS)** A classification system for trading in securities, which replaced the alpha, beta, gamma, and delta classification used on the *London Stock Exchange in January 1991. The old system had developed in a way that, contrary to the original intention, had made it a measure of corporate virility. NMS is the minimum size of the package of shares in a company traded in normal-sized market transactions; there are 12 categories. The main purpose of the system is to fix the size of transactions in which *market makers are obliged to deal, and to set a basis on which the bargains should be published.

**normal retirement age** The age of an individual when he or she retires. This is normally 65 for a man and 60 for a woman in the UK. It is at these ages that state pensions begin. However, other policies can nominate other pre-agreed dates, which the Inland Revenue will accept in certain cases. The inequality between a man's normal retirement age and a woman's retirement age in the UK is controversial and a retirement age of 65 or 63 has been suggested as a European norm for both sexes.

**nostro account** A bank account conducted by a UK bank with a bank in another country, usually in the currency of that country. Compare vostro account.

**notary public** A legal practitioner, usually a solicitor, who is empowered to attest deeds and other documents and notes (see noting) dishonoured *bills of exchange.

**note 1.** A *promissory note. **2.** A negotiable record of an unsecured loan (see commercial paper). The word 'note' is now used in preference to *bond when the principal sum is repayable in less than five years. **3.** A *banknote. **4.** An inscription on an unpaid *bill of exchange (see noting) made by a *notary public.

**note issuance (or purchase) facility (NIF)** A means of enabling short-term borrowers in the *eurocurrency markets to issue euronotes, with maturities of less than one year, when the need arises rather than having to arrange a separate issue of euronotes each time they need to borrow. A **revolving underwriting facility** (**RUF**) achieves the same objective.

**note purchase facility** See note issuance (or purchase) facility.

**notice day** The day on which notice must be given that goods will be supplied to fulfil a commodity-market contract, rather than having it cancelled out by a matching contract.

**notice in lieu of distringas** See stop notice.

**noting** The procedure adopted if a *bill of exchange has been dishonoured by non-acceptance or by non-payment. Not later than the next business day after the day on which it was dishonoured, the holder has to hand it to a *notary public to be noted. The notary re-presents the bill; if it is still unaccepted or unpaid, the notary notes the circumstances in a register and also on a **notarial ticket**, which has to be attached to the bill. The noting can then, if necessary, be extended to a *protest.

**notional income**  Income that is not received as such, but nevertheless has a value, which can be converted into cash terms for taxation purposes. In the UK this would include the *benefits in kind received by an employee.

**not negotiable**  Words marked on a *bill of exchange indicating that it ceases to be a *negotiable instrument, i.e. although it can still be negotiated, the holder cannot obtain a better title to it than the person from whom it was obtained, thus providing a safeguard if it is stolen. A cheque is the only form of bill that can be crossed 'not negotiable'; other forms must have it inscribed on their faces.

**novation**  The replacement of one legal agreement by a new obligation, with the agreement of all the parties. For example, on exchanges using the *London Clearing House (LCH), transactions between members are novated by the LCH, so that one contract is created between the buyer and LCH while a matching contract is created between the seller and LCH (*see* counterparty risk).

**NOW**  Abbreviation for *negotiable order of withdrawal.

**NPV**  **1.** Abbreviation for *net present value.  **2.** Abbreviation for *no-par-value.

**NRV**  Abbreviation for *net realizable value.

**NSB**  Abbreviation for *National Savings Bank.

**NSC**  Abbreviation for National Savings Certificates. *See* National Savings.

**NSCC**  Abbreviation for *National Securities Clearing Corporation.

**nudum pactum**  (Latin: nude contract) An agreement that is unenforceable in British law because no consideration is mentioned. *See* contract.

**numbered account**  A bank account identified only by a number. This service, offered by some Swiss banks at one time, encouraged funds that had been obtained illegally to find their way to Switzerland. A numbered account is now more frequently used to ensure legitimate privacy.

**NV**  Abbreviation for *Naamloze Vennootschap*. It appears after the name of a Dutch company, being equivalent to the British abbreviation plc (denoting a public limited company). *Compare* BV.

**NYMEX**  Abbreviation for *New York Mercantile Exchange.

**NYSE**  Abbreviation for *New York Stock Exchange.

**objectivity** The quality of being able to be independently verified, especially in accounting practice. It has been suggested that accounts produced on a historical cost basis (*see* historical-cost accounting) are objective, whereas those based on *inflation accounting are thought to be rather more subjective. However, such comments tend to overlook the considerable areas of subjectivity in historical cost accounts, such as choice of stock valuation methods, periods of asset life chosen for depreciation, and amounts to be set aside as provisions for bad debts.

**obligation 1.** The duty of a borrower to repay a loan and that of the lender to ensure that repayment is made. **2.** A bond or other promise to pay a sum of money.

**obligatory expenditure** The spending of the European Community, governed by such treaties as the Common Agricultural Policy and the European Regional Development Fund. The European Parliament can add to the amount spent but if it wishes to reduce it, it must obtain the agreement of the Council of Ministers, or reject the whole of the Community Budget in that year.

**occupational pension scheme** A pension scheme open to employees within a certain trade or profession or working for a particular firm. An occupational pension scheme can either be insured or self-administered. If it is insured, an insurance company pays the benefits under the scheme in return for having the premiums to invest. In a self-administered scheme, the pension-fund trustees are responsible for investing the contributions themselves. In order to run an occupational pension scheme, an organization must satisfy the Occupational Pension Board that the scheme complies with the conditions allowing employers to contract out of the *State Earnings-Related Pension Scheme. After 1988 certain regulations relating to occupational pensions schemes were introduced. *See also* personal pension scheme.

**odd lot** *See* round lot.

**OECD** Abbreviation for *Organization for Economic Cooperation and Development.

**off-balance-sheet finance** The use of company funds to hire or lease an expensive piece of equipment rather than purchasing it. This enables a company to make use of the equipment without having to invest capital. The item does not appear on the balance sheet as an asset and therefore the capital employed will be understated, although the profit and loss account will show the rental payments.

**off-balance-sheet reserve** *See* hidden reserve.

**offer** The price at which a seller is willing to sell something. If there is an *acceptance of the offer a legally binding *contract has been entered into. In law, an offer is distinguished from an **invitation to treat**, which is an invitation by one person or firm to others to make an offer. An example of an invitation to treat is to display goods in a shop window. *See also* offer price; quotation.

**offer by prospectus** An offer to the public of a new issue of shares or debentures made directly by means of a *prospectus, a document giving a detailed account of the aims, objects, and capital structure of the company, as well as its past history. The prospectus must conform to the provisions of the Companies Act 1985. *Compare* offer for sale.

**offer document** A document sent to the shareholders of a company that is the subject of a *takeover bid. It gives details of the offer being made and usually provides shareholders with reasons for accepting the terms of the offer.

**offer for sale** An invitation to the general public to purchase the stock of a company through an intermediary, such as an *issuing house or *merchant bank (*compare* offer by prospectus); it is one of the most frequently used means of *flotation. An offer for sale can be in one of two forms: at a fixed price (the more usual), which requires some form of balloting or rationing if the demand for the shares exceeds supply; or an *issue by tender, in which case individuals offer to purchase a fixed quantity of stock at or above some minimum price and the stock is allocated to the highest bidders. In the USA an offer for sale is called a **public offering**. *Compare* introduction; placing; public issue.

**offer price** The price at which a security is offered for sale by a *market maker and also the price at which an institution will sell units in a unit trust. *Compare* bid.

**offer to purchase** *See* takeover bid.

**Office of Fair Trading** A government department that, under the Director General of Fair Trading, reviews commercial activities in the UK and aims to protect the consumer against unfair practices. Established in 1973, it is responsible for the administration of the Fair Trading Act 1973, the Consumer Credit Act 1974, the Restrictive Trade Practices Act 1976, the Estate Agents Act 1979, the Competition Act 1980, the Financial Services Act 1986, and the Control of Misleading Advertisements Regulations 1988. Its five main areas of activity are: consumer affairs, consumer credit, monopolies and mergers, restrictive trade practices, and anti-competitive practices.

**Official List** **1.** A list of all the securities traded on the *main market of the *London Stock Exchange. *See* listed security; listing requirements; Yellow Book. **2.** A list prepared daily by the London Stock Exchange, recording all the bargains that have been transacted in listed securities during the day. It also gives dividend dates, rights issues, prices, and other information.

**official rate** The rate of exchange given to a currency by a government. If the official rate differs from the market rate, the government has to be prepared to support its official rate by buying or selling in the open market to make the two rates coincide.

**official receiver** A person appointed by the Secretary of State for Trade and Industry to act as a *receiver in *bankruptcy and winding-up cases. The High Court and each county court that has jurisdiction over insolvency matters has an official receiver, who is an officer of the court. Deputy official receivers may also be appointed. The official receiver commonly acts as the *liquidator of a company being wound up by the court.

**offset**  **1.** The right that enables a bank to seize any bank-account balances of a guarantor or debtor if a loan has been defaulted upon (*see also* garnishee order).  **2.** A code on the magnetic strip of a plastic card that, together with the *personal identification number (PIN), verifies that the user of the card is entitled to use it.  **3.** The process of cancelling the need to deliver physical commodities sold on a *futures contract by making an equal purchase of the same commodity for the same delivery period.

**offshore banking**  The practice of offering financial services in locations that have attractive tax advantages to non-residents. Offshore banking centres are based in many European countries, e.g. France, Switzerland, the Isle of Man, and Jersey, as well as the Middle East, the Caribbean, and Asia. These locations are often described as *tax havens because they can reduce customers' tax liabilities in entirely legal ways. *See* offshore financial centres.

**offshore financial centres**  Centres that provide advantageous deposit and lending rates to non-residents because of low taxation, liberal exchange controls, and low reserve requirements for banks. Some countries have made a lucrative business out of *offshore banking; the Cayman Islands is currently one of the world's largest offshore centres. In Europe, the Channel Islands and the Isle of Man are very popular. The USA and, more recently, Japan have both established domestic offshore facilities enabling non-residents to conduct their business under more liberal regulations than domestic transactions. Their objective is to stop funds moving outside the country.

**offshore fund**  **1.** A fund that is based in a tax haven (offshore tax haven) outside the UK to avoid UK taxation. Offshore funds operate in the same way as *unit trusts but are not supervised by the Department of Trade and Industry.  **2.** A fund held outside the country of residence of the holder. *See* offshore banking; offshore financial centres.

**Old Lady of Threadneedle Street**  An affectionate name for the *Bank of England, coined by the English politician and dramatist R. B. Sheridan (1751–1816). The street in which the Bank stands (since 1734 in a Renaissance building by George Sampson) probably takes its name from the thread and needle used by the Merchant Taylors, a guild whose hall is in the same street.

**OM**  Abbreviation for the Swedish Options Market, which is based in Stockholm and London; it opened in 1985.

**Ombudsman**  *See* Financial Ombudsman; Parliamentary Commissioner for Administration.

**on demand**  Denoting a *bill of exchange that is payable on presentation. An uncrossed cheque is an example of such a bill.

**one-month money**  Money placed on the *money market for one month, i.e. it cannot be withdrawn without penalty for one month.

**one-year money**  Money placed on the *money market for one year, i.e. it cannot be withdrawn without penalty for one year.

**on stream** Denoting that a specified investment or asset is bringing in the income expected of it.

**OPEC** Abbreviation for *Organization of Petroleum Exporting Countries.

**open cheque** *See* cheque.

**open credit** **1.** Unlimited credit offered by a supplier to a trusted client. **2.** An arrangement between a bank and a customer enabling the customer to cash cheques up to a specified amount at a bank or branches other than the customer's own. This practice is less used since *credit cards and *cash cards were introduced.

**open economy** An economy in which a significant percentage of its goods and services are traded internationally. The degree of openness of an economy usually depends on the amount of overseas trade in which the country is involved or the political policies of its government. Thus the UK economy is relatively open, as the economy is significantly dependent on foreign trade, while the US economy is relatively closed as overseas trade is not very important to its economy.

**open-end credit** The US name for a *revolving credit.

**open-end fund (mutual fund)** A form of *unit trust in which the managers of the trust may vary the investments held without notifying the unit holders. Open-end funds are used in the USA.

**opening prices** The bid prices and offer prices made at the opening of a day's trading on any security or commodity market. The opening prices may not always be identical to the previous evening's *closing prices, especially if any significant events or movements in markets in another time zone have taken place during the intervening period.

**open-market desk** The part of the *Federal Reserve System that conducts *open-market operations under the supervision of the Open Market Committee.

**open-market operations** The purchase or sale by a government of bonds (gilt-edged securities) in exchange for money. This is the main mechanism by which *monetary policy in developed economies operates. To buy (or sell) more bonds the government must raise (or lower) their price and hence reduce (or increase) interest rates. In Keynesian theory, lower interest rates will stimulate investment and so raise national output. However, many economists now believe that this will only have the effect of raising the level of prices (i.e. fuelling *inflation).

**open-market value** The value of an asset on an open market. *See* market value.

**open-mouth operations** The use of public statements by the US *Federal Reserve System to try to implement *monetary policy.

**open outcry** Quoting prices, making offers, bids, and acceptances, and concluding transactions by word of mouth in a *commodity market or *financial futures exchange, usually in a trading *pit. *See also* callover.

**open position** A trading position in which a dealer has commodities, *securities, or currencies bought but unsold or unhedged (*see* hedging), or sales that are neither covered nor hedged. In the former, the dealer has a **bull**

**position**; in the latter, a **bear position**. In either case the dealer is vulnerable to market fluctuations until the position is closed or hedged. *See also* option.

**operating budget** A forecast of the financial requirements for the future trading of an organization, including its planned sales, production, cash flow, etc. An operating budget is normally designed for a fixed period, usually one year, and forms the plan for that period's trading activities. Any divergences from it are usually monitored and, if appropriate, changes can then be made to it as the period progresses.

**operating lease** Any form of lease other than a *finance lease, i.e. one that does not transfer all the benefits and risks of ownership to the lessee.

**operating profit (**or **loss)** The profit (or loss) made by a company as a result of its principal trading activity. This is arrived at by deducting its **operating expenses** from its *trading profit, or adding its operating expenses to its trading loss; in either case this is before taking into account any extraordinary items.

**opportunity cost** The benefits lost by not employing an economic resource in the most profitable alternative activity. For example, the opportunity cost to a self-employed person is the highest salary he or she could earn elsewhere. Economists use the concept of opportunity cost to decide whether or not the allocation of resources is efficient. In the example above, if efficiency is judged by income alone, self-employment is efficient only if the income earned exceeds the best alternative salary, i.e. the opportunity cost. Opportunity cost is a much broader concept than accounting cost, and therefore the former is generally preferred when weighing up the costs and benefits of investment decisions (*see also* cost-benefit analysis). For example, in a situation in which investment in competing and mutually exclusive projects is being considered, the opportunity cost of selecting one project is the revenue obtainable from the next best option.

**option** The right to buy or sell a fixed quantity of a commodity, currency, *security, etc., at a particular date at a particular price (the *exercise price). Unlike futures, the purchaser of an option is not obliged to buy or sell at the exercise price and will only do so if it is profitable; the purchaser may allow the option to lapse, in which case only the initial purchase price of the option (the *option money or *premium) is lost. In London, options in commodity futures are bought and sold on *London FOX, and options on share indexes, foreign currencies, equities, and interest rates are dealt with through the *London International Financial Futures and Options Exchange (LIFFE).

An option to buy is known as a **call option** and is usually purchased in the expectation of a rising price; an option to sell is called a **put option** and is bought in the expectation of a falling price or to protect a profit on an investment. Options, like futures, allow individuals and firms to hedge against the risk of wide fluctuations in prices; they also allow dealers and speculators to gamble for large profits with limited liability.

Professional traders in options make use of a large range of potential strategies, often purchasing combinations of options that reflect particular expectations or cover several contingencies (*see* butterfly; straddle).

**Traded options** can be bought and sold on an exchange, at all times, i.e. there is a trade in the options themselves. Traded options are dealt in on London FOX and LIFFE. **Traditional options**, however, once purchased, cannot be resold. Traditional options in equities are dealt in on the London Stock Exchange, but traded options in equities are now dealt in on LIFFE. In a **European option** the buyer can only exercise the right to take up the option or let it lapse on the *expiry date, whereas with an **American option** this right can be exercised at any time up to the expiry date. European options are therefore cheaper than American options. *See also* exercise notice; hedging; intrinsic value; option to double; time value.

**option dealer** A dealer who buys and sells either traded *options or traditional options on a stock exchange, commodity exchange, or financial futures and options exchange.

**option money** The price paid for an *option. The cost of a call option is often known as the **call money** and that for a put option as the **put money**. In traded options the option money is usually called the *premium.

**option to double** **1.** An *option by a seller to sell double the quantity of securities for which an option has been sold, if so desired. In some markets this is called a **put-of-more option**. **2.** An option by a buyer to buy double the quantity of securities for which an option has been bought, if so desired. In some markets this is called a **call-of-more option**.

**option to purchase** **1.** A right given to shareholders to buy shares in certain companies in certain circumstances at a reduced price. **2.** A right purchased or given to a person to buy something at a specified price on or before a specified date. Until the specified date has passed, the seller undertakes not to sell the property to anyone else and not to withdraw it from sale.

**order** *See* limit; market order; stop-loss order.

**order cheque** *See* cheque.

**order driven** Denoting a market in which prices are determined by the publication of orders to buy or sell shares, with the objective of attracting a counterparty. The *Company Bulletin Board Service was an order-driven market. *Compare* quote driven.

**ordinary resolution** A resolution that is valid if passed by a majority of the votes cast at a general meeting of a British company. No notice that the resolution is to be proposed is required.

**ordinary share** A fixed unit of the *share capital of a company. Shares in publicly owned *listed companies are usually traded on *stock exchanges and represent one of the most important types of security for investors. Shares yield dividends, representing a proportion of the profits of a company (*compare* fixed-interest security; preference share). In the long term, ordinary shares, by means of *capital growth, yield higher rewards, on average, than most alternative forms of securities, which compensates for the greater element of risk they entail. *See also* convertible; growth stocks.

**öre** A monetary unit of Sweden, worth one hundredth of a *krona.

**øre** A monetary unit of Denmark, the Faeroe Islands, Greenland, and Norway. It is worth one hundredth of a *krone.

**Organization for Economic Cooperation and Development (OECD)** An organization formed in 1961, replacing the Organization for European Economic Cooperation (OEEC), to promote cooperation among industrialized member countries on economic and social policies. Its objectives are to assist member countries in formulating policies designed to achieve high economic growth while maintaining financial stability, contributing to world trade on a multilateral basis, and stimulating members' aid to developing countries. Members are Australia, Austria, Belgium, Canada, Denmark, Finland, France, Germany, Greece, Iceland, Ireland, Italy, Japan, Luxembourg, the Netherlands, New Zealand, Norway, Portugal, Spain, Sweden, Switzerland, Turkey, UK, and USA (Yugoslavia participates with a special status). The OECD is based in Paris.

**Organization for European Economic Cooperation (OEEC)** An organization set up after World War II to administer the US Marshall Plan for funding the rebuilding of war-ravaged Europe. Its major achievement was the European Recovery Programme. It became the *Organization for Economic Cooperation and Development (OECD) in 1961.

**Organization of Petroleum Exporting Countries (OPEC)** An organization created in 1960 to unify and coordinate the petroleum policies of member countries and to protect their interests, individually and collectively. Present members are Algeria, Ecuador, Gabon, Indonesia, Iran, Iraq, Kuwait, Libya, Nigeria, Qatar, Saudi Arabia, UAE, and Venezuela.

**organized market** A formal market in a specific place in which buyers and sellers meet to trade according to agreed rules and procedures. Stock exchanges, *financial futures exchanges, and commodity markets are examples of organized markets.

**origin 1.** The country from which a commodity originates. **Shipment from origin** denotes goods that are shipped directly from their country of origin, rather than from stocks in some other place. **2.** The country from which a person comes. A person's country of origin is not necessarily that person's country of *domicile or *residence.

**OTC Bulletin Board** An electronic bulletin board set up by the *National Association of Securities Dealers Inc. in June 1990 for displaying firm and non-firm quotations and unpriced indications of interest of over-the-counter securities (*see* over-the-counter market).

**OTC market** Abbreviation for *over-the-counter market.

**OTOB** Abbreviation for the Austrian Futures and Options Exchange, which opened in 1991. Its prices are given in the Austrian Traded Index (ATX).

**ouguiya** (UM) The standard monetary unit of Mauritania, divided into 5 khoums.

**outcry** *See* callover.

**out-of-the-money option** *See* intrinsic value.

**output tax** The VAT that a trader adds to the price of the goods or services supplied. The trader must account for this output tax to HM Customs and Excise, having first deducted the *input tax.

**outright forward** A contract to buy or sell a currency at a fixed price in the future, without a corresponding offsetting transaction.

**outside broker** A stockbroker who is not a member of a stock exchange but acts as an intermediary between the public and a stockbroker who is a member.

**overbought   1.** Having purchased more of a good than one needs or has orders for.   **2.** Having purchased more securities or commodities than are covered by margins deposited with a broker or dealer. In a falling market, for example, a bull speculator can become overbought without having made a fresh purchase.   **3.** Denoting a market that has risen too rapidly as a result of excessive buying. An overbought market is unstable and likely to fall if unsupported. *Compare* oversold.

**overcapitalization**   A condition in which an organization has too much *capital for the needs of its business. If a business has more capital than it needs it is likely to be overburdened by interest charges or by the need to spread profits too thinly by way of dividends to shareholders. Businesses can now reduce overcapitalization by repaying long-term debts or by buying their own shares.

**overdraft**   A loan made to a customer with a cheque account at a bank or building society, in which the account is allowed to go into debit, usually up to a specified limit (the **overdraft limit**). Interest is charged on the daily debit balance. This is a less costly way of borrowing than taking a *bank loan (providing the interest rates are the same) as, with an overdraft, credits are taken into account. Small agreed overdrafts are available to many banking customers, often with an extra charge, because of the competitive nature of the banking business.

**overfunding**   A policy available to the UK government in which it sells more government securities than it needs to pay for public spending. The objective of the policy is to absorb surplus money and so curb *inflation.

**overheating**   The state of an economy during a boom, with increasing aggregate demand leading to rising prices rather than higher output. Overheating reflects the inability of some firms to increase output as fast as demand; they therefore choose to profit from the excess demand by raising prices.

**overinsurance**   The practice of insuring an item for a greater amount than its value. This is pointless as insurers are only obliged to pay the full value (usually the replacement value) of an insured item and no more, even if the sum insured exceeds this value. If insurers find a policyholder has overinsured an item, the premium for the cover above the true value is returned.

**overinvestment**   Excessive investment of capital, especially in the manufacturing industry towards the end of a boom as a result of over-optimistic expectations of future demand. When the boom begins to fade, the manufacturer is left with surplus capacity and therefore makes no further capital investments, which itself creates unemployment and fuels the imminent recession.

**overnight loan**   A loan made by a bank to a bill *broker to enable the broker to take up *bills of exchange. Initially the loan will be repayable the following day but it is usually renewable. If it is not, the broker must turn to the *lender of last resort, i.e. the Bank of England in the UK.

**overnight money**   *See* day-to-day money.

**overnight repo** A method of overcoming a short-term shortage of funds on the *money market using *repurchase agreements (repos) on an overnight basis. Their use was developed in the USA but they are now used elsewhere.

**overseas company** A company incorporated outside the UK that has a branch or a subsidiary company in the UK. Overseas companies with a place of business in the UK have to make a return to the Registrar of Companies, giving particulars of their memorandum of association, directors, and secretary as well as providing an annual balance sheet and profit and loss account.

**overseas-income taxation** Taxation of income arising outside the national boundaries of the taxing authority. Most countries tax the worldwide income of their permanent residents, as well as the incomes arising in the country to outsiders. This can involve double (or multiple) taxation, for which reliefs are often provided by double-taxation treaties.

**overseas investment** Investment by the government, industry, or members of the public of a country in the industry of another country. For members of the public this is often most easily achieved by investing through foreign stock exchanges.

**overshooting** A jump in the value of an asset followed by a slow adjustment to equilibrium, caused by a change in expectations. It is usually applied to an analysis of the real exchange rates and has been used to explain the extreme volatility of exchange rates in the 1970s and 1980s (for example, between 1980 and 1984 the US dollar rose by around 70% against foreign currencies and between 1985 and 1987 fell by 40%). Overshooting provides an argument for more government intervention in the determination of exchange rates.

**oversold 1.** Having sold more of a product or service than one can produce or purchase. **2.** Denoting a market that has fallen too fast as a result of excessive selling. It may therefore be expected to have an upward reaction.

**oversubscription** A situation that arises when there are more applications for a *new issue of shares than there are shares available. In these circumstances, applications have to be scaled down according to a set of rules devised by the company issuing the shares or their advisors. Alternatively some companies prefer to allocate the shares by ballot (*see* allotment). Oversubscription usually occurs because of the difficulty in arriving at an issue price that will be low enough to attract sufficient investors to take up the whole issue and yet will give the company the maximum capital. Speculative purchases by *stags also make it difficult to price a new issue so that it is neither oversubscribed nor undersubscribed. In the case of **undersubscription**, which is rare, the *underwriter has to take up that part of the issue that has not been bought by the public. Undersubscription can occur if some unexpected event occurs after the announcement of the issue price but before the issue date.

**over-the-counter market (OTC market)** A market in which shares are bought and sold outside the jurisdiction of a recognized stock exchange; it was originally so named in the 1870s, from the practice of buying shares over bank counters in the USA. OTC markets acquired a reputation for providing reduced investor protection but they have since become more formalized. The world's largest OTC market is the US *National Association of Securities Dealers Automated Quotation System (NASDAQ). The UK has considered the OTC market as less than respectable and it disappeared altogether with the formation of the *third market, with its minimal entry requirements, by the London Stock Exchange in 1987. This market was subsequently abolished in 1990 with the introduction of less stringent requirements for the *unlisted securities market (USM).

**overtrading**   Trading by an organization beyond the resources provided by its existing capital. Overtrading tends to lead to *liquidity problems as too much stock is bought on credit and too much credit is extended to customers, so that ultimately there is not sufficient cash available to pay the debts as they arise. The solution is either to cut back on trading or to raise further permanent capital.

**ownership**   Rights over property, including rights of possession, exclusive enjoyment, destruction, etc. In UK common law, land cannot be owned outright, as all land belongs to the Crown and is held in tenure by the 'owner'. However, an owner of an estate in land in fee simple is to all intents and purposes an outright owner. In general, ownership can be split between different persons. For example, a trustee has the legal ownership of trust property but the beneficiary has the equitable or beneficial ownership. If goods are stolen, the owner still has ownership but not possession. Similarly, if goods are hired or pledged to someone, the owner has ownership but no immediate right to possession.

**own resources**   The funds owned outright by the European Community, rather than those contributed by its member states, e.g. 1% of VAT revenues within Europe go direct to the Community's funds.

**PA** **1.** Abbreviation for personal account, used to denote a transaction made by a professional investment advisor for his or her own account rather than for the firm for which he or she works. **2.** Abbreviation for personal assistant. **3.** Abbreviation for *power of attorney.

**pa'anga** (T$) The standard monetary unit of Tonga, divided into 100 seniti.

**Pacific Stock Exchange (PSE)** The only stock market in the USA operating west of the Mississippi; it has trading floors in San Francisco and Los Angeles. It signed a cooperation deal in 1990 with the Taiwan Stock Exchange, seeing its future in linking with other exchanges bordering on the Pacific.

**paid-up capital (fully paid capital)** The total amount of money that the shareholders of a company have paid to the company for their shares. *See* share capital.

**paid-up policy** An *endowment assurance policy in which the assured has decided to stop paying premiums before the end of the policy term. This results in a *surrender value, which instead of being returned in cash to the assured is used to purchase a single-premium *whole (of) life policy. In this way the life assurance protection continues (for a reduced amount), while the policyholder is relieved of the need to pay further premiums. If the original policy was a *with-profits policy, the bonuses paid up to the time the premiums ceased would be included in the surrender value. If it is a unit-linked policy, capital units actually allocated would be allowed to appreciate to the end of the term.

**paid-up share** A share the par value of which has been paid in full. *See* share capital.

**paisa** **1.** A monetary unit of India, Nepal, and Pakistan, worth one hundredth of a *rupee. **2.** A monetary unit of Bangladesh, worth one hundredth of a *taka.

**Panel on Takeovers and Mergers** *See* City Code on Takeovers and Mergers.

**paper** An informal name for securities that can be bought and sold or held as an investment. It is used particularly on the *money market for *debt instruments maturing in less than 90 days. *See* commercial paper; euro-commercial paper.

**paper money** **1.** Legal tender in the form of banknotes. **2.** Banknotes and any form of paper that can be used as money, such as cheques, *bills of exchange, promissory notes, etc., even though they are not legal tender.

**paper profit** A profit shown by the books or accounts of an organization, which may not be a realized profit because the value of an asset has fallen below its book value, because the asset, although nominally showing a profit, has not actually been sold, or because some technicality of book-keeping might show an activity to be profitable when it is not. For example, a share that has risen in value since its purchase might show a paper profit but this would not be a real profit since the value of the share might fall again before it is sold.

**paper trail**  *See* audit trail.

**par**  *See* par value; par of exchange.

**para**  A Yugoslavian monetary unit, worth one hundredth of a *dinar.

**par banking**  The US practice of one bank paying the full face value of a cheque drawn on another bank, without imposing a charge for encashment. Members of the *Federal Reserve System are obliged to comply with the rules of par banking.

**par bond**  A security or financial instrument that is bought and sold at its face value, rather than at a discount or premium.

**parent company**  *See* holding company.

**pari passu**  (Latin: with equal step) Ranking equally. When a new issue of shares is said to rank pari passu with existing shares, the new shares carry the same dividend rights and winding-up rights as the existing shares. A pari passu bank loan is a new loan that ranks on level par with older loans.

**Paris Bourse**  From January 1991, the only stock exchange in France, incorporating the six provincial stock exchanges in Bordeaux, Lille, Lyons, Marseilles, Nancy, and Nantes. The merger recognized the dominance of the Paris Bourse, which accounted for 95% of all trading in French securities. The **CAC** (Cotation Assistée en Continue) electronic trading system was introduced in 1988 and the Relit five-day rolling settlement system was launched in 1990, based on delivery against payment. Trading is carried out through 45 broker members of the exchange; the market's indicator is the **CAC General Index**, based on the prices of 250 shares, with a subsidiary CAC-40 developed for an *index futures contract.

**Paris Club**  *See* Group of Ten.

**Paris Inter Bank Offered Rate (PIBOR)**  The French equivalent of the *London Inter Bank Offered Rate (LIBOR).

**parity**  **1.** An equality between prices of commodities, currencies, or securities on separate markets. **2.** The amount of a foreign currency equivalent to a specified sum of domestic currency at the *par of exchange.

**parity grid**  *See* European Monetary System.

**parking**  Putting company shares that one owns in the name of someone else or of nominees in order to hide their real ownership. This is often illegal. *See also* warehousing.

**Parliamentary Commissioner for Administration**  The Ombudsman responsible for investigating complaints, referred through an MP, by members of the public against maladministration by government departments and certain public bodies. *See also* Financial Ombudsman.

**par of exchange**  The theoretical *rate of exchange between two currencies in which there is equilibrium between the supply and demand for each currency.

The par value lies between the market buying and selling rates. *See also* mint par of exchange.

**par priced** Denoting a security that is trading at its *par value.

**parquet** A colloquial name for the *Paris Bourse.

**partial loss** *See* average.

**participating interest** An interest held by one organization in the shares of another organization, provided these shares are held on a long-term basis for the purpose of exercising some measure of control over the organization's activities. The UK Companies Act 1985 lays down that a holding of 20% or more of the shares of an organization constitutes a participating interest, unless contrary indications are given. Options to buy shares are normally treated as an interest in these shares.

**participating preference share** *See* preference share.

**partly paid shares** Shares on which the full nominal or *par value has not been paid. Formerly, partly paid shares were issued by some banks and insurance companies to inspire confidence, i.e. because they could always call on their shareholders for further funds if necessary. Shareholders, however, did not like the liability of being called upon to pay out further sums for their shares and the practice largely died out. It has been revived for large new share issues, especially in *privatizations, in which shareholders pay an initial sum for their shares and subsequently pay one or more *calls on specified dates (*see also* share capital).

**partnership** An association of two or more people formed for the purpose of carrying on a business. Partnerships are governed by the Partnership Act 1890. Unlike an incorporated *company, a partnership does not have a legal personality of its own and therefore partners are liable for the debts of the firm. **General partners** are fully liable for these debts, **limited partners** only to the extent of their investment. A **limited partnership** is one consisting of both general and limited partners and is governed by the Limited Partnership Act 1907. A **partnership-at-will** is one for which no fixed term has been agreed. Any partner may end the partnership at any time provided that notice of the intention to do so is given to all the other partners. **Nominal partners** allow their names to be used for the benefit of the partnership, usually for a reward but not for a share of the profits. They are not legal partners.

Partnerships are usually governed by a **partnership agreement** (sometimes called a **deed of partnership**) that lays down the way in which profits are to be shared, the procedure to be adopted on the death, retirement, or bankruptcy of a partner, and the rules for withdrawing capital from the partnership. Partners do not draw salaries and are not paid interest on their capital.

**par value (face value; nominal value)** The *nominal price of a share or other security. If the market value of a security exceeds the par value it is said to be **above par**; if it falls below the par value it is **below par**. Gilt-edged securities are always repaid **at par** (usually £100), i.e. at the par value.

**passing a name** The disclosure by a broker of the name of the principal for whom he or she is acting. In some commodity trades, if a broker discloses the name of the buyer to the seller, the buyer's solvency is not guaranteed, although the broker may do so in some circumstances. However, if the broker does not pass the principal's name, it is usual for the broker to guarantee the principal's solvency. Thus, to remain anonymous, a buyer may have to pay an additional brokerage.

**pass-through** *See* Ginnie Mae.

**pataca** The standard monetary unit of Macao, divided into 100 avos.

**patent** The grant of an exclusive right to exploit an invention. In the UK patents are granted by the Crown through the *Patent Office, which is part of the Department of Trade and Industry. An applicant for a patent (usually the inventor or the inventor's employer) must show that the invention is new, is not obvious, and is capable of industrial application. An expert known as a **patent agent** often prepares the application, which must describe the invention in considerable detail. The Patent Office publishes these details if it grants a patent. A patent remains valid for 20 years from the date of application (the **priority date**) provided that the person to whom it has been granted (the **patentee**) continues to pay the appropriate fees. During this time, the patentee may assign the patent or grant licences to use it. Such transactions are registered in a public register at the Patent Office. If anyone infringes the patentee's monopoly, the patentee may sue for an *injunction and *damages or an account of profits. However, a patent from the Patent Office gives exclusive rights in the UK only: the inventor must obtain a patent from the European Patent Office in Munich and patents in other foreign countries to protect the invention elsewhere.

**Patent Office** A UK government office that administers the Patent Acts, the Registered Designs Act, and the Trade Marks Act. It also deals with questions relating to the Copyright Acts and provides an information service about *patent specifications.

**pathfinder prospectus** An outline prospectus concerning the flotation of a new company in the UK; it includes enough details to test the market reaction to the new company but not its main financial details or the price of its shares. Pathfinder prospectuses are known in the USA as **red herrings**.

**pawnbroker** A person who lends money against the security of valuable goods used as collateral. Borrowers can reclaim their goods by repaying the loan and interest within a stated period. However, if the borrower defaults, the pawnbroker is free to sell the goods. The operation of pawnbrokers is governed by the Consumer Credit Act 1974.

**payable to bearer** Describing a *bill of exchange in which neither the payee or endorsee are named. A holder, by adding his or her name, can make the bill *payable to order.

**payable to order** Describing a *bill of exchange in which the payee is named and on which there are no restrictions or endorsements; it can therefore be paid to the endorsee.

**pay and file** A new administration system proposed for UK *corporation tax. From 1 October 1993 companies will be required to pay their corporation tax nine months after the end of their accounting period, with the accounts being submitted some three months later.

**pay-as-you-earn** *See* PAYE.

**payback period** A method of appraising capital projects, in which the principal criterion for acceptance is the length of time the project will take to recover the initial outlay it requires. The assumption is that any further recoveries are then pure profit. This is a relatively unsophisticated method of appraising a capital project (*compare* discounted cash flow; net present value), although it is frequently used in industry. *See also* internal rate of return.

**PAYE** Pay-as-you-earn. This means of collecting tax arose under Schedule E of the UK income-tax legislation on wages and salaries. Because it is often difficult to collect tax at the end of the year from wage and salary earners, the onus is placed on employers to collect the tax from their employees as payments are made to them. There is an elaborate system of administration to ensure that broadly the correct amount of tax is deducted week by week or month by month and that the employer remits the tax collected to the Inland Revenue very quickly. Although technically called pay-as-you-earn, the system would be better called pay-as-you-get-paid.

**payee** A person or organization to be paid. In the case of a cheque payment, the payee is the person or organization to whom the cheque is made payable.

**payer** A person or organization who makes a payment.

**paying agent** An organization that makes payments either of capital or interest to bond-holders. Banks performing this function charge a fee.

**paying banker** The bank on which a *bill of exchange (including a cheque) has been drawn and which is responsible for paying it if it is correctly drawn and correctly endorsed (if necessary).

**paying-in book** A book of slips used to pay cash, cheques, etc., into a bank account. The counterfoil of the slip is stamped by the bank if the money is paid in over the counter.

**payment for honour** *See* acceptance supra protest.

**payment in advance (prepayment)** Payment for goods or services before they have been received. In company accounts, this often refers to rates or rents paid for periods that carry over into the next accounting period.

**payment in due course** The payment of a *bill of exchange when it matures (becomes due).

**payment on account 1.** A payment made for goods or services before the goods or services are finally billed. *See also* deposit. **2.** A payment towards meeting a liability that is not the full amount of the liability. The sum paid will be credited to the account of the payer in the books of the payee as a part-payment of the ultimate liability.

**payment supra protest** *See* acceptance supra protest.

**payment terms** The agreed way in which a buyer pays the seller for goods. The commonest are cash with order or cash on delivery; prompt cash (i.e. within 14 days of delivery); cash in 30, 60, or 90 days from date of invoice; *letter of credit; *cash against documents; *documents against acceptance; or *acceptance credit.

**pay-out ratio** *See* dividend cover.

**payroll tax** A tax based on the total of an organization's payroll. The main function of such a tax would be to discourage high wages or over-employment. The current UK employers' Class 1 *National Insurance contributions constitute such a tax.

**PDR (P/D ratio)** Abbreviations for *price–dividend ratio.

**pegging** **1. (pegging the exchange)** The fixing of the value of a country's currency on foreign exchange markets. *See* crawling peg; fixed exchange rate. **2. (pegging wages)** The fixing of wages at existing levels by government order to prevent them rising during a period of *inflation. The same restraint may be applied to prices (**pegging prices**) in order to control inflation.

**penalty** An arbitrary pre-arranged sum that becomes payable if one party breaches a contract or undertaking. It is usually expressly stated in a **penalty clause** of the contract. Unlike liquidated *damages, a penalty will be disregarded by the courts and treated as being void. Liquidated damages will generally be treated as a penalty if the amount payable is extravagant and unconscionable compared with the maximum loss that could result from the breach. However, use of the terms 'penalty' or 'liquidated damages' is inconclusive as the legal position depends on the interpretation by the courts of the clause in which they appear.

**penni** (plural **pennia**) A monetary unit of Finland, worth one hundredth of a *markka.

**penny** (p) **1.** A monetary unit of the UK, worth one hundredth of a *pound. **2.** A monetary unit of the Republic of Ireland, worth one hundredth of a *punt.

**penny shares** Securities with a very low market price (although they may not be as low as one penny) traded on a stock exchange. They are popular with small investors, who can acquire a significant holding in a company for a very low cost. Moreover, a rise of a few pence in a low-priced share can represent a high percentage profit. However, they are usually shares in companies that have fallen on hard times and may, indeed, be close to bankruptcy. The investor in this type of share is hoping for a rapid recovery or a takeover.

**pension** A specified sum paid regularly to a person who has reached a certain age or retired from employment. It is normally paid from the date of reaching the specified age or the retirement date until death. A widow may also receive a pension from the date of her husband's death.

In the UK, contributory **retirement pensions** are usually paid by the state from the normal retirement age (currently 65 for men and 60 for women), irrespective of whether or not the pensioners have retired from full-time employment (*see* pension age). A non-working wife or widow also receives a state pension based on her husband's contributions. Self-employed people are also required to contribute towards their pensions. The state pays non-contributory retirement pensions to people over 80 if they are not already receiving a retirement pension.

Since 1978 state pensions have been augmented by the *State Earnings-Related Pension Scheme (SERPS) to relate pensions to inflation and to ensure that men and women are treated equally. Employers can contract out of the earnings-related part of the state pension scheme relating to retirement and widows, provided that they replace it with an *occupational pension scheme that complies with the Social Security Act 1986. Employees may also contract out of SERPS by starting their own approved *personal pension scheme.

The private sector of the insurance industry also provides a wide variety of pensions, *annuities, and *endowment assurances. *See also* executive pension plan; single-life pension.

**pensionable earnings** The part of an employee's salary that is used to calculate the final pension entitlement. Unless otherwise stated, overtime, commission, and bonuses are normally excluded.

**pension age** The age at which a *pension becomes payable, irrespective of whether or not the pensioner has retired.

**Pension Benefit Guaranty Corporation** *See* Employment Retirement Income Security Act 1974.

**pensioneer trustee** A person authorized by the Superannuation Funds Office of the Inland Revenue to oversee the management of a *pension fund in accordance with the provisions of the Pension Trust Deed.

**pension funds** State and private pension contributions invested to give as high a return as possible to provide the funds from which pensions are paid. In the UK, pension funds managed by individual organizations work closely with insurance companies and investment trusts, being together the *institutional investors that have a dominant influence on many securities traded on the London Stock Exchange. The enormous amount of money accumulated by these pension funds, which grows by weekly and monthly contributions, needs prudent management; real estate and works of art are often purchased for investment by pension funds in addition to stock-exchange securities. *See also* pensioneer trustee; Superannuation Funds Office; unfunded pension scheme.

**pension mortgage** A *mortgage in which the borrower repays interest only and also contributes to a pension plan designed to provide an eventual tax-free lump sum, part of which is used to pay off the capital at the end of the mortgage term and the rest to provide a pension for the borrower's retirement. This type of mortgage is particularly suitable for the self-employed or those without a company pension.

**pension scheme** Any arrangement the main purpose of which is to provide a defined class of individuals (called members of the scheme) with *pensions. A pension scheme may include benefits other than a pension and may provide a pension for dependants of deceased members. *See also* occupational pension scheme; personal annuity scheme; personal pension scheme.

**Pensions Ombudsman** *See* Financial Ombudsman.

**PEP** Abbreviation for *personal equity plan.

**PEP mortgage** A *mortgage in which the borrower repays only the interest on the loan to the lender, but at the same time puts regular sums into a *personal equity plan (PEP). When the PEPs mature they are used to repay the capital. The PEP mortgage is similar to an endowment mortgage, except that the PEP mortgage does not provide any life-assurance cover. The advantages are that PEP funds are untaxed, unlike endowments, and that the borrower has the flexibility of being able to change the PEP provider each year.

**P/E ratio** Abbreviation for *price–earnings ratio.

**per capita income**  The average income of a group, obtained by dividing the group's total income by its number of members. The **national per capita income** is the ratio of the national income to the population.

**per diem**  (Latin: per day) Denoting a fee charged by a professional person who is paid a specified fee for each day of employment.

**perfecting the sight**  *See* bill of sight.

**peril (risk)**  An event that can cause a financial loss, against which an *insurance contract provides cover. *See also* risk. An **excepted peril** is one that is not normally covered by an insurance policy.

**period bill (term bill)**  A *bill of exchange payable on a specified date rather than on demand.

**period of grace**  The time, usually three days, allowed for payment of a *bill of exchange (except those payable at sight or on demand) after it matures.

**permanent health insurance (PHI)**  A form of health insurance that provides an income (maximum 75% of salary) up to normal retirement age (or *pension age) to replace an income lost by prolonged illness or disability in which the insured is unable to perform any part of his or her normal duties. Premiums are related to age and occupation and normally are fixed; benefits, which are not paid for the first 4–13 weeks of disability, are tax free for one year and thereafter are taxed. *Compare* sickness and accident insurance.

**per mille (per mill; per mil)**  (Latin: per thousand) Denoting that the premium on an insurance policy is the stated figure per £1000 of insured value. Per mille is also used to mean 0.1% in relation to interest rates.

**permission to deal**  Permission by the *London Stock Exchange to deal in the shares of a newly floated company. It must be sought three days after the issue of a *prospectus.

**perpetual annuity**  An *annuity that has been bought to provide an income in perpetuity.

**perpetual debenture**  **1.** A bond or *debenture that can never be redeemed. *See* irredeemable securities. **2.** A bond or debenture that cannot be redeemed on demand.

**perpetual FRN**  A *floating-rate note that is never redeemed. *See also* flip-flop FRN.

**perpetual inventory**  A method of continuous stock control in which an account is kept for each item of stock; one side of the account records the deliveries of that type of stock and the other side records the issues from the stock. Thus, the balance of the account at any time provides a record of either the number of items in stock or their values, or both. This method is used in large organizations in which it is important to control the amount of capital tied up in the running of the business. It also provides a means of checking pilferage. Less sophisticated organizations rely on annual stocktaking to discover how much stock they have.

**perpetual succession**  The continued existence of a corporation until it is legally dissolved. A corporation, being a separate legal person, is unaffected by the death or other departure of any member but continues in existence no matter how many changes in membership occur.

**Perpetuities and Accumulations Act 1964**  An Act reforming the **rule against perpetuities**. This rule exists to prevent a donor of a gift from directing its destination too far into the future and thus creating uncertainty as to the ultimate ownership of the property. Under the old law, the ownership had to become certain within the period of an existing lifetime (i.e. the lifetime of a person living at the date of the gift) plus 21 years. If there was any possibility, however remote, that this would not happen, the gift was void. For example, a gift to 'the first of A's daughters to marry' fails under the old law, unless A is dead or already has a married daughter, because all of A's living daughters may die unmarried and then A might have another daughter (who was not an existing lifetime or life in being at the date of the gift), who might marry more than 21 years after A's death. This was so even if A was a woman past the age of childbearing at the date of the gift. The Perpetuities and Accumulations Act changed the old law by allowing a 'wait and see' period, i.e. by allowing a gift to remain valid until it becomes clear that it will in fact offend against the rule against perpetuities. The Act also allows the donor to choose a perpetuity period of 80 years instead of the uncertain 'life in being plus 21 years'. The Act also allows the age at which a person is to benefit from a gift to be reduced, if this will save the gift from infringing the rule against perpetuities.

**per pro (per proc; p.p.)**  Abbreviations for *per procurationem* (Latin: by procuration): denoting an act by an agent, acting on the authority of a principal. The abbreviation is often used when signing letters on behalf of a firm or someone else, if formally authorized to do so. The firm or person giving the authority accepts responsibility for documents so signed.

**personal accident and sickness insurance**  *See* sickness and accident insurance.

**personal allowances**  Sums deductible from taxable income under an income-tax system to allow for personal circumstances. The principal allowances in the UK system are a personal allowance to which all taxpayers are entitled, a married couple's allowance, a single parent's allowance, and *age relief. The personal allowance for a taxpayer in the year commencing 5 April 1993 is £3445; for those over 64 it is £4200 and for those over 74, £4370. The rates for older taxpayers are reduced for those with a total income in excess of £14,200. *See also* additional personal allowance; separate taxation of a wife's earnings.

**personal annuity scheme**  A contributory *pension scheme designed for people who are self-employed or not covered by an *occupational pension scheme. *See also* pension.

**personal equity plan (PEP)**  A UK government scheme introduced in 1987 under the Finance Act 1986 to encourage individuals to invest directly in UK quoted companies, offering investors certain tax benefits. The investment is administered by an authorized plan manager. Plans are either discretionary (in which the plan manager makes the investment decisions, sometimes called a **managed PEP**) or non-discretionary (in which the investor makes the decisions, a **self-select PEP**). Investors may put in a lump sum or regular monthly amounts. Re-invested dividends are free of *income tax and *capital-gains tax is not incurred, as long as the investment is retained in the plan for at least a complete calendar year. There is a limit of £6000 on the amount an individual can invest in an authorized plan in any one year and a limit of £3000 in a **single-company PEP**.

**personal identification number (PIN)** A number memorized by the holder of a *cash card, *credit card, or *multifunctional card and used in *automated teller machines and *electronic funds transfer at point of sale to identify the card owner. The number is given to the cardholder in secret and is memorized so that if the card is stolen it cannot be used. The number is unique to the cardholder. Banks will not honour *phantom withdrawals if it can be shown that the PIN number was known to a party other than the customer to whom it was allocated.

**Personal Investment Authority (PIA)** A *Self-Regulating Organization (SRO) that, from April 1993, will regulate the activities of investment business carried out mainly with or for private investors. The PIA will take over many of the responsibilities of FIMBRA and LAUTRO and some of the activities of IMRO.

**personal loan** A loan to a private person by a bank or building society for domestic purposes, buying a car, etc. There is usually no security required and consequently a high rate of interest is charged. Repayment is usually by monthly instalments over a fixed period. This is a more expensive way of borrowing from a bank than by means of an *overdraft.

**personal pension scheme (**or **plan)** A *money-purchase pension scheme entered into by an employee, who wishes to contract out of the *State Earnings-Related Pension Scheme (SERPS). An employee may start a personal pension scheme, whether or not the employer has an *occupational pension scheme. Personal pension schemes must provide a half-rate widowers' benefit. They must be approved by the Occupational Pension Board before a person can contract out of SERPS. An employee with a personal pension in place of SERPS or an occupational pension scheme pays National Insurance contributions at the full ordinary rate. The Department of Social Security pays the difference between the lower contracted-out rate and the full ordinary rate for the personal pension scheme.

**personal property (personalty)** Any property other than *real property (realty). This distinction is especially used in distinguishing property for *inheritance tax. Personal property includes money, shares, chattels, etc.

**personal reliefs** *See* income-tax allowances.

**personal representative** A person whose duty is to gather in the assets of the estate of a deceased person, to pay any liabilities, and to distribute the residue. Personal representatives of a person dying testate are known as *executors; those of a person dying intestate are known as *administrators.

**personalty** *See* personal property.

**peseta** (Pta) The standard monetary unit of Spain and Andorra, divided into 100 céntimos.

**pesewa** A monetary unit of Ghana, worth one hundredth of a *cedi.

**peso 1.** The standard monetary unit of Argentina ($), Chile (Ch$), Colombia (Col$), Cuba (CUP), the Dominican Republic (RD$), Guinea-Bissau (PG), Mexico (Mex$), and the Philippines (₱); it is divided into 100 centavos.
**2.** (NUr$) The standard monetary unit of Uruguay, divided into 100 centésimos.

**PET** Abbreviation for *potentially exempt transfer.

**petrodollars** Reserves of US dollars deposited with banks as a result of the steep rises in the price of oil in the 1970s. The export revenues of the oil-exporting nations increased rapidly in this period, leading to large current-account surpluses, which had an important impact on the world's financial system.

**petroleum revenue tax (PRT)** A tax on the profits from oil exploration and mining occurring under the authority of licences granted in accordance with the Petroleum (Production) Act 1934 or the Petroleum (Production) Act (Northern Ireland) 1964. This tax was the principal means enabling the UK government to obtain a share in the profits made from oil in the North Sea.

**petty cash** The amount of cash that an organization keeps in notes or coins on its premises to pay small items of expense. This is to be distinguished from cash, which normally refers to amounts held at banks. Petty-cash transactions are normally recorded in a petty-cash book, the balance of which should agree with the amounts of petty cash held at any given time.

**pfennig** A monetary unit of Germany, worth one hundredth of a *Deutschmark.

**phantom withdrawals** The removal of funds from bank accounts through *automated teller machines (ATMs) by unauthorized means and without the knowledge or consent of the account holder. Banks maintain that such withdrawals are not possible without the collusion, intended or unintended, of account holders by divulging their *personal identification numbers (PINs) to a third party or lending their ATM card to someone else. Many disputes have arisen over so-called phantom withdrawals but no case has so far been proved.

**PHI** Abbreviation for *permanent health insurance.

**Philadelphia Stock Exchange** *See* US stock exchanges.

**Philippines stock exchanges** *See* Manila Stock Exchange.

**physical capital** *See* capital.

**physical controls** Direct measures used by a government to regulate an economy, compared to indirect controls, which influence the price mechanism. For example, the imposition of a quota on a specific import would be a physical control, whereas a surcharge on that import would be an indirect control.

**physical price** The price of a commodity that is available for delivery. In most forward contracts (*see* forward dealing) and *futures contracts the goods are never actually delivered because sales and purchases are set off against each other.

**physicals** *See* actuals.

**PIA** Abbreviation for *Personal Investment Authority.

**piastre** A monetary unit of Egypt, Lebanon, the Sudan, and Syria, worth one hundredth of a *pound.

**PIBOR** Abbreviation for *Paris Inter Bank Offered Rate.

**PIN** Abbreviation for *personal identification number.

**PINC** Abbreviation for *property income certificate.

**pink form (preferential form)** An *application form in a flotation that is printed on pink paper and usually distributed to employees of the company to give them preference in the allocation of shares. Up to 10% of a share issue can be set aside under London Stock Exchange rules for applications from employees or from shareholders in a parent company that is floating a subsidiary.

**pink sheets** The US National Quotation Bureau publications listing the bid and offer prices of the securities available on the *over-the-counter markets.

**Pink 'Un** The colloquial name for the *Financial Times*, the London business newspaper, which is published on pink newsprint.

**pit (trading pit)** An area of a stock market, financial futures and options exchange, or commodity exchange in which a particular stock, financial future, or commodity is traded, especially one in which dealings take place by *open outcry (*see* London International Financial Futures and Options Exchange; callover). A member who is allowed to trade on the floor but wishes to conceal his or her identity may use a **pit broker** to carry out transactions. Dealers in these markets are called **pit traders**.

**placement** *See* placing; private placing.

**placing** The sale of shares by a company to a selected group of individuals or institutions. Placings can be used either as a means of *flotation or to raise additional capital for a quoted company (*see also* pre-emption rights; rights issue). Placings are usually the cheapest way of raising capital on a *stock exchange and they also allow the directors of a company to influence the selection of shareholders. The success of a placing usually depends on the placing power of the company's stockbroker. Placings of *public companies are sometimes called **public placings** (*compare* private placing). In the USA a placing is called a **placement**. *Compare* introduction; issue by tender; offer for sale; public issue.

**Plantation House** An office block in Mincing Lane in the City of London that houses many firms involved in the commodity trade and formerly housed the London Commodity Exchange (*see* London FOX).

**plastic money** A colloquial name for a *credit card, *cash card, or *multifunctional card. It is often shortened to **plastic**.

**Plaza Agreement** *See* Group of Five.

**plc** Abbreviation for *public limited company. This (or its Welsh equivalent) must appear in the name of a public limited company in the UK. *Compare* Ltd.

**pledge** An article given by a borrower (**pledgor**) to a lender (**pledgee**) as a security for a debt. It remains in the ownership of the pledgor although it is in the possession of the pledgee until the debt is repaid. *See also* pawnbroker.

**ploughed-back profits** *See* retained profits.

**PMT** Abbreviation for *post-market trading.

**poison pill** A tactic used by a company that fears an unwanted takeover by ensuring that a successful takeover bid will trigger some event that substantially reduces the value of the company. Examples of such tactics include the sale of some prized asset to a friendly company or bank or the issue of securities with a conversion option enabling the bidder's shares to be bought at a reduced price if the bid is successful. Poison pills are used all over the world but were developed in the USA. *See also* porcupine provisions; staggered directorships.

**polarization** The regulation in the *Financial Services Act 1986 that stipulates that financial intermediaries, such as banks and building societies, must either act as advisers who may not offer their own financial products for sale, or as agents selling their own products; they cannot, as they previously could, do both.

**policy** *See* insurance policy.

**policy mix** A combination of fiscal, monetary, and other policies employed by a government to achieve an economic objective.

**policy proof of interest (PPI)** An insurance policy (usually marine insurance) in which the insurers agree that they will not insist on the usual requirement that the insured must prove an *insurable interest existed in the subject matter before a claim is paid. The possession of the policy is all that is required. These policies are a matter of trust between insurer and insured as they are not legally enforceable.

**poll tax** A tax that is the same for each individual, i.e. a lump sum per head (from Middle Low German *polle*: head). The benefits of such taxes are that they do not distort choices, being an equal levy from everyone's resources whatever their circumstances; however, poll taxes are sometimes criticized as being regressive in that they do not take account of persons' ability to pay. The **community charge**, an alternative to *rates, was a poll tax introduced by the Conservative government in 1990 (1989 in Scotland) and replaced by a *council tax in 1993.

**porcupine provisions (shark repellents)** Provisions made by a company to deter *takeover bids. They include *poison pills, *staggered directorships, etc.

**portable pension** A *pension entitlement that can be moved from one *pension scheme to another without loss, as when a person changes jobs.

**PORTAL market** A market in the USA operated by the *National Association of Securities Dealers Inc. (NASD) since June 1990 for qualified investors to trade privately in unregistered international securities.

**portfolio** **1.** The list of holdings in securities owned by an investor or institution. In building up an investment portfolio an institution will have its own investment analysts, while an individual may make use of the services of a *merchant bank that offers **portfolio management**. The choice of portfolio will depend on the mix of income and capital growth its owner expects, some investments providing good income prospects while others provide good prospects for capital growth. **2.** A list of the loans made by an organization. Banks, for example, attempt to balance their portfolio of loans to limit the risks.

**portfolio insurance (portfolio protection)** The use of a *financial futures and *options market to protect the value of a portfolio of investments. For example, a fund manager may expect the general level of prices to fall on the stock exchange. The manager could protect the portfolio by selling the appropriate number of *index futures, which could then be bought back at a profit if the market falls. Alternately, the manager could establish the value of the portfolio at current prices by buying put options, which would provide the opportunity to benefit if there was a rise in the general level of prices.

**portfolio theory** An analytical approach to the selection and management of a *portfolio of investments. It will include a study of diversification to minimize risk, as well as a historical view of markets (*see* chartist; random-walk theory) to survey price trends. A major aspect of portfolio theory, now that index and equity futures and options can be bought and sold, will be *portfolio insurance. The theory, as well as considering risks and capital growth, will also be concerned with the structure of portfolios in relation to their expected income. *See also* alpha coefficient; beta coefficient; capital asset pricing model.

**POSB** Abbreviation for the Post Office Savings Bank, the former name of the *National Savings Bank.

**position** The extent to which an investor, dealer, or speculator has made a commitment in the market by buying or selling securities, currencies, commodities, etc. *See* long position; open position; short position.

**post-Bang** Denoting the method of operation of the *London Stock Exchange after the *Big Bang of October 1986. It also refers to the widening of all the activities of the London security markets as a result of these changes.

**post-date** To insert a date on a document that is later than the date on which it is signed, thus making it effective only from the later date. A **post-dated** (or **forward-dated**) **cheque** cannot be negotiated before the date written on it, irrespective of when it was signed. *Compare* ante-date.

**post-market trading (PMT)** An automated trading system on screens, operated by the *Chicago Mercantile Exchange.

**Post Office Savings Bank (POSB)** The former name of the *National Savings Bank.

**potentially exempt transfer (PET)** A gift that is not subject to *inheritance tax when it is made, although it may become taxable if the donor dies within a specified period, currently seven years. *See* lifetime transfers.

**pound** **1.** (£) The standard UK monetary unit, divided into 100 pence. It dates back to the 8th century AD when Offa, King of Mercia, coined 240 pennyweights of silver from 1 pound of silver. When *sterling was decimalized in 1971 it was divided into 100 newly defined pence. The pound is also the currency unit of the Falkland Islands (Fk£) and Gibraltar (Gib£). *See also* punt. **2.** The standard monetary unit of Egypt (LE), Lebanon (LL), the Sudan (LSd), and Syria (LS), divided into 100 piastres. **3.** (£C) The standard monetary unit of Cyprus, divided into 100 cents.

**poundage** *See* rates.

**pound cost averaging** A method of accumulating capital by investing a fixed sum of money in a particular share every month (or other period). When prices fall the fixed sum will buy correspondingly more shares and when prices rise fewer shares are bought. The result is that the average purchase price over a period is lower than the arithmetic average of the market prices at each purchase date (because more shares are bought at lower prices and fewer at higher prices).

**poverty trap** A situation in which an increase in the income of a low-earning household causes either a loss of state benefits or an increase in taxation that approximately equals the increase in earnings, i.e. the household faces a marginal tax rate of 100% (in some instances the marginal tax rate can exceed 100%). The poverty trap creates a disincentive to earning and is often demoralizing for those caught in it. Most *progressive tax systems create poverty traps and policies for removing them are difficult to find.

**power of attorney (PA)** A formal document giving one person the right to act for another. A power to execute a *deed must itself be given by a deed. An attorney may not delegate these powers unless specifically authorized to do so.

**p.p.** Abbreviation for *per procurationem*. *See* per pro.

**PPI 1.** Abbreviation for *policy proof of interest. **2.** Abbreviation for *producer price index.

**PPP** Abbreviation for *purchasing power parity.

**preacquisition profit** The retained profit of one company before it is taken over by another company. Preacquisition profits should not be distributed to the shareholders of the acquiring company by way of dividend, as such profits do not constitute income to the parent company but a partial repayment of its capital outlay on the acquisition of the shares.

**preceding-year basis** The basis on which UK taxes are assessed. Income or profits are charged to tax in the year in which they are assessed, which is normally the financial year following the one in which they were earned.

**pre-emption** First refusal: the right of a person to be the first to be asked to enter into an agreement at a specified price; for example, the right to be offered a house at a price acceptable to the vendor before it is put on the open market.

**pre-emption rights** A principle, established in company law, according to which any new shares issued by a company must first be offered to the existing shareholders as the legitimate owners of the company. To satisfy this principle a company must write to every shareholder (*see* rights issue), involving an expensive and lengthy procedure. Newer methods of issuing shares, such as *vendor placings or *bought deals, are much cheaper and easier to effect, although they violate pre-emption rights. In the USA pre-emption rights have now been largely abandoned but controversy is still widespread in the UK.

**preference share** A share in a company yielding a fixed rate of interest rather than a variable dividend. A preference share is an intermediate form of security between an *ordinary share and a *debenture. Preference shares, like ordinary shares but unlike debentures, usually confer some degree of ownership of the company. However, in the event of liquidation, they are less likely to be paid off than debentures, but more likely than ordinary shares. Preference shares may be redeemable (*see* redeemable preference share) at a fixed or variable date; alternatively they may be undated. Sometimes they are *convertible. The rights of preference shareholders vary from company to company and are set out in the articles of association. Voting rights are normally restricted, often only being available if the interest payments are in arrears.

   **Participating preference shares** carry additional rights to dividends, such as a further share in the profits of the company, after the ordinary shareholders have received a stated percentage. *See also* cumulative preference share; non-cumulative preference share; preferred ordinary share.

**preferential creditor** A creditor whose debt will be met in preference to those of other creditors and who thus has the best chance of being paid in full on the bankruptcy of an individual or the winding-up of a company. Preferential creditors, who are usually paid in full after *secured debts and before ordinary creditors, include: the Inland Revenue in respect of PAYE, Customs and Excise in respect of VAT and car tax, the DSS in respect of National Insurance Social Security contributions, the trustees of occupational pensions schemes, and employees in respect of any remuneration outstanding.

**preferential form** *See* pink form.

**preferential payment** A payment made to a *preferential creditor.

**preferred ordinary share** A share issued by some companies that ranks between a *preference share and an *ordinary share in the payment of dividends.

**preferred stock** The US name for a *preference share.

**preliminary expenses** Expenses involved in the formation of a company. They include the cost of producing a *prospectus, issuing shares, and advertising the flotation.

**pre-market** Denoting any trading that takes place before the official opening of a market.

**premium** **1.** The consideration payable for a contract of *insurance or life assurance. **2.** An amount in excess of the nominal value of a share, bond, or other security. **3.** An amount in excess of the issue price of a share or other security. When dealings open for a new issue of shares, for instance, it may be said that the market price will be at a premium over the issue price (*see* stag). **4.** The price paid by a buyer of a traded *option to the seller for the right to exercise the option. Premiums are determined in an exchange or market by *open outcry in a trading *pit, the level reflecting the supply and demand for that particular option at that particular moment. In general, the premium asked for an option consists of two components, its *intrinsic value and its *time value. **5.** The difference between the spot price for a commodity or currency and the forward price. **6.** A bonus given to bank customers as an inducement to open an account.

**premium bonds** UK government securities first issued in 1956 and now administered by the Department for *National Savings. No regular income or capital gain is offered but bonds enter weekly and monthly draws for tax-free prizes of between £50 and £250,000. The prize fund (calculated at 6.5% from 1988) is distributed in a range of prizes, winners being drawn by ERNIE (electronic random number indicating equipment). The chance of winning in each monthly draw is 11 000 to one. Bonds are in £1 denominations with a minimum purchase of £100 and a maximum holding of £10,000. Bonds are repaid at their face value at any time.

**premium income** The total income of an insurance company from insurance policy *premiums.

**present value** *See* future value.

**pre-tax profit** The profit of a company before deduction of corporation tax.

**price control** Restrictions by a government on the prices of consumer goods, usually imposed on a short-term basis as a measure to control inflation. *See also* prices and income policy.

**price–dividend ratio (PDR; P/D ratio)**  The current market price of a company share divided by the dividend per share for the previous year. It is a measure of the investment value of the share.

**price–earnings ratio (P/E ratio)**  The current market price of a company share divided by the *earnings per share (eps) of the company. The P/E ratio usually refers to the annual eps and is expressed as a number (e.g. 5 or 10), often called the **multiple** of the company. Loosely, it can be thought of as the number of years it would take the company to earn an amount equal to its market value. High multiples, usually associated with low *yields, indicate that the company is growing rapidly, while a low multiple is associated with dull no-growth stocks. The P/E ratio is one of the main indicators used by fundamental analysts to decide whether the shares in a company are expensive or cheap, relative to the market.

**price index**  *See* Retail Price Index.

**price–net tangible assets ratio**  The current market price of a company share divided by its *net tangible assets. The higher the ratio, the more attractive the share as an investment.

**prices and income policy**  A government policy to curb *inflation by directly imposing wage restraint and *price controls. Some less interventionist governments prefer indirect methods using fiscal and monetary policies.

**price support**  A government policy of providing support for certain basic, usually agricultural, products to stop the price falling below an agreed level. Support prices can be administered in various ways: the government can purchase and stockpile surplus produce to support the price or it can pay producers a cash payment as a *subsidy to raise the price they obtain through normal market channels. *See also* Common Agricultural Policy.

**primary dealer  1.** A *money-market dealer in government (gilt-edged) stocks; they have been established in London markets since the *Big Bang in October 1986. They deal direct with the Bank of England, by whom they are supervised, and can bid for *tap stocks when required, as well as having an obligation to maintain a market in all government stocks. There were 27 primary dealers in 1986, but only 20 in 1992. They have to some extent taken over the role of the *government broker. They are also known as **gilt-edged dealers**. **2.** *See* reporting dealer.

**primary market**  *See* secondary market.

**prime cost**  The total of the direct costs incurred in making a product. These include material costs, direct labour costs, and direct expenses. The prime cost may be expressed per product or per year (or other period). The total production cost will also include an item for the indirect overhead costs.

**prime rate**  The rate of interest at which US banks lend money to first-class borrowers. It is similar in operation to the *base rate in the UK. Competitive markets have forced many banks, both in the USA and the UK, to offer business customers credit at below prime rates. The main difference between US and UK practice is that the US prime rate is approximately equal to the dollar three-month *London Inter Bank Offered Rate (LIBOR) plus 1%, whereas the UK base rate is approximately equivalent to the sterling three-month LIBOR.

**principal** **1.** A person on whose behalf an agent or broker acts. **2.** A sum of money on which *interest is earned.

**principles of taxation** A set of criteria, largely determined by the economist Adam Smith (1723–90), for determining whether a given tax or system of taxation is good or bad. The main principles are that taxes should be equitable and certain. Subsidiary principles are that they should distort choices that would otherwise be made as little as possible and that the cost of collection should be as low as possible. Some economists argue that a further principle might be that the tax should be effective in redistributing income.

**priority percentage (prior charge)** The proportion of any profit that must be paid to holders of fixed-interest capital (*preference shares and loan stock; *see* debenture) before arriving at the sums to be distributed to ordinary shareholders. These percentages help to assess the security of the income of ordinary shareholders and are related to the gearing of the company's capital (*see* capital gearing; leverage).

**prior-year adjustment** An adjustment to the profit and loss account of an organization necessitated by matters relating to earlier years, which give a misleading view of the position. Such an adjustment might arise as a result of under- or overvaluation of assets or liabilities or because of changes in accounting policies. For the purpose of accounting standards the term is limited to material adjustments arising from either changes in accounting policies or the correction of fundamental errors. Minor adjustments to estimates are not prior-year adjustments. Prior-year adjustments are to be made by adjusting the opening balances of reserves.

**private bank** **1.** A *commercial bank owned by one person or a partnership (*compare* joint-stock bank). Popular in 19th-century Britain, they have been superseded by joint-stock banks. They still exist in the USA. **2.** A bank that is not a member of a *clearing house and therefore has to use a clearing bank as an agent. **3.** A bank that is not owned by the state.

**private limited company** Any *limited company that is not a *public limited company. Such a company is not permitted to offer its shares for sale to the public and it is free from the rules that apply to public limited companies.

**private placing** The selling of shares in a private company direct to investors, often without the intermediary of a stockbroker. In the USA it is called a **private placement**. *See also* placing.

**private sector** The part of an economy that is not under government control. In a mixed economy most commercial and industrial firms are in the private sector, run by private enterprise. *Compare* public sector.

**private-sector liquidity** *See* money supply.

**private treaty** Any contract made by personal arrangement between the buyer and seller or their agents, i.e. not by public auction.

**privatization** The process of selling a publicly owned company (*see* nationalization) to the private sector. Privatization may be pursued for political as well as economic reasons. The economic justification for privatization is that a company will be more efficient under private ownership, although most economists would argue that privatization will only achieve this if it is accompanied by increased competition. Recently, privatizations in the form of *share offers to the general public have been advocated as a means of increasing the participation of individuals in the capitalist system. The process can also be called **denationalization**.

**probate** A certificate issued by the Family Division of the High Court, on the application of *executors appointed by a will, to the effect that the will is valid and that the executors are authorized to administer the deceased's estate. When there is no apparent doubt about the will's validity, probate is granted in **common form** on the executors filing an affidavit. Probate granted in common form can be revoked by the court at any time on the application of an interested party who proves that the will is invalid. When the will is disputed, probate in **solemn form** is granted, but only if the court decides that the will is valid after hearing the evidence on the disputed issues in a **probate action**.

**probate price** The price of shares or other securities used for *inheritance-tax purposes on the death of the owner. The price is taken as either one quarter of the interval between the upper and lower quotations of the day on which the owner died added to the lower figure or as half way between the highest and lowest recorded bargains of the day, whichever is the lower.

**probate value** The value of the assets at the time of a person's death; the value of each asset has to be agreed with the Capital Taxes Office of the Inland Revenue for the purposes of calculating *inheritance tax.

**procuration** *See* per pro.

**produce** *See* commodity.

**produce broker** *See* commodity broker.

**producer price index (PPI)** A measure of the rate of *inflation among goods purchased and manufactured by UK industry (replacing the former **wholesale price index**). It measures the movements in prices of about 10 000 goods relative to the same base year. *Compare* Retail Price Index.

**productive expenditure** Money spent by a government on public services, schools, hospitals, etc., i.e. for benefits in the future as opposed to the immediate benefits that follow from current consumption.

**products-guarantee insurance** An insurance policy covering financial loss as a consequence of a fault occurring in a company's product. A product-guarantee claim would be made, for example, to pay for the cost of recalling and repairing cars that are found to have a defective component. This type of policy would not pay compensation to customers or members of the public injured as a result of the defect. Such claims would be met by a *products-liability insurance.

**products-liability insurance** An insurance policy that pays any compensation the insured is legally liable to pay to customers who are killed, injured, or have property damaged as a result of a defect in a product that they have manufactured or supplied. Costs incurred as a consequence of the defect that are not legal *damages would not be covered by a policy of this kind. A *products-guarantee insurance is intended to cover these costs.

**professional-indemnity insurance** A form of third-party insurance that covers a professional person, such as a solicitor, surveyor, accountant, businessman or businesswoman, etc., against paying compensation in the event of being successfully sued for professional negligence. This can include the giving of defective advice if the person professes to be an expert in a given field. *See also* public-liability insurance.

**profit  1.** For a single transaction, the excess of the selling price of the article or service being sold over the costs of providing it.  **2.** For a period of trading, the surplus of net assets at the end of a period over the net assets at the start of that period, adjusted where relevant for amounts of capital injected or withdrawn by the proprietors. As profit is notoriously hard to define, it is not always possible to derive one single figure of profit for an organization from an accepted set of data.

**profit and loss account  1.** An *account in the books of an organization showing the profits (or losses) made on its business activities with the deduction of the appropriate expenses.  **2.** A statement of the profit (or loss) of an organization derived from the account in the books. It is one of the statutory accounts that, for most limited companies, has to be filed annually with the UK Registrar of Companies. The profit and loss account usually consists of three parts. The first is a trading account, showing the total sales income less the costs of production, etc., and any changes in the value of stock or work in progress from the last accounting period. This gives the *gross profit (or loss). The second part gives any other income (apart from trading) and lists administrative and other costs to arrive at a *net profit (or loss). From this net profit before taxation the appropriate corporation tax is deducted to give the net profit after taxation. In the third part, the net profit after tax is appropriated to dividends or to reserves. The UK Companies Act 1985 gives a choice of four formats, one of which must be used to file a profit and loss account for a registered company.

**profit forecast**  A forecast by the directors of a public company of the profits to be expected in a stated period. If a new flotation is involved, the profit forecast must be reported on by the reporting accountants and the sponsor to the share issue. An existing company is not required to make a profit forecast with its *accounts, but if it does it must be reported on by the company's auditors.

**profit margin**  The ratio of the net profit of an organization to its *turnover.

**profit sharing**  The distribution of part of the profits of a company to its employees, in the form of either cash or shares in the company. There are many workers' participation schemes that use profit sharing as a means of increasing the motivation of employees; some schemes relate the share of the profit to salary or wages, others to length of service, and yet others give equal shares to all who have been employed by the company for a minimum period.

**profit taking**  Selling commodities, securities, etc., at a profit, either after a market rise or because they show a profit at current levels but will not do so if an expected fall in prices occurs.

**program trading**  Trading on international stock exchanges using a computer program to exploit differences between stock *index futures and actual share prices on world equity markets. The programs used trigger trading automatically once certain limits are reached. It was said to account for some 10% of the daily turnover (1989–90) on the New York Stock Exchange and has been partly blamed for the market crash in October 1987. Subsequently the New York Stock Exchange imposed limits on program trading.

**progressive tax**  A tax in which the rate of tax increases with increases in the tax base. The most common of these is *income tax but progressive rates are also applied to National Insurance contributions, *inheritance tax, and to a limited extent *corporation tax. Such taxes are generally linked to the ability-to-pay principle. *Compare* proportional tax.

**progress payment**  An instalment of a total payment made to a contractor, when a specified stage of the operation has been completed.

**promissory note**  A document that is a negotiable instrument and contains a promise to pay a certain sum of money to a named person, to that person's order, or to the bearer at a specified time in the future. It must be unconditional, signed by the maker, and delivered to the payee or bearer. They are widely used in the USA but are not in common use in the UK. A promissory note cannot be reissued, unless the promise is made by a banker and is payable to the bearer, i.e. unless it is a *banknote.

**promoter**  A person involved in setting up and funding a new company, including preparing its articles and memorandum of association, registering the company, finding directors, and raising subscriptions. The promoter is in a position of trust with regard to the new company and may not make an undisclosed profit or benefit at its expense. A promoter may be personally liable for the fulfilment of a contract entered into by, or on behalf of, the new company before it has been formed.

**prompt cash**  Payment terms for goods or services in which payment is due within a few days (usually not more than 14) of delivery of the goods or the rendering of the service.

**prompt day (prompt date)  1.** The day (date) on which payment is due for the purchase of goods. In some commodity spot markets it is the day payment is due and delivery of the goods may be effected.  **2.** The date on which a contract on a commodity exchange, such as the *London Metal Exchange, matures.

**property**  *See* personal property; real property.

**property bond**  A bond issued by a life-assurance company, the premiums for which are invested in a fund that invests in property.

**property income certificate (PINC)**  A certificate giving the bearer a share in the value of a particular property and a share of the income from it. PINCs can be bought and sold.

**property insurance**  Insurance covering loss, damage, or destruction of any form of item from personal jewellery to industrial plant and machinery. Property-insurance policies are a form of *indemnity in which the insurer undertakes to make good the loss suffered by the insured. The policy may state the specific compensation payable in the event of loss or damage; if it does not, the policy will normally pay the intrinsic value of the insured object, taking into account any appreciation or depreciation on the original cost. Such policies usually have a maximum sum for which the insurers are liable.

**property tax**  A tax based on the value of property owned by the taxpayer.

**proportional tax**  A tax in which the amount of tax paid is proportional to the size of the tax base, i.e. a tax with a single rate. *Compare* progressive tax.

**proportional treaty (quota share reinsurance treaty)** A *reinsurance agreement in which the risks are transferred in direct proportion to the premiums paid over.

**proprietary network** A network of *automated teller machines (ATMs) available for use only by the customers of a specific bank or financial institution or some other limited group.

**proprietary company** *See* Pty.

**prospectus** A document that gives details about a new issue of shares and invites the public to buy shares or debentures in the company. A copy must be filed with the Registrar of Companies. The prospectus must conform to the provisions of the Companies Act 1985, describe the aims, capital structure, and any past history of the venture, and may contain future *profit forecasts. There are heavy penalties for knowingly making false statements in a prospectus.

**protected bear** *See* covered bear.

**protest** A certificate signed by a *notary public at the request of the holder of a *bill of exchange that has been refused payment or acceptance. It is a legal requirement after *noting the bill (*see also* acceptance supra protest). The same procedure can also be used for a *promissory note that has been dishonoured.

**provision** An amount set aside out of profits in the accounts of an organization for a known liability (even though the specific amount might not be known) or for the diminution in value of an asset. Common provisions are for bad debts (*see* provision for bad debts) and for depreciation (*see* provision for depreciation) and also for accrued liabilities. According to the UK Companies Act 1981 notes must be given to explain every material provision in the accounts of a limited company.

**provisional liquidator** A person appointed by a court after the presentation of a winding-up petition on a company (*see* compulsory liquidation). The provisional liquidator, whose powers are limited, has to protect the interests of all the parties involved until the winding-up order is made. The *official receiver is normally appointed to this post. *See also* liquidator.

**provision for bad debts** A sum credited to an *account in the books of an organization to allow for some of the debtors not paying their debts in full. This amount is normally deducted from the total debtors in the balance sheet.

**provision for depreciation** A sum credited to an *account in the books of an organization to allow for the *depreciation of a fixed asset. The aggregate amounts set aside from year to year are deducted from the value of the asset in the balance sheet to give its *net book value.

**proximate cause** The dominant and effective cause of an event or chain of events that results in a claim on an insurance policy. The loss must be caused directly, or as a result of a chain of events initiated, by an insured peril. For example, a policy covering storm damage would also pay for items in a freezer that deteriorate because of a power cut caused by the storm, which is the proximate cause of the loss of the frozen food.

**proxy** A person who acts in the place of a member of a company at a company meeting at which one or more votes are taken. The proxy need not be a member of the company but it is quite common for directors to offer themselves as proxies for shareholders who cannot attend a meeting. Notices calling meetings must state that a member may appoint a proxy and the appointment of a proxy is usually done on a form provided by the company with the notice of the meeting; it must be returned to the company not less than 48 hours before the meeting. A **two-way proxy form** is printed so that the member can state whether the proxy should vote for or against a particular resolution. A **special proxy** is empowered to act at one specified meeting; a **general proxy** is authorized to vote at any meeting.

**PRT** Abbreviation for *petroleum revenue tax.

**prudence concept** A principle of accounting designed to ensure that unrealized profits are not distributed to shareholders by way of dividend. According to this principle, unrealized profits are not taken account of until they are realized; on the other hand foreseeable losses are taken account of as soon as they can be foreseen. Some accountants find it difficult to reconcile this concept with the 'true and fair view' required of published accounts; the prudence concept must give a view with a pessimistic bias. However, most accountants accept that taking a 'true and fair view' means doing so in accordance with the prudence concept.

**prudent insurer** A theoretical insurer who needs to know all the *material facts before entering into a contract of insurance. The insured must not conceal any information that a prudent insurer would need to know in assessing a risk.

**PSBR** Abbreviation for *Public Sector Borrowing Requirement.

**PSL** Abbreviation for private-sector liquidity, a concept formerly used as a measure of the *money supply.

**Pty** Abbreviation for proprietary company, the name given to a *private limited company in Australia and the Republic of South Africa. The abbreviation Pty is used after the name of the company as Ltd is used in the UK. It is also used in the USA for an insurance company owned by outside shareholders.

**public company** A company whose shares are available to the public through a stock exchange. *See* public limited company.

**public corporation** A state-owned organization set up either to provide a national service (such as the British Broadcasting Corporation) or to run a nationalized industry (such as the British Coal Corporation, formerly the National Coal Board). The chairman and members of the board of a public corporation are usually appointed by the appropriate government minister, who retains overall control and accountability to parliament. The public corporation attempts to reconcile public accountability for the use of public finance, freedom of commercial operation on a day-to-day basis, and maximum benefits for the community.

**public debts** The debts of the *public sector of the economy, including the *national debt.

**public deposits** The balances to the credit of government departments held at the Bank of England.

**public examination** *See* bankruptcy.

**public finance** **1.** The financing of the goods and services provided by national and local government through taxation or other means. **2.** The economic study of the issues involved in raising and spending money for the public benefit.

**public finance accountant**  A member of the Chartered Institute of Public Finance and Accountancy. The principal function of the members of this body is to prepare the financial accounts and act as management accountants for government agencies, local authorities, nationalized industries, and such bodies as publicly owned health and water authorities. As many of these bodies are non-profitmaking and are governed by special statutes, the skills required of public sector accountants differ from those required in the private sector.

**public issue**  A method of making a *new issue of shares, loan stock, etc., in which the public are invited, through advertisements in the national press, to apply for shares at a price fixed by the company. *Compare* introduction; issue by tender; offer for sale; placing.

**public-liability insurance**  An insurance policy that pays compensation to a member of the public and court costs in the event of the policyholder being successfully sued for causing death, injury, or damage to property by failing to take reasonable care in his or her actions or those of any employees. A business whose work brings it into contact with the public must have a public-liability policy. *See also* professional-indemnity insurance.

**public limited company (plc)**  A company registered under the Companies Act 1980 as a public company. Its name must end with the initials 'plc'. It must have an authorized share capital of at least £50,000, of which at least £12,500 must be paid up. The company's memorandum must comply with the format in Table F of the Companies Regulations 1985. It may offer shares and securities to the public. The regulation of such companies is stricter than that of private companies. Most public companies are converted from private companies, under the re-registration procedure in the Companies Act.

**public offering**  The US name for an *offer for sale.

**public placing**  *See* placing.

**public policy**  The interests of the community. If a contract is (on common-law principles) contrary to public policy, this will normally make it an *illegal contract. In a few cases, however, such a contract is void but not illegal, and is treated slightly more leniently (for example, by severance). Contracts that are illegal because they contravene public policy include any contract to commit a crime or a tort or to defraud the revenue, any contract that prejudices national safety or the administration of justice, and any immoral contract. Contracts that are merely void include contracts in restraint of trade.

**public sector**  The part of an economy in a mixed economy that covers the activities of the government and local authorities. This includes education, the National Health Service, the social services, public transport, the police, local public services, etc., as well as state-owned industries and *public corporations. *Compare* private sector.

**Public Sector Borrowing Requirement (PSBR)**  The amount by which UK government expenditure exceeds its income (i.e. the **public sector deficit**); this must be financed by borrowing (e.g. by selling gilt-edged securities) or by printing money. As an indicator of government fiscal policy the PSBR has acquired increased status since the late 1970s. By that time many economists had come to accept that a high PSBR is inflationary or leads to the crowding out of private expenditure; this remains a widely held view. While printing money simply causes prices to rise (*see* quantity theory of money), selling gilts has the effect of raising interest rates, reducing private investment, and curbing private expenditure. *See also* Central Government Borrowing Requirement.

**public sector deficit** *See* Public Sector Borrowing Requirement.

**public trustee** A state official in charge of the Public Trust Office, a trust corporation set up for certain statutory purposes. Being a corporation sole, the office exists irrespective of the person performing it. The public trustee may act as *administrator of small estates, as *trustee for English trusts where required, and as *receiver when directed to do so by a court. Another duty is to hold funds of registered *Friendly Societies and trade unions.

**public works** Government-sponsored construction work, especially that undertaken during a *recession or a depression on such activities as house building or road building. It is aimed at increasing the level of employment and aggregate demand. *See also* pump priming; reflation.

**published accounts** Accounts of organizations published according to UK law. The most common, according to the UK Companies Act 1981, are the accounts of *limited companies, which must be provided for their shareholders and filed with the Registrar of Companies at Companies House, Cardiff. The accounts comprise the *balance sheet, the *profit and loss account, the statement of *source and application of funds, the *directors' report, and the *auditors' report. In the case of *groups of companies, consolidated accounts are also required. *Small companies and *medium-sized companies, as defined by the Act, need not file some of these documents.

**puisne mortgage** A legal *mortgage of unregistered land that is not protected by the deposit of title deeds. It should instead be protected by registration.

**pul** An Afghan monetary unit, worth one hundredth of an *afghani.

**pula** (P) The standard monetary unit of Botswana, divided into 100 thebe.

**pumping** The colloquial name for the injection of money into the US banking system by the *Federal Reserve Bank to force down interest rates.

**pump priming** An addition to aggregate demand generated by a government in order to set off the *multiplier process. It usually involves allowing government expenditure to exceed receipts, thus creating a *budget deficit. Pump priming was widely employed by governments in the post-war era in order to maintain full employment; however, it became discredited in the 1970s when it failed to halt rising unemployment and was even held to be responsible for *inflation.

**punt** (Ir£) The Irish pound: the standard monetary unit of the Republic of Ireland, divided into 100 pence.

**punter** A speculator on a stock exchange, financial futures market, or commodity market, especially one who hopes to make quick profits.

**purchased life annuity** An *annuity in which a single premium purchases an income to be paid from a specified future date for the rest of the policyholder's life.

**purchasing power parity (PPP)**  Parity between two currencies at a *rate of exchange that will give each currency exactly the same purchasing power in its own economy. The belief that exchange rates adjust to reflect PPP dates back at least to the 17th century, but in the short term, at least, is demonstrably false (*see* overshooting). It may well hold in the long term, and is often used as a benchmark to indicate the levels that exchange rates should achieve (although measurement is difficult and controversial).

**pure endowment assurance**  An assurance policy that promises to pay an agreed amount if the policyholder is alive on a specified future date. If the policyholder dies before the specified date no payment is made and the premium payments cease. The use of the word 'assurance' for this type of contract is questionable as there is no element of life-assurance cover.

**pure risk**  An insurance risk that will lead to loss if certain events occur; it is therefore one that can be calculated and have premiums calculated for it.

**put-of-more option**  *See* option to double.

**put option**  *See* option.

**put through**  Two deals made simultaneously by a *market maker on the London Stock Exchange, in which a large quantity of shares is sold by one client and bought by another, the market maker taking a very small turn.

**pya**  A monetary unit of Myanmar, worth one hundredth of a *kyat.

**pyramiding**  The snowballing effect that derives from a holding company acquiring a number of subsidiary companies.

**qindar** An Albanian monetary unit, worth one hundredth of a *lek.

**qualified acceptance** An *acceptance of a *bill of exchange that varies the effect of the bill as drawn. If the holder refuses to take a qualified acceptance, the drawer and any endorsers must be notified or they will no longer be liable. If the holder takes a qualified acceptance, all previous signatories who did not assent from liability are released.

**qualified report** An *auditors' report in which the auditors, for one reason or another, have been unable to satisfy themselves that the accounts give a true and fair view of a company's affairs. For smaller companies, in which internal control cannot be perfect, qualified reports are not uncommon. However, it is normally regarded as a serious matter for a public limited company to receive a qualified report.

**qualifying distribution** A dividend or other distribution of the assets of a company to a member of the company, on which UK advance corporation tax must be made as laid down by the Income and Corporation Taxes Act 1988.

**qualifying policy** A life-assurance policy that the UK Inland Revenue has agreed is eligible for tax relief on the premiums and under which the proceeds are normally tax-free of the sum assured. Tax relief on life-assurance premiums was abolished on 13 March 1984, therefore policies eligible for life-assurance premium relief have now disappeared. *Compare* non-qualifying policy.

**quango** Acronym for quasi-autonomous non-governmental organization. Such bodies, some members of which are likely to be civil servants and some not, are appointed by a minister to perform some public function at the public expense. While not actually government agencies, they are not independent and are usually answerable to a government minister.

**quantity theory of money** A theory, first proposed by the philosopher David Hume (1711–76), stating that the price level is proportional to the quantity of money in the economy. Formally, it is usually stated in the equation: $MV = PT$, where $M$ is the quantity of money, $V$ is its velocity of circulation, $P$ is the price level, and $T$ the number of transactions in the period. Milton Friedman (1912– ) made this equation the central pivot of *monetarism, with the additional assumption that $V$ is more or less constant; thus, for a given number of transactions, the relationship between $M$ and $P$ is direct. This implies that any increase in the *money supply will lead to an increase in the price level, i.e. to inflation. *See* demand for money; monetary policy.

**quarter days** Four days traditionally taken as the beginning or end of the four quarters of the year, often for purposes of charging rent. In England, Wales, and

Northern Ireland they are Lady Day (25 March), Midsummer Day (24 June), Michaelmas (29 September), and Christmas Day (25 December). In Scotland they are Candlemas (2 February), Whitsuntide (15 May), Lammas (1 August), and Martinmas (11 November).

**quarter up**  The means of arriving at the *probate price of a share or other security.

**quasi-contract**  A legally binding obligation that one party has to another, as determined by a court, although no formal contract exists between them.

**quasi-loan**  An arrangement between two parties in which one party agrees to settle a financial obligation of the other party on condition that a reimbursement will follow.

**quetzal**  (Q) The standard monetary unit of Guatemala, divided into 100 centavos.

**quick assets**  See liquid assets.

**quid pro quo**  (Latin: something for something) Something given as compensation for something received. *Contracts require a quid pro quo; without a *consideration they would become unilateral agreements.

**quorum**  The smallest number of persons required to attend a meeting in order that its proceedings may be regarded as valid. For a company, the quorum for a meeting is laid down in the articles of association.

**quota**  **1.** A share of a whole that must not be exceeded.  **2.** A fixed amount of a product or commodity that may be imported into or exported from a country as laid down by a government in an attempt to control the market in that product or commodity.  **3.** A fixed amount of funds allocated by the *International Monetary Fund to its participating member countries.

**quota share reinsurance treaty**  See proportional treaty.

**quotation**  **1.** The representation of a security on a recognized *stock exchange (see listed company). A quotation allows the shares of a company to be traded on the stock exchange and enables the company to raise new capital if it needs to do so (see flotation; listing requirements; rights issue).  **2.** An indication of the price at which a seller might be willing to offer goods for sale. A quotation does not, however, have the status of a firm *offer.  **3.** A *quoted price.

**quoted company**  See listed company.

**quoted price**  The official price of a security or commodity. On the London Stock Exchange, quoted prices are given daily in the *Official List. Quoted prices of commodities are given by the relevant markets and recorded in the financial press.

**quote driven**  Denoting an electronic stock-exchange system in which prices are determined by the quotations made by *market makers or dealers. The London Stock Exchange and the US *National Association of Securities Dealers Automated Quotation System use quote-driven arrangements. Compare order driven.

**raider** An individual or organization that specializes in exploiting companies with undervalued assets by initiating hostile *takeover bids.

**rally** A rise in prices in a market, such as a stock exchange or commodity market, after a fall. This is usually brought about by a change of sentiment. However, if the change has occurred because there are more buyers than sellers, it is known as a **technical rally**. For example, unfavourable sentiment might cause a market to fall, in turn causing sellers to withdraw at the lower prices. The market will then be sensitive to the presence of very few buyers, who, if they show their hand, may bring about a technical rally.

**ramping** The practice of trying to boost the image of a security and the company behind it by buying the securities in the market with the object of raising demand; if the price rises, the ramper may be able to make a quick profit by selling.

**rand** (R) The standard monetary unit of South Africa and Namibia, divided into 100 cents.

**random-walk theory** The theory that share prices move, for whatever reason, without any memory of past movements and that the movements therefore follow no pattern. This theory is used to refute the predictions of *chartists, who do rely on past patterns of movements to predict present and future prices.

**ratchet effect** An irreversible change to an economic variable, such as prices, wages, exchange rates, etc. For example, once a price or wage has been forced up by some temporary economic pressure, it is unlikely to fall back when the pressure is reduced. This rise may be reflected in parallel sympathetic rises throughout the economy, thus fuelling *inflation.

**rate** **1.** To assess the creditworthiness of an individual or organization. *See* credit rating; rating agency. **2.** *See* rates. **3.** *See* interest rate.

**rateable value** *See* rates.

**rate anticipation swap** An *interest-rate swap in which the swap is related to predicted interest-rate changes. *See also* swap.

**rate capping** *See* rates.

**rate of exchange (exchange rate)** The price of one currency in terms of another. It is usually expressed in terms of how many units of the home country's currency are needed to buy one unit of the foreign currency. However, in some cases, notably in the UK, it is expressed as the number of units of foreign currency that one unit of the home currency will buy. Two rates are usually given, the buying and selling rate; the difference is the profit or commission charged by the organization carrying out the exchange.

**rate of interest**  *See* interest rate.

**rate of return**  The annual amount of income from an investment, expressed as a percentage of the original investment. This rate is very important in assessing the relative merits of different investments. It is therefore important to note whether a quoted rate is before or after tax, since with most investments, the after-tax rate of return is most relevant. Also, because some rates are payable more frequently than annually, it may be important, in order to make true comparisons, to consider the annual percentage rate (APR), which most investment institutions are required to state by law.

**rate of turnover**  The frequency, expressed in annual terms, with which some part of the assets of an organization is turned over. The total sales revenue is often referred to as *turnover and in order to see how frequently stock is turned over, the sales revenue (or if a more accurate estimate is needed the cost of goods sold) is divided by the average value of the stock to give the number of times the stock is turned over. This provides a reasonable measure in terms of stock. However, some accountants divide the sales figure by the value of the fixed assets to arrive at turnover of fixed assets. This is less realistic, although it does express the relationship of sales to the fixed assets of the organization, which in some organizations could be significant.

**rates**  A local-authority tax calculated as a poundage on the rateable value of property in the area of the rating authority. The **poundage** is fixed annually by the rating authority as the number of pence that must be paid for each pound of rateable value. Under the Rates Act 1984, the Secretary of State for the Environment is empowered to limit the rates a local council can charge ratepayers (a process known as **rate capping**). The **rateable value** (or **net annual rentable value**) is determined by the Board of Inland Revenue for each property by deducting, from the rack rent that the property would earn, certain allowable costs. Domestic rates were replaced in the UK by the community charge (*see* poll tax), which, in turn, was replaced by the *council tax.

**rate support grant**  Central government funding in the UK of local government authorities to supplement income from local taxes. The grant helps local authorities to maintain services and taxes at levels comparable to other authorities.

**rating agency**  An agency that assesses the creditworthiness of organizations that issue securities, bonds, etc. *See* credit rating.

**reaction**  A reversal in a market trend as a result of overselling on a falling market (when some buyers are attracted by the low prices) or overbuying on a rising market (when some buyers are willing to take profits).

**realignment**  The process that occurs in the *European Monetary System when one or more currencies devalue. The exchange rate of each European currency is determined by the Exchange Rate Mechanism, which allows it to fluctuate between narrow fixed limits. In 1992, the Italian, British, and Spanish governments were unable to support their currencies above their floor values and they had to be allowed to float. This involved a realignment of these currencies against the other European currencies, i.e. they were devalued, with a view to re-entering the EMS at lower levels. Later in the year Portugal devalued.

**real interest rate** The actual interest rate less the current rate of inflation. For example, if a building society is paying 5% interest and the rate of inflation is 3%, the real growth of a deposit held for a year in the building society is 2% – this is the real rate of interest. Real interest rates are used to calculate more accurate pre-tax returns on investment, i.e. by discounting inflation.

**real investment** Investment in capital equipment, such as a factory, plant and machinery, etc., or valuable social assets, such as a school, a dam, etc., rather than in such paper assets as securities, debentures, etc.

**realizable asset** *See* liquid assets.

**realization account** An *account used to record the disposal of an asset or assets and to determine the profit or loss on the disposal. The principle of realization accounts are that they are debited with the book value of the asset and credited with the sale price of the asset. Any balance therefore represents the profit or loss on disposal.

**realized profit (or loss)** A profit (or loss) that has arisen from a completed transaction (usually the sale of goods or services or other assets). In accounting terms, a profit is normally regarded as having been realized when an asset has been legally disposed of and not when the cash is received, since if an asset is sold on credit the asset being disposed of is exchanged for another asset, a debtor. The debt may or may not prove good but that is regarded as a separate transaction.

**real property (realty)** Any property consisting of land or buildings as distinct from *personal property (personalty).

**real terms** A representation of the value of a good or service in terms of money, taking into account fluctuations in the price level. Economists are usually interested in the relationship between the prices of goods in real terms, i.e. by adjusting prices according to a price index or some other measure of inflation.

**real-time operation** A computer operation in which time is significant. Either it is essential that the computer coordinates its activities with external events (e.g. in the control of industrial processes) or any delay in response should be minimal (e.g. in such point of sale terminals as airline reservation systems).

**realtor** The US name for an estate agent or land agent.

**realty** *See* real property.

**real value** A monetary value expressed in *real terms.

**rebate 1.** A discount offered on the price of a good or service, often one that is paid back to the payer, e.g. a tax rebate is a refund to the taxpayer. **2.** A discount allowed on a *bill of exchange that is paid before it matures.

**receivables** Sums of money due to a business from persons or businesses to whom it has supplied goods or services in the normal course of trade.

**receiver** A person exercising any form of *receivership. In *bankruptcy, the *official receiver becomes receiver and manager of the bankrupt's estate. Where there is a *floating charge over the whole of a company's property and a crystallizing event has occurred, an **administrative receiver** may be appointed to manage the whole of the company's business. The administrative receiver will have wide powers under the Insolvency Act to carry on the business of the company, take possession of its property, commence *liquidation, etc. A receiver appointed in respect of a *fixed charge can deal with the property covered by the charge only, and has no power to manage the company's business.

**receivership** A situation in which a lender holds a mortgage or charge (especially a *floating charge) over a company's property and, in consequence of a default by the company, a receiver is appointed to realize the assets charged in order to repay the debt.

**receiving order** Formerly, an order made during the course of bankruptcy or insolvency. It is now called a bankruptcy order (*see* bankruptcy).

**recession** A slowdown or fall in the rate of growth of *gross national product. A severe recession is called a **depression**. Economic growth usually follows a cycle from boom to recession and back again (known as the business cycle). Recession is associated with falling levels of *investment, rising unemployment, and sometimes falling prices.

**reciprocity** A form of negotiation in which one party agrees to make a concession in return for a reciprocal, or broadly equivalent, action by the other. Most international economic negotiations take this form. For example, agreements to lower protectionist barriers over markets are nearly always made on a reciprocal basis. Economists often argue that this is inefficient, since unilateral action is frequently beneficial by itself.

**Recognized Investment Exchange (RIE)** A body authorized in the UK under the Financial Services Act 1986 to conduct investment management activities on behalf of clients, with the approval of the *Securities and Investment Board; the *London Stock Exchange, *London FOX, and *London International Financial Futures and Options Exchange (LIFFE) are RIEs.

**Recognized Professional Body (RPB)** An organization registered with the *Securities and Investment Board as having statutory recognition for regulating their professions; the RPBs are the Chartered Association of Certified Accountants (ACCA), Institute of Actuaries, Institute of Chartered Accountants in England and Wales, Institute of Chartered Accountants in Ireland, Institute of Chartered Accountants for Scotland, the Insurance Brokers Registration Council (IBRC), the Law Society, the Law Society of Northern Ireland, and the Law Society of Scotland.

**recourse** *See* without recourse.

**recourse agreement** An agreement between a hire-purchase company and a retailer, in which the retailer undertakes to repossess the goods if the buyer fails to pay the regular instalments.

**recovery stock** A share that has fallen in price but is believed to have the potential of climbing back to its original level.

**redeemable gilts** *See* gilt-edged security.

**redeemable preference share** A *preference share that a company reserves the right to redeem, either out of profits or out of the proceeds of a further issue of shares. It may or may not have a fixed redemption date.

**redeemable trust certificate** *See* unit trust.

**redemption** The repayment at maturity of a *bond (*see also* gilt-edged security) or other document certifying a loan by the borrower to the lender (or whoever owns the bond at that date). Thus the **redemption date** specifies when repayment takes place and is usually printed on the bond certificate itself.

**redemption date** *See* redemption.

**redemption yield** *See* yield.

**red herring** A colloquial name in the USA for a *pathfinder prospectus.

**rediscounting** The discounting of a *bill of exchange or *promissory note that has already been discounted by someone else, usually by a *discount house. A *central bank, acting as *lender of last resort, may be said to be rediscounting securities submitted to it by brokers in the money market, as the securities will have already been discounted in the market. In some cases the US *Federal Reserve Bank will rediscount a financial instrument that has already been discounted by a local bank.

**reducing-balance depreciation** *See* depreciation.

**redundancy payment** A payment made to an employee who has been made redundant. The Employment Protection (Consolidation) Act 1978 requires employers to make redundancy payment to all employees dismissed because of redundancy.

**referee** **1.** A person who will, if asked, provide a **reference** for an applicant for a job. An approach to a referee can be in writing or by telephone and the referee should be given a brief job description of the job the applicant is trying to secure. **2.** A person appointed by two arbitrators who cannot agree on the award to be made in a dispute to be settled by arbitration. The procedure for appointing a referee in these circumstances is usually laid down in the terms of arbitration. **3.** A person or organization named on some *bills of exchange as a **referee** (or **reference**) **in case of need**. If the bill is dishonoured its holder may take it to the referee for payment.

**refer to drawer** Words written on a cheque that is being dishonoured by a bank, usually because the account of the person who drew it has insufficient funds to cover it and the manager of the bank is unwilling to allow the account to be overdrawn or further overdrawn. Other reasons for referring to the drawer are that the drawer has been made bankrupt, that there is a garnishee order against the drawer, that the drawer has stopped it, or that something in the cheque itself is incorrect (e.g. it is wrongly dated, words and figures don't agree, etc.). The words 'please re-present' may often be added, indicating that the bank may honour the cheque at a second attempt.

**refinance bill** *See* third-country acceptance.

**refinance credit** A credit facility enabling a foreign buyer to obtain credit for a purchase when the exporter does not wish to provide it. The buyer opens a credit at a branch or agent of his or her bank in the exporting country, the exporter being paid by sight draft on the buyer's credit. The bank in the exporting country accepts a *bill of exchange drawn on the buyer, which is discounted and the proceeds sent to the bank issuing the credit. The buyer only has to pay when the bill on the bank in the exporting country matures.

**refinancing**  The process of repaying some or all of the loan capital of a firm by obtaining fresh loans, usually at a lower rate of interest.

**reflation**  A policy aimed at expanding the level of output of the economy by government stimulus, either by *fiscal or *monetary policy. This could involve increasing the money supply and government expenditure on investment, public works, subsidies, etc., or reducing taxation and interest rates. Usually advocated in times of increasing unemployment, this policy is favoured by Keynesian economists. Monetarists argue that reflation can only lead to *inflation.

**refugee capital**  *Hot money belonging to a foreign government, company, or individual that is invested in the country offering the highest interest rate, usually on a short-term basis.

**regional bank  1.** A US bank that operates in one state or several states but in a limited geographical region. Bank holding companies of significant size with subsidiary banks in separate US states covering a wider region are often known as **super-regional banks**. **2.** A local Japanese bank.

**regional stock exchanges**  Stock exchanges established in regional financial centres, whose importance varies with the importance of the main market of the country. Founded in the formative years of capitalism to raise money for local projects, many have succumbed to the *globalization of the markets. However, some, especially in the USA, Japan, and Germany, have survived. In the UK subsidiary exchanges exist in Birmingham, Bristol, Leeds, Manchester, Glasgow, and Belfast; all of these were originally independent but are now branch offices of the *London Stock Exchange. None still have trading floors (the last to close was Birmingham in 1989).

**registered capital**  *See* share capital.

**registered company**  A company incorporated in the UK by the Registrar of Companies in accordance with the Companies Act. It may be a public limited company or a private limited or unlimited company.

**registered name**  The name in which a UK company is registered. The name, without which a company cannot be incorporated, will be stated in the memorandum of association. Some names are prohibited by law and will not be registered; these include names already registered and names that in the opinion of the Secretary of State for Trade and Industry are offensive. The name may be changed by special resolution of the company and the Secretary of State may order a company to change a misleading name. The name must be displayed at each place of business, on stationery, and on bills of exchange, etc., or the company and its officers will be liable to a fine.

**registered office**  The official address of a UK company, to which all correspondence can be sent. Any change must be notified to the Registrar of Companies within 14 days and published in the *London Gazette*. Statutory registers are kept at the registered office, the address of which must be disclosed on stationery and in the company's annual return.

**registered stock**  *See* inscribed stock.

**register of charges** **1.** The register maintained by the Registrar of Companies on which certain charges must be registered by companies. A charge is created when a company gives a creditor the right to recover a debt from specific assets. The types of charge that must be registered in this way, and the details that must be given, are set out in the Companies Act 1985. Failure to register the charge within 21 days of its creation renders it void, so that it cannot be enforced against a liquidator or creditor of the company. The underlying debt remains valid, however, but ranks only as an unsecured debt. **2.** A list of charges that a company must maintain at its registered address or principal place of business. Failure to do so may render the directors and company officers liable to a fine. This register must be available for inspection by other persons during normal business hours.

**register of companies** *See* company; registered company; Registrar of Companies.

**register of debenture-holders** A list of the holders of *debentures in a UK company. There is no legal requirement for such a register to be kept but if one exists it must be kept at the company's registered office or at a place notified to the Registrar of Companies. It must be available for inspection, to debenture-holders and shareholders free of charge and to the public for a small fee.

**register of members** A list of the *members of a company, which all UK companies must keep at their *registered office or where the register is made up, provided that this address is notified to the Registrar of Companies. It contains the names and addresses of the members, the dates on which they were registered as members, and the dates on which any ceased to be members. If the company has a share capital, the register must state the number and class of the shares held by each member and the amount paid for the shares. As legal, rather than beneficial, ownership is registered, it is not always possible to discover from the register who controls the shares. The register must be available for inspection by members free of charge for at least two normal office hours per working day. Others may inspect it on payment of a small fee. The register may be rectified by the court if it is incorrect.

**registrar** The appointed agent of a company whose task is to keep a register of share and stock holders of that company. The functions of registrar are often performed by a subsidiary company of a bank.

**Registrar of Companies** An official charged with the duty of registering all the companies in the UK. There is one registrar for England and Wales and one for Scotland. The registrar is responsible for carrying out a wide variety of administrative duties connected with registered companies, including maintaining the **register of companies** and the *register of charges, issuing certificates of incorporation, and receiving annual returns.

**registration fee** A small fee charged by a company whose shares are quoted on a stock exchange when it is requested to register the name of a new owner of shares.

**regressive tax** A tax in which the rate of tax decreases as income increases. Indirect taxes fall into this category. Regressive taxes are said to fall more heavily on the poor than on the rich; for example, the poor spend a higher proportion of their incomes on VAT than the rich. A *proportional tax may also be regressive; because of the theory of the marginal utility of money (i.e. the next pound is of more value to the poor than to the rich), it is thought that a flat rate of tax bears unfairly on the poor.

**regulated company**  *See* company.

**regulation**  The imposition by a government of controls over the decisions of individuals or firms. Usually it refers to the control of industries in which there is monopoly or oligopoly, in order to prevent firms from exploiting their market power at the expense of the public. Regulation may be seen as an alternative to *nationalization. For example, the types of industries that have formerly been nationalized in the UK have usually been regulated in the USA. The main vehicle for regulation in the UK has been the *Monopolies and Mergers Commission. *See also* deregulation.

**reinstatement of the sum insured**  The payment of an additional premium to return the sum insured to its full level, after a claim has reduced it. Insurance policies are, in effect, a promise to pay money if a particular event occurs. If a claim is paid, the insurance is reduced by the claim amount (or if a total loss is paid, the policy is exhausted). If the policyholder wishes to return the cover to its full value, a premium representing the amount of cover used by the claim must be paid. In the case of a total loss the whole premium must be paid again.

**reinsurance**  The passing of all or part of an insurance risk that has been covered by an insurer to another insurer in return for a premium. The contract between the parties is usually known as a **reinsurance treaty**. The policyholder is usually not aware that reinsurance has been arranged as no mention is made of it on the policy. Reinsurance is a similar process to the bookmaker's practice of laying off bets with other bookmakers when too much money is placed on a particular horse. Very often an insurer will only accept a risk with a high payout if a total loss occurs (e.g. for a jumbo jet) in the sure knowledge that the potential loss can be reduced by reinsurance. *See also* facultative reinsurance.

**reintermediation**  *See* disintermediation.

**related party**  An individual, partnership, or company that has the ability to control, or exercise significant influence over, another organization.

**remitting bank**  The bank to which a person requiring payment of a cheque or other financial document has presented the cheque or other document for payment. In the UK this is often known as the **collecting bank**.

**remuneration**  **1.** A sum of money paid for a service given. *See* auditor (for **auditors' remuneration**). **2.** A salary.

**renounceable documents**  Documents that provide evidence of ownership, for a limited period, of unregistered shares. A letter of *allotment sent to shareholders when a new issue is floated is an example. Ownership of the shares can be passed to someone else by *renunciation at this stage.

**rentes**  Non-redeemable government bonds issued by several European governments, notably France. The interest, which is paid annually, for ever, is called **rente**.

**rentier**  A person who lives on income from *rentes or on receiving rent from land. The meaning is sometimes extended to include anyone who lives on income derived from assets rather than a wage or salary.

**renting back**  *See* lease-back.

**renunciation**  **1.** The surrender to someone else of rights to shares in a rights issue. The person to whom the shares are allotted by letter of *allotment fills in the **renunciation form** (usually attached) in favour of the person to whom the rights are renounced.  **2.** The disposal of a unit-trust holding by completing the renunciation form on the reverse of the certificate and sending it to the trust managers.

**reorganization**  **1.** The process of restructuring a US company that is in financial difficulties. Protection against creditors can be sought under *Chapter 11 of the Bankruptcy Code while such a reorganization back to profitability is being undertaken. If creditors cannot agree on a plan, the company's assets are liquidated and the proceeds distributed by the Bankruptcy Court.  **2.** The restructuring of a larger organization without the formation of a new company.

**repatriation**  **1.** The return of a person to his or her country of origin.  **2.** The return of capital from a foreign investment to investment in the country from which it originally came. Exchange controls may limit an individual's ability to transfer funds in this way.

**repayment mortgage**  A *mortgage in which the borrower's regular payments consist of both capital repayments and interest.

**repayment supplement**  A tax-free payment of interest by the UK Inland Revenue on delayed income tax or capital-gains tax refunds. The general rule is that the interest runs from one year after the end of the tax year in which the overpayment arose or the end of the tax year in which it was paid, whichever is the later.

**replacement cost**  The price at which the assets of an organization could be replaced, broadly in their existing state. The significance of the replacement cost is in *current-cost accounting; instead of valuing assets at their historical cost, less depreciation where appropriate, assets are valued at their current cost, which in most cases is taken to be the replacement cost.

**repo**  Short for repurchase agreement. *See* repurchase.

**reporting accountants**  A firm of accountants who report on the financial information provided in a *prospectus. They may or may not be the company's own auditors. It is usual for reporting accountants to have had previous experience of new issues and the preparation of prospectuses.

**reporting dealer**  A dealer with whom the US *Federal Reserve Bank does daily business in buying or selling government securities in *open-market operations. There are about 40 such dealers in New York. A reporting dealer is also known as a **primary dealer**.

**report of the auditor(s)**  *See* auditors' report.

**repossession**  The taking back of something purchased, for nonpayment of the instalments due under a *hire-purchase agreement. Foreclosing a mortgage on a house is sometimes also referred to as repossessing the house (*see* foreclosure).

**representations**  Information given by a person wishing to arrange insurance about the nature of the risk that is to be covered. If it contains a material fact it must be true to the best knowledge and belief of the person wishing to be insured. *See* utmost good faith.

**repurchase 1.** The purchase from an investor of a unit-trust holding by the trust managers. **2. (repurchase agreement** or **repo**) An agreement (in full a **sale–repurchase agreement**) in which a security is sold and later bought back at an agreed price. The seller is paid in full and makes the agreement to raise ready money without losing the holding. The buyer negotiates a suitable repurchase price to enable a profit to be earned equivalent to interest on the money involved. Repurchase agreements originated in arrangements between the US *Federal Reserve Bank and the *money market, but are now widely used by large companies in the USA and also in Europe. Repos may have a term of only a few days – or even overnight. *See also* overnight repo; retail repo.

**required reserves** The amounts that US banks are obliged to hold against their liabilities. It is a specified proportion of the deposits and other liabilities.

**rescission** The right of a party to a contract to have it set aside and to be restored to the position he or she was in before the contract was made. This is an equitable remedy, available at the discretion of the court. The usual grounds for rescission are mistake, misrepresentation, undue influence, and unconscionable bargains (i.e. those in which the terms are very unfair). No rescission will be allowed where the party seeking it has taken a benefit under the contract (affirmation), or where it is not possible to restore the parties to their former position (restitutio in integrum), or where third parties have already acquired rights under the contract.

**reserve** Part of the *capital of a company, other than the share capital, largely arising from retained profit or from the issue of share capital at more than its nominal value. Reserves are distinguished from *provisions in that for the latter there is a known diminution in value of an asset or a known liability, whereas reserves are surpluses not yet distributed and, in some cases (e.g. share premium account or capital redemption reserve), not distributable. The directors of a company may choose to earmark part of these funds for a special purpose (e.g. a **reserve for obsolescence** of plant). However, reserves should not be seen as specific sums of money put aside for special purposes as they are represented by the general net assets of the company. Reserves are subdivided into *retained earnings (revenue reserves), which are available to be distributed to the shareholders by way of dividends, and *capital reserves, which for various reasons are not distributable as dividends, although they may be converted into permanent share capital by way of a bonus issue.

**reserve asset ratio** A former requirement that UK banks had to keep reserves in proportion to their total assets. Abandoned in 1981, it was used in the previous decade as a crude means of monetary control. A similar ratio is still enforced in the USA, while UK banks are now required to hold a specified average of their liquid assets.

**reserve assets** Money held at banks but not required or committed to outstanding loans, and therefore available to cover shortfalls of cash. In the USA it is money held by the US banks with the *Federal Reserve System.

**Reserve Bank** *See* Federal Reserve Bank.

**reserve capital (uncalled capital)** That part of the issued *capital of a company that is held in reserve and is intended only to be called up if the company is wound up.

**reserve currency** A foreign currency that is held by a government because it has confidence in its stability and intends to use it to settle international debts. The US dollar and the pound sterling fulfilled this role for many years but the Japanese yen and the Deutschmark are now preferred by most governments.

**reserve for obsolescence** *See* reserve.

**reserve price** The price below which a seller is not prepared to sell, especially at an auction.

**reserve requirement** The *cash ratio of a bank: the percentage of its assets that must be held in cash; in the USA this is usually 12.5%.

**reserves** **1.** In the UK, the amount of gold and convertible currencies held at the *Bank of England, together with credits at the *International Monetary Fund. **2.** In other countries, similar assets held by a government-controlled *central bank. **3.** *See* reserve.

**reserves market** The dealings of the *Federal Open Market Committee with other US banks.

**reserves multiplier** The method used in the US *Federal Reserve System to calculate the level of deposits to be held by banks.

**reserve tranche** The 25% of its quota to which a member of the *International Monetary Fund has unconditional access, for which it pays no charges, and for which there is no obligation to repay the funds. The reserve tranche corresponds to the 25% of quota that was paid not in the member's domestic currency but in *Special Drawing Rights (SDRs) or currencies of other IMF members. It counts as part of the member's foreign reserves. As before 1978 it was paid in gold, it was known as the **gold tranche**. Like all IMF facilities it is available only to avert balance of payments problems, although for the reserve tranche the IMF has no power either to challenge the member's assessment of need or to impose a corrective policy. Further funds are available through credit tranches but these are subject to certain conditions (*see* conditionality). Use of the reserve tranche was heaviest in the 1970s, when members needed it to gain access to the IMF's Oil Facilities (1974–76) and the USA made a record level of reserve-tranche purchases (1978).

**residence** The country in which an individual resides for tax purposes. Under UK tax legislation residence is decided for each tax year. In determining the residential status of a person in any one year the factors taken into account include:
(i) the amount of time spent in the UK;
(ii) the previous residential status of the individual;
(iii) the lengths of visits and their nature in earlier years and, in some cases, those anticipated in following years;
(iv) the availability of accommodation in the UK.
The UK also has the concept 'ordinary resident', which denotes a habitual residence and requires examination of the individual's pattern of life over a number of years. It is also possible for an individual to be resident for tax purposes in more than one country in any one year.

**residuary legatee** A person to whom a testator's estate is left, after specific bequests have been satisfied. If a will leaves £3000 to A, £10,000 to B, and the rest of the estate to C, then C is the residuary legatee.

**resolution** A binding decision made by the members of a company. If a motion is put before the members of a company at a general meeting and the required majority vote in favour of it, the motion is passed and becomes a resolution. A resolution may also be passed by unanimous informal consent of the members. An **ordinary resolution** may be passed by a bare majority of the members. The Companies Act prescribes this type of resolution for certain actions, such as the removal of a director. Normally, no particular length of notice is required for an ordinary resolution to be proposed, beyond the notice needed to call the meeting. However, ordinary resolutions of the company require **special notice** if a director or an auditor is to be removed or if a director who is over the statutory retirement age is to be appointed or permitted to remain in office. In these circumstances 28 days' notice must be given to the company and the company must give 21 days' notice to the members. An **extraordinary resolution** is one for which 14 days' notice is required. The notice should state that it is an extraordinary resolution and for such a resolution 75% of those voting must approve it if it is to be passed. A **special resolution** requires 21 days' notice to the shareholders and a 75% majority to be effective. The type of resolution required to make a particular decision may be prescribed by the Companies Acts or by the company's articles. For example, an extraordinary resolution is required to wind up a company voluntarily, while a special resolution is required to change the company's articles of association.

**respondentia bond** *See* hypothecation.

**restitution** The legal principle that a person who has been unjustly enriched at the expense of another should make restitution, e.g. by returning property or money. This principle is not yet fully developed in English law but has a predominant place in the law of Scotland and the USA.

**restrictive endorsement** An endorsement on a *bill of exchange that restricts the freedom of the endorsee to negotiate it.

**retail banking** Mass-market banking in which personal and domestic customers use local branches of the *commercial banks. It typically offers a wide range of such services as personal loans, mortgages, pensions, and insurance as well as providing *current accounts and savings accounts. Cash cards and credit cards are also provided. In most nationwide banking systems it is still the most profitable part of a bank's activities.

**Retail Price Index (RPI)** An index of the prices of goods and services in retail shops purchased by average households, expressed in percentage terms relative to a base year, which is taken as 100. For example, if 1987 is taken as the base year for the UK (i.e. average prices in 1987 = 100), then in 1946 the RPI stood at 7.4, and in 1990 at 126.1. The RPI is published by the Central Statistical Office on a monthly basis and includes the prices of some 130 000 different commodities. The RPI is one of the standard measures of the rate of *inflation. In the USA and some other countries the RPI is known as the **consumer price index**. *See also* GDP deflator; producer price index; tax and price index.

**retail repo** A *repurchase agreement involving a loan to a bank rather than to a company or an individual.

**retained earnings (retentions)**  Profits earned to date but not yet distributed to shareholders by way of dividends. Such earnings are also called revenue reserves (*see* reserve) and form an important part of the *capital of most companies.

**retained profits (ploughed-back profits)**  The part of the annual profits of an organization that are not distributed to its owners but are invested in the assets of the organization. Retained profits are normally the means that enable organizations to grow; it is usually easier to retain profits than to raise new capital.

**retirement pension**  *See* pension.

**retirement relief**  A relief from *capital-gains tax given to persons disposing of business assets or shares in trading companies in which they are full-time working directors. To be eligible a person must be 60 years of age or over or have retired due to ill-health.

**retiring a bill**  The act of withdrawing a *bill of exchange from circulation when it has been paid on or before its due date.

**return**  The income from an investment, frequently expressed as a percentage of its cost. *See also* return on capital employed.

**returned cheque**  A cheque on which payment has been refused and which has been returned to the bank on which it was drawn. If the reason is lack of funds, the bank will mark it *refer to drawer; if the bank wishes to give the customer an opportunity to pay in sufficient funds to cover it, they will also mark it 'please re-present'. The collecting bank will then present it for payment again, after letting the customer know that the cheque has been dishonoured.

**return on capital employed (ROCE; return on imputed capital)**  The profits of an organization expressed as a percentage of the *capital employed. This is an important indicator of the efficiency with which the assets of the organization are used; it provides a useful comparison of companies in the same industry or, for the investor, a comparison between various industrial sectors. However, it is important to know what is meant by capital. Frequently, return on capital is calculated by comparing the profits with the *book value of the net assets. This tends to undervalue the assets, so that a capital figure based on market value would be more helpful, although not as readily obtainable. It is also important to know whether the profit given is before or after tax and whether or not adequate provision has been made for any bad debts. *See also* return on equity.

**return on equity (ROE)**  The net income of an organization expressed as a percentage of its equity capital.

**Reuters**  A worldwide agency dealing in news, financial information, and trading services. It was founded in 1851 as a subscription information service for newspapers. It now provides a wide range of financial prices.

**revalorization of currency**  The replacement of one currency unit by another. A government often takes this step if a nation's currency has been devalued frequently or by a large amount. *Compare* revaluation of currency.

**revaluation of assets**  A revaluation of the assets of a company, either because they have increased in value since they were acquired or because *inflation has made the balance-sheet values unrealistic. The Companies Act 1985 makes it obligatory for the directors of a company to state in the directors' report if they believe the value of land differs materially from the value in the balance sheet. The Companies Act 1980 lays down the procedures to adopt when fixed assets are revalued. The difference between the net book value of a company's assets before and after revaluation is shown in a **revaluation reserve account** or, more commonly in the USA, an **appraisal-surplus account** (if the value of the assets has increased).

**revaluation of currency** An increase in the value of a currency in terms of gold or other currencies. It is usually made by a government that has a persistent balance of payments surplus. It has the effect of making imports cheaper but exports become dearer and therefore less competitive in other countries; revaluation is therefore unpopular with governments. *Compare* devaluation; revalorization of currency.

**revaluation reserve account** *See* revaluation of assets.

**revenue account** **1.** An *account recording the income from trading operations or the expenses incurred in these operations. **2.** A budgeted amount that can be spent for day-to-day operational expenses, especially in public-sector budgeting. *Compare* capital account.

**reverse takeover** **1.** The buying of a larger company by a smaller company. **2.** The purchasing of a public company by a private company. This may be the cheapest way that a private company can obtain a listing on a stock exchange, as it avoids the expenses of a *flotation and it may be that the assets of the public company can be purchased at a discount. However, on the *London Stock Exchange there are regulations stipulating that the nature of the target company's business must be compatible with that of the private company. Usually the name of the public company is changed to that of the private company, who takes over the listing.

**reverse yield gap** *See* yield gap.

**reversionary annuity** *See* contingent annuity.

**reversionary bonus** A sum added to the amount payable on death or maturity of a *with-profits policy for life assurance. The bonus is added if the life-assurance company has a surplus or has a profit on the investment of its life funds. Once a reversionary bonus has been declared it cannot be withdrawn if the policy runs to maturity or to the death of the insured. However, if the policy is cashed, the bonus is usually reduced by an amount that depends on the length of time the policy has to run.

**revocable letter of credit** *See* letter of credit.

**revolving credit** A bank credit that is negotiated for a specified period; it allows for *drawdown and repayment within that period. Repaid amounts can be redrawn up to the agreed limit of the credit. At the end of the loan period there is a *bullet repayment of the principal and any outstanding interest; alternatively, a repayment schedule is negotiated for the outstanding principal and interest. In the USA a revolving credit is called an **open-end credit**. *See also* convertible revolving credit.

**rial** **1.** (Rls) The standard monetary unit of Iran, divided into 100 dinars. **2.** (RO) The standard monetary unit of Oman, divided into 1000 baizas.

**RIE** Abbreviation for *Recognized Investment Exchange.

**riel** The standard monetary unit of Cambodia, divided into 100 sen.

**rigging a market** An attempt to make a profit on a market, usually a security or commodity market, by overriding the normal market forces. This often involves taking a *long position or a *short position in the market that is sufficiently substantial to influence price levels, and then supporting or depressing the market by further purchases or sales.

**rights issue** A method by which quoted companies on a stock exchange raise new capital, in exchange for new shares. The name arises from the principle of *pre-emption rights, according to which existing shareholders must be offered the new shares in proportion to their holding of old shares (a **rights offer**). For example in a 1 for 4 rights issue, shareholders would be asked to buy one new share for every four they already hold. As rights are usually issued at a discount to the market price of existing shares, those not wishing to take up their rights can sell them in the market (*see* rights letter; renunciation). *See also* excess shares. *Compare* bought deal; vendor placing; scrip issue.

**rights letter** A document sent to an existing shareholder of a company offering shares in a *rights issue on advantageous terms. If the recipient does not wish to take advantage of the offer, the letter and the attendant rights may be sold on a stock exchange (*see* renunciation).

**rights offer** *See* rights issue.

**Riksbanken** Sweden's *central bank.

**ringgit** (M$) The Malaysian dollar: the standard monetary unit of Malaysia, divided into 100 sen.

**ring trading** *See* callover.

**risk** **1.** The possibility of suffering some form of loss or damage (*see also* peril). If it is one that can be described sufficiently accurately for a calculation to be made of the probability of it happening, on the basis of past records, it is called an **insurable risk**. Fire, theft, accident, etc., are all insurable risks because underwriters can assess the probability of having to pay out a claim and can therefore calculate a reasonable *premium. If the risk is met so infrequently that no way of calculating the probability of the event exists, no underwriter will insure against it and it is therefore an **uninsurable risk** (*see also* actuary). **2.** The possibility of suffering a loss in trading. The **credit risk** is the risk a trader takes when offering credit or it may involve the risk of a bank withdrawing its credit facilities. A **systematic risk** involves the risk of a failure in a whole system, such as the *clearing-house system in commodity markets. The **delivery risk** involves the danger that a supplier will not deliver goods or services as contracted or will deliver late.

**risk-adjusted assets** The assets, shown on the balance sheet of a bank, that have had a risk weighting applied to them. Since 1922 banks have been required to hold *capital adequacy ratios that take account of the different weights of risk attached to loans, foreign exchange, government securities, cross-border loans, and mortgages. The system also takes account of assets that are held off the balance sheet, such as letters of credit, interest-rate swaps, and currency options, which also have to have risk weightings applied to them. Major changes were brought about in 1992 through the *Bank for International

Settlements; these are likely to affect the calculation and measurement of a bank's capital adequacy position when fully formulated.

**risk capital (venture capital)** Capital invested in a project in which there is a substantial element of risk, especially money invested in a new venture or an expanding business in exchange for shares in the business. It is not a loan.

**risk management** The control of an individual's or company's chances of losing on an investment. Managing the risk can involve taking out insurance against a loss, hedging a loan against interest-rate rises, and protecting an investment against a fall in interest rates (*see* financial futures). A bank will always try to manage the risks involved in lending by adjusting the level of charges and interest rates to compensate for a percentage of losses.

**risk premium (market-risk premium)** The difference between the expected *rate of return on an investment and the risk-free return (e.g. on a government stock) over the same period. If there is any risk element at all, the rate of return would be higher than that if no risk is involved.

**riyal** **1.** (SRIs) The standard monetary unit of Saudi Arabia, divided into 100 halalah. **2.** (QR) The standard monetary unit of Qatar, divided into 100 dirhams. **3.** (YRIs) The standard monetary unit of Yemen, divided into 100 fils.

**ROCE** Abbreviation for *return on capital employed.

**ROE** Abbreviation for *return on equity.

**rolled-up coupon** A certificate of interest (*see* coupon) on a bond or other security, in which the interest is ploughed back to increase the capital value of the original bond, rather than being drawn as cash.

**rolling settlement** The practice on many stock markets of settling a transaction a fixed number of days after the trade is agreed. On the London Stock Exchange, however, the practice is to have two- or three-week accounts for dealings with a fixed day for settlement after the close of the account.

**roll-over CD** A *certificate of deposit in which the maturity is divided into short periods to make it easier to sell on the secondary market. They are sometimes known as **roly-poly CDs**.

**roll-over credit** A medium- or long-term bank loan in which the rate of interest varies with short-term money-market rates (such as LIBOR) because the bank has raised the loan by short-term money-market or *interbank market borrowing.

**roll-over relief** A relief from capital-gains tax allowing tax on the disposal of an asset to be postponed by deducting the capital gain from the base cost of another asset acquired by the person making the original disposal. The effect is that the gain on the disposal of the second asset will be increased because the consideration for the purchase of the asset is treated as artificially reduced by the gain on the earlier asset. This type of relief is available in a variety of transactions in which the person disposing of the asset will not be in funds to pay the tax, e.g. the replacement of business assets and the formation of companies in exchange for shares. *See also* employee share-ownership plan.

**roll-up funds** An offshore investment fund using securities with *rolled-up coupons designed to avoid *income tax. However, these funds are now assessed for income tax as if the coupons were paid in cash.

**roly-poly CD** *See* roll-over CD.

**rotation of directors** Under the articles of association of most UK companies, one third of the directors are obliged to retire each year (normally at the annual general meeting), so that each director retires by rotation every three years. Retiring directors may be re-elected.

**rouble** The standard monetary unit of Russia and all the other former Soviet republics, except Estonia and Ukraine; it is divided into 100 kopeks.

**round lot** A round number of shares or a round amount of stock for which market makers will sometimes offer better prices than for **odd lots**.

**roundtripping** A transaction that enables a company to borrow money from one source and lend it at a profit to another, by taking advantage of a short-term rise in interest rates.

**Royal Mint** The organization in the UK that has had the sole right to manufacture English coins since the 16th century. Controlled by the Chancellor of the Exchequer, it was formerly situated in the City of London but moved to Llantrisant in Wales in 1968. It also makes banknotes, UK medals, and some foreign coins.

**royalty** A payment made for the right to use the property of another person for gain. This may be an *intellectual property, such as a book or an invention (*see* patent). It may also be paid to a landowner, who has granted mineral rights to someone else, on sales of minerals extracted from the land. A royalty is regarded as a wasting asset as copyrights, patents, and mines have limited lives.

**RPB** Abbreviation for *Recognized Professional Body.

**RPI** Abbreviation for *Retail Price Index.

**RUF** Abbreviation for revolving underwriting facility. *See* note issuance facility.

**rufiyaa** (Rf) The standard monetary unit of the Maldives, divided into 100 laari.

**rule against perpetuities** *See* Perpetuities and Accumulations Act 1964.

**running-account credit** A personal credit agreement that enables a person to receive loans from time to time from a bank or other lender provided that a specified credit limit is not exceeded. Interest is charged on the amount loaned during any period.

**running broker** A bill broker who does not himself discount *bills of exchange but acts between bill owners and discount houses or banks for a commission.

**running yield** *See* yield.

**run to settlement** Denoting a *futures contract in a commodity that has run to its settlement day without being set off by a corresponding sales or purchase contract so that delivery of the physical goods must be made or taken.

**rupee** **1.** The standard monetary unit of India (Re, plural Rs), Pakistan (PRs), and Nepal (NRs), divided into 100 paisa. **2.** The standard monetary unit of Sri Lanka (SL Rs), Mauritius (Mau Re; plural Mau Rs), and the Seychelles (SR), divided into 100 cents.

**rupiah** (Rp) The standard monetary unit of Indonesia, divided into 100 sen.

**SA 1.** Abbreviation for *société anonyme*. It appears after the name of a French, Belgian, or Luxembourg company, being equivalent to the British abbreviation plc (i.e. denoting a public limited company). **2.** Abbreviation for *sociedad anónima*. It appears after the name of a Spanish public company. **3.** Abbreviation for *sociedade anónima*. It appears after the name of a Portuguese public company. *Compare* Sarl.

**sacrifice** Loss of welfare as a result of paying a tax. One of the principles of taxation is that a tax should be formulated so that it involves **equality of sacrifice** on the part of the taxpayers. It is assumed that taxpayers with equal incomes will sacrifice equal amounts of welfare by paying identical taxes.

**SAEF** Abbreviation for *Stock Exchange Automatic Execution Facility.

**safe custody** A service offered by most UK commercial banks, in which the bank holds valuable items belonging to its customers in its strong room. These items are usually documents, such as house deeds and bearer bonds, but they may also include jewellery, etc. The bank is a bailee for these items and its liability will depend on whether or not it has charged the customer for the service and the terms of the customer's own insurance (in the case of jewellery, etc.). In a **safe deposit** the customer hires a small lockable box from the bank or safe-deposit company, to which access is provided during normal banking hours. The customer keeps the key to the box.

**saitori** Members of the *Tokyo Stock Exchange who act as intermediaries between brokers. They cannot deal on their own account or for non-members of the exchange; they may only be allowed to deal in a limited number of stocks.

**salaried partner** A partner in a *partnership who by agreement draws a regular salary.

**salary** A regular payment, usually monthly, made by an employer, under a contract of employment, to an employee.

**sale and lease-back** *See* lease-back.

**sale by instalments** *See* hire purchase.

**sale by tender** *See* issue by tender.

**sale–repurchase agreement** *See* repurchase.

**sales tax** A tax based on the selling price of goods. Such taxes are not now generally favoured, since they have a cascade effect, i.e. if goods are sold on from one trader to another the amount of sales tax borne by the ultimate buyer becomes too great. *VAT was largely designed to meet this objection.

**Samurai bond**  A *bond issued in Japan by a foreign institution. It is denominated in yen and can be bought by non-residents of Japan.

**sandbag**  A stalling tactic used by an unwilling target company in a takeover bid. The management of the target company agrees to have talks with the unwelcome bidder, which it protracts for as long as possible in the hope that a *white knight will appear and make a more acceptable bid.

**S&L**  Abbreviation for *savings and loan association.

**S&P 500**  Abbreviation for *Standard and Poor's 500 Stock Index.

**Sanmekai**  The Japanese group of *City Banks that sets short-term interest rates.

**sans recours**  *See* without recourse.

**São Paulo Stock Exchange**  The most important of the ten stock exchanges in Brazil, called the Bolsa de Valores de São Paulo (BOVESPA); together with the older Rio de Janeiro market it accounts for 90% of Brazilian equity trading. The São Paulo Exchange issues the 83-company BOVESPA index. São Paulo is also the home of an early futures market, Bolsa de Mercadorias de São Paulo, set up in 1917 and now noted for gold trading.

**Sarl.**  **1.** Abbreviation for *società a responsabilità limitata*. It appears after the name of an Italian company, being equivalent to the British abbreviation Ltd (i.e. denoting a private limited liability company).  **2.** Abbreviation for *société à responsabilité limitée*. It appears after the name of a French private limited company. *Compare* SA.

**SAS**  Abbreviation for *statement of auditing standards.

**satang**  A Thai monetary unit, worth one hundredth of a *baht.

**save-as-you-earn (SAYE)**  A method of making regular savings (not necessarily linked to earnings), which carries certain tax privileges. This method has been used to encourage tax-free savings in building societies or National Savings and also to encourage employees to acquire shares in their own organizations.

**savings**  Money set aside by individuals, either for some special purpose or to provide an income at some time in the future (often after retirement). Money saved can be placed in a *savings account with a bank or building society, invested in *National Savings, or used to purchase *securities. Savings are also used to buy *pensions, *annuities, and *endowment assurance.

**savings account**  A bank or building-society account designed for the investment of personal savings. There are a wide variety available, offering different terms and conditions and interest rates. The rates tend to be higher than old-fashioned deposit accounts and interest-bearing current accounts. Some accounts offer instant access to funds, while others require that notice be given, typically 30, 60, or 90 days. In general terms, interest rates vary according to the sum invested and the length of the notice period.

**savings and loan association (S&L)**  The US equivalent of a UK *building society. It usually offers loans with a fixed rate of interest and has greater investment flexibility than a UK building society.

**savings bank** A bank that specializes in setting up *savings accounts for relatively small deposits. In the UK the *National Savings Bank and *building societies perform this function. In the USA, *savings and loan associations do so.

**savings bonds** *See* National Savings.

**savings certificate** *See* National Savings.

**savings ratio** The ratio of *savings by individuals and households to *disposable income. Savings are estimated in the *national income accounts by deducting consumers' expenditure from disposable income. Variations in the savings ratio reflect the changing preferences of individuals between present and future consumption. Countries, such as Japan, with very high savings ratios have tended to experience faster growth in GDP than countries, such as the USA, with low savings ratios.

**SAYE** Abbreviation for *save-as-you-earn.

**schedule** **1.** The part of legislation that is placed at the end of a UK Act of Parliament and contains subsidiary matter to the main sections of the Act. **2.** One of several schedules of income tax forming part of the original income-tax legislation, now used to classify various sources of income for tax purposes. Some of the schedules are further subdivided into cases. The broad classification is: Schedule A, rents from property in the UK; Schedule B, income from commercial woodlands; Schedule C, interest paid by public bodies; Schedule D, Case 1, profits from trade; Case II, profits from professions or vocations; Case III, interest not otherwise taxed; Case IV, income from securities outside the UK; Case V, income from possessions outside the UK; Case VI, other annual profits and gains; Schedule E, Cases I, II, and III, emoluments of offices or employments (the cases depending on the residential status of the taxpayer); Schedule F, dividends paid by UK companies. **3.** Working papers submitted with tax returns or tax computations. **4.** Any scale of rates. **5.** A plan for undertaking some enterprise, especially one that details the timing of events.

**scheme of arrangement** *See* arrangement.

**schilling** (S) The standard monetary unit of Austria, divided into 100 groschen.

**SCM** Abbreviation for *smaller companies market.

**scorched earth policy** An extreme form of *poison pill in which a company that believes it is to be the target of a *takeover bid makes its balance sheet or profitability less attractive than it really is by a reversible manoeuvre, such as borrowing money at an exorbitant rate of interest.

**S corporation** *See* sub-chapter S.

**SCOUT** Abbreviation for Shared Currency Option Under Tender, a currency *option especially designed for companies who are tendering for the same overseas job in a foreign currency. To save each of them having to hedge the currency risk separately, SCOUT enables them to share the cost of a single option.

**screen trading** Any form of trading that relies on the use of a computer screen rather than personal contact as in *floor trading, *pit trading, ring trading, etc. On the London Stock Exchange the *Stock Exchange Automatic Execution Facility (SAEF) is an example. *See also* automated screen trading.

**scrip** The certificates that demonstrate ownership of *stocks, *shares, and *bonds (capital raised by sub*scrip*tion), especially the certificates relating to a *scrip issue.

**scrip issue (bonus issue; capitalization issue; free issue)** The issue of new share certificates to existing shareholders to reflect the accumulation of profits in the reserves of a company's balance sheet. It is thus a process for converting money from the company's reserves into issued capital. The shareholders do not pay for the new shares and appear to be no better off. However, in a 1 for 3 scrip issue, say, the shareholders receive one new share for every three existing shares they own. This automatically reduces the price of the shares by 25%, catering to the preference of shareholders to hold lower-priced shares rather than *heavy shares; it also encourages them to hope that the price will gradually climb to its former value, which will, of course, make them 25% better off. In the USA this is known as a **stock split**.

**SDR-linked deposit** A special deposit in a private bank account of *Special Drawing Rights. As SDRs are equivalent to a form of currency (*see* International Monetary Fund) these can be used to pay debts and banked much like other financial instruments.

**SDRs** Abbreviation for *Special Drawing Rights.

**SEAQ** Abbreviation for *Stock Exchange Automated Quotations System.

**SEATS** Abbreviation for *Stock Exchange Alternative Trading Service.

**SEC** Abbreviation for *Securities and Exchange Commission.

**secondary bank** **1.** A name sometimes given to *finance houses. **2.** Any organization that offers some banking services, such as making loans, offering secondary mortgages, etc., but that does not offer the usual commercial-bank services of cheque accounts, etc.

**secondary market** A market in which existing securities are traded, as opposed to a **primary market**, in which securities are sold for the first time. In most cases a *stock exchange largely fulfils the role of a secondary market, with the flotation of *new issues representing only a small proportion of its total business. However, it is the existence of a flourishing secondary market, providing *liquidity and the spreading of *risks, that creates the conditions for a healthy primary market.

**second mortgage** A *mortgage taken out on a property that is already mortgaged. Second and subsequent mortgages can often be used to raise money if the value of the property has increased considerably since the first mortgage was taken out. As the deeds of the property are usually held by the first mortgagee (lender), the second mortgagee undertakes a greater risk and therefore usually demands a higher rate of interest. The second mortgagee usually registers the second mortgage to protect himself against subsequent mortgages. In the UK, the Land Registry will issue a certificate of second charge in the case of registered land.

**second of exchange** *See* bills in a set.

**second-tier market** A market for stocks and shares in which *listing requirements for the companies are less stringent than those on a *main market. Although a second-tier market needs to be effectively regulated, conditions of entry and reporting are less expensive. In the UK the *unlisted-securities market was a second-tier market. *See also* over-the-counter market.

**secret reserve** *See* hidden reserve.

**secured** **1.** Denoting a loan (**secured loan**) in which the lender has an asset to which recourse can be made if the borrower defaults on the loan repayments. **2.** Denoting a creditor (**secured creditor**) who has a charge on the property of the debtor. *See* fixed charge; floating charge.

**secured debenture** A *debenture secured by a charge over the property of a company, such as mortgage debentures (secured on land belonging to the company). Usually a trust deed sets out the powers of the debenture holders to enforce their security in the event of the company defaulting in payment of the principal or the interest. It is usual to appoint a *receiver to realize the security.

**secured liability** A debt against which the borrower has provided sufficient assets as security to safeguard the lender in case of non-repayment.

**Securities and Exchange Commission (SEC)** A US government agency that closely monitors the activities of stockbrokers and traders in securities. It also monitors takeovers in the USA. If a person or organization acquires 5% or more of the equity of another company it must notify the SEC of the purchase within 10 days. *See also* creeping takeover.

**Securities and Futures Authority Ltd (SFA)** The *Self-Regulating Organization formed from the merger of The *Securities Association Ltd (TSA) and the *Association of Futures Brokers and Dealers Ltd (AFBD) in April 1991. It is responsible for regulating the conduct of brokers and dealers in securities, *options, and futures, including most of those on the *London Stock Exchange and the *London International Financial Futures and Options Exchange.

**Securities and Investment Board (SIB)** A regulatory body set up by the Financial Services Act 1986 to oversee London's financial markets (e.g. the stock exchange, life assurance, unit trusts). Each market has its own *Self-Regulating Organization (SRO), which reports to the SIB. The prime function of the SIB is to protect investors from fraud and to ensure that the rules of conduct established by the government and the SROs are followed. However, as the structure of City institutions and their regulation is not fixed for all time, the role of the SIB has to be capable of adapting to changing practices. Moreover, some City activities are outside its control; for example, takeovers remain under the supervision of the Takeover Panel (*see* City Code on Takeovers and Mergers). Members of the SIB are appointed jointly by the Secretary of State for Trade and Industry and the Governor of the Bank of England from leading City institutions; while this understandably leads to suggestions of partisanship, it is doubtful whether outsiders would have sufficient understanding of City practices to be effective as regulators. The SIB is authorized to grant recognition to investment institutions and is financed by the fees paid to achieve this recognition.

**Securities Association Ltd, The (TSA)** The former *Self-Regulating Organization responsible for regulating the conduct of brokers and dealers in securities, options, and futures. It included most member firms of the *London Stock Exchange. In April 1991 it merged with the *Association of Futures Brokers and Dealers Ltd to form the *Securities and Futures Authority Ltd (SFA).

**Securities Exchange of Thailand (SET)**  One of the *dragon markets of the Pacific; its share trading dates from 1962 with the foundation of the Bangkok Stock Exchange. The SET itself was established in 1975 and is regulated by the Thai Ministry of Finance.

**securities house**  A large stockbroker-based financial institution, many of which have grown since the 1980s to provide investors with facilities of all types on a global scale. They encompass the activities of brokers, dealers, market makers, researchers, and traders.

**Securities Industry Automation Corporation (SIAC)**  The US corporation that provides the *National Securities Clearing Corporation with the data-processing and electronic communications facilities required to act as a *clearing house for both New York's stock exchanges.

**Securities Investor Protection Corporation (SIPC)**  A US corporation to which all members of the *National Association of Securities Dealers Inc. belong; its function is to provide compensation for investors who suffer a loss as a result of the activities of a market maker or dealer.

**securitization**  The process that enables borrowing and lending by banks to be replaced by the issue of such securities as *eurobonds. A bank borrows money from savers (investors) and lends to borrowers, charging fees to both for its service as well as making a turn on the interest payments. If a borrower can borrow directly from an investor, by issuing them with a bond (or equity), the costs to both borrower and lender can be reduced. Securitization has occurred increasingly in the 1980s as technology has improved and investors have become more sophisticated.

**securitized mortgage**  A *mortgage that has been converted into a marketable security, which can be sold to an investor. One advantage of selling on mortgages and other loans in this way is that it enables banks to move assets from their balance sheets, thus boosting their *cash ratios. Securitization of mortgages is strictly controlled by the regulating authorities.

**securitized paper**  A financial instrument, such as a bond or note, which results from a borrower and investor agreeing on an exchange of funds by *securitization.

**security**   **1.** An asset or assets to which a lender can have recourse if the borrower defaults on any loan repayments. In the case of loans by banks and other moneylenders the security is sometimes referred to as *collateral.   **2.** A financial asset, including shares, government stocks, debentures, bonds, unit trusts, and rights to money lent or deposited. It does not, however, include insurance policies. *See also* bearer security; dated security; fixed-interest security; gilt-edged security; listed security; marketable security.

**seed capital**  The small amount of initial capital required to fund the research and development necessary before a new company is set up. The seed capital should enable a persuasive and accurate *business plan to be drawn up.

**self-employed taxpayers**  Persons who are not employees and who are in business on their own account. They are taxed on the profits of their business rather than by *PAYE and their national-insurance contributions differ from those of employees.

**Self-Employment Individuals Retirement Act**  *See* Keogh plan.

**self-financing** Denoting a company that is able to finance its capital expenditure from undistributed profits rather than by borrowing.

**self-liquidating** **1.** Denoting an asset that earns back its original cost out of income over a fixed period. **2.** Denoting a loan in which the money is used to finance a project that will provide sufficient yield to repay the loan and its interest and leave a profit. **3.** Denoting a sales-promotion offer that pays for itself. For example, if a seller of tea bags offers a free tea mug in exchange for a specified number of vouchers, each taken from a box of tea bags, the seller expects the extra number of tea-bag boxes sold during the promotion to pay for the costs of buying and despatching the mugs.

**Self-Regulating Organization (SRO)** One of several organizations set up in the UK under the Financial Services Act 1986 to regulate the activities of investment businesses and to draw up and enforce specific codes of conduct. Five SROs were originally recognized by the *Securities and Investment Board, to whom they report, which was reduced to four in 1991 on the merger of The *Securities Association Ltd (TSA) and the *Association of Futures Brokers and Dealers Ltd (AFBD) to form the *Securities and Futures Authority Ltd (SFA). The other three SROs are: the **Financial Intermediaries, Managers and Brokers Regulatory Association Ltd (FIMBRA)**, which regulates organizations marketing and managing securities, unit trusts, and unit-linked life assurance policies, as well as independent financial advisors; the **Life Assurance and Unit Trust Regulatory Organization (LAUTRO)**, which regulates institutions offering life assurance and unit trusts as principals; and the **Investment Managers Regulatory Organization (IMRO)**, which regulates any institution that offers investment management.
  From April 1993 a *Personal Investment Authority (PIA) will regulate the activities of investment business carried out mainly with or for the private investor.

**self-select PEP** *See* personal equity plan.

**self-tender** A *tender offer in which a company approaches its shareholders in order to buy back some or all of its shares. There are two circumstances in which this operation can be of use. One is in the case of a hostile bid: the directors may wish to buy back shares in their company in order to reduce the chances of the bidder being able to buy a controlling interest in the company. The other circumstance is that the board may wish to show increased earnings per share; if they are unable to increase their profits it may be appropriate for them to reduce the number of shares in the company.

**sellers over** A market in commodities, securities, etc., in which buyers have been satisfied but some sellers remain. This is clearly a weak market, with a tendency for prices to fall. *Compare* buyers over.

**selling out** The selling of securities, commodities, etc., by a broker because the original buyer is unable to pay for them. This invariably happens after a fall in market price (the buyer would have taken them up and sold them at a profit if the market had risen). The broker sells them at the best price available and the original buyer is responsible for any difference between the price realized and the original selling price, plus the costs of selling out. *Compare* buying in.

**selling short** *See* short selling.

**sen 1.** A monetary unit of Cambodia, worth one hundredth of a *riel. **2.** A monetary unit of Malaysia, worth one hundredth of a *ringgit. **3.** A former monetary unit of Japan (still used as a unit of account), worth one hundredth of a *yen.

**sene** A monetary unit of Western Samoa, worth one hundredth of a *tala.

**seniti** A monetary unit of Tonga, worth one hundredth of a *pa'anga.

**sensitive market** A market in commodities, securities, etc., that is sensitive to outside influences because it is basically unstable. For example, a poor crop in a commodity market may make it sensitive, with buyers anxious to cover their requirements but unwilling to show their hand and risk forcing prices up. News of a hurricane in the growing area, say, could cause a sharp price rise in such a sensitive market.

**separate assessment** Before April 1990, an election that could be made by one party to a marriage in the UK enabling each party to pay his or her own tax. Unlike an election for *separate taxation of a wife's earnings, this saved no tax. It merely allocated the total tax payable by the married couple as a single unit to the two parties for payment.

**separate taxation of a wife's earnings** Before April 1990, an election that could be made by both parties to a marriage in the UK enabling the earned income of the wife to be treated separately from that of her husband. The normal principle of income tax was that a married couple were treated as one and the total income of both was deemed to be that of the husband. Thus a married woman's income was taxed at her husband's marginal rate. By separate taxation of a wife's earnings, both parties could be treated as single persons (thus foregoing the married man's allowance) and the wife's earned income was treated as hers, although her *unearned income continued to be treated as that of her husband. For this election to be effective, the combined incomes of the two parties had to be such that more was saved by not combining the incomes than was lost by converting the married man's allowance to a single person's allowance. Since April 1990 husband and wife have been assessed independently (*see* independent taxation).

**SEPON Ltd** Abbreviation for *Stock Exchange Pool Nominees Ltd.

**Serious Fraud Office (SFO)** A body established in 1987 to be responsible for investigating and prosecuting serious or complex frauds in England, Wales, and Northern Ireland. The Attorney General appoints and superintends its director. Serious and complex fraud cases can go straight to the Crown Court without committal for trial. That court can hold preparatory hearings to clarify issues for the jury and settle points of law.

**SERPS** Abbreviation for *State Earnings-Related Pension Scheme.

**service** An economic *good consisting of labour, advice, managerial skill, etc., rather than a *commodity. **Services to trade** include banking, insurance, transport, etc. **Professional services** encompass the advice and skill of accountants, lawyers, architects, business consultants, doctors, etc. **Consumer services** include those given by caterers, cleaners, mechanics, plumbers, etc. Industry may be divided into extractive, manufacturing, and service sectors. The **service industries** make up an increasing proportion of the national income.

**service contract (service agreement)** An employment contract between an employer and employee, usually a senior employee, such as a director, executive manager, etc. Service contracts must be kept at the registered office of a company and be open to inspection by members of the company. The Companies Acts 1980 and 1985 prohibit service contracts that give an employee guaranteed employment for more than five years, without the company having an opportunity to break the employment as and when it needs to. This measure prevents directors with long service agreements from suing companies for loss of office in the event of a takeover or reorganization. *See also* compensation for loss of office; golden parachute.

**servicing a loan** Paying the interest on a loan.

**SES** Abbreviation for *Stock Exchange of Singapore.

**SESDAQ** Abbreviation for Stock Exchange of Singapore Dealing and Automated Quotation System. *See* Stock Exchange of Singapore.

**SESI** Abbreviation for Stock Exchange of Singapore Index. *See* Stock Exchange of Singapore.

**SET** Abbreviation for *Securities Exchange of Thailand.

**set-off** An agreement between the parties involved to set off one debt against another or one loss against a gain. A banker is empowered to set off a credit balance on one account against a debit balance on another if the accounts are in the same name and in the same currency. It is usual, in these circumstances, for the bank to issue a **letter of set-off**, which the customer countersigns to indicate agreement. A letter of set-off is also needed if the accounts are not in the same name, e.g. differently named companies in the same group.

**settlement** **1.** The payment of an outstanding account, invoice, charge, etc. **2.** The payment of outstanding dues on the *London Stock Exchange at the end of an *account. *See also* account day (settlement day). **3.** A disposition of land, or other property, made by deed or will under which a *trust is set up by the settlor. The settlement names the beneficiaries and the terms under which they are to acquire the property. **4.** The document in which such a disposition is made. **5.** The voluntary conclusion of civil litigation or an industrial dispute, as a result of agreement between the parties.

**settlement day** *See* account day.

**settlement price** The price at which an *index futures or option contract is settled on the *London International Financial Futures and Options Exchange. Officially known as the **Exchange Delivery Settlement Price (EDSP)**, the settlement price is calculated on the last day of the delivery month and forms the basis for the cash settlement.

**settlor** A person declaring or creating a *settlement or *trust. For tax purposes any person providing money or property for a settlement will be regarded as the settlor.

**seven-day money** Money that has been invested in the *money market for a term of seven days. Special interest rates are quoted for seven-day money.

**several liability** *See* joint and several liability.

**severance payment** *See* compensation for loss of office; redundancy payment.

**SFA** Abbreviation for *Securities and Futures Authority Ltd.

**SFO** **1.** Abbreviation for *Superannuation Funds Office. **2.** Abbreviation for *Serious Fraud Office.

**share** One of a number of titles of ownership in a company. Most companies are limited by shares, thus if a company fails an investor has a liability that is limited to the amount paid for (or owing on) the shares. A share confers on its owner a legal right to the part of the company's profits (usually by payment of a *dividend) and to any voting rights attaching to that share (*see* voting shares; A shares). Companies are obliged to keep a public record of the rights attaching to each class of share. The common classes of shares are: *ordinary shares, which have no guaranteed amount of dividend but carry voting rights; and *preference shares, which receive dividends (and/or repayment of capital on winding-up) before ordinary shares, but which have no voting rights. Shares in public companies may be bought and sold in an open market, such as a stock exchange. Shares in a private company are generally subject to restrictions on sale, such as that they must be offered to existing shareholders first or that the directors' approval must be sought before they are sold elsewhere. *See also* cumulative preference share; deferred ordinary share; founders' shares; partly paid shares; preferred ordinary share; redeemable preference share; subscription shares; term shares.

**share account** **1.** In the UK, a building society deposit account with no fixed investment period; it usually demands one month's notice for withdrawals but will often pay up to £250 without notice. **2.** In the USA, an account with a *credit union that pays dividends rather than interest.

**share capital** That part of the *capital of a company that arises from the issue of *shares. Every company must commence with some share capital (a minimum of two shares). The **authorized share capital** (**registered capital** or **nominal capital**) of a company is the total amount of capital it is authorized to raise according to its articles of association. The **issued share capital** or **subscribed share capital** is the amount of the authorized capital that shareholders have subscribed. If the shareholders have subscribed the full *par value of the share, this will constitute the **fully paid share capital**. If they have subscribed only a proportion of the issued share capital, this is called the **called-up capital**. Some capital may be subscribed on application or on allotment or as separate calls. The shares do not become fully paid until the last call has been made. *See also* reserve capital.

**share certificate** A document that provides evidence of ownership of shares in a company. It states the number and class of shares owned by the shareholder and the serial number of the shares. It is stamped by the common seal of the company and usually signed by at least one director and the company secretary. It is not a negotiable instrument. *See* bearer security.

**share exchange** A service offered by most unit-trust managements and life-assurance companies, in which the trust or company takes over a client's shareholding and invests the proceeds in unit-trust funds, etc., of the client's choice. The client is thereby saved the trouble and expense of disposing of the shares and if the shares are absorbed into the trust's or company's own portfolio the client may receive a better price than would be possible on the market (i.e. the offer price rather than the bid price).

**share-for-share offer**  A *takeover bid in which the directors of one company offer shares in that company as the payment for acquiring the shares in the target company. If the offer is accepted the shareholders of both companies will become the owners of the newly formed combination.

**shareholder**  An owner of shares in a limited company or limited partnership. A shareholder is a member of the company.

**shareholders' equity**  *See* net asset value.

**share index**  *See* Chambre Agent General Index; Commerzbank Index; Dow Jones Industrial Average; Financial Times Share Indexes; Nikkei Stock Average; Hang Seng Index.

**ShareLink**  A telephone service for dealing in shares originally established in 1987 to take advantage of the privatization boom. It was set up by British Telecom and Albert E. Sharp, a firm of Birmingham stockbrokers, and was the subject of a management buyout in 1992.

**share option**  **1.** A benefit sometimes offered to employees, especially new employees, in which they are given an option to buy shares in the company for which they work at a favourable fixed price or at a stated discount to the market price.  **2.** *See* option.

**share premium**  The amount payable for shares in a company and issued by the company itself in excess of their nominal value (*see* nominal price). Share premiums received by a company must be credited to a **share premium account**, which cannot be used for paying dividends to the shareholders, although it may be used to make *scrip issues.

**share premium account**  *See* share premium.

**share register**  The register kept by a limited company in which ownership of shares in that company is recorded, together with the full names, addresses, extent of holding, and class of shares for each shareholder. Entry in the register constitutes evidence of ownership. Thus, a shareholder who loses a share certificate can obtain a replacement from the company provided that proof of identity is supplied and that the holding is recorded in the register.

**share splitting**  The division of the share capital of a company into smaller units. The effect of a share split is the same as a *scrip issue although the technicalities differ. Share splits are usually carried out when the existing shares reach such a high price (*see* heavy share) that trading in them becomes difficult.

**share transfer**  *See* transfer deed.

**share warehousing**  The practice of building up a holding of the shares of a company that is to be the target for a takeover. The shares are bought in the name of nominees in relatively small lots and 'warehoused' until the purchaser has built up a significant interest in the company.

**shark repellents**  *See* porcupine provisions.

**shark watcher**  A business consultant who specializes in helping companies to identify raiders and to provide early warning of *share warehousing and other manoeuvres used as preliminaries to takeovers.

**shelf registration**  A measure to allow larger US companies to register advance details of new securities with the *Securities and Exchange

Commission (SEC), without specifying a date of issue. When companies need the capital, they issue securities 'off the shelf', without having to wait for SEC clearance of the application.

**shell company**  **1.** A non-trading company, with or without a stock-exchange listing, used as a vehicle for various company manoeuvres or kept dormant for future use in some other capacity.  **2.** A company that has ceased to trade and is sold to new owners for a small fee to minimize the cost and trouble of setting up a new company. Some business brokers register such companies with the sole object of selling them to people setting up new businesses. The name and objects of such a company can be changed for a small charge.

**sheqel**  (NIS) New Israeli sheqel: the standard monetary unit of Israel, divided into 100 agorot.

**Shibosai bond**  A *Samurai bond sold direct by a company to investors, without using a stockbroker.

**shilling**  The standard monetary unit of Kenya (KSh), Somalia (So.Sh.), Tanzania (TSh), and Uganda (USh), divided into 100 cents.

**Shogun bond**  A bond sold on the Japanese market by a foreign institution and denominated in a foreign currency. *Compare* Samurai bond.

**short bill**  A *bill of exchange that is payable at sight, on demand, or within ten days.

**short covering**  The purchasing of goods that have been sold short (*see* short position) so that the open position is closed. A dealer in commodities, securities, or foreign exchanges hopes to cover shorts at below the selling price in order to make a profit. Dealers cover their shorts when they expect the market to turn or when it has already started to move upwards.

**short-dated gilt**  *See* gilt-edged security.

**short hedging**  *See* hedging.

**shorting**  Establishing a *short position.

**short position**  A position held by a dealer in securities (*see* market maker), commodities, currencies, etc., in which sales exceed holdings because the dealer expects prices to fall, which will enable the shorts to be covered at a profit. *Compare* long position.

**shorts**  **1.** *See* gilt-edged security.  **2.** Securities, commodities, currencies, etc., of which a dealer is short, i.e. has a *short position.

**short selling**  Selling commodities, securities, currencies, etc., that one does not have. A short seller expects prices to fall so that the short sale can be bought in at a profit before delivery has to be made. A short seller is a *bear.

**short-term capital**  Capital raised for a short period to cover an exceptional demand for funds over a short period. A bank loan, rather than a debenture, is an example of short-term capital.

**short-term instrument**  A *negotiable instrument that matures in three months or less.

**short-term interest rates**  The rates of interest on **short-term loans**, i.e. loans that are made for a short period. Banks will usually pay higher rates for short-term loans, in which no withdrawal is permitted until the money is withdrawn on an agreed date, usually within three months. However, when banks are asked to make loans for a short term (usually less than one year), their interest rate charged may be lower than for a long-term loan, which will involve a higher risk.

**short-term monetary support (STMS)**  Funds available to a member country of the European Community for three months. These funds are provided by the central banks of other members to offset problems one state may be having in relation to exchange-rate pressures. *Compare* medium-term financial assistance.

**show stopper**  A legal action taken by the target firm in an unwelcome takeover bid that seeks a permanent injunction to prevent the bidder from persisting in takeover activities, on the grounds that the bid is legally defective in some way.

**shut-down cost**  The costs to be incurred in closing down some part of an organization's activities.

**SIAC**  Abbreviation for *Securities Industry Automation Corporation.

**SIB**  Abbreviation for *Securities and Investment Board.

**sickness and accident insurance**  A form of health insurance in which the benefits are paid after eight days for a total of 140 weeks after the onset of an illness or accident that prevents the insured from working. Premiums can increase each year and renewal can be refused if a claim has been made. *Compare* permanent health insurance.

**side deal**  A private deal between two people, usually for the personal benefit of one of them, as a subsidiary to a transaction between the officials of a company, government, etc. For example, the chairman of a public company may agree to encourage the board to welcome a takeover bid, because of a personal profit agreed in some side deal with the bidder. Side deals are rigorously investigated by the Panel on Takeovers and Mergers (*see* City Code on Takeovers and Mergers).

**sight bill**  *See* at sight.

**sight deposit**  Money deposited in a bank account that can be withdrawn without notice, e.g. money withdrawn by cheque from a current account. In the USA it is known as a *demand deposit.

**sight draft**  Any *bill of exchange that is payable on sight, i.e. on presentation, irrespective of when it was drawn.

**SIMEX**  Abbreviation for *Singapore International Monetary Exchange.

**simple interest**  *See* interest.

**sine die**  (Latin: without a day) Denoting an adjournment of an action, arbitration, etc., indefinitely.

**Singapore International Monetary Exchange (SIMEX)**  A commodities futures exchange in Singapore launched in 1984; it is linked with the *Chicago Mercantile Exchange and uses *eurodollars for its main contracts.

**Singapore Stock Exchange**  *See* Stock Exchange of Singapore (SES).

**Single Act** The legislation passed in 1985 in the European Community that commits all member states to an integrated method of trading with no frontiers between countries by 31 December 1992. In practice, some of its terms on harmonization, such as the insurance market, will take considerably longer to implement. The main creation of the Single Act is the Single Market for trading in goods and services within the Community.

**single-capacity system** *See* dual-capacity system.

**single company PEP** *See* personal equity plan.

**single-life pension** A pension or *annuity that is paid for the lifetime of the beneficiary only. *Compare* joint-life and last-survivor annuities.

**single-premium assurance** A life-assurance or pension policy in which the insured pays only one capital sum rather than regular premiums. *See also* investment bond.

**single-tax system** A system of taxation in which there would be only one major tax, usually a *comprehensive income tax, instead of several taxes, such as income tax, capital-gains tax, and national insurance, as in the UK. Arguments in favour of such taxes are that they should be less avoidable and should simplify administration. On the other hand the present variety of taxes is designed for a variety of purposes and flexibility may be lost in a single-tax system.

**sinking fund** A fund set up to replace a *wasting asset at the end of its useful life. Usually a regular annual sum is set aside to enable the fund, taking into account interest at the expected rate, to replace the exhausted asset at a specified date. Some have argued that amounts set aside for *depreciation of an asset should be equal to the annual amounts needed to be placed in a notional sinking fund.

**SIPC** Abbreviation for *Securities Investor Protection Corporation.

**six-month money** Money invested on the *money market for a period of six months. If it is withdrawn before the six months have elapsed there may be a heavy penalty, although if the market has moved in favour of the recipient of the funds, this penalty may be negligible.

**skip-day** The two-day period allowed before payment has to be made for a security purchased on the US *money market.

**sliding peg** *See* crawling peg.

**slush fund** Money set aside by an organization for discreet payments to influential people for preferential treatment, advance information, or other services for the benefit of the organization. Slush funds are normally used for purposes less blatant than bribes, but sometimes not much less.

**small companies rate** A rate of UK *corporation tax for companies earning less than a specified profit in a specified year that is less than the full rate of corporation tax. The rate of tax and the limits vary from year to year; in 1992, for example, a company earning less than £250,000 paid 25% tax, compared to the full rate of 33%.

**small company** A company, as defined by the UK Companies Act 1985, that falls below any two of the following three size criteria: (a) gross assets £700,000; (b) turnover £1,400,000; (c) average number of employees 50. These companies, if not *public limited companies or banking, insurance, or shipping companies, may file very abbreviated accounts (*see* modified accounts) with the Registrar of Companies (excluding even a profit and loss account), although they must provide their own shareholders with the full statutory information. *Compare* medium-sized company.

**smaller companies market (SCM)**  A market for the stocks and shares of *unlisted securities in Ireland.

**small loan company**  The US equivalent of a *finance house for private consumers, i.e. one that lends money to consumers to enable them to make purchases on an instalment plan.

**Small Order Execution System (SOES)**  The US *National Association of Securities Dealers' automatic system for executing customers' orders of 1000 or fewer shares in securities traded on NASDAQ.

**small print**  Printed matter on a document, such as a life-assurance policy or hire-purchase agreement, in which the seller sets out the conditions of the sale and the mutual liabilities of buyer and seller. The use of a very small type size and unintelligible jargon is often intended to obscure the legal rights and safeguards from the buyer. This unfair practice has largely been remedied by the various Acts that provide consumer protection. *See also* cooling-off period.

**smart card**  A plastic card that contains electronically stored information enabling its user to access to a system, usually for obtaining cash from an *automated teller machine. It can also be used as an identification card that gains the bearer access to a computer system, hotel room, office, etc.

**smart money**  Money invested by experienced and successful people, especially those with inside information about a particular project or investment opportunity.

**SMI**  Abbreviation for Swiss Market Index. *See* Swiss Options and Financial Futures Exchange; Swiss stock exchanges.

**snake**  A European monetary system adopted in 1972, in which the exchange rate between the participants was restricted by a fluctuation limit of 2¼%. The participants were the Belgian franc, Danish krone, French franc, Irish punt, Dutch guilder, German Deutschmark, and Italian lira, the dominating currency being the Deutschmark. It was originally called a snake-in-the-barrel or -tunnel to indicate that the rates of exchange could 'snake' about within the limits imposed by the barrel (tunnel). Sterling did not participate in this arrangement, which was replaced in 1979 by the *European Monetary System.

**social security**  A government system for paying allowances to the sick and the unemployed, as well as maternity benefits and retirement pensions. Other low-income members of society are also eligible, such as the disabled and single-parent families. Since 1988 in the UK this has been the responsibility of the Department of Social Security, which also administers the *National Insurance scheme that funds the social security payments.

**Social Security Act 1986**  UK legislation that laid the foundations for freeing the pensions industry by allowing employees to opt out of *occupational pension schemes run by their employers and create their own *personal (and portable) pension schemes. It was not completely enacted until 1988 because its consumer-protection clauses were bound up in the later *Financial Services

Act 1986. The Social Security Act 1990 went further in introducing consumer protection for pension plans and introduced the pensions Ombudsman.

**sociedad anónima** *See* SA.

**sociedade anónima** *See* SA.

**società a responsabilità limitata** *See* Sarl.

**società per azioni** *See* SpA.

**société anonyme** *See* SA.

**société à responsabilité limitée** *See* Sarl.

**Society for Worldwide Interbank Financial Telecommunications (SWIFT)** A communications system that advises member banks to transfer funds from one member to another. Based in Brussels, the SWIFT network of terminals links 1500 banks in Europe, USA, Africa, Asia, Australia, and Latin America. It is not a payment system, but an information and instruction network. It began operations in 1977 and is run by a non-profitmaking organization.

**SOFFEX** Abbreviation for *Swiss Options and Financial Futures Exchange.

**SOFS** Abbreviation for *Small Order Execution System.

**soft commodity** *See* commodity.

**soft currency** The currency of a country that has a weak *balance of payments and for which there is relatively little demand. *Compare* hard currency.

**soft dollars** *See* hard dollars.

**soft loan** A loan with an artificially low rate of interest. Soft loans are sometimes made to developing nations by industrialized nations for political reasons.

**sol** (S/) The standard monetary unit of Peru, divided into 100 centavos.

**solicitor's letter** A letter written by a solicitor to a debtor who has failed to settle a debt. The letter usually threatens to take the matter to court, unless payment is received by a specified date.

**solo (sola)** A single *bill of exchange of which no other copies are in circulation.

**solvency** **1.** The financial state of a person or company that is able to pay all debts as they fall due. **2.** The amount by which the assets of a bank exceed its liabilities.

**solvency margin** The difference between the assets and the liabilities of an insurance company. This margin is carefully regulated by the insurance industry's supervisory organization LAUTRO (*see* Self-Regulating Organization).

**solvency ratio** **1.** The ratio of a bank's own assets to its liabilities. **2.** A ratio used by the UK Department of Trade and Industry to evaluate the stability of insurance companies; it is the ratio of the company's net assets to its non-life premium income.

**source and application (disposition) of funds**  A statement showing how an organization has raised finance for a specified period and how that finance has been applied. Sources of funds are typically trading profits, issues of shares or loan stock, sales of fixed assets, and borrowings. Applications are typically trading losses, purchases of fixed assets, dividends paid, and repayment of borrowings. Any balancing figure represents an increase or decrease in *working capital.

**sovereign loan**  A loan made by a bank to a foreign government, often the government of a third-world country. The attendant risk is sometimes called **sovereign risk**.

**SpA**  Abbreviation for *società per azioni*. It appears after the name of a public limited company in Italy, being equivalent to the British abbreviation plc. *Compare* Sarl.

**special clearing**  The clearing of a cheque through the UK banking system in less than the normal three days, for a small additional charge. A cheque for which a special clearing has been arranged can usually be passed through the system in one day.

**Special Commissioners**  A body of civil servants who are specialized tax lawyers appointed by the Lord Chancellor after consultation with the Lord Advocate to hear appeals against assessments to income tax, corporation tax, and capital-gains tax. A taxpayer may generally choose to appeal to the Special Commissioners, rather than the *General Commissioners, particularly in cases in which legal matters rather than questions of fact are at issue.

**special crossing**  A crossing on a *cheque in which the name of a bank is written between the crossing lines. A cheque so crossed can only be paid into the named bank.

**special deposits**  Deposits that the UK government may instruct the clearing banks to make at the Bank of England, as a means of restricting credit in the economy. The less money the clearing banks have at their disposal, the less they are able to lend to businesses. A similar system has been used by the Federal Reserve System in the USA.

**Special Drawing Rights (SDRs)**  The standard unit of account used by the *International Monetary Fund (IMF). In 1970 members of the IMF were allocated SDRs in proportion to the quotas of currency that they had subscribed to the fund on its formation. There have since been further allocations. SDRs can be used to settle international trade balances and to repay debts to the IMF itself. On the instructions of the IMF a member country must supply its own currency to another member, in exchange for SDRs, unless it already holds more than three times its original allocation. The value of SDRs was originally expressed in terms of gold, but since 1974 it has been valued in terms of its members' currencies. SDRs provide a credit facility for IMF members in addition to their existing credit facilities (hence the name); unlike these existing facilities they do not have to be repaid, thus forming a permanent addition to members' reserves and functioning as an international reserve currency. *Compare* European Currency Unit.

**specialist**  A dealer on the New York Stock Exchange who has been appointed by the exchange to maintain an orderly market in certain assigned securities. Specialists operate as market makers and are required to perform four functions: to quote prices, execute orders, create liquidity in the market, and match bids and offers by bringing together buyers and sellers.

**special Lombard rate** The day-to-day rate of interest fixed by the German Bundesbank when its normal rates (*see* Lombard rate) have been suspended for any reason.

**special manager** A person appointed by the court in the liquidation of a company or bankruptcy of an individual to assist the *liquidator or *official receiver to manage the business of the company or individual. The powers of the special manager are those invested in him or her by the court.

**special notice** *See* resolution.

**special resolution** *See* resolution.

**specie** Money in the form of coins, rather than banknotes or bullion.

**specific charge** *See* charge; fixed charge.

**speculation** The purchase or sale of something for the sole purpose of making a capital gain. For professional speculators the security, *financial futures and options, commodity, and foreign-exchange markets are natural venues as they cater for speculation as well as investment and trading. Indeed, speculators help to make a market viable by providing liquidity and by smoothing out price fluctuations.

**speculative risk** An insurance risk that cannot be calculated and formulated – and is outside the so-called 'law of large numbers', e.g. outside human control – and is therefore difficult or impossible to assess for insurance cover.

**split** *See* share splitting.

**split-capital investment trust (split-level trust; split trust)** An *investment trust with a limited life in which the equity capital is divided into various classes of income shares and capital shares. Holders of income shares receive all or most of the income earned plus a predetermined capital value on liquidation. Holders of capital shares receive little or no income but are entitled to all of the assets remaining after repayment of the income shares.

**sponsor** The *issuing house that handles a new issue for a company. It will supervise the preparation of the *prospectus and make sure that the company is aware of the benefits and obligations of being a public company.

**spot currency market** A market in which currencies are traded for delivery within two days, as opposed to the *forward dealing exchange market in which deliveries are arranged for named months in the future. The rate of exchange for spot currency is the **spot rate**.

**spot goods** Commodities that are available for delivery within two days, as opposed to futures (*see* futures contract) in which deliveries are arranged for named months in the future. The price of spot goods, the **spot price**, is usually higher than the forward price, unless there is a glut of that particular commodity but an expected shortage in the future.

**spot month** The month during which goods bought on a futures contract will become available for delivery.

**spot price** *See* spot goods.

**spot rate**   *See* spot currency market.

**spread   1.** The difference between the buying and selling price made by a
*market maker on the stock exchange.   **2.** The diversity of the investments in a
*portfolio. The greater the spread of a portfolio the less volatile it will be.
**3.** The simultaneous purchase and sale of commodity futures (*see* futures
contract) in the hope that movement in their relative prices will enable a profit
to be made. This may include a purchase and sale of the same commodity for
the same delivery, but on different commodity exchanges (*see* straddle), or a
purchase and sale of the same commodity for different deliveries.

**Square Mile**   The colloquial name for the commercial district of the City of
London, traditionally the square mile north of the Thames between Waterloo
Bridge and Tower Bridge. It has been the principal financial district of the UK,
with office blocks clustering around the Stock Exchange, the Bank of England,
Lloyds, and the commodity markets in Mincing Lane. Recent developments
have seen a spread eastwards to the London Docklands redevelopment area
and westwards to occupy former newspaper offices in Fleet Street.

**squeeze   1.** Controls imposed by a government to restrict inflation. An
**income (pay) squeeze** limits increases in wage and salaries, a **credit squeeze**
limits the amounts that banks and other moneylenders can lend, a **dividend
(profits) squeeze** restricts increases in dividends.   **2.** Any action on a market
that forces buyers to come into the market and prices to rise. In a **bear
squeeze**, bears are forced to cover in order to deliver. It may be restricted to a
particular commodity or security or a particular delivery month may be
squeezed, pushing its price up against the rest of the market.

**SRO**   Abbreviation for *Self-Regulating Organization.

**SSAP**   Abbreviation for *statements of standard accounting practice.

**stabilizers**   Economic measures used in a free economy to restrict swings in
prices, production, employment, etc. Such measures include progressive
income tax, control of interest rates, government spending, unemployment
benefits, and government retraining schemes.

**stag**   A person who applies for shares in new issues in the hope that the price
when trading begins will be higher than the issue price. Often measures will be
taken by the issuers to prevent excessive stagging; it is usually illegal for
would-be investors to attempt to obtain large numbers of shares by making
multiple applications. Issuers will often scale down share applications to
prevent such quick-profit taking, e.g. by *ballot.

**staggered directorships**   A measure used in the defence against unwanted
takeover bids. If the company concerned resolves that the terms of office served
by its directors are to be staggered and that no director can be removed from
office without due cause, a bidder cannot gain control of the board for some
years, even with a controlling interest in the share capital. *See* poison pill.

**STAGS**   Abbreviation for Sterling Transferable Accruing Government Securities.
These European sterling bonds are backed by a holding of Treasury stock. They
are *deep-discount bonds paying no interest.

**stale bull**   A dealer or speculator who has a *long position in something,
usually a commodity, which is showing a paper profit but which the dealer
cannot realize as there are no buyers at the higher levels. The dealer may be

fully committed financially and unable to increase his or her bull position so that no further trading is possible.

**stale cheque** *See* cheque.

**stamp duty** A tax on specific transactions collected by stamping the legal documents giving rise to the transactions. The most common in the UK were the stamp duties on the transfer of land and of securities. The stamp duty on the transfer of securities was abolished in 1992.

**Standard and Poor's 500 Stock Index (S&P 500)** The widest general-market index of stocks produced by the US credit-rating agency Standard and Poor; it is made up of 425 shares in US industrial companies and 75 stocks in railway and public-utility corporations.

**standby agreement** An agreement between the *International Monetary Fund and a member state, enabling the member to arrange for immediate drawing rights in addition to its normal drawing rights in such cases of emergency as a temporary balance of payments crisis.

**standby credit** A *letter of credit that guarantees a loan or other form of credit facility. The bank that issues it promises to refund the amount borrowed if the borrower defaults on repayment. It calls for a certificate of default by the applicant. In a *note issuance facility a standby credit is a third-party guarantee to honour an issue to an investor who may have a low credit rating.

**standing order** An instruction by a customer to a bank (**banker's order**) or building society to pay a specified amount of money on a specified date or dates to a specified payee. Standing orders are widely used for such regular payments as insurance premiums, subscriptions, etc. *See also* credit transfer.

**standstill agreement** **1.** An agreement between two countries in which a debt owed by one to the other is held in abeyance until a specified date in the future. **2.** An agreement between an unwelcome bidder for a company and the company, in which the bidder agrees to buy no more of the company's shares for a specified period. **3.** An arrangement between banks who have loans to a company in trouble, in which they each agree to maintain their existing credit facilities and not to force the company into receivership by acting alone.

**state banks** Commercial banks in the USA that were established by state charter rather than federal charter (*compare* national banks). The rules governing their trading are controlled by state laws and there are therefore differences in practices from state to state. State banks are not compelled to join the *Federal Reserve System, although national banks are. State banks are regulated by state banking departments and by the *Federal Deposit Insurance Corporation (FDIC). Even if they choose not to join the Federal Reserve System, they must abide by its rules, particularly on consumer credit protection.

**State Earnings-Related Pension Scheme (SERPS)** A scheme, started in 1978, run by the UK government to provide a pension for every employed person in addition to the basic state flat-rate pension. The contributions are paid from part of the National Insurance payments made by employees and employers. Payment of the pension starts at the state retirement age (65 for men, 60 for women) and the amount of pension received is calculated using a formula based on a percentage of the person's earnings. Persons who wish to contract out of SERPS may subscribe to an *occupational pension scheme or a *personal pension scheme.

**statement of affairs** A statement showing the assets and liabilities of a person who is bankrupt or of a company in liquidation.

**statement of auditing standards (SAS)** A statement that lays down accepted US auditing standards. It was issued by the Auditing Standards Board of the American Institute of Certified Public Accountants, members of which have to explain any deviation from the SAS in their audit reports.

**statement of changes in financial position** The US equivalent of the UK *source and application (disposition) of funds.

**statement of source and application of funds** *See* source and application (disposition) of funds.

**statements of standard accounting practice (SSAP)** Statements issued by the Accounting Standards Committee to guide accountants on how to deal with such matters as depreciation, stock, mergers, leases, etc., in accounts in order to minimize disparity of treatment of the same transactions in different companies. These statements do not have the force of law but they represent the best accountancy practice; auditors are expected to follow them as presenting a 'true and fair view', unless it would be misleading to do so. In 1990 the Accounting Standards Committee was replaced by the Accounting Standards Board, which confirmed all existing SSAPs.

**static risk** An insurance risk the magnitude of which can be assessed because it has a direct natural cause, e.g. fire, theft, or disaster caused by adverse weather.

**status enquiry** *See* banker's reference.

**statute-barred debt** A debt that has not been collected within the period allowed by law. *See* limitation of actions.

**statutory books** The books of account that the Companies Act 1985 requires a company to keep. They must show and explain the company's transactions, disclose with reasonable accuracy the company's financial position at any time, and enable the directors to ensure that any accounts prepared therefrom comply with the provisions of the Act. They must also include entries from day to day of all money received and paid out together with a record of all assets and liabilities and statements of stockholding (where appropriate).

**statutory company** *See* company.

**statutory damages** *See* damages.

**statutory meeting** A meeting held in accordance with the Companies Act 1985. This normally refers to the annual general meeting of the shareholders, although it could refer to any other meeting required to be held by statute.

**statutory report** A report required to be made by statute. This normally refers to the annual report and accounts required to be laid before the members of a company by the Companies Act 1985.

**stepped preference share** A *preference share that earns a predetermined income, which rises steadily by a set amount each year to the winding-up date; there is also a predetermined capital growth.

**sterilization** The process of offsetting the inflationary-deflationary effects that result when a government intervenes in foreign-exchange markets. If a nation's currency is depreciating and its government wishes to intervene to stabilize the exchange rate, it can sell its reserves of foreign currency and buy its own currency. However, buying its own currency will take money out of circulation, which could cause interest rates to rise, followed by recession. Sterilization is the process of expanding the money supply in these circumstances to prevent increases in interest rates and any consequent recession. Conversely, if a government intervenes to prevent a currency from appreciating, sterilization would involve reducing the money supply.

**sterling** The UK *pound, as distinguished from the pounds of other countries. The name derives from the small star *steorra* (Old English) that appeared on early Norman pennies.

**Sterling Transferable Accruing Government Securities** *See* STAGS.

**Sterling Warrant Into Gilt-edged Stock (SWING)** A warrant issued by the Bank of England giving the holder an option to buy or sell a specified *gilt-edged security.

**STI** Abbreviation for *Straits Times (Industrial) Index.

**STMS** Abbreviation for *short-term monetary support.

**stock   1.** In the UK, a fixed-interest security (*see* gilt-edged security) issued by the government, local authority, or a company in fixed units, often of £100 each. They usually have a *redemption date on which the *par value of the unit price is repaid in full. They are dealt in on stock exchanges at prices that fluctuate, but depend on such factors as their *yield in relation to current interest rates and the time they have to run before redemption. *See also* tap stock.   **2.** The US name for an *ordinary share.   **3.** The stock-in-trade of an organization.   **4.** Any collection of assets, e.g. the stock of plant and machinery owned by a company.

**stockbroker** An agent who buys and sells securities on a stock exchange on behalf of clients and receives remuneration for this service in the form of a *commission. Before October 1986 (*see* Big Bang), stockbrokers on the *London Stock Exchange were not permitted by the rules of the Stock Exchange to act as *principals (*compare* stockjobber) and they worked for a fixed commission laid down by the Stock Exchange. Since October 1986, however, many London stockbrokers have taken advantage of the new rules, which allow them to buy and sell as principals, in which capacity they are now known as *market makers. This change has been accompanied by the formal abolition of fixed commissions, enabling stockbrokers to vary their commission in competition with each other. Stockbrokers have traditionally offered investment advice, especially for their *institutional investors.

**stock exchange (stock market)** A market for the sale and purchase of securities, in which the prices are controlled by the laws of supply and demand. The first stock exchange was in Amsterdam, where in 1602 shares in the United East India Company could be traded. UK exchanges date from 1673, with the first daily official price lists being issued in London in 1698. Stock markets have developed hand-in-hand with capitalism, gradually growing in complexity and importance. Their basic function is to allow public companies, governments, local authorities, and other incorporated bodies to raise capital by selling securities to investors. They perform valuable secondary functions in allowing those investors to buy and sell these securities, providing liquidity, and reducing the risks attached to investment. Stock markets were abolished after World War II in communist-dominated states but with the collapse of communism many restarted. The major international stock exchanges are based in London, New York, and Tokyo. Outside the UK and English-speaking countries, a stock exchange is usually known as a *bourse.

**Stock Exchange Alternative Trading Service (SEATS)** A *London Stock Exchange system for trading in less liquid securities, which commenced in November 1992. It replaced the *Company Bulletin Board Service (commenced in April 1992), and allows for the registration of single *market makers. By enabling a combination of quote and order displays, SEATS complements the competing *Stock Exchange Automated Quotations System (SEAQ).

**Stock Exchange Automated Quotations System (SEAQ)** A computerized system used on the *London Stock Exchange to record the prices at which transactions in securities have been struck, thus establishing the market prices for these securities; these prices are made available to brokers through *TOPIC. When a bargain is concluded, the details must be notified to the central system within certain set periods during the day. **SEAQ International** is the system used on the London Stock Exchange for non-UK equities; it operates on similar lines to SEAQ.

**Stock Exchange Automatic Execution Facility (SAEF)** A computerized system used on the *London Stock Exchange to enable a broker to execute a transaction in a security through an SAEF terminal, which automatically completes the bargain at the best price with a *market maker, whose position is automatically adjusted. The price of the transaction is then automatically recorded on a trading report and also passes into the settlement system. The system has greatly reduced the administrative burden on brokers and market makers but has been criticized for eliminating the personal element between brokers and market makers on the floor of the exchange.

**Stock Exchange Daily Official List** A record of all the bargains made on the *London Stock Exchange. It also provides details of dividend dates, rights issues, prices, etc., of all *listed companies. It is also known as the *Official List.

**Stock Exchange of Hong Kong** *See* Hong Kong stock exchanges.

**Stock Exchange of Singapore (SES)** One of the four *tiger markets of South East Asia whose origin goes back to the early years of the century. In its present form it dates from 1973, after Malaysia's decision to sever its currency link with Singapore. It was further modified after the Malaysian government forced companies to delist from the SES in 1990. Its main indicator is the *Straits Times (Industrial) Index, and there is also the less-used Stock Exchange of Singapore Index (SESI). The Overseas China Banking Corporation also calculates an index. A computerized over-the-counter market, the Central Limit Order Book (CLOB) International, was opened in 1990, a year after the main market had changed to electronic trading. A second-tier market has operated since February 1987 as the **Stock Exchange of Singapore Dealing and Automated Quotation System** (**SESDAQ**). Regulation is by the central bank and the Monetary Authority of Singapore under the Securities Industry Act 1986, passed after the collapse in 1985 of the Pan-Electric Industries conglomerate.

**Stock Exchange Pool Nominees Ltd (SEPON Ltd)**  The official nominee company that holds all stocks and shares sold during the course of settlement on the *London Stock Exchange, to facilitate the allocation of holdings. *See* TALISMAN.

**Stockholm Stock Exchange (Stockholm Fondbors)**  The main stock exchange in Sweden, which is regulated by the Bank Inspection Board and the *Riksbanken (central bank). Taxation on share trading from 1984 drove much trading to London and New York, with 45% of the turnover in Swedish equities being traded outside Sweden. The non-socialist government elected in 1991 is expected to abolish the tax.

**stockjobber (jobber)**  A *market maker on the *London Stock Exchange prior to the Big Bang (October 1986). Stockjobbers were only permitted to deal with the general public through the intermediary of a *stockbroker. This single-capacity system was replaced by the *dual-capacity system of market makers after the Big Bang. Formerly, jobbers, whose liability was traditionally unlimited, earned their living by the **jobbers' turn**, the difference between the prices at which they were prepared to buy and sell. After the Big Bang most of the London firms of stockjobbers were absorbed into larger financial institutions, usually banks.

**stock market**  **1.** *See* stock exchange.  **2.** A market in which livestock are bought and sold.

**stock of money**  *See* money supply.

**stock option**  *See* option.

**stock split**  *See* scrip issue.

**stock symbol**  A short form of the full title of a security, used for quick and convenient identification, especially on screen-based trading systems.

**stock watering**  The creation of more new shares in a company than is justified by its tangible assets, even though the company may be making considerable profits. The consequences of this could be that the dividend may not be maintained at the old rate on the new capital and that if the company were to be liquidated its shareholders may not be paid out in full.

**stop-loss order**  An order placed with a broker in a security or commodity market to close an *open position at a specified price in order to limit a loss. It may be used in a volatile market, especially by a speculator, if the market looks as if it might move strongly against the speculator's position.

**stop-loss treaty**  A *reinsurance treaty in which the insurer is refunded by the reinsurer for any claims in excess of a specified proportion of the premiums received.

**stop notice**  A court procedure available to protect those who have an interest in shares but have not been registered as company members. The notice prevents the company from registering a transfer of the shares or paying a dividend upon them without informing the server of the notice. It was formerly known as **notice in lieu of distringas**.

**stop order**  An order placed with a broker in a security or commodity market to buy if prices rise to a specified level or sell if they fall to another specified level.

**stotinka**  A monetary unit of Bulgaria, worth one hundredth of a *lev.

**straddle**  A strategy used by dealers in traded options or futures. In the traded option market it involves simultaneously purchasing put and call options; it is most profitable when the price of the underlying security is very volatile. *Compare* butterfly. In commodity and currency futures a straddle may involve buying and selling options or both buying and selling the same commodity or currency for delivery in the future, often on different markets. Undoing half the straddle is known as **breaking a leg**.

**straight**  *See* eurobond.

**straight-line method of depreciation**  *See* depreciation.

**Straits Times (Industrial) Index (STI)**  The main price indicator on the *Stock Exchange of Singapore; it comprises 30 industrial shares and is issued daily by the Straits Times Newspaper Group.

**strap**  A triple *option on a share or commodity market, consisting of one put option and two call options at the same price and for the same period. *Compare* strip.

**street-name stocks**  The US name for nominee stocks (*see* nominee shareholding).

**striking price**  **1.** The price fixed by the sellers of a security after receiving bids in a *tender offer (for example, in the sale of gilt-edged securities or a new stock-market issue). Usually, those who bid below the striking price receive nothing, while those who bid at or above it receive some proportion of the amount they have bid for.  **2.** *See* exercise price.

**strip**  A triple *option on a share or commodity market, consisting of one call option and two put options at the same price and for the same period. *Compare* strap.

**stripped bond**  A bond or stock that has been subjected to *dividend stripping.

**sub-chapter S**  A heading in the US Internal Revenue Code that deals with corporations having fewer than 35 shareholders. Such a corporation can elect for its shareholders to pay income tax on a personal basis rather than the corporation paying corporation tax. It is thus known as an **S corporation** or a small-business corporation.

**subordinated debt**  A debt that can only be claimed by an unsecured creditor, in the event of a liquidation, after the claims of secured creditors have been met. In **subordinated unsecured loan stocks** loans are issued by such institutions as banks, in which the rights of the holders of the stock are subordinate to the interests of the depositors. Debts involving *junk bonds are always subordinated to debts to banks, irrespective of whether or not they are secured.

**subpoena**  (Latin: under penalty) An order made by a court instructing a person to appear in court on a specified date to give evidence, or to produce specified documents. The party calling for the witness must pay any reasonable expenses. Failure to comply with a subpoena is contempt of court.

**subrogation**  The principle that, having paid a claim, an insurer has the right to take over any other methods the policyholder may have for obtaining compensation for the same event. For example, if a neighbour is responsible for breaking a person's window and an insurance claim is paid for the repair, the insurers may, if they wish, take over the policyholder's legal right to claim the cost of repair from the neighbour.

**subscribed share capital** *See* share capital.

**subscriber** A person who signs the memorandum of association of a new company and who joins with other members in the company in paying for a specified quantity of shares in the company, signing the articles of association, and appointing the first directors of the company.

**subscription shares** **1.** Shares in a building society that are paid for by instalments; they often pay the highest interest rates. **2.** The shares bought by the initial *subscribers to a company.

**subsidiary company** *See* group of companies.

**subsidy** A payment made by a government to specified traders either to enable them to continue in business or to sell their products at a lower price than would have been possible without the subsidy.

**sucre** (S/.) The standard monetary unit of Ecuador, divided into 100 centavos.

**sugar terminal market** *See* London FOX.

**sum insured** The maximum amount the insurers will pay in the event of a claim.

**sunk capital** The amount of an organization's funds that has been spent and is therefore no longer available to the organization, frequently because it has been spent on either unrealizable or valueless assets.

**superannuation** An occupational pension scheme. Contributions are deducted from an employee's salary by the employer and passed to an insurance company or the trustees of a pension fund. After retirement, the employee receives a pension payment from the scheme.

**Superannuation Funds Office (SFO)** The department of the UK Inland Revenue that deals with all forms of pension funds and benefits from pensions.

**supplementary special deposit scheme** *See* corset.

**supply and demand** *See* market forces.

**supply estimate** A request by the UK government for parliament's permission to use a specified sum of money, to be provided by the *Consolidated Fund, for use by a government department or some other body requiring money for public purposes.

**supra protest** *See* acceptance supra protest.

**surrender value** The sum of money given by an insurance company to the insured on a life policy that is cancelled before it has run its full term. The amount is calculated approximately by deducting from the total value of the premiums paid any costs, administration expenses, and a charge for the life-assurance cover up to the cancellation date. There is little or no surrender value to a life policy in its early years. Not all life policies acquire a surrender value; for example, *term assurance policies have no surrender value.

**sushi bond** A bond issued in Japan in a foreign currency but which is classified as a domestic Japanese bond. It is useful for institutions whose holdings of foreign bonds are limited.

**suspense account** A temporary account in the books of an organization to record balances to correct mistakes or balances that have not yet been finalized (e.g. because a particular deal has not been concluded).

**swap** The means by which a borrower can exchange the type of funds most easily raised for the type of funds required, usually through the intermediary of a bank. For example, a UK company may find it easy to raise a sterling loan when they really want to borrow Deutschmarks; a German company may have exactly the opposite problem. A swap will enable them to exchange the currency they possess for the currency they need. The other common type of swap is an *interest-rate swap, in which borrowers exchange fixed- for floating-interest rates. Swaps are most common in the *eurocurrency markets.

**swap line** A line of credit between two central banks in different countries, when securities of equal value are exchanged but the borrowing bank repays on a forward contract.

**sweep facility** A service provided by a bank which automatically transfers funds above a certain level from a current account to a higher-interest earning account. The process can work in reverse when funds in the current account fall below a certain level. The purpose is to provide the customer with the greatest amount of interest, with the minimum personal intervention.

**SWIFT** Abbreviation for *Society for Worldwide Interbank Financial Telecommunications.

**SWING** Abbreviation for *Sterling Warrant Into Gilt-edged Stock.

**swing line** A short-term and very short notice credit that can be used to cover shortfalls in other credit arrangements, such as commercial paper.

**Swiss Options and Financial Futures Exchange (SOFFEX)** A *financial futures exchange based in Zurich. Its contracts include *index futures based on the **Swiss Market Index (SMI)**. It was set up by the stock exchanges in Zurich, Basle, and Geneva, with the help of five banks, in 1988.

**Swiss stock exchanges** Zurich is the largest of the eight stock exchanges in Switzerland, with Geneva, Basle, and Berne ranking next in importance. Numbers may be reduced with the introduction of full electronic trading in 1993. The price level is given daily by the **Swiss Market Index (SMI)**.

**switching** **1.** Using the cash from the sale of one investment to purchase another. This may, or may not, involve a liability for capital-gains tax, depending on the circumstances. **2.** Closing an *open position in a commodity market and opening a similar position in the same commodity but for a different delivery period. For example, a trader may switch a holding of sugar for October delivery FOB to an equal quantity of sugar for March delivery FOB for the next year. **3.** A country's intervention in the international currency market to stop an outflow of its currency. **4.** Exporting and importing through a third nation, where the currency paying for the goods can be easily exchanged into one acceptable to the seller.

**switching discount** A discount offered to holders of a unit trust who wish to switch to another unit trust managed by the same group.

**syndicate** **1.** A group of bankers, insurers, contractors, etc., who join together to work on a large project (*see also* syndicated loan). **2.** A number of *Lloyd's underwriters who accept insurance risks as a group; each syndicate is run by a syndicate manager or agent. The **names** in the syndicate accept an agreed share of each risk in return for the same proportion of the premium. The names do not take part in organizing the underwriting business. Although a syndicate underwrites as a group, each member is financially responsible for only his or her own share.

**syndicated loan** A very large loan made to one borrower by a group of banks headed by one lead bank, which usually takes only a small percentage of the loan itself, syndicating the rest to other banks and financial institutions. The loans are usually made on a small margin. The borrower can reserve the right to know the names of all the members of the syndicate. If the borrower states which banks are to be included, it is known as a **club deal**.

**systemic risk** *See* risk.

**Taiwan Stock Exchange** One of the *tiger markets of the Pacific, in which share trading dates from 1962 in Taipei, after the formation of a Securities and Exchange Commission in 1960. Trading is mainly in local stocks. An *over-the-counter market was launched in 1982.

**taka** (Tk) The standard monetary unit of Bangladesh, divided into 100 paisa.

**takeover bid (offer to purchase)** An offer made to the shareholders of a company by an individual or organization to buy their shares at a specified price in order to gain control of that company. In a welcome takeover bid the directors of the company will advise shareholders to accept the terms of the bid. This is usually known as a *merger. If the bid is unwelcome, or the terms are unacceptable, the board will advise against acceptance (*see* hostile bid). In the ensuing **takeover battle**, the bidder may improve the terms offered and will then usually write to shareholders outlining the advantages that will follow from the successful takeover. In the meantime bids from other sources may be made (*see* grey knight; white knight) or the original bidder may withdraw as a result of measures taken by the board of the *target company (*see* poison pill; porcupine provisions). In an **unconditional bid**, the bidder will pay the offered price irrespective of the number of shares acquired, while the bidder of a **conditional bid** will only pay the price offered if sufficient shares are acquired to provide a controlling interest. Takeovers in the UK are subject to the rules and disciplines of the *City Code on Takeovers and Mergers.

**Takeover Panel** *See* City Code on Takeovers and Mergers.

**taker** The buyer of a traded *option. *Compare* writer.

**tala** (WS$) The standard monetary unit of Western Samoa, divided into 100 sene.

**TALISMAN** Abbreviation for Transfer Accounting Lodgement for Investors and Stock Management. This is the *London Stock Exchange computerized transfer system, which covers most UK securities; it also covers claims for dividends on shares being transferred. It is operated by a special company set up for the purpose, the Stock Exchange Pool Nominees Ltd, known as SEPON Ltd.

**talon** A printed form attached to a *bearer bond that enables the holder to apply for a new sheet of *coupons when the existing coupons have been used up.

**tambala** A monetary unit of Malawi, worth one hundredth of a *kwacha.

**tangible assets** Assets that can be touched, i.e. physical objects. However, tangible assets usually also include leases and company shares. They are therefore the fixed assets of an organization as opposed to such assets as goodwill, patents, and trademarks, which are even more intangible than leases and shares.

**Tanshi company** A Japanese company that deals on the money markets.

**tap issue** The issue of UK government securities or bills to selected market makers, usually to influence the price of gilts. The government can control their volume and price, like turning a tap on or off.

**tap stock** A gilt-edged security from an issue that has not been fully subscribed and is released onto the market slowly when its market price reaches predetermined levels. **Short taps** are short-dated stocks and **long taps** are long-dated taps.

**target company** A company that is subject to a *takeover bid.

**target price** *See* Common Agricultural Policy.

**tariff office** An insurance company that bases its premiums on a tariff arranged with other insurance companies. A **non-tariff office** is free to quote its own premiums.

**TAURUS** Abbreviation for Transfer and Automated Registration of Uncertified Stock. This was the *London Stock Exchange's computerized system designed to enable stocks and shares to be transferred without the use of contract notes or share certificates. It was abandoned in March 1993 leaving London behind its continental competitors; a new system will be devised.

**taxable income** Income liable to taxation. It is calculated by deducting *income-tax allowances and any other tax-deductible expenses from the taxpayer's gross income.

**tax allowance** *See* income-tax allowances.

**tax and price index (TPI)** A measure of the increase in taxable income needed to compensate taxpayers for any increase in retail prices. As an index of the rate of *inflation, it is similar to the *Retail Price Index, but in addition to measuring price changes it includes changes in average tax liability; for example, a cut in income tax will cause the TPI to rise by less than the RPI.

**taxation** A levy on individuals or corporate bodies by central or local government in order to finance the expenditure of that government and also as a means of implementing its fiscal policy. Payments for specific services rendered to or for the payer are not regarded as taxation. In the UK, an individual's income is taxed by means of an *income tax (*see also* PAYE), while corporations pay a *corporation tax. Capital profits are taxed by means of a *capital-gains tax while gifts, made during an individual's lifetime or on death, are taxed by means of an *inheritance tax. *See also* council tax; direct taxation; indirect taxation; poll tax; VAT.

**taxation brackets** Figures between which taxable income or wealth is taxed at a specified rate. For example, taxable incomes between, say, £2001 and £23,700 are liable to tax at 25%, while income in excess of £23,700 is taxed at 40%. *See also* bracket indexation.

**tax avoidance (tax planning)** Minimizing tax liabilities legally and by means of full disclosure to the tax authorities. *Compare* tax evasion.

**tax base**  The specified domain on which a tax is levied, e.g. an individual's income for *income tax, the estate of a deceased person for *inheritance tax, the profits of a company for *corporation tax.

**tax burden**  The amount of tax suffered by an individual or organization. This may not be the same as the tax actually paid because of the possibility of shifting tax or the normal *incidence of taxation. As an example of the latter case, *inheritance tax is paid by the personal representatives of the deceased but the tax burden falls on the heirs, since their inheritance is reduced.

**tax clearance**  An assurance, obtained from the UK Inland Revenue, that a proposed transaction, for example the reorganization of a company's share capital, will, if executed, not attract tax.

**tax credit**  **1.** Relief given for tax that has been notionally borne, as in UK dividends (*see* advance corporation tax) or when foreign tax has been paid and can be set off against a UK tax liability (*see* double taxation).  **2.** More generally, any tax deducted at source that is available to set against a tax liability.

**tax credit system**  A taxation system in which individuals are given tax allowances dependent on their needs; if tax on their income is less than the total of their tax credits, they can be paid the excess credits. *See also* negative income tax.

**tax-deductible**  Denoting a payment, allowance, benefit, etc., that can be deducted from a person's total income in calculating the *taxable income.

**tax deposit certificate**  A certificate issued by the UK Inland Revenue to a taxpayer who has made an advance payment in anticipation of future income tax, capital-gains tax, or corporation tax. The initial payment must not be less than £2000 and has to be made to a tax-collection office. The certificates bear interest, which is liable to tax. The interest rate depends on whether the certificate is withdrawn for cash or surrendered to meet a tax demand. A higher rate is paid on the latter. Interest normally runs to the date of encashment but if the certificate is used to pay tax, it runs only to the due date of payment of the liability, not the actual date of payment.

**tax evasion**  Minimizing tax liabilities illegally, usually by not disclosing that one is liable to tax or by giving false information to the authorities. Evasion is liable to severe penalties. *Compare* tax avoidance.

**Tax Exempt Special Savings Account (Tessa)**  A UK account with a savings institution (bank, building society, etc.), the interest or bonus on which, provided special conditions are met, is exempt from UK income tax. The tax exemption is lost if: (a) the deposits to the account exceed £3000 in the first year, more than £1800 in any subsequent year, or a maximum of £9000 in total; (b) the account holders' rights are assigned or used as security for a loan; (c) withdrawals exceed 75% of the interest or bonuses credited to the account prior to the withdrawal.

**tax exile**  A person with a high income or considerable wealth who chooses to live in a *tax haven to avoid high taxation in his or her own country.

**tax-free**  Denoting a payment, allowance, benefit, etc., on which no tax is payable.

**tax haven** A country or independent area that has a low rate of tax and therefore offers advantages to retired wealthy individuals or to companies that can arrange their affairs so that their tax liability falls at least partly in the low-tax haven. In the case of individuals, the cost of the tax saving is usually residence in the tax haven for a major part of the year (*see* tax exile). For multinational companies, an office in the tax haven, with some real or contrived business passing through it, is required. Monaco, Liechtenstein, the Bahamas, and the Cayman Islands are examples of tax havens.

**tax holiday** A period during which a company, in certain countries, is excused from paying corporation tax or profits tax (or pays them on only part of its profits) as an export incentive or an incentive to start up a new industry.

**tax loss** A loss made by an organization in one period, that can be carried forward to another period to reduce the tax payable by that organization in the subsequent period.

**tax planning** *See* tax avoidance.

**Tax Reform Act 1986** US legislation introduced to restrict the benefits of overseas *tax credits against US tax liabilities. Under this Act, income from foreign sources is categorized into one of several baskets, on which foreign tax credits are separately calculated. These baskets include: (a) interest, dividends, rents, royalties, etc.; (b) interest that has borne a high withholding tax (foreign tax of at least 5%); (c) financial services income; (d) shipping income. Where income from a foreign source does not fall into a particular basket, it is included in a 'general limitation income' basket.

**tax relief** A deduction from a taxable amount, usually given by statute. In the UK, income-tax reliefs are given in respect of income from tax-exempt sources (e.g. PEPs, Tessas, NSCs), as well as tax-deductible expenses, personal allowances, mortgage interest (*see* mortgage interest relief at source), and covenants. *See* income-tax allowances.

The reliefs against *capital-gains tax include the annual exemption (currently £5800), exemption from the proceeds of the sale of an only or a principal private residence, and retirement relief.

For *inheritance tax there is an annual relief (currently £3000) as well as relief in respect of gifts between spouses and gifts to political parties and charities; agricultural and business reliefs are also available.

**tax return** A form upon which a taxpayer makes an annual statement of income and personal circumstances enabling claims to be made for personal allowances. In the UK an income-tax return also requires details of *capital gains in the year. The onus is on the taxpayer to give the Inland Revenue the appropriate information even if the taxpayer receives no tax return. The completed return is used by the Inspector of Taxes to assess the appropriate tax liability.

Separate returns are required for *inheritance tax purposes and by the Customs and Excise in respect of VAT and excise duties.

**tax shelter** Any financial arrangement made in order to avoid or minimize taxes.

**tax year** *See* fiscal year.

**technical analysis** *See* investment analyst.

**technical rally**  *See* rally.

**technical reserves**  The assets held by an insurance company against future claims or losses.

**telegraphic transfer (TT)**  A method of transmitting money overseas by means of a transfer between banks by cable or telephone. The transfer is usually made in the currency of the payee and may be credited to the payee's account at a specified bank or paid in cash to the payee on application and identification.

**Telerate**  A US financial news and information service, partly owned and operated by the Dow Jones Corporation. It is also available in some other countries.

**Teletext Output Price Information Computer**  *See* TOPIC.

**teller**  The US name for a bank or building society cashier, i.e. someone who accepts deposits and pays out cash over the counter to customers.

**temporary assurance**  *See* term assurance.

**tender**  A means of auctioning an item of value to the highest bidder. Tenders are used in many circumstances, e.g. for allocating valuable construction contracts, for selling shares on a stock market (*see* offer for sale; issue by tender), or for the sale of government securities (*see* gilt-edged security).

**tender offer**  A US practice of offering securities to the public by inviting them to tender a price; the securities are then sold to the highest bidder.

**tender panel**  A group of banks who are asked to subscribe as a *syndicate for the issue of *euronote facilities.

**tenor**  The time that must elapse before a *bill of exchange or *promissory note becomes due for payment, as stated on the bill or note.

**term**  **1.** The period of time before a security expires or is redeemed.  **2.** *See* term assurance.  **3.** A clause in a contract that refers to a particular obligation between the contracting parties.

**term assurance (temporary assurance; term insurance)**  A life-assurance policy that provides a payment on death within a specified period of time (the term). No benefit is paid if the insured person dies outside the term. This form of insurance is often used to cover the period of a loan, mortgage, etc. *See also* decreasing term assurance.

**term bill**  *See* period bill.

**terminable annuity**  *See* certain annuity.

**terminal bonus**  An additional amount of money added to payments made on the maturity of an insurance policy or on the death of an insured person, because the investments of the insurer have produced a profit or surplus. Bonuses of this kind are paid at the discretion of the life office and usually take the form of a percentage of the sum assured.

**terminal date**  The date on which a *futures contract expires.

**terminal loss relief**  A tax loss made in the closing year of a business's life, which may be carried back and set against profits of earlier years.

**terminal market** A commodity market in a trading centre, such as London or New York, rather than a market in a producing centre, such as Calcutta or Singapore. The trade in terminal markets is predominantly in *futures contracts, but *spot goods may also be bought and sold.

**term insurance** *See* term assurance.

**term loan** A fixed-period loan, usually for one to ten years, that is paid back by the borrower in regular (often monthly) instalments with interest. This is the most common form of business loan; it may be secured or unsecured.

**term shares** Shares that cannot be sold for a given period (term). They are usually shares in a building society that cannot be cashed on demand and consequently carry a higher rate of interest.

**term structure of interest rates** The relationship between the *yields on fixed-interest securities (such as government bonds) and their maturity dates. One important factor affecting the term structure relates to expectations of changes in interest rates. For example, if both short-term and long-term bonds have the same yield initially and subsequently investors expect interest rates to fall, long-term bonds will appear relatively attractive, because, being fixed-interest securities, they will continue to pay their stated rates of interest for a long period, after market interest rates have declined. *Arbitrage will then ensure that their prices will rise and their yields will fall; thus yields on short-term bonds will exceed those on long-term bonds. A graph showing the relationship between the number of years to maturity and the yield is called the *yield curve. Other factors that may also affect the term structure include *liquidity preference and *hedging pressure, especially as *index futures and *interest-rate futures are now widely available on *financial futures exchanges.

**Tessa** Abbreviation for *Tax Exempt Special Savings Account.

**testacy** The state of a person who has died leaving a valid will. Such a person is said to have died **testate**.

**testator** A person who makes a will. The feminine form is **testatrix**.

**Thailand Stock Market** *See* Securities Exchange of Thailand.

**thebe** A monetary unit of Botswana, worth one hundredth of a *pula.

**thin capitalization** A form of company capitalization in which the capital of a company consists of too few shares and too much loan stock in the view of the tax authority. Some countries reserve the right in such cases to treat some of the interest on the loan stock as if it were a dividend, thus denying the right to a tax deduction on the interest payment.

**third-country acceptance (refinance bill)** An international trade *time draft drawn on a country other than that of the importer or exporter. *See also* banker's acceptance.

**third market** A market established by the London Stock Exchange in January 1987 for the trading of shares unsuited either to the *main market or the *unlisted-securities market (USM). The market was abolished on 31 December 1990 and combined with a reorganized USM. It had the object of specifying less stringent listing standards than either the main or unlisted markets, in order to attract the formerly unregulated *over-the-counter market, which was outside the jurisdiction of the London Stock Exchange. Investment in the third market was generally much more risky, because much less information was available on the companies.

**threshold price**   *See* Common Agricultural Policy.

**thrifts (thrift institutions)**   US non-banking savings institutions that also gave mortgage finance to home buyers. In the late 1980s the US government had to inject millions of dollars to shore up these institutions, which had found themselves in trouble by relying on short-term deposits to finance long-term lending.

**TIBOR**   Abbreviation for *Tokyo Inter Bank Offered Rate.

**tick (point)**   The smallest increment of price fluctuation in a commodity market. For example, on LIFFE interest-rate futures, the **tick size** is 0.01% of the nominal value of the trading unit. Thus, for example, on a three-month euromark futures contract, the trading unit is DM1,000,000; for each tick up or down, the **tick value** is the tick size multiplied by the trading unit multiplied by the length of the contract in years, i.e. $0.0001 \times 1,000,000 \times 3/12 = \text{DM25}$. If the contract was a futures purchase and the gain was 25 ticks, the profit would be DM625.

**tied loan**   A loan made by one nation to another on condition that the money loaned is spent buying goods or services in the lending nation. It thus helps the lending nation, by providing employment, as well as the borrowing nation.

**tiger markets**   The colloquial name for the four most important markets in the Pacific Basin after Japan. They are Hong Kong, South Korea, Singapore, and Taiwan. *Compare* dragon markets.

**Tigers**   *See* TIGR.

**tight money**   *See* dear money.

**TIGR**   Abbreviation for Treasury Investment Growth Receipts. These *zero-coupon bonds are linked to US Treasury bonds. Denominated in dollars, their semi-annual compounding yield is taxed in the UK as income in the year of encashment or redemption. They are often known as **Tigers**.

**time bargain**   A contract in which securities have to be delivered at some date in the future.

**time deposit**   A deposit of money in an interest-bearing account for a specified period. In the USA, a time deposit requires at least 30 days' notice of withdrawal. A time-deposit account can have a maturity period of anything from seven days to seven years.

**time draft**   A *bill of exchange drawn on and accepted by a US bank. *See also* banker's acceptance.

**time value**   The market value of an *option over and above its *intrinsic value. Thus the time value represents the value of the possibility that the option will be worth exercising before it expires. Clearly, an option's value declines with the passage of time, and its value at expiry will be nil if it is not in the money. At expiry the value of an option, if any, consists solely of its intrinsic value.

**toea**   A monetary unit of Papua New Guinea, worth one hundredth of a *kina.

**tokkin** A special investment fund on the Japanese stock markets owned by companies using their cash surpluses to generate extra income, although their main business is not in the financial markets.

**Tokyo Inter Bank Offered Rate (TIBOR)** The Japanese equivalent of the *London Inter Bank Offered Rate.

**Tokyo Stock Exchange (TSE)** The largest and most important of the eight stock exchanges in Japan, accounting for some 85% of the turnover in Japanese securities. The market is split into three sections. The first section lists some 1200 of the largest issues in the market. Around 70% of first-section companies are also listed in the markets in Osaka and Nagoya. The second section has around 400 stocks, with less stringent listing requirements, similar to the *unlisted-securities market in the UK. Foreign shares are traded on the third section of the market. The TSE also has an *over-the-counter market in shares registered with the Japanese Securities Dealers Association. A computerized trading system for over-the-counter stocks was established in late 1991. TSE members are either regulars, who deal in securities as principals, or agents (saitori), who can only act as intermediaries between regular members. Dealing is now mainly electronic through the Computerized Order Routing and Execution System (**CORES**), although about 150 first-section stocks are still traded by *open outcry on the exchange floor. The main market indicator is the *Nikkei Stock Average of 225 Japanese industrial companies.

**tombstone** A newspaper or magazine advertisement showing the parties involved in an acquisition, merger, new issue, large syndicated loan, or other major financial deal. The advertisements are very simple, do not directly canvass for business, and resemble the brief information usually found on a gravestone. They are usually paid for by the borrower rather than the financial institutions involved.

**TOPIC** Abbreviation for Teletext Output Price Information Computer. This computerized communication system provides brokers and market makers on the *London Stock Exchange with information about share price movements and bargains as they are transacted. Input is from the *Stock Exchange Automated Quotations System (SEAQ).

**top slicing** A method of assessing the taxable gain on a life-assurance policy. The proceeds of the policy plus all capital withdrawals, less the premiums paid, are divided by the number of years for which the policy has been in force. This amount is added to any other income for the year in which the chargeable event occurred; if this places the taxpayer in a higher tax band, the whole gain is charged at the appropriate marginal rate, i.e. the tax rate in that band less the basic rate of tax. If the sum does not exceed the basic rate tax, no further tax is due.

**top up** To increase the benefits due under an existing insurance scheme, especially to increase the provision for a pension when a salary increase enables the insured to pay increased premiums.

**Toronto Stock Exchange (TSE)** The main exchange for Canadian shares; it is larger than either the Montreal or Vancouver markets. The Toronto exchange is computerized and was the first to link with a foreign exchange (the *American Stock Exchange). The main indicators are the Toronto 35 index and the wider TSE 300 Composite index.

**total-absorption costing** A method of arriving at the cost of producing goods and services that allocates to them not only such direct costs as labour and materials but also the other costs of the organization, such as general overheads and head-office costs. This method ensures, if the goods can be sold at the resulting price, that all costs will be covered. However, opportunities may be lost to make some contribution to overheads if they are not fully covered. *Compare* marginal costing.

**total income** The income of a taxpayer from all sources. This is often referred to as **statutory total income**, which consists of income from sources based on the income of the current year and income from other sources based on income of the preceding year. This artificial concept is used to calculate a person's income tax for a given year.

**total profits** The income of a company from all sources, including capital gains. This figure, after deduction of annual charges, is used to calculate the corporation tax payable by the company. Dividends from UK companies are not included in the figure.

**touch** The largest available spread or difference between the bid and offer prices of a security.

**touch screen** A system of *screen trading in which the operator uses a finger or other pointer to touch the screen in order to activate the system instead of using a keyboard or other system of entry.

**town clearing** *See* Association for Payment Clearing Services.

**TPI** Abbreviation for *tax and price index.

**trade** **1.** The activity of selling goods or services in order to make a profit. Profits from trade are taxed under *income tax or *corporation tax on income, rather than under *capital-gains tax or corporation tax on capital gains. The concept of trade is difficult to define for taxation purposes (*see* badges of trade). **2.** To buy or sell in a market.

**trade balance** *See* balance of trade.

**trade barrier** Any action by a government that restricts free trading between organizations within that country and the world outside. Tariffs, quotas, embargoes, sanctions, and restrictive regulations all present barriers to free trade.

**trade bill** A *bill of exchange used to pay for goods. They are usually either held until they mature, as they do not command a favourable discount rate compared to bank bills, or they are discounted by banks.

**trade bloc** A group of nations united by trade agreements between themselves. The EC forms a trade bloc.

**trade credit** Credit given by one company to another; it usually results when a supplier of goods or services allows the customer a period (e.g. 14 days, 90 days) before expecting an invoice to be settled.

**trade creditor** One who is owed money by an organization for having provided goods or services to that organization.

**trade debt** A debt that arises during the normal course of trade.

**traded months** Those months of the year used in a futures market (*see* futures contract) for stipulating that goods must be delivered or taken up.

**traded option** *See* option.

**trade gap** A deficit in a nation's *balance of payments.

**trade investment** Shares in or loans made to another company with a view to facilitating trade with the other company.

**trademark** A distinctive symbol that identifies particular products of a trader to the general public. The symbol may consist of a device, words, or a combination of these. A trader may register a trademark at the Register of Trade Marks, which is held at the Patent Office (*see* patent). The trader then enjoys the exclusive right to use the trademark in connection with the goods for which it was registered. Any manufacturer, dealer, importer, or retailer may register a trademark. Registration is initially for seven years and is then renewable. The right to remain on the register may be lost if the trademark is not used or is misused. The owner of a trademark may assign it or, subject to the Registrar's approval, allow others to use it. If anyone uses a registered trademark without the owner's permission, or uses a mark that is likely to be confused with a registered trademark, the owner can sue for an *injunction and *damages or an account of profits.

**trading account** The part of a *profit and loss account in which the cost of goods sold is compared with the money raised by their sale in order to arrive at the gross profit.

**trading floor** An area in a stock exchange, commodity market, financial futures and options market, etc., in which dealers trade by personal contact. In some markets the trading floors are being replaced by *screen trading.

**trading pit** *See* pit.

**trading post** The base on the *trading floor from which a *specialist on a US stock exchange operates.

**trading profit** The profit of an organization before deductions for such items as interest, directors' fees, auditors' remuneration, etc.

**traditional option** *See* option.

**tranche** (French: slice) A part or instalment of a large sum of money. In the International Monetary Fund the first 25% of a loan is known as the **reserve** (formerly **gold**) **tranche**. In **tranche funding**, successive sums of money become available on a prearranged basis to a new company, often linked to the progress of the company and its ability to reach the targets set in its *business plan.

**tranche CD** A *certificate of deposit that has one maturity date but is sold by the issuing bank in portions (*tranches) to other investors.

**transfer 1.** The movement of money from one bank account to another. **2.** The movement of funds through the banking system's *clearing house. **3.** A large movement of dollars in the USA through the *fedwire system. **4.** The conveyance of property ownership by the transfer of deeds. **5.** The change of title of ownership of stocks and shares from one owner to a new one by *transfer deed.

**transferable**  Denoting a deed or other document the ownership of which can be transferred freely, e.g. a *negotiable instrument.

**Transfer Accounting Lodgement for Investors**  See TALISMAN.

**Transfer and Automated Registration of Uncertified Stock**  See TAURUS.

**transfer deed**  A deed that is used to transfer property from one person to another. On the *London Stock Exchange a **stock transfer form** has to be signed by the seller of registered securities to legalize the transaction. This is dealt with by the computerized *TALISMAN system.

**transferee**  A person to whom an asset is transferred.

**transfer form**  See transfer deed.

**transfer of value**  The reduction in the value of a person's estate by a gratuitous transfer. Such transfers are subject to *inheritance tax in most cases if made in a given period before the date of the donor's death.

**transferor**  A person who transfers an asset to another (the transferee).

**transfer payment (transfer income)**  A payment made or income received in which no goods or services are being paid for. Pensions, unemployment benefits, subsidies to farmers, etc., are transfer payments; they are excluded in calculating *gross national product.

**transfer pricing**  A means of allocating costs between units of a large organization or multinational company for goods or services supplied. The pricing may be based on allocating true profits to the individual units, although, in the case of multinational companies, the price may be chosen to avoid paying excessive taxes or duties in one particular country.

**transfer risk**  The risk that goods sold on credit to a foreign buyer may not be paid for in full or on time as a result of a change in exchange-control regulations in the buyer's country.

**transfer stamp**  An impressed stamp on documents relating to the transfer of securities or land, as an acknowledgment that the *stamp duty has been paid.

**transparency**  An essential condition of a free market in securities, in which transaction prices and volumes of trade are visible for all to see.

**traveller's cheque**  A cheque issued by a bank, building society, travel agency, credit-card company, etc., to enable a traveller to obtain cash in a foreign currency when abroad. They may be cashed at banks, exchange bureaus, restaurants, hotels, some shops, etc., abroad on proof of identity. The traveller has to sign the cheque twice, once in the presence of the issuer and again in the presence of the paying bank, agent, etc. Most traveller's cheques are covered against loss.

**treasurer**  A person who is responsible for looking after the money and other assets of an organization. This may include overseeing the provision of the organization's finances as well as some stewardship over the way in which the money is spent.

**treasure trove**  Gold or silver found on land that has been hidden deliberately and that has no known owner. Treasure trove belongs to the Crown but the finder is recompensed for its value.

**Treasury**  The UK government department responsible for the country's financial policies and management of the economy. The First Lord of the Treasury is the Prime Minister, but the Treasury is run by the Chancellor of the Exchequer.

**Treasury bill**  A *bill of exchange issued by the Bank of England on the authority of the UK government that is repayable in three months. They are issued by tender each week to the *discount houses in units of £5000 to £100,000. They bear no interest, the yield being the difference between the purchase price and the redemption value. The US Treasury also issues Treasury bills.

**Treasury bill rate**  The rate of interest obtainable by buying a *Treasury bill at a discount and selling it at its redemption value.

**Treasury bill tender**  A weekly sale of Treasury bills to UK *discount houses by the Bank of England. The cost of the bills is set by the **Treasury bill tender rate**.

**Treasury bond**  A bond issued by the US Treasury.

**Treasury Investment Growth Receipts**  *See* TIGR.

**Treasury stocks**  *See* gilt-edged security.

**treaty**  **1.** Any formal agreement between nations. A **commercial treaty** relates to trade between the signatories.  **2.** A transaction in which a sale is negotiated between the parties involved (**by private treaty**) rather than by auction.  **3.** An agreement, usually in reinsurance, in which a reinsurer agrees automatically to accept risks from an insurer, either when a certain sum insured is exceeded or on the basis of a percentage of every risk accepted. With such a treaty an insurer has the confidence and capacity to accept larger risks than would otherwise be possible, as the necessary reinsurance is already arranged.

**trial balance**  A listing of the balances on all the *accounts of an organization with debit balances in one column and credit balances in the other. If the processes of double-entry book-keeping have been accurate, the totals of each column should be the same. If they are not the same, checks must be carried out to find the discrepancy. The figures in the trial balance after some adjustments, e.g. for closing stocks, prepayments and accruals, depreciation, etc., are used to prepare the final accounts (profit and loss account and balance sheet).

**trinh**  A monetary unit of Vietnam, worth one thousandth of a *dông.

**true and fair view**  Auditors of the published accounts of companies both in the UK and internationally are required by law to form an opinion as to whether the accounts they audit show a 'true and fair view' of the organization's affairs. 'True' implies that the accounts contain no false statements, 'fair' implies that the aggregate of facts shown by the 'true' statements is not misleading because, for instance, of omissions.

**trust**  **1.** An arrangement enabling property to be held by a person or persons (the *trustees) for the benefit of some other person or persons (the beneficiaries). The trustee is the legal owner of the property but the beneficiary has an equitable interest in it. A trust may be intentionally created or it may be imposed by law (e.g. if a trustee gives away trust property, the recipient will hold that property as constructive trustee for the beneficiary). Trusts are commonly used to provide for families and in commercial situations (e.g. pensions trusts). **2.** A monopoly formed in the USA, in which the owners of merging corporations gave their stock to a board of trustees, who were empowered to act on their behalf. Such monopolies were largely outlawed by the antitrust laws.

**trust bank** A Japanese bank that both lends and accepts savings; it also carries out trust activities, usually involving property or pension funds.

**trust corporation** **1.** A body allowed by law to act as a trustee for a will. **2.** (or **trust company**) In the USA, a non-banking organization that can engage in banking activities provided it is chartered by the state authorities. US trust companies can be members of the *Federal Reserve System.

**trust deed** The document creating and setting out the terms of a *trust. It will usually contain the names of the trustees, the identity of the beneficiaries, and the nature of the trust property, as well as the powers and duties of the trustees. Trusts of land must be declared in writing; trusts of other property need not be although there is often a trust deed to avoid uncertainty.

**trustee** A person who holds the legal title to property but who is not its beneficial owner. Usually there are two or more trustees of a *trust and for some trusts of land this is necessary. The trustee may not profit from the position but must act for the benefit of the beneficiary, who may be regarded as the real owner of the property. Either an individual or a company may act as trustee. It is usual to provide for the remuneration of trustees in the trust deed, otherwise there is no right to payment. Trustees may be personally liable to beneficiaries for loss of trust property.

**trustee in bankruptcy** A person who administers a bankrupt's estate and realizes it for the benefit of the creditors (*see* bankruptcy).

**trustee investments** Investments in which trustees are authorized to invest trust property. In the UK the Trustees Investment Act 1961 regulates the investments of trust property that may be made by trustees. The Act applies unless excluded by a trust deed executed after the Act was passed. Half of the trust fund must be invested in **narrow-range securities**, largely specified in fixed-interest investments. The other half may be invested in **wider-range securities**, most importantly ordinary shares in companies quoted on the London Stock Exchange. In some cases, trustees must take advice before investing. The Act considerably enlarged the range of trustee investments.

**trust fund** A fund consisting of the assets belonging to a *trust, including money and property, that is held by the *trustees for the beneficiaries.

**trust letter** A document that assigns goods to a bank as security against a loan and enables the borrower to regain title of the goods in order to sell them to pay off the loan.

**trust receipt** A document given by a bank holding a borrower's goods as security against a loan (*see* trust letter), when the borrower takes possession of these goods in order to sell them to pay off the loan.

**Truth in Lending Act** US consumer protection legislation, dating from 1969, that required lenders to state how they calculated interest on loans and other charges and to express them as an *annual percentage rate. The Act also allows the borrower a 'cooling-off' period, authorizing withdrawal from a financial agreement on a mortgage, within three days of signing a consumer credit agreement.

**TSA** Abbreviation for The *Securities Association Ltd, which has now been replaced by the *Securities and Futures Authority Ltd (SFA).

**TSE 1.** Abbreviation for *Tokyo Stock Exchange. **2.** Abbreviation for *Toronto Stock Exchange.

**tugrik** The standard monetary unit of Mongolia, divided into 100 möngös.

**turn** The difference between the price at which a *market maker will buy a security (*see* bid) and the price at which the market maker will sell it (*see* offer price), i.e. the market maker's profit.

**turnover 1.** The total sales figure of an organization for a stated period. Turnover is defined in the UK Companies Act 1985 as the total revenue of an organization derived from the provision of goods and services, less trade discounts, VAT, and any other taxes based on this revenue. **2.** More generally, the rate at which at some asset is turned over, e.g. stock turnover is obtained by dividing the total sales figure by the value of the particular asset. **3.** The total value of the transactions on a market or stock exchange in a specified period.

**turnover tax** A tax on the sales made by a business, i.e. on its turnover. *See* sales tax.

**turn-round rate** The total cost of a transaction on a commodity market, including the broker's commission and the fee charged by the *clearing house.

**twenty-four-hour trading** Round-the-clock dealings in securities, bonds, and currency. In practice, it is not normally carried out from any one office of a securities house; instead, the dealers in one time zone pass on their position to associates in another time zone. Thus, a London office may pass its position to its New York office, which is passed, in turn, to Tokyo, and back to London. Twenty-four-hour trading has been encouraged by the rise in cross-border share trading, which rose from around 6% of world equity trading in 1979 to more than 15% at the end of the 1980s.

**two-tier tender offer** A tender offer in a takeover in which shareholders are offered a high initial offer for sufficient shares to give the bidder a controlling interest in the company, followed by an offer to acquire the remaining shares at a lower price. Bidders use this technique in order to provide an incentive to shareholders to accept the initial offer quickly. Such offers are usually for a combination of cash and shares in the bidder's own company.

**uberrima fides** (Latin: utmost good faith) The basis of all insurance contracts. *See* utmost good faith.

**UK Balance of Payments** An annual publication of the Central Statistical Office. It is often known as the *Pink Book*.

**UK National Accounts** A monthly publication of the Central Statistical Office. It is often known as the *Blue Book*. It provides figures for the *gross domestic product and separate accounts of production, income, and expenditure.

**ULS** Abbreviation for unsecured loan stock. *See* unsecured debenture.

**ultra vires** (Latin: beyond the powers) Denoting an act of an official or corporation for which there is no authority. The powers of officials exercising administrative duties and of companies are limited by the instrument from which their powers are derived. If they act outside these powers, their action may be challenged in the courts. A company's powers are limited by the objects clause in its memorandum of association. It it enters into an agreement outside these objects, the agreement may be unenforceable, although a third party may have a remedy under the Companies Act 1985 if it was dealing with the company in good faith (or there may be other equitable remedies).

**umbrella fund** An *offshore fund consisting of a *fund of funds that invests in other offshore funds.

**unamortized cost** **1.** The historical cost of a fixed asset less the total depreciation shown against that asset up to a specified date. **2.** The value given to a fixed asset in the accounts of an organization after a revaluation less the total depreciation shown against that asset since it was revalued.

**unappropriated profit** The part of an organization's profit that is neither allocated to a specific purpose nor paid out in *dividends.

**unbundling** The takeover of a large conglomerate with a view to retaining the core business as a going concern and selling off some or all of the subsidiary businesses to help pay for the takeover.

**uncalled capital** *See* reserve capital.

**uncertificated units** A small number of units purchased for an investor in a *unit trust by reinvestment of dividends. If the number of units is too small to warrant the issue of a certificate they are held on account for the investor and added to the total when the holding is sold.

**uncleared effects** Financial documents lodged with a bank for collection, still held by the bank pending the completion of the collection.

**unconditional bid**   *See* takeover bid.

**unconfirmed letter of credit**   *See* letter of credit.

**unconscionable bargain**   *See* catching bargain.

**undated security**   A *fixed-interest security that has no *redemption date. *See* Consols.

**undercapitalized**   Denoting an organization that has insufficient capital or reserves for the amount of business it undertakes.

**undersubscription**   *See* oversubscription.

**underwrite**   **1.** To guarantee an issue of *commercial paper, *euronote, etc., especially by a bank. **2.** To carry out a detailed investigation of the risks involved in making a loan to a particular borrower, especially by a bank. *See also* underwriter.

**underwriter**   **1.** A person who examines a risk, decides whether or not it can be insured, and, if it can, works out the premium to be charged, usually on the basis of the frequency of past claims for similar risks. Underwriters are either employed by insurance companies or are members of *Lloyd's (*see also* syndicate). The name arises from the early days of marine insurance, when a merchant would, as a sideline, *write* his name *under* the amount and details of the risk he had agreed to cover on a slip of paper. **2.** A financial institution, usually an *issuing house or *merchant bank, that guarantees to buy a proportion of any unsold shares when a *new issue is offered to the public. Underwriters usually work for a commission (usually 2%), and a number may combine together to buy all the unsold shares, provided that the minimum subscription stated in the *prospectus has been sold to the public. *See also* underwrite.

**undischarged bankrupt**   A person whose *bankruptcy has not been discharged. Such persons must not obtain credit (above £250) without first informing their creditors that they are undischarged bankrupts, become directors of companies, or trade under another name. Undischarged bankrupts may not hold office as a JP, MP, mayor, or councillor. A peer who is an undischarged bankrupt may not sit in the House of Lords.

**undisclosed factoring**   A form of *factoring in which the seller of goods does not wish to disclose that a factor is being used. In these circumstances, the factor buys the goods that have been sold (rather than the debt their sale incurred) and, as an *undisclosed principal, appoints the original seller to act as an agent to recover the debt. The factor assumes responsibility in the case of non-payment so that from the point of view of the seller, the factor offers the same service as in normal factoring.

**undisclosed principal**   A person who buys or sells through an agent or broker and remains anonymous. The agent or broker must disclose that such deals are being made on behalf of an undisclosed principal; if the agent or broker does not do so, the agent or broker may be treated in law as the principal and in some circumstances the contract may be made void.

**undistributable reserves**   *See* capital reserves.

**undistributed profit**  Profit earned by an organization but not distributed to its shareholders by way of dividends. Such sums are available for later distribution but are frequently used by companies to finance their trade.

**undue influence**  Unfair pressure exerted on a person to sign a contract that is not a true expression of that person's aims or requirements at the time, but is to the advantage of another party (either a party to the contract or a third party). Such a contract may be set aside by a court.

**unearned income**  Income not derived from trades, professions, or vocations, or from the emoluments of office. In the UK, until 1984, it was thought that as investment income was more permanent than earned income and did not depend on the labours of the taxpayer, it should be taxed more heavily than earned income. This was achieved by an investment-income surcharge, which was an extra 15% over the normal rate of income tax. In the UK both earned and unearned income are now taxed at the same rates.

**unfavourable balance**  A *balance of trade or *balance of payments deficit.

**unfranked income**  Any type of income from investments that is not *franked investment income.

**unfunded pension scheme**  A government pension scheme in which contributions from those in employment provide the funds for paying the pensioners.

**unilateral relief**  Relief against *double taxation given by the UK authorities for tax paid in another country with which the UK has no double-taxation agreement.

**uninsurable risk**  *See* risk.

**unissued share capital**  The difference between the nominal *share capital of a company and the issued share capital.

**unitary taxation**  A form of corporation tax used in some states of the USA for international corporations operating within their jurisdiction. Tax is computed taking into account not only the corporation's worldwide profits but also their payroll, sales revenue, and fixed assets in that state.

**unit banking**  A system of banking in which a bank must be a single enterprise without branches. In the USA there are many thousands of unit banks, which are often independently owned and maintained. Some states insist on unit banking, but unit banks are common even in those states that permit branch banking.

**United Nations Common Fund for Commodities (CFC)**  A fund set up by the United Nations Conference on Trade and Development in 1989 to provide finance for international commodity organizations to enable buffer stocks to be maintained and to carry out research into the development of commodity markets.

**unit investment trust**  *See* unit trust.

**unitization**  The process of changing an *investment trust into a *unit trust.

**unit-linked policy**  A life-assurance policy in which the benefits depend on the performance of units in an *asset-backed fund. In this way a small investor can benefit from investment in a *managed fund without making a large financial commitment. As they are linked to the value of assets in the underlying fund, unit-linked policies can go up or down in value. Policyholders can surrender the policy at any time and the *surrender value is the selling price of the units purchased by the date of cancellation (less expenses).

**unit of account 1.** A function of money enabling its users to calculate the value of their transactions and to keep accounts. **2.** The standard unit of currency of a country. **3.** An artificial currency used only for accounting purposes; the EC employs such a unit for fixing its farm prices (see green currencies).

**unit trust 1.** A *trust formed in the UK to manage a portfolio of stock-exchange securities, in which small investors can buy units. This gives the small investor access to a diversified portfolio of securities, chosen and managed by professional *fund managers, who seek either high capital gains or high yields, within the parameters of reasonable security. The trustees, usually a commercial bank, are the legal owners of the securities and responsible for ensuring that the managers keep to the terms laid down in the trust deed. Prices of unit trusts are quoted daily, the difference between the bid and offer prices providing a margin for the management costs and the costs of buying and selling on the *London Stock Exchange. Basic-rate tax is deducted from the dividends paid by unit trusts and capital gains on the sale of a holding are subject to capital-gains tax, although transactions involved in creating the portfolio are free of capital-gains tax. UK unit trusts are authorized and controlled by the Department of Trade and Industry and most belong to the *Unit Trust Association. In the USA unit trusts are called **mutual funds** (see also open-end fund). Many trusts are now available, specializing in various sectors of the market, both at home and abroad; there is also a wide spectrum of trusts catering for both those seeking growth and those seeking income. See also unit-linked policy. **2.** A trust scheme (also called a **unit investment trust**) in the USA in which investors purchase **redeemable trust certificates**. The money so raised is used by the trustees to buy such securities as bonds, which are usually held until they mature. Usually both the number of certificates issued and the investments held remain unchanged during the life of the scheme, but the certificates can be sold back to the trustees at any time.

**Unit Trust Association (UTA)** An association formed to agree standards of practice for the managers of unit trusts for the protection of unit-trust holders and to act as the representative body of **Managers of Authorized Unit Trusts** in dealings with the government and other authorities. It also coordinates control of commissions and charges and has a register of approved agents for selling unit trusts as intermediaries.

**universal banking** Banking that involves not only services related to loans and savings but also those involved in making investments in companies. Universal banking is most common in Germany, Switzerland, and the Netherlands. The Glass–Steagal Act 1933 prohibits universal banking in the USA, although this is under market pressures to change. In the UK, it has been largely avoided as it often leads the banker to become a shadow director of the company in which the bank has invested and to which it is also lending.

**unlimited company** See company.

**unlimited liability** A liability to pay all the debts incurred by a business. This occurs if the business is carried on by a sole trader or by a *partnership. In the case of a *limited company, there is a firm distinction between a person's business liabilities and that person's personal liabilities.

**unliquidated damages**  *See* damages.

**unlisted company**  *See* unquoted company.

**unlisted securities**  Securities (usually *equities) in companies that are not on an official stock-exchange list. They are therefore not required to satisfy the standards set for listing (*see* listed security). Unlisted securities are usually issued in relatively small companies and their shares usually carry a high degree of risk. In London, unlisted securities are traded on the *unlisted-securities market (USM) and other exchanges have their own USMs. The existence of a USM enables owners of small companies to realize their investments and raise capital, without having to satisfy the more stringent requirements of the *main market. For full listing a company has to have a capital of at least £700,000, a three-year trading record, and 25% of the equity has to be available to the public. For unlisted securities the capital figure is the same but only 10% of the equity need be available for purchase on the USM, and there is a minimum two-year trading period.

**unlisted-securities market (USM)**  A market established by the *London Stock Exchange in 1980 to trade in shares of small companies, not suitable for the *main market (although most USM companies ultimately aim for promotion). The USM is cheaper to join, and the listing requirements are less stringent (*see* unlisted securities). There are currently under 370 companies traded on the USM, compared to over 7000 on the main market. Between 1987 and 1990 the London Stock Exchange also had a *third market dealing in unlisted securities. This merged with the USM in 1990. In December 1992 the London Stock Exchange proposed to abolish the USM at the end of 1995, with no new entrants permitted after June 1993. *Compare* over-the-counter market.

**unquoted company**  A company whose securities (*see* unquoted securities) are not normally available to the public on a stock exchange.

**unquoted securities**  Securities that are not dealt in on any stock exchange. On the London Stock Exchange there are rules for occasional unofficial trading in unquoted securities of small companies or new ventures. Unquoted securities are usually shown in balance sheets valued at cost or market value (if this can be ascertained).

**unsecured creditor**  A person who is owed money by an organization but who has not arranged that in the event of non-payment specific assets would be available as a fund out of which that person could be paid in priority to other creditors.

**unsecured debenture**  A *debenture or loan stock (unsecured loan stock is sometimes abbreviated to **ULS**) in which no specific assets have been set aside as a fund out of which the holders could be paid either interest or repayment of capital in priority to other creditors in the event of non-payment.

**unsecured debt**  A debt that is not covered by any kind of collateral.

**unvalued policy**  An insurance policy for property that has a sum insured shown for each item although the insurers do not acknowledge that this figure is its actual value. As a result, if a claim is made the insured must provide proof of the value of the item lost, damaged, or stolen before a payment will be made. *Compare* valued policy.

**upstream** Denoting a loan from a subsidiary company to its parent, for example a loan from a subsidiary of a bank to its holding company to enable the holding company to pay its dividends.

**usance** **1.** The time allowed for the payment of short-term foreign *bills of exchange. It varies from country to country but is often 60 days. **2.** Formerly, the rate of interest on a loan.

**USM** Abbreviation for *unlisted-securities market.

**US stock exchanges** The nine stock exchanges in the USA: the *New York Stock Exchange, *American Stock Exchange, *National Association of Securities Dealers Automated Quotation System, *Pacific Stock Exchange, National Stock Exchange (a small New York exchange dealing in smaller companies not listed elsewhere), Philadelphia Stock Exchange (the oldest exchange in the USA, founded 1790), Boston Stock Exchange, Midwest Stock Exchange, and the Cincinnati Stock Exchange.

**UTA** Abbreviation for *Unit Trust Association.

**utmost good faith (uberrima fides)** The fundamental principle of insurance practice, requiring that a person wishing to take out an insurance cover must provide all the information the insurer needs to calculate the correct premium for the risk involved. Nothing must be withheld from the insurers, even if they do not actually ask for the information on an application form. The principle is essential because an insurer usually has no knowledge of the facts involved in the risk they are being asked to cover; the only source of information is the person requiring the insurance. If an insured person is found to have withheld information or given false information, the insurer can treat the policy. as void and the courts will support a refusal to pay claims.

**valium holiday (valium picnic)** A colloquial name for a non-trading day on a stock exchange or other commercial market; i.e. a market holiday.

**valorization** The raising or stabilization of the value of a commodity or currency by artificial means, usually by a government. For example, if a government wishes to increase the price of a commodity that it exports it may attempt to decrease the supply of that commodity by encouraging producers to produce less, by stockpiling the commodity itself, or, in extreme cases, by destroying part of the production.

**value added** The value added to goods or services by a step in the chain of original purchase, manufacture or other enhancement, and retail. For example, if a manufacturer acquires a partly made component, the value added will be the combination of labour and profit that increase the value of the part before it is sold. *See* VAT.

**value-added tax** *See* VAT.

**value date** **1.** The date on which specified funds become available for use. **2.** The date on which a transaction actually takes place. **3.** The date on which foreign exchange is due to be delivered.

**valued policy** An insurance policy in which the value of the subject matter is agreed when the cover starts. As a result, the amount to be paid in the event of a total-loss claim is already decided and does not need to be negotiated. *Compare* unvalued policy.

**value for money audit** An audit of a government department, charity, or other non-profitmaking organization to assess whether or not it is functioning efficiently and giving value for the money it spends.

**value received** Words that appear on a *bill of exchange to indicate that the bill is a means of paying for goods or services to the value of the bill. However, these words need not appear on a UK bill as everyone who has signed a UK bill is deemed to have been a party to it for value.

**value to business** The net current replacement cost of an asset of a business.

**value transferred** The amount by which a donor's estate is diminished by making a *transfer of value. The term is used in the computation of *inheritance tax.

**variable life assurance** A *unit-linked policy in which the policyholder can vary the amount of life assurance cover provided.

**variable-rate mortgage** A *mortgage in which the rate of interest is varied from time to time by the mortgagee (lender) according to market conditions.

**variable-rate security** A security in which the interest rate varies with market rates. *Floating-rate notes, eurobonds, and 90-day *certificates of deposit are examples of variable-rate securities.

**variance analysis** An analysis of the difference between a budgeted cost, income, or profit and the actual amounts. This forms the basis of **variance accounting**.

**variation margins** The gains or losses on open contracts in futures markets, calculated on the basis of the closing price at the end of each day. They are credited by the *clearing house to its members' accounts and by its members to their customers' accounts.

**VAT** Abbreviation for value-added tax. Although this is theoretically a tax on *value added, in practice it resembles a sales tax in that each trader adds the tax to sale invoices issued and accounts for the tax so collected to Customs and Excise. However, the trader is permitted to deduct the amount of tax paid on invoices received for goods and services (but not for wages and salaries). Thus VAT is a form of *indirect taxation, its burden being borne not by traders but by the ultimate consumers of their goods and services. The system is designed to avoid the cascade in which tax is paid on tax, as goods and services pass through long chains of activity; in VAT, all goods and services ultimately bear only the rate of tax applicable to the final sale to the consumer. VAT was introduced in the UK in 1973 to comply with its partners in the EC. In the UK all goods and services bear VAT at a rate of 17½% (since April 1991), unless they are *zero-rated or exempt.

**vatu** (VT) The standard monetary unit of Vanuatu.

**vault cash** The actual cash present in any bank to enable it to make day-to-day payments to customers.

**velocity of circulation** The average number of times that a unit of money is used in a specified period, approximately equal to the total amount of money spent in that period divided by the total amount of money in circulation. The **income velocity of circulation** is the number of times that a particular unit of currency forms part of a person's income in a specified period. It is given by the ratio of the *gross national product to the amount of money in circulation. The **transactions velocity of circulation** is the number of times that a particular unit of currency is spent in a money transaction in a specified period, i.e. the ratio of the total amount of money spent in sales of goods or services to the amount of money in circulation.

**vendor placing** A type of *placing used as a means of acquiring another company or business. For example, if company X wishes to buy a business from company Y, it issues company X shares to company Y as payment with the prearranged agreement that these shares are then placed with investors in exchange for cash. Vendor placings have been popular with some companies as a cheaper alternative to a *rights issue. *See also* bought deal.

**venture capital** *See* risk capital.

**vertical integration** *See* integration.

**vertical spread** A strategy used with *options, consisting of buying a long call option and a short call option with the same exercise date.

**vested benefit** A benefit owing to a member of a pension scheme, whether or not the member is employed by the organizers of the scheme.

**vested interest** **1.** In law, an interest in property that is certain to come about rather than one dependent upon some event that may not happen. For example, a gift to 'A for life and then to B' means that A's interest is **vested in possession**, because A has the property now. B's gift is also vested (but not in possession) because A will certainly die sometime and then B (or B's estate if B is dead) will inherit the property. A gift to C 'if C reaches the age of 30' is not vested, because C may die before reaching that age. An interest that is not vested is known as a **contingent interest**. **2.** An involvement in the outcome of some business, scheme, transaction, etc., usually in anticipation of a personal gain.

**visibles** Earnings from exports and payments for imports of goods, as opposed to services (such as banking and insurance). The *balance of trade is made up of visibles and is sometimes called the **visible balance.**

**volume** **1.** The space occupied by something. **2.** A measure of the amount of trade that has taken place, usually in a specified period. On the *London Stock Exchange, for example, the number of shares traded in a day is called the volume and the value of these shares is called the *turnover. In commodity markets, the daily volume is usually the number of lots traded in a day.

**voluntary arrangement** A procedure provided for by the Insolvency Act 1986, in which a company may come to an arrangement with its creditors to pay off its debts and to manage its affairs so that it resolves its financial difficulties. This arrangement may be proposed by the directors, an administrator acting under an *administration order, or a *liquidator. A qualified insolvency practitioner must be appointed to supervise the arrangement. This practitioner may be the administrator or liquidator, in which case a meeting of the company and its creditors must be called to consider the arrangement. The proposals may be modified or approved at this meeting but, once approved, they bind all those who had notice of the meeting. The court may make the necessary orders to bring the arrangement into effect. The arrangement may be challenged in court in the case of any irregularity. The aim of this legislation is to assist the company to solve its financial problems without the need for a winding-up (*see* liquidation).

**voluntary liquidation (voluntary winding-up)** *See* creditors' voluntary liquidation; members' voluntary liquidation.

**vostro account** A bank account held by a foreign bank with a UK bank, usually in sterling. *Compare* nostro account.

**voting shares** Shares in a company that entitle their owner to vote at the annual general meeting and any extraordinary meetings of the company. Shares that carry **voting rights** are usually *ordinary shares, rather than *A shares or *debentures. The company's articles of association will state which shares carry voting rights.

**wafer seal** A modern form of seal used on such documents as deeds. It is usually a small red disc stuck onto the document to represent the seal. Almost any form of seal agreeable to all the parties concerned is now acceptable in place of sealing wax.

**wagering contract** *See* gaming contract.

**waiter** An attendant at the *London Stock Exchange and at *Lloyd's, who carries messages and papers, etc. The name goes back to the 17th-century London coffee houses from which these institutions grew, in which the waiters also performed these functions.

**Wall St  1.** The street in New York in which the *New York Stock Exchange is situated.  **2.** The New York Stock Exchange itself.  **3.** The financial institutions, collectively, of New York, including the stock exchange, banks, money markets, commodity markets, etc.

**warehousing  1.** The storage of goods in a warehouse.  **2.** Building up a holding of shares in a company prior to making a *takeover bid, by buying small lots of the shares and 'warehousing' them in the name of nominees. The purpose is for the bidder to remain anonymous and to avoid having to make the statutory declaration of interest. This practice is contrary to the *City Code on Takeovers and Mergers.

**war loan** A government stock issued during wartime; it has no redemption date, pays only 3½% interest, and stands at less than half its face value.

**warrant  1.** A security that offers the owner the right to subscribe for the *ordinary shares of a company at a fixed date, usually at a fixed price. Warrants are themselves bought and sold on *stock exchanges and are equivalent to stock options. Subscription prices usually exceed the market price, as the purchase of a warrant is a gamble that a company will prosper. They have proved increasingly popular in recent years as a company can issue them without including them in the balance sheet.  **2.** A document that serves as proof that goods have been deposited in a public warehouse. The document identifies specific goods and can be transferred by endorsement. Warrants are frequently used as security against a bank loan. Warehouse warrants for warehouses attached to a wharf are known as **dock warrants** or **wharfinger's warrants**.

**warranty  1.** A statement made clearly in a contract (**express warranty**) or, if not stated clearly, understood between the parties to the contract (**implied warranty**). An unfulfilled warranty does not invalidate the contract but could lead to the payment of damages. *See also* floating warranty.  **2.** A condition in an insurance policy that confirms that something will or will not be done or that a certain situation exists or does not exist. If a warranty is breached, the insurer is entitled to refuse to pay claims, even if they are unconnected with the breach. For example, if a policy insuring the contents of a house has a warranty that certain locks are to be used on the doors and windows and these are found not to have been used, the insurers could decline to settle a claim for a burst pipe. In practice, however, this does not happen as insurers have agreed that they will only refuse to pay claims if the breach of warranty has affected the circumstances of the claim. **3.** A manufacturer's written promise to repair or replace a faulty product, usually free of charge, during a specified period subsequent to the date of purchase. This is often called a **guarantee**.

**wash sale** A US name for the sale and purchase by a single investor, or a group in collusion, of a block of securities either simultaneously or in a short space of time to establish a loss or a gain; it may also be used to create the impression that the security in question is trading actively. It is similar to the practice known in the UK as *bed and breakfast. See also* crossing.

**wasting asset** An asset that has a finite life; for example, a lease may lose value throughout its life and become valueless when it terminates. It is also applied to such assets as plant and machinery, which wear out during their life and therefore lose value.

**watered stock** *See* stock watering.

**WDV** Abbreviation for *written-down value.

**wealth** The value of the assets owned by an individual or group of individuals. Economics began as the study of wealth (e.g. Adam Smith's *The Wealth of Nations*) and how it changes during a given period. Keynesian theory tended to place a greater emphasis on *income as the object of study in macroeconomics but it has since been accepted that income only tends to affect the behaviour of individuals as it affects their wealth.

**wealth tax** An annual tax charged in some countries on the accumulated wealth (or net assets) of an individual. A wealth tax is almost impossible to administer fairly owing to the complexities of valuing an individual's assets at a particular time.

**weighted average (weighted mean)** An arithmetic average that takes into account the importance of the items making up the average. For example, if a person buys a commodity on three occasions, 100 tonnes at £70 per tonne, 300 tonnes at £80 per tonne, and 50 tonnes at £95 per tonne, the purchases total 450 tonnes; the simple average price would be $(70 + 80 + 95)/3 = £81.7$. The weighted average, taking into account the amount purchased on each occasion, would be $[(100 \times 70) + (300 \times 80) + (50 \times 95)]/450 = £79.4$ per tonne.

**weighted ballot** A *ballot held if a new issue of shares has been oversubscribed, in which the allocation of shares is based on the number of shares applied for and biased towards either the smaller investor or the larger investor.

**white knight** A person or firm that makes a welcome *takeover bid for a company on improved terms to replace an unacceptable and unwelcome bid from a *black knight. If a company is the target for a takeover bid from a source of which it does not approve or on terms that it does not find attractive, it will often seek a white knight, whom it sees as a more suitable owner for the company, in the hope that a more attractive bid will be made. *Compare* grey knight.

**whole (of) life policy** A life-assurance policy that pays a specified amount on the death of the life assured. Benefits are not made for any other reason and the cover continues until the death of the life assured, provided the premiums continue to be paid, either for life or until a specified date. They may be *with-profits or *unit-linked policies.

**wholesale banking** Interbank lending as well as lending to or by other large financial institutions, pension funds, and government agencies. In the USA, wholesale banking also refers to the provision of banking services to the large corporate businesses at special rates.

**wholesale deposit** A large deposit obtained by a bank, financial institution, or large corporate business.

**wholesale market** The *money market between banks; the interbank market for short-term loans.

**wider-range securities** *See* trustee investments.

**wife's earnings** *See* separate taxation of a wife's earnings.

**will** A document giving directions as to the disposal of a person's property after death. It has no effect until death and may be altered as many times as the person (the *testator) wishes. To be binding, it must be executed in accordance with statutory formalities. It must be in writing, signed by the testator or at the testator's direction and in the testator's presence. It must appear that the signature was intended to give effect to the will (usually it is signed at the end, close to the last words dealing with the property). The will must be witnessed by two persons, who must also sign the will. The witnesses must not be beneficiaries.

**windbill** *See* accommodation bill.

**winding-up** *See* liquidation.

**winding-up order** An order given by a British court, under the Insolvency Act 1986, compelling a company to be wound up.

**windmill** *See* accommodation bill.

**window  1.** An opportunity to borrow or invest that may be only temporary and should therefore be taken while it is available.  **2.** A period during the day during which interbank transfers and clearance may be enacted.

**window dressing** Any practice that attempts to make a situation look better than it really is. It has been used extensively by accountants to improve the look of balance sheets. For example, banks used to call in their short-term loans and delay making payments at the end of their financial years, in order to show spuriously high cash balances. It can also take the form of writing down goodwill (since goodwill is not tax-deductible and does not count as risk-based bank capital as recognized and regulated by the Bank for International Settlements) and accounting for trademarks and exceptional items. These practices now fall within the remit of the *Accounting Standards Board.

**WIP** Abbreviation for *work in progress.

**withholding tax**  Tax deducted at source from *dividends or other income paid to non-residents of a country. If there is a *double-taxation agreement between the country in which the income is paid and the country in which the recipient is resident, the tax can be reclaimed.

**without prejudice**  Words used as a heading to a document or letter to indicate that what follows cannot be used in any way to harm an existing right or claim, cannot be taken as the signatory's last word, cannot bind the signatory in any way, and cannot be used as evidence in a court of law. For example, a solicitor may use these words when making an offer in a letter to settle a claim, implying that the client may decide to withdraw the offer. It may also be used to indicate that, although agreement may be reached on the terms set out in the document on this occasion, the signatory is not bound to settle similar disputes on the same terms.

**without-profits policy**  A life-assurance or pension policy that does not share in the profits of the life-assurance office that issued it. *Compare* with-profits policy.

**without recourse (sans recours)**  Words that appear on a *bill of exchange to indicate that the holder has no recourse to the person from whom it was bought, if it is not paid. It may be written on the face of the bill or as an endorsement. If these words do not appear on the bill, the holder does have recourse to the drawer or endorser if the bill is dishonoured at maturity.

**with-profits bond**  An investment bond that has a cash-in value to some extent protected by the payment and accrual of bonuses.

**with-profits policy**  A life-assurance or pension policy that has additional amounts added to the sum assured, as a result of a surplus or profit made on the investment of the fund or funds of the life-assurance office in which the policyholder is entitled to share. *Compare* unit-linked policy; without-profits policy.

**won**  (W) The standard monetary unit of North Korea and South Korea, divided into 100 chon.

**working capital**  The part of the capital of a company that is employed in its day-to-day trading operations. It consists of *current assets (mainly trading stock, debtors, and cash) less current liabilities (mainly trade creditors). In the normal trade cycle – the supply of goods by suppliers, the sale of stock to debtors, payments of debts in cash, and the use of cash to pay suppliers – the working capital is the aggregate of the net assets involved, sometimes called the **working assets**.

**work in progress (WIP)**  Partly manufactured goods or partly completed contracts. For accounting purposes, work in progress is normally valued at its cost by keeping records of the cost of the materials and labour put into it, together with some estimate of allocated overheads. In the case of long-term contracts, the figure might also include an element of profit. In the USA the usual term is **work in process**.

**World Bank**  The name by which the *International Bank for Reconstruction and Development combined with its affiliates, the *International Development Association and the *International Finance Corporation, is known.

**writ** An order issued by a court. A **writ of summons** is an order by which an action in the High Court is started. It commands the defendant to appear before the court to answer the claim made in the writ by the plaintiff. It is used in actions in tort, claims alleging *fraud, and claims for *damages in respect of personal injuries, death, or infringement of *patent. A **writ of execution** is used to enforce a judgment; it is addressed to a court officer instructing that officer to carry out an act, such as collecting money or seizing property. A **writ of delivery** is a writ of execution directing a sheriff to seize goods and deliver them to the plaintiff or to obtain their value in money, according to an agreed assessment. If the defendant has no option to pay the assessed value, the writ is a **writ of specific delivery**.

**write** **1.** To cover an insurance risk, accepting liability, under an insurance contract as an *underwriter. **2.** To sell a traded option.

**write off** **1.** To reduce the value of an asset to zero in a balance sheet. An expired lease, obsolete machinery, or an unfortunate investment would be written off. **2.** To reduce to zero a debt that cannot be collected (*see* bad debt). Such a loss will be shown in the *profit and loss account of an organization.

**writer** The seller of a traded option. *Compare* taker.

**written-down value (WDV)** The value of an asset for accounting purposes after deducting amounts for depreciation or, in the case of tax computations, for capital allowances.

**wrongful trading** Trading during a period in which a company had no reasonable prospect of avoiding insolvent *liquidation. The liquidator of a company may petition the court for an order instructing a director of a company that has gone into insolvent liquidation to make a contribution to the company's assets. The court may order any contribution to be made that it thinks proper if the director knew, or ought to have known, of the company's situation. A director would be judged liable if a reasonably diligent person carrying out the same function in the company would have realized the situation: no intention to defraud need be shown. *See* fraudulent trading.

**xd** Abbreviation for ex dividend (*see* ex-).

**xu** A monetary unit of Vietnam, worth one hundredth of a *dông.

**Yankee bond** A *bond issued in the USA by a foreign borrower.

**yard** **1.** An informal word for one billion. **2.** An informal name for 100 dollars.

**yearling bond** A UK local-authority bond that is redeemable one year after issue.

**yearly savings plans** The National Savings Yearly Plans were introduced by the Department for *National Savings in 1984. Savers make 12 monthly payments of between £20 and £400; this entitles them to a **Yearly Plan Certificate**, which earns maximum tax-free interest if held for four years, annual interest being compounded.

**year of assessment** *See* fiscal year.

**Yellow Book** The colloquial name for *Admission of Securities to Listing,* a book issued by the Council of the *London Stock Exchange that sets out the regulations for admission to the *Official List and the obligations of companies with *listed securities.

**yen** (¥) The standard monetary unit of Japan, (formerly) divided into 100 sen.

**yield** **1.** The income from an investment expressed in various ways. The **nominal yield** of a fixed-interest security is the interest it pays, expressed as a percentage of its *par value. For example, a £100 stock quoted as paying 8% interest will yield £8 per annum for every £100 of stock held. However, the **current yield** (also called the **interest yield**, **running yield**, **earnings yield**, or **flat yield**) will depend on the market price of the stock. If the 8% £100 stock mentioned above was standing at a market price of £90, the current yield would be $100/90 \times 8 = 8.9\%$. As interest rates rise, so the market value of fixed-interest stocks (not close to redemption) fall in order that they should give a competitive current yield. The capital gain (or loss) on redemption of a stock, which is normally redeemable at £100, can also be taken into account. This is called the **yield to redemption** (**redemption yield** or **maturity yield**). The redemption yield consists approximately of the current yield plus the capital gain (or loss) divided by the number of years to redemption. Thus, if the above stock had nine years to run to redemption, its redemption yield would be about $8.9 + 10/9 = 10\%$. The yields of the various stocks on offer are usually listed in commercial papers as both current yields and redemption yields, based on the current market price. However, for an investor who actually owns stock, the yield will be calculated not on the market price but the price the investor paid for it. The annual yield on a fixed-interest stock can be stated exactly once it has been purchased. This is not the case with *equities, however, where neither the dividend yield (*see* dividend) nor the capital gain (or loss) can be forecast, reflecting the greater degree of risk attaching to investments in equities. Yields on fixed-interest securities and equities are normally quoted gross, i.e. before deduction of tax. **2.** The income obtained from a tax.

**yield curve** A curve on a graph in which the *yield of fixed-interest securities is plotted against the length of time they have to run to maturity. The yield curve usually slopes upwards, indicating that investors expect to receive a premium for holding securities that have a long time to run. However, when there are expectations of changes in interest rate, the slope of the yield curve may change (*see* term structure of interest rates).

**yield gap** The difference between the average annual dividend yield on *equities and the average annual yield on long-dated *gilt-edged securities. Before the 1960s equity yields usually exceeded gilt yields, reflecting the greater degree of risk involved in an investment in equities. In the 1960s rising equity prices led to falling dividend yields causing a **reverse yield gap**. This was accepted as equities were seen to provide a better hedge against *inflation than fixed-interest securities; thus their greater risk element is compensated by the possibility of higher capital gains.

**yield to redemption** *See* yield.

**yuan** (Y) The standard monetary unit of the People's Republic of China, divided into 10 jiao or 100 fen.

**zaïre** (Z) The standard monetary unit of Zaïre, divided into 100 makuta (singular, likuta).

**Zebra** A discounted *zero-coupon bond, in which the accrued income is taxed annually rather than on redemption.

**zero-coupon bond** A type of *bond or preference share that offers no interest payments but which is sold at a discount to its redemption value. Thus, in effect, the interest is paid at maturity in the redemption value of the bond. Investors sometimes prefer zero-coupon bonds as they may confer more favourable tax treatment. *See also* deep-discount bond; TIGR; Zebra.

**zero-rated** Denoting goods or services that are taxable for VAT, but with a tax rate of zero. A distinction is made between exempt goods and services (such as postage stamps) and zero-rated goods or services (such as food, books, and children's clothes) as exempt goods are outside the VAT system and there is no opportunity to offset input tax, whereas zero-rated goods and services are within the system, providing an opportunity for offsetting input tax.

**zloty** (Zl) The standard monetary unit of Poland, divided into 100 groszy.